DATE DUE

The publisher gratefully acknowledges the generous contribution to this book provided by the Sue Tsao Endowment Fund in Chinese Studies of the University of California Press Foundation.

Tears from Iron

ASIA: LOCAL STUDIES/GLOBAL THEMES

Jeffrey N. Wasserstrom, Kären Wigen, and Hue-Tam Ho Tai, Editors

Tears from Iron

*Cultural Responses to Famine
in Nineteenth-Century China*

Kathryn Edgerton-Tarpley

With a Foreword by Cormac Ó Gráda

UNIVERSITY OF CALIFORNIA PRESS
Berkeley · Los Angeles · London

University of California Press, one of the most
distinguished university presses in the United States,
enriches lives around the world by advancing scholarship in the humanities, social sciences, and natural
sciences. Its activities are supported by the UC Press
Foundation and by philanthropic contributions from
individuals and institutions. For more information,
visit www.ucpress.edu.

University of California Press
Berkeley and Los Angeles, California

University of California Press, Ltd.
London, England

Library of Congress Cataloging-in-Publication Data

Edgerton-Tarpley, Kathryn, 1970–.
  Tears from iron : cultural responses to famine in
nineteenth-century China / Kathryn Edgerton-Tarpley :
with a foreword by Cormac Ó Gráda.
    p.   cm — (Asia : local studies/global themes ;
15)
  Includes bibliographical references and index.
  ISBN 978-0-520-25302-5 (cloth : alk. paper)
    1. Famines—China—History—19th century.
2. China—Social conditions—History—19th
century.   I. Title.

HC430.F3E34   2008
363.80951'09034—dc22   2007040156

Manufactured in the United States of America

16   15   14   13   12   11   10   09   08   07
10   9   8   7   6   5   4   3   2   1

Contents

List of Illustrations

Commonly Used
Chinese Terms

QING CURRENCY, WEIGHTS, AND MEASURES

Currency

1 *liang* = 1 tael = 1 ounce of silver

1 *qian* = 0.1 *liang*

1 *wen* = 0.01 *liang* = the standard copper unit of account.
Nineteenth-century English-language sources usually translate
wen as "cash" or as "copper coin." Theoretically, 1 "string"
of a thousand copper cash was supposed to exchange for 1
tael of silver; but during the late 1870s the exchange rate was
actually between 1 tael to 1,275 cash and 1 tael to 1,500 cash.

1 *yuan* = a Chinese dollar. In 1876–79 1 yuan was worth about
0.65 tael.

Capacity

1 *shi* = 1 Chinese bushel = 103.6 liters

1 *dou* = 1 peck = 0.1 shi

1 *sheng* = 1 pint = 0.01 shi, or slightly less than 1 English pint

Weight

   1 *dan* = 1 picul = 133⅓ English pounds

   1 *jin* = 1 catty = 1 Chinese pound or 1⅓ English pounds

Area

   1 *mu* = 0.0615 hectare or ⅙ acre

   1 *qing* = 100 mu

Length and Distance

   1 *li* = 0.5 kilometers or ⅓ mile

   1 *chi* = 1 Chinese foot = 31.3 centimeters

OTHER TERMS

   fu = prefecture, the largest administrative division of a province

   zhou = department, a smaller administrative division of a province

   xian = county, the lowest administrative unit of a province

   Hubu = the Board of Revenue, in charge of monetary policy and fiscal matters

   yamen = the headquarters of a senior official at any level of the administrative hierarchy

   daotai = a circuit intendant, or the lowest provincial official privileged to memorialize the emperor

   lijin = *likin,* a trade tax on goods in transit

REIGN PERIODS OF THE QING DYNASTY (1644–1911)

   Shunzhi, 1644–61

   Kangxi, 1662–1722

   Yongzheng, 1723–35

   Qianlong, 1736–96

   Jiaqing, 1796–1820

Daoguang, 1821–50
Xianfeng, 1851–61
Tongzhi, 1862–74
Guangxu, 1875–1908
Xuantong, 1908–11

Acknowledgments

The foundational ideas for this book emerged in graduate seminars taught by Jeffrey Wasserstrom, Lynn Struve, and Lawrence Friedman, and my work owes a great deal to all three. I am especially grateful to Jeff for fostering my interest in transnational history and for his wise counsel since I left Indiana, and to Lynn for influencing my thinking about cultural responses to disaster in important ways. I also appreciate the helpful suggestions made by George Wilson, Maureen Coulter, George Alter, and James Riley at Indiana University, and the years of encouragement and insight offered by Vera Schwarcz, who played a key role in inspiring me to study Chinese history.

I am deeply grateful to Henrietta Harrison for reading my manuscript in its unfinished form and offering invaluable comments and critiques, as well as for sharing her expertise on late-Qing Shanxi. Lillian Li, Helen Dunstan, David Johnson, Rudolf Wagner, and R. Bin Wong have all offered useful suggestions concerning sections of my work presented at conferences, and Andrea Janku, Barbara Mittler, and Jeffrey Snyder-Reinke have kindly shared their works-in-progress with me and influenced my thinking about food, famine, and the *Shenbao*. Many thanks as well to Margaret Kelleher, Cormac Ó Gráda, and Mary Daly for taking the time to meet with me during my stay in Ireland and for helping me to navigate the enormous amount of source material on the Irish famine. I also greatly appreciate the insightful suggestions and critiques offered by the two outside readers who reviewed my manuscript after its submission.

I am also eager to express my gratitude for the help offered to me by professors, librarians, local historians, and elderly villagers in China, without which I simply could not have written this book. I am particularly indebted to Xia Mingfang, Zhu Hu, and Li Wenhai at the Qing Research Institute of the People's University of China, who shared their extensive knowledge of sources on the North China Famine and familiarized me with the lay of the land of disaster studies in the People's Republic of China (PRC). I thank the Shanghai Library for granting permission to use famine illustrations from their collection in this book, and for Feng Jinniu's and Wang Heming's assistance at that library. I also appreciate the help offered by Wang Xianming at Shanxi University, and Bi Xinxin, Bi Yuan, Zhai Wang, Cao Cairui, Zhang Jie, and Zhang Zhibin in Taiyuan. Thanks as well to Wu Jun for sharing his extensive collection of rubbings of stele inscriptions regarding the famine, to Hao Ping, Xiang Kai, Niu Xuejie, and Wang Xueqiao for helping me locate and photograph some of the extant steles; to Wang Yongnian for introducing me to recently published famine folklore; to Tao Fuhai for sharing his rich collection of local famine sources; to Andrew Kaiser in Taiyuan for information on Shanxi-based missionaries; and to Wang Xinsen and other directors of local-history offices for familiarizing me with local historiography of the famine in Shanxi. My warmest thanks also to Tan Wenfeng, a writer with a passion for bringing rural Shanxi to life. Tan introduced me to many of the elderly villagers who shared haunting famine stories passed down to them by their grandparents, thus allowing me to glimpse how the famine was remembered by the ordinary people who suffered most during the disaster. I also want to convey my appreciation for the help and guidance provided by Hsiung Ping-chen, He Hanwei, and Chen Tsun-Kung at the Academia Sinica in Taiwan, and the help of staff at the archival collection of the School of Oriental and African Studies in London, at the Baptist Missionary Archives in Oxford, and at the National Library of Ireland.

I could not have conducted the research for this book without substantial financial support from many different organizations. The J. William Fulbright Foreign Scholarship Board and the Social Science Research Council funded my initial research in China, Taiwan, London, and Ireland, and a National Endowment for the Humanities Summer Stipend allowed me to return to Beijing and Shanxi to conduct additional research in 2004. Moreover, an American Fellowship from the American Association of University Women made it possible for me to devote a full year entirely to writing my dissertation, and a National Endowment for the

Humanities fellowship provided me with six crucial months to finish revising the manuscript for publication.

Finally, my greatest debt is to my husband, Van, who has read and reread countless drafts of this book and has provided me with invaluable support and encouragement throughout the writing process, and to my parents, Ron and Becky Edgerton, who taught me to love books, ideas, and good stories.

Foreword

Most readers of this book will know the famine that devastated China during the Great Leap Forward (1959–61) as the greatest of all time. Not all will know that the North China famine of 1876–79 (known in China at the time and for long afterward as the Incredible Famine) that is the subject of this book may have been the *second* greatest ever. Curiously, estimates of excess mortality in 1959–61 (from 15 million to over 30 million), range much more widely than those in 1876–79—when between 9.5 million and 13 million are supposed to have died.[1] Specialist estimates of mortality during the Great Leap Forward famine have tended to fall over time, and a figure of 15 to 18 million now seems the most plausible.[2] On that reckoning, the *relative* human cost of the earlier famine was considerably greater, given that China's population was 650 million in the late 1950s but little more than half that (365 million) on the eve of the Incredible Famine. Thus the claim by American socialist

1. This estimate, originally suggested by the China Famine Relief Fund, has been widely recycled since. See, e.g., R. H. Tawney, *Land and Labour in China* (London: G. Allen and Unwin, 1932), 76; Lillian Li, "Introduction: Food, Famine, and the Chinese State," *Journal of Asian Studies*, 41(4), August 1982, 687; Mike Davis, *Late Victorian Holocausts* (London: Verso, 2001), 113.

2. Daniel Houser, Barbara Sands, and Erte Xiao, "Three Parts Natural, Seven Parts Man-made: Bayesian Analysis of China's Great Leap Forward Demographic Disaster," www.sas.upenn.edu/~exiao/china.pdf, downloaded 12 October 2006; C. Ó Gráda, "Making Famine History," *Journal of Economic Literature*, XLV(1) March 2007, 5–38. This figure does not include "missing" or delayed births.

James Maurer in 1912 that "1876 witnessed the commencement of a drought in the two great provinces of Honan and Shansi which has probably never been surpassed as the cause of such a vast amount of human suffering" may still hold true, or almost true.[3] Almost certainly, the Incredible Famine was much more intense in its epicenter in Shanxi (as Shansi province is now known) than the Great Leap Forward famine was even in the worst hit provinces of Anhui or Sichuan.

My purpose in this foreword is to offer some further famine-historical context to this major catastrophe. As Kathryn Edgerton-Tarpley makes clear, the North China famine struck at a time when outsiders regarded famine as what Felix Greene dubbed "a tragic but inescapable fact of Chinese life."[4] China's economy was in decline and particularly vulnerable to shocks. The Qing Manchu regime was already severely weakened, still recovering from the Taiping Rebellion of the 1850s and 1860s, under attack from the north and the east, and unsure about its compromise with globalization. Economic historian Angus Maddison reckons that Chinese GDP per head was 12 percent less on the eve of the famine than at mid-century.[5] Away from the coast, communications were still difficult and costly.[6] Moreover, there is good reason to believe that the area worst hit by the famine had fallen behind relative to the rest of China in the preceding decades.

In such circumstances, it might be tempting to attribute the Incredible Famine to poverty and overpopulation alone. But as Edgerton-Tarpley shows, even allowing for the difficult economic context, the policy response of the authorities to the crisis was belated and inadequate. The British-run *North China Herald* savagely lambasted the "dominating mandarins" of Beijing for the "aggravation of a serious dearth into a famine" (a phrase that might have been lifted straight from Book IV of Adam Smith's *Wealth of Nations*), but its editorials offered no panacea: in precisely these same years, the poor of India were dying by the millions under a regime that practiced to the letter the teachings advocated in the *Herald*. The notion that government mismanagement of the trade in foodgrains alone was responsible for the Incredible Famine forgets that the market is no substitute for the free transfer of resources from the rich

---

3. James H. Maurer, *The Far East* (Reading, PA: Press of Sentinel Printing Co., 1912), 15.

4. Felix Greene, *A Curtain of Ignorance* (Garden City, NY: Doubleday, 1964), 93.

5. Available at www.ggdc.net/maddison.

6. John Watt, "The Effect of Transportation on Famine Prevention," *China Quarterly*, 6 (1960), 76–80.

to those who lack the funds to purchase food at *any* price. Mere maintenance of smoothly functioning markets would not have absolved the
Chinese elite of their moral responsibilities. The half-truth that in the
1840s "Ireland died of political economy" has a wider resonance.

Tears from Iron illustrates that while the causes of famine may differ,
many of the symptoms are distressingly similar. Common features include
an increase in crime and antisocial behavior, moral-economy resistance in
the form of food riots, an initial increase in philanthropy followed by donor
fatigue, a weakening of family bonds, an upsurge in child desertion, and
an increase in the numbers of suicides and infanticides. Famines lay bare
the inequalities between rich and poor that are ignored or taken for granted
in normal times. Invariably, they produce a hierarchy of suffering; some
groups may well benefit from them. Much of what happens during
famines is the result of cruel choices dictated by the ethics of the lifeboat:
the survival of some (mostly likely the stronger) means the sacrifice of others (most likely the weaker). All these features were in evidence in China
in the late 1870s and they are vividly and expertly described herein.

Like most other severe famines, the Incredible Famine occurred in the
wake of back-to-back harvest failures. Even poor communities are usually resilient and prudent enough to cope with one harvest deficit—they
have to be, since such deficits are common. The poor suffer, but they survive with the help of a range of coping mechanisms. Other famous examples of famines due to back-to-back shortfalls, or bang bang famines
(an expression coined by famine demographer Tim Dyson), include the
Great North European Famine of the 1310s, the Great Irish Famine of
the 1840s, and the Berar famine of the 1860s. Northern China suffered
from severe droughts in 1876, 1877, and 1878. The link between these
droughts and a global El Niño Southern Oscillation (ENSO) event has
been highlighted by Mike Davis in *Late Victorian Holocausts*.

Tears from Iron also corroborates the view that famines are usually
subject to significant regional disparities, even in relatively small countries. For example, the excess death toll in Ireland in the 1840s ranged
from negligible along most of the east coast to one-in-four along much
of the west coast. Indeed, the Incredible Famine is sometimes described
as the Shansi (Shanxi) Famine because it was at its fiercest in the provinces of Shanxi and Henan in northern China. Much of the country was
relatively unaffected. In particular, most of Anhui, the focus of so many
Chinese famines, seems to have escaped relatively lightly, as did Sichuan,
a virtual hecatomb in 1959–61.

Some of the famine symptoms described here are not quite so universal, however. *Tears from Iron* offers compelling evidence of two particularly gruesome features of the Incredible Famine. First, it describes several incidents of voluntary servitude. This was an extreme coping mechanism, indeed, and one with a long history during famines. Like much else about famine, it is mentioned in the Old Testament; in Genesis, destitute Egyptians pleaded with Joseph, the Pharaoh's agent: "Why should we die before your eyes, both we and our land? Buy us and our land for bread, and we and our land will be servants unto Pharaoh" (Gen. 47: 19). Famine-induced traffic in humans was quite common in the ancient world and in nineteenth-century Africa (though not, apparently, in medieval or early-modern Europe). Nor did it end in China with the famine of 1876–78: in Henan a famine in the 1920s led to numerous sales of women and children as servants, prostitutes, or second wives. Parents parted with their children with the greatest reluctance; some of those forced to sell their children were "self-respecting industrious farmer folks, who think highly of their children and would only part with them in case of the greatest suffering." A measure of the severity of famine in a region was the number of children sold. In his graphic account of the Henan famine of 1942–43, *Time* reporter Theodore White described parents tying children to a tree "so they would not follow them as they went in search for food" and "larger" children being sold for less than ten dollars.[7]

The horror of these coping mechanisms is brought home by the implication that the alternative was even worse: for those who endured it, voluntary slavery was a means of survival. In Angola the suppression of the practice in the nineteenth century was linked to the slaughter during famines of people formerly sold as slaves. "They were simply taken out and knocked on the head to save them from starvation." Similarly, in early twentieth-century northern Nigeria, former slaves "set free" during a famine by masters who could no longer maintain them were particularly vulnerable. For such unfortunates, the abolition of the traffic in humans was a mixed blessing. This prompts a macabre thought: had Irish landlords and farmers been allowed to enslave their laborers in the 1840s, would they have evicted fewer of them?[8]

Second, as highlighted in chapter 9, rumors of cannibalism were a notable feature of the Incredible Famine, in the double sense that some people were said to have consumed the corpses of those who predeceased them,

7. *Time*, 26 October 1942; 22 March 1943.
8. For a more detailed account see C. Ó Gráda, *Famine: A Short History* (Princeton, NJ: Princeton University Press, forthcoming), ch. 2.

and others were accused of killing for the express purpose of eating their (mainly young) victims. It is likely that in this case, as in others, many of the stories about cannibalism were metaphorical rather than literal in character, that cannibalism was a trope used to emphasize the scale of the disaster and the threat it posed for Confucian family relations. The evidence for cannibalism in Russia in 1921–22 and in 1932–33 is more clearcut, and at the height of the Leningrad siege-famine of 1941–42 hundreds of people were tried for it.[9] In 1943, just a decade and a half before the Great Leap Forward famine, Theodore White wrote about a mother in Henan province who was charged with eating her little girl, and who denied only that she had killed her. Evidence of cannibalism during the Bengal famine of 1943–44 or during the Great Irish Famine of the 1840s is lacking, however. In Calcutta the taboo against eating meat of any kind was so strong that many victims refused the rations offered to them by compassionate soldiers. Again, the relative paucity of reliable evidence for cannibalism in China in 1959–61 is noteworthy. Is this because the Great Leap famine was less intense, or is it because there had been an intervening "civilizing process" that ruled out cannibalism even in extremis?

The several contemporary woodcuts of famine scenes reproduced here are shocking, and were meant to be so. They recall the graphic and sometimes repugnant illustrations of famine in Bengal in 1943–44 by campaigning Bengali artists such as Zainul Abedin and Chittaprasad, and the celluloid images of Sunil Janah, reproduced in the Calcutta *Statesman* and elsewhere. These too were intended to provoke public action and private compassion—and did so, albeit too late to prevent mass mortality.[10] Pictorial representations of famine in Europe tend to be rather sanitized and anodyne by comparison: compare James Mahony's well-known pictures of the Great Irish Famine in the *Illustrated London News*. In Europe it is through the medium of the printed word that the full sense

9. B. M. Patinaude, *The Big Show in Bololand: The American Relief Expedition to Soviet Russia in the Famine of 1921* (Stanford, CA: Stanford University Press, 2002), 262–70; R. W. Davies and S. G. Wheatcroft, *The Years of Hunger: Soviet Agriculture 1931–1933* (Houndsmills, UK: Palgrave Macmillan, 2004), 421–24; John Barber and Andrei Dzeniskevich, eds., *Life and Death in Besieged Leningrad, 1941–44* (Houndsmills, UK: Palgrave Macmillan, 2005), 223–24; Ó Gráda, *Famine*.

10. Compare Peter Gray, "British Public Opinion and the Great Irish Famine 1845–49" in *The Famine Lectures: Léachtaí and Ghorta,* ed. Breandán Ó Conaire (Boyle, Ireland: Comhdháil an Chraoibhín, 1997), 77–106; Nikhil Sarkar, ed., *A Matter of Conscience: Artists Bear Witness to the Great Bengal Famine of 1943* (Calcutta: Punascha, 1998; originally published in Bengali in 1994); Ian Stephens, *Monsoon Morning* (London: Benn, 1966). See too David Heiden, *Dust to Dust: A Doctor's View of Famine in Africa* (Philadelphia: Temple University Press, 1992); and Sebastião Salgado, *Sahel: The End of the Road* (Berkeley: University of California Press, 2004).

of the horrors endured is best represented; in their depiction of the conflicts and the gruesome choices that famines entail, perhaps the famine scenes in Goya's Disasters of War come closest to these Chinese woodcuts. (Interestingly, the woodcuts were reproduced in London in 1878, with translated captions, as part of a campaign by British philanthropists to raise funds in aid of China. Alas, they too were reproduced too late to prevent disaster.)[11]

Tears from Iron devotes particular attention to the impact of the famine on women. Today there is a widespread belief—often reflected in the publicity campaigns of disaster-relief and development agencies and in the writings of campaigning journalists—that women (and children) are particularly vulnerable during famines. According to Agence France-Presse in 2003, "despite international efforts to avert more suffering caused by food shortages in Ethiopia, women and children are still dying of malnutrition and diseases." In southern Sudan in 1999 victims of famine were "children, women, men at an average of six per day." The "principal victims" of famine in North Korea in the 1990s were deemed to be "children, women and the elderly." David Arnold's classic *Famine: Social Crisis and Historical Change* also "feminizes" famine, arguing that its burden fell, and falls, "with exceptional severity upon women."

As Edgerton-Tarpley clearly shows, this feminization of famine, so commonplace nowadays, is nothing new. Yet, the demographic evidence shows that females are more likely to survive famines than males. A sympathetic and close observer of the Irish famine noted in 1849: "No one has yet . . . been able to explain why it is that men and boys sink sooner under famine than the other sex; still, so it is; go where you will, every officer will tell you, it is so. In the same workhouse, in which you will find the girls and women looking well, you will find the men and boys in a state of the lowest physical depression; equal care in every way being bestowed on both sexes."[12] The reason for this female advantage during famines, for which statistical evidence is plentiful, is almost certainly physiological.[13] Females store a much higher proportion of body fat and

11. "Pictures Illustrating the Terrible Famine in Honan That Might Draw Tears from Iron," in *The Famine in China: Illustrations by a Native Artist*, China Famine Relief Fund (London: Kegan Paul, 1878).

12. S. Godolphin Osborne, *Gleanings from the West of Ireland* (London: Boone, 1850), 19.

13. Kate Macintyre, "Famine and the Female Mortality Advantage," in *Famine Demography: Perspectives from the Past and Present*, ed. Tim Dyson and C. Ó Gráda (Oxford: Oxford University Press, 2002), 240–60; Violetta Hionidou, *Famine and Death in Occupied Greece, 1941–1944* (Cambridge: Cambridge University Press, 2006), 165–77.

a lower proportion of muscle—an encumbrance in famine conditions—than males. Also, Edgerton-Tarpley's sources imply that women were more likely to be bought and sold as sex objects and domestic servants during famines than men: paradoxically, this too might contribute, even in a small way, to the greater survival rate of females.

Sometimes the famine historian is placed in a predicament rather like that of the surgeon treating seriously ill patients, or the NGO worker distributing famine relief. There has to be concern for the victims, but the job must get done. Kathryn Edgerton-Tarpley gets the balance between empathy and scholarship exactly right.

Cormac Ó Gráda, University College Dublin

Introduction

The fields lack green grass and households lack smoke from kitchen chimneys. People catch rats or spread their nets for birds or grind wheat stubble into powder or use dry grass to make cakes. Alas! How can this be considered food?

When people die, others eat them. People who eat people die. People's deaths result in pestilence. People with the pestilence die and people eat the plague victims and more people die. Deaths come one after the other.

Between 1876 and 1879, the most lethal drought-famine in imperial China's long history of famines and disasters struck the five northern provinces of Shanxi, Henan, Shandong, Zhili, and Shaanxi. The drought in the Yellow River basin began in 1876 and worsened dramatically with the almost total failure of rain in 1877. By the time the rains returned late in 1878, 9 to 13 million of the affected area's population of about 108 million people had perished.[1] In Shanxi Province, the epicenter of the famine, mountainous terrain and transportation difficulties made relief work especially difficult. Over a third of the province's prefamine population of 15 to 17 million people either starved to death, perished of famine-related diseases, or fled during the disaster. In some counties, population loss approached 80 percent, and the formerly prosperous province did not regain its pre-1877 population until after 1950.[2] The North China Famine, referred to in Chinese as the Dingwu qihuang 丁戊奇荒 (Incredible Famine of 1877–78), or simply Guangxu sannian 光绪三年 (The third year of the Guangxu emperor's reign), had local, national, and global implications.[3] The famine forced a series of hideous moral choices on starving families in the southern half of Shanxi Province, where the famine was most severe. Striking only a decade after the Qing state finally suppressed three mid-century rebellions that had threatened to topple the dynasty, the famine also presented a serious cri-

sis for an empire already beleaguered by foreign aggression, internal unrest, and fiscal woes. The severity and scope of the disaster galvanized
into action not only the Qing court and the officials in charge of relieving the famished northern provinces but also Chinese and Western philanthropists living in the treaty port of Shanghai. The catastrophe received
widespread coverage in Chinese- and English-language newspapers published in Shanghai. As the most lethal of the drought-famines that also
affected India, Brazil, Korea, Egypt, and southern Africa in the late 1870s,
the disaster drew attention as well from newspapers and missionary journals in Europe and North America.[4]

During the worst period of the famine, Xie Jiafu and Tian Zilin, two
Chinese philanthropists from a wealthy city near Shanghai, designed and
printed a small booklet titled *Henan qihuang tieleitu* (The Incredible
Famine in Henan: Pictures to draw tears from iron). The booklet comprised a dozen woodblock print illustrations of famine conditions in
Henan Province, each accompanied by an eight-character heading and
a poetic lament. The epigraphs for this introduction come from the
laments accompanying Xie Jiafu's original set of illustrations and a larger
compilation published in 1881. The disturbing illustrations were aimed
at rousing people to contribute to relief efforts by moving even "people
of iron" (*tieren*) to shed tears upon viewing them. The emaciated men
and women in one print struggle to subsist on tree bark and grass roots,
while family members in another illustration weep as they sell their children to human traders. China's first modern newspaper, the Shanghai-
based *Shenbao*, introduced the illustrations to its treaty-port readers and
praised them as an innovative method of raising famine relief funds.[5] In
1878 the booklet of "pictures to draw tears from iron" was translated
into English and published in London. British members of the Committee of the China Famine Relief Fund hoped it would "help to carry home
to English hearts a sense of the dire distress from which these unhappy
people are now suffering, and to call forth from benevolent persons in
this country also, a practical expression of sympathy."[6]

The famine itself, as well as Xie Jiafu's illustrations, did indeed draw
tears from all audiences. Local literati in Shanxi, high officials in the capital, treaty-port reformers in Shanghai, and Anglo-American missionary
relief workers all included descriptions of sleepless nights, fervent prayers,
tears, wails, and laments in their accounts of the famine. Even the child
emperor and other members of the imperial family reportedly wept and
lost sleep over the misery experienced by famine victims. The genesis and
the focus of these tears, however, differed substantially among the vari-

ous observers of the "Incredible Famine," just as the meaning of the famine itself varied considerably according to the cultural, social, geographic, and temporal context within which it was viewed.

The lack of consensus over theories of famine causation and over definitions of moral versus immoral responses to the disaster presaged the more extreme breakdown in consensus following the famine over what values were crucial to Chinese identity. The famine thus reveals competing contexts for the consideration of trauma in a key period of transition in late-Qing China. Observers from different levels of Chinese society often shared the assumption that the arrival of the disaster might stem from Heaven's anger over human, particularly official, misconduct. At the same time, they offered diverse interpretations of the famine's fundamental meaning. Local observers in southern Shanxi, for example, viewed the famine primarily as a threat to the Confucian family system and its emphasis on female chastity and filial piety, while members of Shanghai's treaty-port elite saw the disaster as a call for national reform. In the imperial capital one group of conservative Qing officials used discussions of the famine to emphasize the paternalistic obligations of a good Confucian ruler. Their rivals, reform-minded officials anxious to strengthen China by importing Western technology, saw foreign aggression as a greater threat than famine and wanted to limit government spending on relief efforts accordingly. British newspaper editors and foreign missionaries, on the other hand, frequently viewed the disaster as irrefutable evidence of the corruption and incompetence of Qing officialdom. This book contributes to a better understanding of both the famine itself and the complexity of the crises confronting late-nineteenth-century China.

A key focus of the book is to analyze disparate cultural and political responses to the Incredible Famine. Perhaps because the image of innocent human beings starving to death is so disturbing, a famine provides a particularly vivid window through which to view a culture's response to disaster. As historian Paul Greenough has suggested, "disasters such as floods and famines activate discussion of the culture's ultimate values, [its] concepts of good and bad, legitimate and illegitimate."[7] A major famine tests and stretches the values and assumptions of any society, but the images used to describe a famine, and the definitions of what actions constitute moral and immoral responses to the impossible choices that famines force people to make, vary from culture to culture. Throughout the book I address several questions. How did people from different levels of late-Qing society interpret famine causation, define heroes and villains during the crisis, and determine which members of a starving family were most or least expendable? What actions did local, central-government, and treaty-port observers in China consider to be effective responses to famine? What culturally specific images did observers of the disaster use to describe the devastation in the north? And how has the famine been remembered and made use of in the People's Republic of China (PRC)?

The heart of this book is an analysis of ground-level famine narratives from Shanxi Province, where the disaster was most severe. I put these local accounts in dialogue with broader debates over the famine's meaning. As I delved into the disturbing, often fragmented sources from the North China Famine, I found that the famine itself resembled an unmovable block of iron that weighed heavily on the society and government of late-Qing China. It was an inescapable fact whose simple telling conveyed little of its true horror, a chunk of iron that could not be dissolved by tears. The catastrophe cast its shadow over multiple facets of late-Qing society and returned to haunt the country again in the early 1960s. By the end of this project, following the famine where it led me demanded that I discuss trauma and memory, class relations in late-Qing Shanxi, "famine foods" and folklore, granaries and grain routes, Qing state ideology, theories of famine causation, opium cultivation, factional politics in the imperial capital, the sale of women, gender and familial relations during times of crisis, famine demographics, cannibalism, press coverage of disasters, visual depictions of starvation, philanthropic traditions in Jiangnan, early Chinese nationalism, and treaty-port reform movements.[8] Such a project quickly threatens to become abstract. Continual return to local sources such as famine songs and poems, county gazetteers, stone stele inscriptions, historical fiction, and folk stories told by the elderly villagers and local historians I interviewed in Shanxi, however, kept me grounded in the famine suffering itself.

THE INCREDIBLE FAMINE IN CHINA'S
HISTORY AND HISTORIOGRAPHY

In spite of the attention it received in the 1870s, throughout most of the twentieth century the Incredible Famine was all but forgotten by Chinese and foreign scholars alike. The only book-length studies of this enormous disaster are Paul Richard Bohr's on missionary relief efforts during the famine, published in 1972, and He Hanwei's useful but brief Chinese-language overview, which appeared in 1980.[9] The famine is rarely covered in PRC or American textbooks on Chinese history. Few

Chinese people outside the scholarly community have even heard the term *Dingwu qihuang* (Incredible Famine of 1877–78), though older people in southern Shanxi are quite familiar with the phrase *Guangxu sannian* (Third year of the emperor Guangxu's reign [1877]). Considering that the famine killed millions of Chinese people, left once wealthy northern provinces like Shanxi permanently altered, and garnered international as well as national and local attention in the 1870s, this is a striking omission. Both local and national discussions of the disaster were, however, rapidly buried under layer upon layer of new upheavals—China's loss to Japan in the 1895 Sino-Japanese War, the invasion by eight allied armies after the Boxer Rebellion, the 1911 Revolution, the May 4th Movement, the Japanese invasion of Manchuria and then of China proper, civil war between the Communists and the Nationalists, and the Communist Revolution. Nineteenth- and twentieth-century Chinese history was marked by one enormous disaster after another, and the horror of mass starvation was repeatedly ignored in favor of focusing on disasters with clearer-cut heroes and villains.

It was not until nearly eighty years after the Incredible Famine, when China was once again threatened by famine, that the horrors of Guangxu 3 were drawn back into public memory. Between 1959 and 1961, as many as thirty million Chinese people died due to the massive famine induced by Mao's failed Great Leap Forward and exacerbated by natural disasters.[10] As part of their attempt to deal with what was until the late 1970s termed simply the "three difficult years" (*san nian kunnan shiqi*), provincial officials in Shanxi sent local historians out into the countryside to collect primary documents about the Qing-era famine. In 1961 and 1962 many of the famine songs, poems, stele inscriptions, and other famine sources collected by local scholars were published in a two-volume work that is a gold mine for anyone interested in local memories of the famine.[11] The rush to locate sources about the famine of 1876–79 slowed after descriptions of that disaster were no longer needed to offset the horrors of the Mao-era famine. Since all attempts to collect and publish historical records became dangerous once Mao's Great Proletarian Cultural Revolution and its "Anti–Four Olds" campaign began in 1966, little scholarship on the famine was published in China between 1966 and 1981. Yet due to the concerted effort of Shanxi's local history offices to seek out and hand-copy sources that dealt with the Incredible Famine, a large number of these sources survived the Cultural Revolution. Once historical scholarship came back into favor in the early 1980s, many of the county-level "Literary and Historical Materials" offices in Shanxi began to publish articles about 1877 that were based on documents collected twenty years earlier.[12]

In the 1980s, Chinese historians working on the national level took a new interest in researching the cluster of major natural disasters that plagued China during the late-Qing period. As the most lethal famine in pre-Communist Chinese history and the first Chinese famine to attract national and international news coverage and relief efforts, the North China Famine has recently received more and more attention. Post–Cultural Revolution scholarly literature on this famine has shifted away from using the disaster as a prime example of the corruption and heartlessness embedded in the "old feudal society." Instead, Xia Mingfang and other scholars examine the Incredible Famine and other late-Qing disasters as keys to understanding why China fell behind Europe and the United States during the nineteenth century and why late-Qing efforts to "modernize" came to naught.[13] Perhaps because natural disasters are now viewed in this light, when Premier Jiang Zemin invited eight leading historians to meet with him in 1998 to discuss key problems of Chinese and world history and to publish a book of essays stemming from their discussion, one of the eight topics selected was "Disasters in Modern [1839–1911] China and Social Stability."[14]

It is not only in the PRC that the field of famine studies has burgeoned over the past few decades. Amartya Sen's entitlement approach has demonstrated that famines often result from maldistribution of food rather than from absolute scarcity, while Mike Davis has contributed a sweeping assessment of the global implications of an array of nineteenth-century famines. Moreover, historians of late imperial China have published groundbreaking scholarship on the Qing state's impressive famine-relief bureaucracy and on how Qing principles and policies concerning the goal of "nourishing the people" compared to those of contemporary European states.[15] Yet very little has been written on how Chinese observers of famine experienced, described, and reacted to the horror of watching millions of their compatriots starve to death.

The wealth of cultural and interdisciplinary scholarship on the Great Irish Famine of 1845–49 provides provocative new questions and approaches useful for exploring the human and social side of famine in nineteenth-century China. Thirty years before the North China Famine, blight destroyed Ireland's potato harvests four times over the course of five years, causing a catastrophic food shortage for Ireland's potato-dependent poor. That Ireland was ruled by the wealthiest nation in the nineteenth-century world did nothing to prevent an astounding two and a half million of Ireland's eight million people from either perishing of hunger or disease or fleeing the country.[16] The "Great Hunger" holds a different place in the historical narrative of Ireland than does the Incredible Famine in China's modern history. Rather than being superseded in public memory by invasions and revolutions, the Great Irish Famine quickly became a major linchpin in Ireland's nationalist historiography. Some Irish nationalists accused the British of carrying out genocide by continuing to export grain out of Ireland during the potato blight. The Irish famine continues to be a defining moment for Irish identity today.[17] A great deal of multidisciplinary scholarship on the famine has been published since 1995, when Ireland commemorated the famine's 150th anniversary. Among those works, Margaret Kelleher's gendered approach to representations of the Irish famine, Cormac Ó Gráda's demographic and economic research on the Great Hunger, Peter Gray's work on famine and British ideology, and Chris Morash's semiotic analysis have all proved vital to my examination of cultural responses to famine.[18]

While different theoretical approaches allowed me to explore various aspects of the North China Famine, I found it impossible to grasp the totality of the famine through any one theory, or even through a combination of many analytic approaches. One or more aspects of this "block of iron" always eluded or simply refused to fit into a given approach. This difficulty in neatly analyzing the famine may have something to do with the nature of famine itself. Chinese and Irish observers who experienced either famine firsthand consistently claimed that the horrors they witnessed were simply beyond the power of words to express. Scholars of Ireland's Great Hunger often argue that famine defies articulation. "The Famine seems to arrest all possibility of meaning and to resist notions of retrieval and restitution," observe Scott Brewster and Virginia Crossman in their essay on the Irish famine. "Symptomatically wavering between silence and speech, forgetting and remembering, the Famine exemplifies history as trauma."[19]

Twenty years after the North China Famine, an educated observer named Liu Xing tried to make sense of the horrors he had witnessed while the famine raged in his native place in southern Shanxi. Recalling that "thousands and tens of thousands" of people had starved to death in surrounding villages, he wrote: "At that time, I thought vainly about who to resent and blame." Liu Xing traced the arrival of the drought to Heaven's anger at human misdeeds.[20] While his explanation allowed Liu to find meaning in the disaster, he was unable to fit all aspects of the catastrophe into his framework. Some shards of memory fiercely resisted incorporation into his causal explanation. The same pattern holds true for modern scholarly approaches to famine, obviously including my own. To get at the meaning of the famine, then, this book offers a dialogue among many different approaches.

In addition, this exploration of how culture is involved in giving meaning to disaster is fundamentally comparative and cross-cultural. Famine texts themselves demanded that I maintain a hybrid focus on the local and the global, the particular and the universal, and the individual and the broader society. Liu Xing, for example, witnessed the famine in southern Shanxi firsthand and left us a searing description of drought, disease, and death on the local level. But he could not grasp the scope of the disaster as it engulfed all of Shanxi. Likewise Zeng Guoquan, the famine-era governor of Shanxi, was intimately aware of the havoc the famine wrecked on the province and on North China as a whole, but paid little heed to the critical dialogue and impetus for reform that the famine inspired among his treaty-port compatriots. British newspaper editors in Shanghai, for their part, were so focused on how railroads and free trade could have prevented the famine that they were blind to the role that opium and imperialism played in bringing it about. Among all the observers in China during the 1870s, Chinese philanthropists in Shanghai and other wealthy Jiangnan cities most clearly illustrate the influence of cross-cultural conversation in their interpretations of the famine. The treaty-port reformers who kept one eye focused on Chinese texts and traditions while turning the other eye across the sea to London and British India provided a model for my own work. Throughout the book, then, late-Qing discussions of the Incredible Famine are compared and contrasted with nineteenth-century British readings of famines in China, Ireland, and India.

I also aim to offer what Mary Daly, a scholar of the Irish famine, terms that "blend of analysis and emotion" vital for those who study famine and trauma.[21] As part of my commitment to the sufferers, I translate fairly lengthy portions of famine songs and laments so that those who actually experienced the famine can to some extent speak for themselves through this work.

THEMES

Themes that run throughout this book include the tough choices the famine forced on individuals, families, and the Qing state; the famine as a referendum on the efficacy of Qing rule; the role the foreign presence played in different levels of Chinese discussions of famine causation and prevention; and diverse interpretations of key "icons of starvation" that appear in all types of famine texts from the 1870s.

Both local and Qing-government documents about the Guangxu 3 disaster highlight the agonizing choices the famine forced people to make. Gazetteer accounts and famine folktales from Shanxi depict filial sons who must choose between feeding their starving children or their elderly parents, young women compelled to either starve to death or give up their chastity by selling their bodies, and younger brothers, adult children, and daughters-in-law forced to decide whether to preserve their own lives or perish so that older or male family members might survive. Xie Jiafu's "pictures to draw tears from iron" offer visual depictions of such choices.

The richness and complexity of a famine folktale passed down to eighty-five-year-old Tan Ruhua by her maternal grandmother capture several of the themes that dominate local discussions of the disaster as experienced in Shanxi:

> In Guangxu 3 it didn't rain and the harvests failed. The people were starving. In one family there were only two brothers left; their parents had already perished. The elder brother knew that one of them had to survive to carry on the family line, so he decided it was necessary to kill his younger brother and eat him. He began to sharpen a knife on a stone, and ordered his younger brother to boil some water. His younger brother asked, "Elder brother [gege], why are you sharpening the knife?" The elder brother glared at him and answered, "To kill a man with!"
>
> So the younger brother began to boil the water. But while doing so, he found one red bean [hong dou] at the bottom of the pot that somehow had been overlooked before. Instead of eating the bean himself, he brought it to his elder brother and said: "Gege, you eat this. You're not strong enough to kill a man!"
>
> When his elder brother saw this, he realized his brother's goodness and did not kill him. So one red bean saved a life.[22]

This story demonstrates that although the will to survive may compel people in any society to jettison many cultural values, culture continues to influence even the choices that mark a complete breakdown of ethics.[23] Like many other accounts in this study, the story of the two brothers and the red bean shows that the moral choices forced on starving families were shaped by Confucian precepts as understood in the late-Qing period. It offers an example of both the incredible abnormalities brought about by the famine and the frantic efforts of people in Shanxi to cling to cultural and social norms in spite of the chaos all around them.

The famine also compelled the beleaguered Qing state to make difficult choices about how best to use its limited resources. Famine-related official memorials and imperial edicts demonstrate that the disaster set off bitter debates among high officials over which of the many crises besetting the empire—Western and Japanese aggression along China's southeastern seacoast, Russian and Muslim threats to the empire's northwestern frontier, or the famine—was most urgent and most deserving of government aid.[24]

A key assertion made by Anglo-American observers in the 1870s, by PRC historians in the 1960s and the early 1980s, and to a lesser extent, by Chinese journalists and reformers in late-Qing Shanghai was that the Qing government's relief efforts during the Incredible Famine were a miserable failure. This charge stands in striking contrast to Pierre-Etienne Will's and R. Bin Wong's superb studies of Qing famine relief policies in the eighteenth and early nineteenth centuries, which document the impressive scope and effectiveness of the Qing granary system and famine-relief bureaucracy up to 1850. This book takes a critical look at nineteenth-century British and Mao-era critiques of Qing efforts by examining how local literati, provincial officials, and Jiangnan philanthropists evaluated the central government's response to the famine. I find considerable conflict over what measures various observers—including different groups of Qing officials—expected the state to take during the famine. A combination of factors such as divisions among metropolitan officials with competing priorities, a weak throne incapable of providing decisive imperial oversight, fiscal limitations, and the demise of the high-Qing granary system impeded the Qing state's ability to deal with the 1877 disaster in a timely manner, in spite of its generally good intentions.

Another theme that appears repeatedly in both late-Qing and PRC discussions of the famine is the symbolic and practical role that foreigners played in bringing about the famine or introducing new methods of famine prevention. For local literati in Shanxi, foreigners were essentially absent from discussions of the disaster. In the imperial capital, officials in rival camps disagreed over how best to deal with the foreign powers, but they agreed that the West was first and foremost a threat. In the Shanghai imagination, to the contrary, the foreign presence was not wholly negative. The treaty-port Chinese-language press portrayed foreigners as competitors who might humiliate Chinese philanthropists by outdoing them in organizing famine-relief efforts, but also as a useful source of new relief methods and new technologies that could strengthen and enrich the country and prevent future famines. Different interpretations of the foreign presence during the famine serve as yet another example of the breakdown in consensus exacerbated by the disaster.

I am also interested in the images that observers of the famine selected to express the horror of mass starvation. Cross-cultural studies of trauma demonstrate that while suffering is a universal and defining human experience, the meanings and modes of the experience of suffering are greatly diverse. In their essay on cultural appropriations of suffering, for example, anthropologist Arthur Kleinman and sinologist Joan Kleinman show how a *New York Times* photograph so famous that it became a virtual "icon of starvation" for Americans actually placed a distinctively Western slant on the portrayal of famine. By personifying a collective catastrophe, this photo of a starving Sudanese girl-child abandoned by all but vultures allows the Sudanese famine to be "culturally represented in an ideologically Western mode: it becomes the experience of a lone individual."[25] In the Chinese case, images of intrafamilial cannibalism and the sale of famished women run throughout local, imperial, and treaty-port accounts of the Incredible Famine.

I examine the diverse meanings that these disturbing "icons of starvation" took on for late-Qing observers residing in different parts of the empire, as well as for twentieth-century Chinese educators who revived the images during the 1960s.

OVERVIEW

Part 1 of this book sets the scene and brings the experience of the famine to life for readers. After introducing the lay of the land of late-Qing Shanxi, I narrate the famine's course by drawing on a haunting account written by a literate survivor from southern Shanxi. Part 2 establishes the various competing contexts within which the Incredible Famine was discussed. I compare and contrast how local, official, foreign, and treaty-port observers answered the basic questions of what caused the famine and what measures could most effectively put an end to it.

Part 3 focuses more explicitly on the "semiotics of starvation." I employ the idea that signs and key words act as "cultural units" that take on different meanings according to the cultural or social system within which they are used in order to analyze the diverse meanings that key famine images took on during and after the disaster. Chapters 7 and 8 contribute directly to the ongoing dialogue on the "feminization of famine." I explore why women more often than men were selected to signify the horror of the famine, and ask how feminized famine images shaped the range of responses expected of Chinese women during the disaster. Chapter 9 analyzes how the meaning of a particularly disturbing famine image, that of intrafamilial cannibalism, changed over time.

Finally, the epilogue brings the story of the famine up to the present by introducing a colorful drama about the 1877 disaster that is now performed for tourists who visit the walled city of Pingyao in Shanxi, and by analyzing how that drama interprets the Incredible Famine in a way indicative of China's twenty-first-century concerns.

PART I

Setting the Scene

CHAPTER I

Shanxi, Greater China, and the Famine

It was in Shanxi Province that the Incredible Famine threw its longest shadow. The province lost between one-third and one-half of its pre-famine population of between fifteen and seventeen million people to starvation, disease, and flight. Even today elderly villagers recall terrifying stories of how starving family members killed and ate one another during the disaster. Before the famine struck, however, Shanxi had been thriving. As one of the few parts of China not severely affected by one of the three gigantic mid-nineteenth-century rebellions, in the early 1870s the province was home to the lucrative Hedong saltworks, an impressive banking network, and merchants powerful enough to dominate China's trade with Mongolia and Russia. How, then, did the drought that struck between 1876 and 1878 result in a devastating famine that brought such a wealthy and strategically important part of the empire to its knees? To address that question, I look closely at prefamine conditions in Shanxi and, more broadly, consider how the formidable challenges facing the Qing Empire in the late nineteenth century hampered the state's ability to prevent a drought from escalating into a major famine.

THE LAY OF THE LAND: SHANXI BEFORE THE FAMINE

Only a decade before the famine, the Reverend Alexander Williamson of the National Bible Society of Scotland and his colleague Jonathan Lees of the London Missionary Society took a nine-hundred-mile journey

through the North China provinces of Zhili, Shanxi, Shaanxi, and Henan. Some seventy years earlier, between 1793 and 1795 a Zhili native
named Li Sui spent two years traveling through forty-eight prefectures,
counties, and cities of Shanxi overseeing examinations as the secretary
to the provincial education commissioner (*xuezheng*). Both Williamson
and Li Sui published detailed descriptions of their travels in prefamine
Shanxi. Their accounts reveal the prosperity that characterized the province in the late-Qing period.[1]

Located on a loess plateau about two hundred miles west of Beijing,
Shanxi Province is approximately the size of England and Wales combined. The Shanxi plateau rises nearly four thousand feet above the plain
of Zhili, and the province is cut off from the North China plain and the
seacoast by mountains. The Yellow River marks Shanxi's border with
Shaanxi Province to the west and Henan Province to the south, and mountains and the outermost Great Wall mark Shanxi's northern border with
the Mongol areas of Suiyuan and Chahar (today's Inner Mongolia). In
the center of the province lies the densely populated Taiyuan basin, home
to both the provincial capital and Qing Shanxi's wealthy banking institutions. The Fen River flows from the mountains north of Taiyuan toward the southwest, finally joining the Yellow River south of Qing-era
Pingyang Prefecture. That river did not dry up during the drought, so
the fortunate farmers who owned land along the river were able to irri-
gate a few crops. The southernmost agricultural region in the province
is the Yuncheng basin, a populous area known for its enormous salt lake
and the important saltworks.[2]

Li Sui and the Williamson party both entered Shanxi via the great
Guguan Pass, a mountainous stretch of about 130 miles that served as
the principal eastern entrance into Shanxi. Li Sui arrived at the pass in
June of 1793, after leaving his former post in Jiangsu Province and traveling by cart through Shandong and Zhili. He was impressed by what
he saw in Pingding, the area just across the pass from Zhili. The people
of Pingding were educated and cultured, he wrote. Moreover, the area
was very rich in iron ore, so the poor there made a living by mining iron.[3]

Williamson, Lees, a Chinese preacher, a servant, and several carters
set out from Beijing in September 1866. After traversing the level plain
of Zhili for about a week, they left the imperial highway at Jingding and
turned west, entering the Taihang mountains that separate Zhili from
Shanxi. Although they transported heavy cartloads of Christian books
over the rugged Guguan Pass, Williamson's party suffered no mishaps
and took only about five days to traverse the mountain ranges and enter

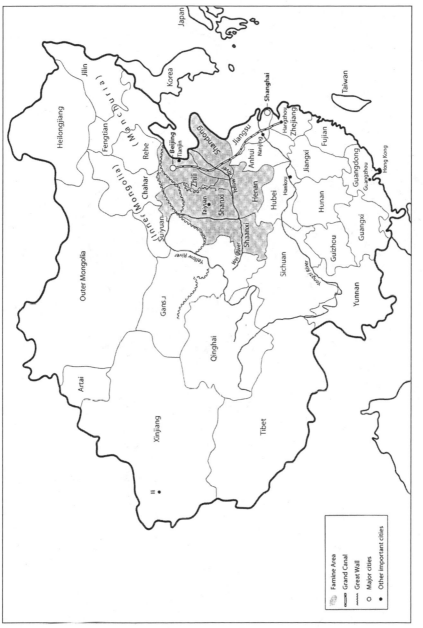

Map 1. The Qing Empire and the North China Famine (Graphic Services, Indiana University)

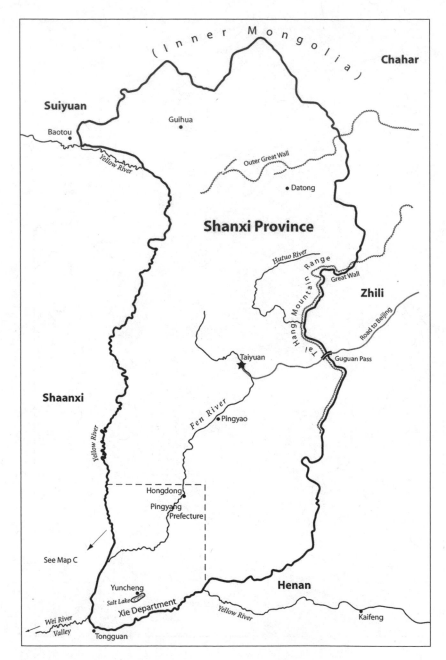

Map 2. Late-Qing Shanxi (Graphic Services, Indiana University)

the plain of Taiyuan.[4] Eleven years later the narrow road through the Guguan Pass became the major artery through which the government attempted to move thousands of piculs of tribute grain from the port of Tianjin into Shanxi to prevent mass starvation there. The pass proved tragically inadequate for this purpose. A report written by R. J. Forrest, the chairman of the China Famine Relief Committee at Tianjin, described the road in terms that would have been unimaginable to Williamson back in 1866:

> The most frightful disorder reigned supreme along this route. Huai-lu Hien [xian], the starting-point, was filled with officials and traders, all intent on getting their convoys over the pass. Fugitives, beggars, and thieves absolutely swarmed. The officials were powerless to create any sort of order among the mountains. The track was frequently worn out, and until a new one was made, a dead block ensued. Camels, oxen, mules, and donkeys were hurried along in the wildest confusion; and so many perished or were killed by the desperate people in the hills for the sake of their flesh, that the transit could only be carried on by the banded vigilance of the interested owners of grain, assisted by the trained bands or militia. . . . Broken carts, scattered grain-bags, dying men and animals, so frequently stopped the way, that it was often necessary to prevent for days together the entry of convoys on the one side, in order to let the trains from the other come over.[5]

The scenes of chaos and death that Forrest witnessed in the Guguan Pass in the late 1870s were repeated throughout southern and central Shanxi. Before the famine, Li Sui and later Williamson described those same areas as thriving and prosperous. Li Sui, while celebrating the Lantern Festival holiday in Taiyuan, witnessed the liberal use of coal. Every year the people of Taiyuan marked the festival night by piling up towers of coal several feet (*chih*) high in their doorways and burning them, he wrote. The towers were called "Fire Pagodas," he reported, and they made the night streets look as bright as day.[6] Williamson devoted pages of admiring prose to the "great and varied" nature of Shanxi's mineral resources, particularly its abundant iron and coal supplies. "At almost every road falling into the imperial highway from the north, we met donkeys laden with coal," he wrote. "We saw pit after pit, collier villages, and all the accessories of coal-mining on the hill-sides. . . . The blocks piled up at the mouths of the pits."[7]

The Shanxi Li Sui described was a place of good food, wine, and well-dressed women. He enjoyed delicious dark-purple grapes in Wen Shui and drank the famous wine made in Fenzhou with enthusiasm, but was perhaps most impressed by the variety of food available in Zezhou Prefecture in southeastern Shanxi. It was said that Shanxi people went their whole lives without tasting crab, he wrote (presumably because the province was far from the sea), but in Zezhou, which traded with nearby Henan, people could enjoy crab, not to mention papaya and many other fruits.[8] Li Sui also noted the wealth of Jiang Department (Jiangzhou) in southwestern Shanxi, the section of the province that would be most severely affected by the North China Famine. Jiangzhou City was a market hub where crowds of merchants converged, he reported. Since it overlooked the Fen River, people could travel by boat from the city to the Yellow River. People in Jiangzhou, continued Li, valued extravagance to the point that young men and women wore trailing garments of fine silk. Shanxi residents called the area "Little Suzhou," presumably because it reminded them of the wealthy South China city famous for its canals, silk production, and beautiful women. Later in his diary Li claimed that all throughout Shanxi it was the custom for men to labor while women enjoyed leisure. Not only the women of wealthy families, he stated disapprovingly, but also poor women who lived in narrow alleys all powdered their faces and oiled their hair.[9] During the 1870s similar critiques of female extravagance were prominent in famine accounts written by local literati in Shanxi.

Williamson's account of prefamine Shanxi emphasized the unusual size and wealth of Shanxi's population. "In Shanxi the cities are more numerous and more populous than anywhere else," he wrote. "The villages of Shanxi are very numerous; they are generally surrounded with high mud-walls, and full of goods of every description, and of people giving not a few indications of wealth and prosperity." Williamson described Taiyuan, the provincial capital, as "a large and noble city" with a population of about 250,000 people. Well-kept walls, a moat, and eight city gates (each with a "splendid" tower) enclosed streets from fifty to seventy feet wide and many good shops. He visited an imperial gun and cannon foundry whose workers were paid a wage of one hundred cash per day as well as food. Eleven years later women and children would be sold on the streets for less than that sum.[10]

Williamson was even more impressed by the province's thriving trade networks, evidenced by the abundance of foreign goods in Shanxi's market towns. "I saw foreign goods in all their busy cities and markets, such as Manchester cottons, Russian woolen goods, matches, needles, etc.," he stated. "I was surprised to find everywhere such quantities of Russian cloth; they evidently carry on a most extensive trade through Mongolia.

We met Russian-speaking Chinamen in several cities. . . . I found also that camel-hire through Central Asia was remarkably inexpensive." He also commented on the wealth of the Yuncheng basin, in the far southwestern corner of the Shanxi plateau. Yuncheng City had a population of 80,000 to 100,000, Williamson estimated. He described the saltworks at the nearby salt lake as a thriving place that employed three hundred different salt merchant firms and produced a sizable revenue for both the Qing government and Shanxi merchants.[11]

Li Sui also emphasized the important role that trade played in Shanxi's economy, though he was less enthusiastic than Williamson would be later about its benefits. In Fenzhou and Pingyang prefectures, areas in south-central and southwestern Shanxi that would suffer terribly during the famine, most people depended on trade to make a living, he claimed. Li Sui identified three types of people who got rich through trade rather than farming. Wealthy financiers who established accounting offices (*zhangju*) in Beijing and other large cities made huge profits by charging high interest rates on loans to officials waiting for appointment to office. Expectant officials who had passed the examinations still needed substantial amounts of cash to pay for gifts and favors that might help them procure a good post.[12]

While the wealthiest merchant families in Fenzhou and Pingyang got rich by playing on the hopes of expectant officials, other entrepreneurs established pawnshops that preyed on the commoners in their own locales. According to Li Sui, the pawnshop owners in Pingyang and Fenzhou were anything but scrupulous. If one brought them gold, "they said it was impure, if pearls, they said they were like rice, if a fur coat, they said it was moth-eaten, if clothing, they said it was tattered. [They] speak evil of all objects so that they can lessen their value," he explained. People who wanted to redeem their possessions had to pay 30 percent more than they had initially received for the objects, and those who could not redeem belongings within two or three years lost them forever. "In name," he railed, pawnshops "are convenient for people, but actually [they are] worms robbing the commoners."[13] Contrary to Li Sui's view, famine accounts written during the 1870s demonstrate that starving families saw the chance to pawn jewelry, furniture, and clothing as a lifeline that provided cash to buy food at famine prices. Yet as the disaster worsened, so many people tried to pawn their possessions that pawnshops were overwhelmed and eventually had to close their doors.[14]

Li Sui also described the muleteers who transported goods and people around the province, traveling over one hundred *li* per day, or 30,000 *li* per year.[15] During the Incredible Famine, this segment of Shanxi's population fared no better than the pawnshop owners or peasantry. Muleteers and carters lost their jobs in the 1870s because the animals they depended on to make a living were either commandeered by famine relief officials in charge of transporting grain into Shanxi or stolen and eaten by famished people.

Williamson's and Li Sui's descriptions of Shanxi before the famine, as well as recent scholarship by historian Henrietta Harrison, highlight the crucial role that trade and other nonagricultural pursuits played in late-Qing Shanxi. Because of the mountainous terrain in Shanxi, only about 20 percent of the land in the Qing period was cultivable.[16] As noted by Li Sui, even as early as the 1790s a large proportion of Shanxi's population did not depend primarily on agriculture for employment. While poor in cultivable land, the province was rich in natural mineral resources including coal, iron ore, salt, tin, copper, marble, and agates. Many families thus made their living working in coal mines, iron foundries, saltworks, lime and pottery kilns, and paper-making centers.[17]

Trade was even more crucial to Shanxi's economy, and young men were often expected to leave their home villages to work as merchants. Shanxi forms a natural corridor linking central China to Mongolia and the northwestern frontier. The imperial troops that the Williamson party witnessed passing through Shanxi in large numbers in 1866 were the most recent in a long line of troops whose presence contributed to the growth of Shanxi's trade networks. During the Ming period (1368–1644), Mongolia was China's main strategic frontier. Shanxi merchants made a fortune after winning government permission to operate the salt and tea trades in return for provisioning the frontier armies. After the Manchus made both Mongolia and China part of the Qing empire in the mid-seventeenth century, Shanxi merchants entered Mongolia and played an important role in the Sino-Mongolia trade. Once the Qing signed the Sino-Russian Treaty of Kiakhta in 1728, the extensive trade with Russia conducted at the Mongolian border town of Kiakhta also came to be controlled by Shanxi merchants.[18] In return for Chinese tea, silk, and cotton, they imported horses, sheep, and woolen cloth from Mongolia and Russia. They also marketed Shanxi's abundant supply of salt, iron, and coal to other areas in China proper.[19]

The merchant-run financial institutions that Li Sui observed in the 1790s became even more wealthy and powerful in the second half of the nineteenth century. Great trading houses used their profits to develop the Shanxi *piaohao*, one of China's main banking networks from 1850 to 1911. The Shanxi banks held and transferred government funds and acted as multipurpose intermediaries between the government and the money market.[20] Having begun in the 1820s, this banking system increased in scale during the Taiping Rebellion, when many provinces started remitting their tax receipts through the Shanxi banks because tax silver could not be safely shipped through rebel-occupied areas. Shanxi's trading houses and banks, based in the Yuncheng and Taiyuan basins, also established branch offices in Hankou, Shanghai, and other major cities in southern and central China.[21]

Famine folktales about the Incredible Famine highlight the importance of merchants in late-Qing Shanxi. A story that Chai Fengju from southern Shanxi's Dingcun Village heard as a child from her grandmother reconfirms that male family members frequently worked as merchants in other provinces. According to Mrs. Chai, during the Guangxu 3 famine, there was no rain for three years, and after a time purchasing a young child as a servant or future concubine cost only two eggs. A man named Zhang Yongsheng had a wife and two small children. Desperate to save her family, Zhang's wife willingly sold herself to a human trader from South China for 1,000 coins. Luckily a merchant who had just returned with a lot of money earned by selling goods in South China ran into the human trader on the road. To his horror, he recognized the woman purchased by the trader as his younger sister, who clung to him and cried when she saw him. When the merchant tried to redeem her, the trafficker initially refused because she was very pretty. Only after the merchant offered the trader every bit of his silver did the trafficker relinquish the sister and allow her to return home.[22]

Few traces of late-Qing Shanxi's wealth, influence, and strategic importance are evident in the hundreds of letters and reports that foreign and Chinese relief workers wrote about Shanxi during the famine years. Missionaries who entered the plain of Taiyuan in late 1877, for example, wrote of encountering "the silence of stupefied misery." R. J. Forrest described how women struggled to bury their dead children, while dogs and crows feasted on those who had perished alone. "Gangs of desperadoes" terrorized those who dared to leave their homes, he wrote, and in each ruined house were found "the dead, the dying, and the living huddled together on the same stone bed."[23] The Shanghai newspaper *Shenbao* published equally disturbing reports for a Chinese audience. Early in 1878 it reported that a filial son from a decent family had beaten his famished step-brothers to death for stealing the pittance of food he had procured for his starving mother, and then had confessed his crime to the authorities in the hope that he and his mother might obtain food by being thrown into prison. [24]

Famine-related depictions of Shanxi shaped perceptions of the province not only among nineteenth-century observers but also among modern scholars who study the famine. Even now it is difficult to find English- or Chinese-language scholarship on the disaster that portrays late-Qing Shanxi as anything but a drought-ridden, miserably poor, and inaccessible part of China. Chinese publications on Shanxi during the Incredible Famine routinely begin with descriptions of the province's mountainous terrain and transportation difficulties.[25] The most detailed English-language discussion of the famine, Paul Richard Bohr's book on missionary relief efforts, is heavily influenced by missionary depictions of Shanxi. Like the foreign relief workers who saw the province at its worst, Bohr highlights the "narrow, winding and often impassable roads over tortuous countryside" that separated Shanxi from the coast. Due to severe deforestation and soil erosion in Shanxi, he concludes, "even in normal times, farmers could barely eke out a living from this barren land." Mike Davis's more recent work on late-nineteenth-century famines also introduces Shanxi as "an impoverished, landlocked province."[26]

Sadly, such descriptions of Shanxi came to fruition in the early twentieth century. In the decades after the 1911 Republican revolution, Shanxi was ranked as one of China's poorest provinces, and its mid-nineteenth-century surpluses gave way to yearly deficits of over seventy-five million Chinese yuan.[27] It continues to lag far behind China's thriving coastal regions.

No single cause accounts for Shanxi's decline. As Harrison has demonstrated, both the central government's decision to focus more attention on the southeast coast than on inland North China and the adverse effects of Mongolian independence and the Russian Revolution on the trade networks so crucial to Shanxi merchants played important roles in turning Shanxi "from a major trading corridor into an isolated and inaccessible province."[28] Some aspects of Shanxi's decline, however, can be traced back to the Incredible Famine of 1876–79.

THE WAGES OF FAMINE

The North China Famine had a considerable impact on Shanxi and on the late-Qing empire as a whole. The disaster wrought additional damage on already weakened national and provincial finances. The customs official and historian of China H. B. Morse calculated that between 1876 and 1878 the Qing government granted more than eighteen million taels of tax remissions, equal to "more than one-fifth of one year's receipts of the imperial treasury," to drought-stricken Shanxi, Henan, Shaanxi, and Zhili. Revenues from the northern provinces remained low for several years afterwards as they struggled to rebuild their tax bases. The central government also allocated more than five million taels in direct aid for famine relief, and ordered provinces outside the famine area to loan additional relief money to the drought-stricken provinces.[29] More than 2.2 million *mu* of Shanxi Province's roughly 56.4 million *mu* of cultivatable land was abandoned during the famine, so no taxes could be collected from those areas. This had a serious effect on the provincial treasury. Even before the famine, Shanxi's annual expenditures had exceeded its revenue by some two million taels per year, but after the famine this jumped to an annual deficit of roughly five million taels.[30]

In addition to adversely affecting national and provincial finances, famine conditions hindered long-distance trade between Shanxi and its neighbors and within the province itself. The long drought made some waterways in Shanxi and Henan unnavigable, forcing salt merchants and others who ordinarily relied on water transport for at least part of their journeys to switch to far costlier land routes. Overland trade routes were also disrupted. The government commandeered as many boats, camels, carts, mules, and horses as possible in order to transport grain into the province. Moreover, both officials and merchants found it increasingly difficult to procure fodder for pack animals during the drought, and those that survived were in danger of being slaughtered and eaten by the starving populace. It thus became increasingly difficult for Shanxi merchants to transport their goods for sale elsewhere. The sharp decline in commerce during the famine is reflected in the 54.9 percent decrease between 1876 and 1878 in provincial transit tax (*lijin*) revenues.[31]

Local markets and industries suffered as well. In south and central Shanxi the local markets for salt, paper, silk, coal, and iron collapsed as people spent an increasing percentage of their income to buy food at famine prices. Local industries were also hurt by a loss of affordable labor because roughly a third of the province's prefamine population died or fled. Li Wenhai and three colleagues, in their book on ten great disasters in China's modern history, argue that Shanxi's traditional iron and silk industries never recovered from the ravages of the Incredible Famine. Jincheng County, for example, had nearly a thousand iron foundries in the 1850s, but only half that number after the famine. Moreover, the number of silk worker families in the Zezhou area is said to have de-

clined from "over a thousand" to only one.[32] The famed Hedong saltworks, which had so impressed Williamson, also declined during and after the famine due to high transport and labor costs and low demand.[33]

The demographic impact of the Incredible Famine is the most disturbing aspect of the disaster. While reliable data are lacking, all estimates posit population loss in the millions. In his March 1879 report,
R. J. Forrest used data collected by foreign relief workers to estimate that
9.5 million people had died due to the famine—roughly 5.5 million in
Shanxi, 2.5 million in Zhili, 1 million in Henan, and 500,000 in Shandong. Estimates increased in the years following the catastrophe. In 1922
the Peking United International Famine Relief Committee reckoned that
between 9 and 13 million deaths had occurred. That is the range most
commonly cited in later studies of the famine.[34]

Shanxi bore the brunt of famine-related demographic loss. He Hanwei demonstrates that while the population of Shanxi, Henan, and
Shaanxi grew rapidly from the 1760s to the 1850s, between 1850 and
1898 Shanxi's population actually declined by about 31 percent, Shaanxi's
by 29 percent, and Henan's by 7.5 percent. While Shaanxi and to a lesser
degree Henan had already experienced serious population losses before
the famine because of the Northwest Muslim rebellion (discussed later
in the chapter), in Shanxi's case the dramatic population decrease was
primarily attributable to the famine.[35]

Estimates of population loss in Shanxi during the famine vary widely.
Toward the end of the disaster Shanxi's governor, Zeng Guoquan, wrote
that nearly half of the people of Shanxi had died since the famine had
begun and that deaths were continuing due to epidemic disease.[36] The
edition of the Shanxi provincial gazetteer compiled shortly after the
famine under Zeng Guoquan's order and published in 1892 stated that
based on the province's population registers, no fewer than ten million
people had died during the famine.[37] Foreign relief workers gave a lower
but still sickening approximation: roughly 5.5 million of Shanxi's prefamine population of 15 million had "perished of famine and the subsequent pestilence."[38] Liu Rentuan's recent gazetteer-based study of the
famine's impact on Shanxi's population from 1877 through 1953 finds
that both the province's prefamine population and famine-related loss
were higher than the foreign estimates but lower than Zeng Guoquan's.
Liu states that Shanxi's population dropped from 17.2 to 9.6 million between 1876 and 1880—an astounding 44.2 percent loss.[39] It is impossible to ascertain from gazetteer records how many of Shanxi's missing
millions died during the famine and how many migrated to other areas.

Liu Rentuan also charts demographic shifts within Shanxi itself. Southwestern Shanxi, which was so prosperous before the disaster, suffered the greatest losses. Liu puts the prefamine population of southwestern Shanxi at 5.9 million, or 34.3 percent of Shanxi's total 1876 population of 17 million. By 1880 this area had lost 3.9 million people to death or flight, or roughly 66 percent of its 1876 population, and its proportion of the province's total population had fallen to 20.4 percent. There was heavy immigration into this depopulated area after the famine, but the region never regained its former preeminence in either population density or wealth. Even in 1953, when China's first modern census was conducted, the southwestern area constituted only 22.4 percent of Shanxi's total population. Liu argues that the famine hampered the province's development in the late nineteenth and early twentieth centuries. He attributes the dramatic decline in capital accumulation among Shanxi's rural and urban population to population loss, and asserts that the damage to the material wealth of Shanxi society also delayed cultural change in the province.[40]

PRC scholars argue that the Incredible Famine, in combination with other natural disasters that struck late-Qing China, impaired national as well as provincial economic development during the late-Qing period. Xia Mingfang, for example, asserts that the Self Strengthening Movement (1861–95), which aimed to enrich and strengthen China by fostering industrialization, was seriously hampered by a series of costly and destructive floods and droughts that drained the Qing treasury and diverted the attention of progressive officials away from modernization efforts. By demonstrating that natural disasters significantly impeded primitive capital accumulation and the development of commodity and labor markets in late-nineteenth-century China, Xia's research expands to the national level Liu's assertion that the famine hampered capital accumulation in Shanxi.[41] Mike Davis takes the discussion of the impact of "natural" disasters to a global level. The devastating famines that struck China, India, and Brazil in the late nineteenth century, he argues, both resulted from and hastened the transformation of "former 'core' regions of eighteenth-century subcontinental power systems" into "famished peripheries of a London-centered world economy."[42]

Whether one focuses on the local, provincial, national, or global level, the effects of the North China Famine were serious and long lasting. As the epicenter of this famine, Shanxi was particularly devastated. Contrary to the assumption often made in scholarship on the disaster, however, prefamine Shanxi was not a poor, isolated, or backward part of

China. Its banking and trading networks were of national importance, and its traditional industries provided its people with many nonagricultural employment opportunities. Shortly before the drought, Shanxi appeared to be in better economic shape than neighboring provinces. How, then, did the drought that struck the province in the mid-1870s result in such a destructive and unprecedented famine?

CONTEXT AND CAUSATION: AN EMPIRE IN CRISIS

The severe drought that struck North China in the late 1870s was the catalyst but not the underlying cause of the Incredible Famine. Droughts were nothing unusual in Shanxi, or in North China generally. Qing rulers and officials might well have agreed with economist and philosopher Amartya Sen's assertion that "droughts may not be avoidable, but their effects can be." They were well aware of the "high degree of uncertainty" concerning climate and water resources in the north, and throughout the eighteenth century and well into the nineteenth they took impressive measures to prevent droughts from escalating into famines.[43] The drought that began in 1875 was more prolonged and affected a much wider area than was usual even for North China. Nevertheless, in a "vast, integrated, and highly commercialized economy such as that of the Qing," a serious regional dearth did not have to result in a major famine.[44] Had such a serious drought occurred in the eighteenth century, when the Qing state's power and commitment to storing and distributing grain were at their apex, the state could have significantly reduced, though perhaps not wholly prevented, the ensuing devastation.

In contrast, by the late nineteenth century the Qing state had been considerably weakened by the mid-century rebellions, the pressure of foreign imperialism, and a lack of strong leadership. It was no longer capable of intervening in food crises to the extent that it had a century earlier. The government's failure to act in a timely manner was particularly problematic for grain-poor provinces like Shanxi that depended on early government intervention and on regional grain trade networks to obtain sufficient grain during a subsistence crisis.

Before the decline of the Qing granary system, which began in the 1790s and reached crisis levels after 1850, Qing officials relied on state and community granaries to keep grain prices down and to provide emergency relief during subsistence crises. As historians Pierre-Etienne Will and R. Bin Wong explain, "ever-normal granaries" (*changping cang*) were run by officials who bought and sold grain with the state's money. Granary officials sought to cushion the impact of seasonal price fluctuations by buying up cheap grain immediately after the harvest and reselling it at low prices during the lean period before the new harvest arrived. Ever-normal granaries also served as emergency food banks that softened the impact of natural disasters by distributing granary reserves to the poor. In addition to the grain stored in ever-normal granaries, during the eighteenth century, grain-poor provinces like Shanxi stored between 20 and 40 percent of their total reported provincial grain reserves in semi-official or nonofficial community and charity granaries (*shecang* and *yicang*). These granaries were supposed to be run by local gentry and to rely on contributions from wealthy families rather than from the government.[45]

The Qing granary system was vital to the welfare of drought-prone northern provinces. Pierre-Étienne Will's overview of the relief campaign carried out by the Qing state during the serious drought that struck Zhili and northern Shandong from 1743 to 1744 provides a vivid example of the high-Qing government's ability to prevent a natural calamity from escalating into a full-blown catastrophe. During the 1743 drought, Zhili, unlike late-Qing Shanxi, had sufficient reserves in its ever-normal granaries to keep people alive until government grain issues could arrive.[46] Moreover, once local reserves were exhausted, the high-Qing state kept some two million people alive for eight months by granting ten successive "allocations" of grain to Zhili. Due to the "very narrow margin of surplus in North China," nearly 75 percent of the relief grain the government rushed into Zhili had to be imported from tribute depots or granaries from other regions of the empire—53.3 percent from Yangzi valley provinces and 21 percent from areas in Mongolia and Manchuria.[47]

As this eighteenth-century example demonstrates, it was crucial for grain-poor northern provinces like Shanxi to establish transport networks that could quickly import surplus grain from South China or from northern areas outside the Great Wall. More than a century before the North China Famine, mountainous Shanxi lost the ability to cultivate enough grain to feed its burgeoning population. Over the course of the eighteenth and nineteenth centuries the province imported more and more grain. Highly conscious of the instability of the food supply in Shanxi and neighboring provinces, activist Qing officials in the eighteenth century strove to increase the grain reserves at three strategic transportation nodes where the Yellow River meets the Wei River or the Fen River along Shanxi's far southern border with Shaanxi and Henan.[48]

The Qing government experimented with transporting tribute grain from Henan up the Yellow River into Yuncheng or from Zhili through the Taihang mountains into Taiyuan, but the difficulty of moving grain upstream or through the narrow Guguan Pass made those two routes impractical. They were used only in times of severe emergency. Normally, officials and merchants imported grain into Shanxi from the west and north. From the eighteenth century on, the province depended heavily on grain surpluses from neighboring Shaanxi's Wei River valley and from newly cultivated land north of the Great Wall.[49]

Shanxi's wealthy grain merchants played a vital role in ensuring that the province imported enough grain. During the eighteenth and nineteenth centuries they regularly transported grain from central Shaanxi into the heavily populated Yuncheng area of southern Shanxi. After shipping Shaanxi rice and wheat in large boats down the Wei River, upon reaching the Yellow River border with Shanxi, merchants transferred the grain into smaller boats and transported it upstream via Shanxi's Fen River or carted it overland to Yuncheng.[50] Through their well-established trade networks, Shanxi merchants also procured grain from areas north of the province's main population centers and the Great Wall. Grain dealers transported grain surpluses from southern Inner Mongolia and northern Shanxi overland a thousand *li* (more than three hundred miles) to the Taiyuan basin. Merchants and Qing officials also attempted to move grain from the fertile Hetao region of Inner Mongolia to southern Shanxi via the Yellow River. The distances involved and the difficulties of navigating the river's often violent current, however, meant that importing sufficient grain from the north remained a problematic and costly endeavor. Until the mid-nineteenth century, Shanxi imported more grain from Shaanxi's Wei River valley than from areas "outside the wall."[51]

Beginning in the 1860s the Qing government's brutal suppression of the Northwest Muslim rebellion in Shaanxi and Gansu (1862–73) destabilized the Wei River valley and seriously hampered its ability to produce grain surpluses. The purchasing power of people in southern and central Shanxi enabled the province to import sufficient grain for more than a decade after the depletion of the vital Wei valley surplus, but grain-hungry Shanxi was gradually forced to import more and more grain from the less accessible surplus areas of Inner Mongolia.[52]

In sum, in spite of Shanxi's serious transportation difficulties and the province's inability to grow enough grain to support its own population, a combination of well-stocked government granaries and the wealth and flexibility of Shanxi's trading networks enabled officials and merchants to deal with annual grain shortages and years of dearth fairly successfully in the eighteenth and much of the nineteenth centuries. During the

Incredible Famine, however, Shanxi's ability to procure sufficient grain collapsed completely and spectacularly. The Qing government tried desperately to ship tribute grain into Shanxi from the east via the Guguan Pass, but as detailed accounts by contemporary observers reveal, those efforts were doomed.

Fiscal problems also contributed to the late-Qing state's inability to get grain into Shanxi in a timely manner. During the eighteenth century, high-Qing officials maintained an effective granary system and mustered enormous amounts of cash and grain relief during famines, in large part because the state's generous fiscal reserves normally remained at around twenty million taels. By the time drought struck North China in the 1870s, the Qing treasury had suffered major reversals. The decline in fiscal reserves began in the late eighteenth century, when the state spent some one hundred million taels to suppress the White Lotus Rebellion of 1796–1804. By the early nineteenth century, tax collection became more and more difficult, and the imperial clan had grown from 2,000 members in the early-Qing period to 30,000 members, their maintenance costing several million taels a year. As the century progressed, the cost of maintaining the Yellow River dikes grew tremendously because of increasingly serious flooding brought about by ecological destruction.[53] Paying indemnities to victorious Western powers after military confrontations, and financing coastal defense projects aimed at improving China's ability to repel maritime invaders, brought additional fiscal pressures.

Above all, it was the mid-century rebellions that began in the 1850s that depleted both national and provincial resources, leaving them woefully ill-prepared to deal with a major drought. The combined fiscal impact of the Taiping Rebellion (1851–64), Nian Rebellion (1853–68), and two major rebellions waged by Muslims in Southwest and Northwest China (1855–73) was enormous. According to some calculations, military expenses constituted nearly three-fourths of total governmental expenditures. The Taiping war devastated some of China's richest Yangzi valley provinces and cut off the capital from the land tax and salt monopoly revenues of thirteen provinces. Simultaneously, the Nian rebels disrupted administration in large sections of four northern provinces, and the Muslim revolts in the southwest and northwest depopulated entire areas.[54]

The monumental effort to suppress the mid-century rebellions wreaked havoc on the Qing granary system so important to ensuring North China's food supply. The empire-wide granaries that had stored as much as forty-eight million piculs of reserve grain during the high-Qing period

had less than twenty million piculs left by the 1850s.[55] Will and Wong
assert that the Qing granary system never fully recovered from the devastating civil unrest that began in that decade. "Ultimately," they write,
"benevolent methods of promoting social welfare to ensure social stability lost some of their appeal in the face of the dramatic political challenges posed by the mid-century rebellions. The food supply priorities of
the state shifted to provisioning large numbers of troops."[56] By the 1870s,
then, the high-Qing state's formidable eighteenth-century ability to deal
with food crises had for the most part been replaced by a makeshift system run by local elites who lacked the state's power to maintain large
granary reserves and carry out vital interregional grain transfers.[57]

The decades of warfare also had a significant, if indirect, impact on
Shanxi's ability to deal with the 1870s drought and ensuing famine. Four
of the five famine-stricken provinces—Shandong, Zhili, Henan, and
Shaanxi—were ravaged by rebel forces and their Qing opponents during the decades immediately preceding the famine. Shanxi escaped most
of the active warfare, though Pingyang Prefecture and other southern
areas were briefly invaded by the Taiping army in 1853 and by Nian
troops in 1868.[58] The heavy financial burden of supporting the Qing
state's war effort, however, threw the province's finances into disarray.
Because Shanxi was a wealthy province relatively unscathed by the wars,
it was expected to contribute a great deal to the struggle to suppress the
various rebels. Li Wenhai and his colleagues estimate that Shanxi's annual revenue in the decades preceding the disaster was about three million taels, but the annual amount the province had to raise for tribute,
military expenses, local armies, and official salaries came close to five
million taels.[59]

After the famine the new governor of Shanxi, Zhang Zhidong, argued that Shanxi had fallen into fiscal insolvency because of the massive expenses it had paid beginning with the Taiping Rebellion. During
the decades of warfare, wrote Zhang, Shanxi's treasury and its wealthy
merchants had repeatedly been called on to lend money and goods to
finance China's military efforts. In addition, a constant stream of soldiers and officials had passed through Shanxi on their way to the conflicts
in the northwest, forcing Shanxi to feed and house all of them. Zhang
estimated the total aid Shanxi sent to other areas of the country during
this time at fifty to sixty million taels.[60] Due to the extensive aid that
wealthy Shanxi had provided from 1850 on, by the time the drought arrived in 1875, the provincial treasury and granaries had few reserves to
fall back on.

The mid-century rebellions also had adverse effects on some of Shanxi's rich merchants. The destruction the Taiping war caused in the Jiangnan region hurt the Shanxi merchants who conducted much of their business there, and they were also pressured to contribute money for military expenses.[61] Moreover, during the 1860s Shanxi's merchants began to lose their monopoly of Sino-Russian overland trade via Mongolia. Preoccupied with quelling the rebellions within its borders, the Qing government buckled under pressure to sign an unequal treaty with Russia that opened the empire's northern frontier to Russia's political and commercial influence and reframed the rules for frontier trade. The Sino-Russian Treaty of Peking (1860) and the ensuing Sino-Russian Overland Trade Regulations (1862) established a favorable system for Russian merchants who traded in Mongolia, thereby cutting in on Han (primarily Shanxi-based) merchants. Worse still, the Russian government legalized the maritime tea trade. At the expense of overland trade routes, Russian ships carried tea and other Chinese goods from Canton and Shanghai to Odessa, bypassing Shanxi merchants altogether.[62]

In short, the nearly three decades of warfare that preceded the North China Famine drained national and provincial treasuries, disrupted trade and commerce across large regions of the country, and took the government's attention away from vital matters such as maintaining granary reserves, roads, and dikes. When the drought spread across North China in the late 1870s, it caught both the Qing state and the exhausted provincial governments in the north unprepared.

A lack of strong leadership was yet another factor that hindered the late-Qing state's response to the drought. Will's study of the government's effective relief effort during the drought of 1743–44 highlights the importance of imperial oversight and activism. "The fact that the emperor had proclaimed his interest in the efficient conduct of relief operations had swept away all the obstacles that might have prevented the use of the channels of communication (and deliberation) reserved for important government business," writes Will.[63] In contrast, during the late 1870s there was no strong imperial voice, and no one person or group had the authority and confidence to set a clear policy.

Questions about the legitimacy of the Guangxu emperor's succession arose in 1875, only a year before the great drought began. When the young Tongzhi emperor died of smallpox in 1875 without leaving an heir, Empress Dowager Cixi selected her three-year-old nephew, Zaitian, as successor to the throne.[64] Her choice shocked Qing officialdom because the child was the late Tongzhi emperor's cousin from the same generation. According to the dynastic law of succession the new emperor should have been selected from the generation below the deceased emperor so that he could perform sacrifices on the latter's behalf. As historian William Ayers has explained, the hasty enthronement of Cixi's nephew as the Guangxu emperor "created an undercurrent of criticism that lasted for more than four years while the empress dowager was trying to consolidate her power anew and forestall the growth of opposition."[65] The weak throne was "able to play a kind of balancing politics by playing off opposing political groups to magnify the significance of its decision making power," states historian Richard Horowitz, but was "unable to drive policy forward."[66]

The lack of a strong ruler on the throne enhanced the importance of the Grand Council and the Zongli Yamen during the famine years. The Grand Council, a supervising and coordinating high privy inner-court body that originated in the mid-Qing era, was in charge of drafting imperial edicts and presenting them to the emperor (or dowager empresses) for approval.[67] The Zongli Yamen (office for the management of affairs with the various countries) was the powerful coordinating bureau established in 1861 to take charge of all matters concerning the Western powers. During the 1860s and the early 1870s Prince Gong and Wenxiang, two influential members of both the Grand Council and the Zongli Yamen, used the latter as a political base from which to push forward self-strengthening policies such as purchasing Western weapons and establishing shipyards and arsenals. Wenxiang, a Manchu grand councilor, was the pre-eminent figure in the Yamen from its inception in 1861 until the eve of the famine. Prince Gong, the Xianfeng emperor's younger brother and the Tongzhi emperor's uncle, was named "deliberative prince" and put in charge of advising the dowager empresses on affairs of state after his brother's death in 1861.[68]

Between 1865 and 1875, however, Cixi increasingly checked Prince Gong's influence and ability to steer Qing policy. In 1875 Prince Gong failed to have his son installed as the successor to the Tongzhi emperor and watched as his brother's son and Cixi's nephew took the throne instead.[69] Then in 1876 Wenxiang died, depriving the Yamen of one of its most influential leaders. "Between 1875 and 1880," Lolan Wang Grady writes, "the decision-making group in the Grand Council and the Tsungli Yamen was much less cohesive than it had been prior to 1875."[70] The day after Wenxiang's death, Prince Gong wrote a poem that interweaves his grief over the great statesman's death with his anxiety about the drought spreading across North China:

In the midst of the great drought, we wait in vain for the timely rain,
Dark clouds have hidden the lustre of the bright star;
You, who have toiled tirelessly for the country both at home and beyond,
Have brought honor to your banner, such that it is known to the Emperor;
Righteousness and caution have guided your steps throughout your life,
In assisting us for twenty years you have sworn the oath of loyalty and
    sincerity,
But from this day on, my eyes shall not want for tears.[71]

Bereft of strong guidance from either the throne or the Zongli Yamen,
the Qing government in the late 1870s had more difficulty than usual in
implementing a famine policy requiring large-scale expenditures. Bureaucratic responsibility for financial matters was divided among many
different government organs, including the Board of Revenue, the Grand
Council, the Imperial Household Department, and the Zongli Yamen in
the capital, and the imperially appointed treasurers in each province. "Any
crisis or reform proposal threatened to degenerate into an acrimonious
debate," states Horowitz, "making the swift resolution of problems, and
the consistent pursuit of policy difficult and perhaps impossible."[72]

During the worst years of the famine, then, the succession crisis had
weakened the throne, Wenxiang's leadership had ended, Prince Gong and
the Zongli Yamen no longer led the formation of new policies, and the
most influential officials in the realm were bitterly divided over which
crisis presented the greatest threat to Qing rule. In spite of these problems, the grim fiscal and political realities facing late-nineteenth-century
China forced Qing rulers and their ministers to make excruciating
choices about how best to use the country's depleted resources.

The years preceding the famine were anxious ones for the Qing empire. The 1856–60 Anglo-French War on China (the Arrow War), the
harsh terms the victors imposed on China in the Treaty of Tianjin (1858),
and the burning and looting of the treasured imperial Summer Palace
outside Beijing by British troops in 1860 accentuated the threat posed
by the West.[73] The decade of relatively calm Sino-Western relations that
followed the Arrow War came to an explosive end in 1870, both because
of Britain's rejection of revisions that would have softened the punitive
character of the Treaty of Tianjin and, more infamously, because of the
Tianjin Massacre and its aftermath.[74] The Tianjin catastrophe occurred
when tensions between French and Chinese Catholics on one hand and
Chinese officials and commoners on the other boiled over in June of that
year. A Chinese crowd angered by French arrogance and by rumors that
French Catholic nuns were mistreating Chinese orphans killed between

thirty and forty Chinese converts and twenty-one foreigners, including two French officials and several nuns and priests. In addition to the damage done to Sino-French relations, the incident led to increased conflict between opposing groups within the Chinese bureaucracy. Self-strengtheners hoped to avoid another war by pursuing a conciliatory policy with the foreign powers involved, while the most anti-foreign wing of the Chinese bureaucracy viewed such a policy as tantamount to selling China's soul. After rancorous debate, the Qing government agreed to execute eighteen Chinese found guilty of conducting attacks and to pay a total of 492,500 taels to compensate for foreign loss of life and property damage.[75]

In addition to defending China's eastern seaboard from foreign aggression, Qing rulers in the 1870s also had to deal with serious threats to the empire's northwestern frontier. Xinjiang, the inner-Asian frontier that Qing emperors had struggled to conquer in the mid-eighteenth century, was thrown into turmoil by the Muslim revolts that convulsed Shaanxi and Gansu from 1862 to 1872. After much of Xinjiang fell to the Muslim rebel commander Ya'qub Beg in 1870, Russia, eager to ensure that Ya'qub did not support the independence of the Central Asian Islamic states Russia was then in the process of conquering, invaded and occupied Xinjiang's rich Ili valley in 1871. Qing rulers viewed Xinjiang as their first line of defense in the northwest and feared both Russian territorial designs and the regional instability that might result from continued Muslim control. Once the Qing forces under Zuo Zongtang finally overcame the Chinese Muslims in Shaanxi and Gansu in 1873, the government set its sights on recovering Xinjiang.[76]

But as Zuo Zongtang awaited the imperial court's permission to launch the campaign to retake Xinjiang, yet another challenge, on the southeastern coast, arose to demand the government's attention and money. In April of 1874 a Japanese "punitive expedition" landed on the eastern coast of Taiwan under the pretext of punishing members of the Botan tribe for killing shipwrecked sailors from the Ryukyu Islands and Japan. Japan apparently aimed to assert its control over the Ryukyu Islands, which were a tributary of China, and to challenge Qing sovereignty over those areas of Taiwan dominated by aboriginal groups. The Qing government responded by appointing Shen Baozhen, the director of the Fuzhou Dockyard, to be imperial commissioner in charge of maritime defense of Taiwan. Shen was given permission to purchase foreign arms and negotiate a foreign loan of up to six million taels, but he soon realized that his forces could not defeat the Japanese navy and its ironclad ships. The impasse was broken only when China agreed to pay a 500,000-tael indemnity to Japan and to refrain from condemning Japan's actions.[77]

The realization that China was unprepared to respond forcefully to a naval challenge posed by a much smaller Asian neighbor shocked Qing officialdom and raised the question of which was more urgent, the threat to China's seacoast or the danger along the northwestern frontier. In November 1874, less than a week after the Taiwan crisis was resolved, officials from the Zongli Yamen submitted a memorial to the throne proposing "dramatic reforms" in the empire's coastal defense capabilities. The imperial court circulated the Yamen's memorial to leading provincial and metropolitan officials and solicited their responses, thus initiating a major policy debate over whether coastal or frontier defense was more critical.[78] The debate highlights the fact that by the mid-1870s, both the Qing court and many high officials had come to see foreign military aggression rather than domestic unrest as the more serious threat to Qing survival.

The Zongli Yamen's memorial expressed the fear that foreigners who had observed China's inability to defend Taiwan might take advantage of the dynasty's military weakness to launch an attack. It recommended that the country's highest officials submit their views on the needs of coastal defense and suggest ways to find additional funding for military training, modern weapons, and shipbuilding.[79] In response Li Hongzhang, the powerful official responsible for defending China's northern ports, boldly suggested that the government should abandon the costly campaign to recover Xinjiang and use the money saved to fund a more effective coastal defense program, which he estimated would cost ten million taels per year. "Nonrecovery of Xinjiang will not hurt us physically or spiritually," he wrote, "whereas lack of preparedness in coastal defense renders our basic trouble even more difficult."[80]

While some officials wrote in support of Li's arguments, other prominent statesmen including leaders in the Zongli Yamen sided with Zuo Zongtang, the influential official in charge of the Xinjiang campaign. Zuo asserted that it was strategically vital to recover Xinjiang. If Xinjiang were lost, the empire would not be able to defend Mongolia, he claimed, and the loss of Mongolia would endanger the security of the capital. Zuo agreed that the Western powers were a threat, but he opposed shifting funds from frontier to coastal defense. Because Russia had both territorial and commercial designs while the Western maritime nations were primarily interested in trade, he reasoned, the Russians represented the more serious threat to China.[81]

The policy debate of 1874–75 impacted the government's ability and willingness to deal effectively with the massive famine that struck only two years later. The court backed Zuo Zongtang's position that it was imperative to recover Xinjiang from Muslim and Russian rule, thereby rejecting Li Hongzhang's proposal to shift funds from the Xinjiang campaign to coastal defense. And it responded only vaguely and ineffectually to the Zongli Yamen's request that the government find additional funds for coastal defense projects.[82] Li and the Yamen became all the more determined, therefore, to guard the already scarce resources earmarked for coastal defense and other self-strengthening projects. During the famine they attempted to prevent transfer of the considerable funds under their jurisdiction from coastal defense to famine relief.[83]

Moreover, the costly campaign to recover Xinjiang coincided with the worst years of the Incredible Famine, thus making it all the more difficult for the state to fund relief efforts for the starving people of North China. For the three-year period from 1875 to the end of 1877, Zuo Zongtang received a total of 26.7 million taels, or 8.9 million taels per year, for the Xinjiang campaign. These funds came from foreign loans, Board of Revenue grants previously earmarked for coastal defense, and money contributed by twelve different provinces. Then between 1878 and 1881, additional interprovincial revenue assistance totaling 25.6 million taels went toward prosecution of the war, making a total of 52.3 million taels for the entire campaign.[84] In comparison, according to the Shanxi provincial gazetteer compiled shortly after the famine, between 1877 and 1879 a little over 10.7 million taels of relief silver and roughly one million piculs of relief grain were distributed in Shanxi.[85]

During the Incredible Famine, Shanxi, and to a lesser extent four other northern provinces, faced a crisis so severe that starving families were forced to choose which family members to save and which to abandon. The late-Qing state faced equally tough choices in the late 1870s. By that point many high officials viewed defending China against foreign assaults—whether along the eastern seacoast or the northwestern frontier—as more urgent than relieving the starving northern provinces. Famine relief was of central importance only to a group of moralistic censors and low-ranking officials known as the Pure Current (Qingliu). Qingliu spokesmen, however, generally lacked the power to get their suggestions approved over the objections of higher-ranking officials.

The comparatively low priority placed on famine relief for North China corroborates Kenneth Pomeranz's argument that beginning in the

1860s, the Qing state gradually abandoned inland North China in order to focus its resources on coastal (or frontier) areas where the threat
of imperialism was more dangerous, thereby turning what had been a
core region of the empire into an impoverished periphery. "The foreign
onslaught destroyed basic principles of Ming-Qing statecraft, particularly a commitment to social reproduction that had often required rich
areas to subsidize the infrastructure of poorer ones," states Pomeranz.
Instead, "resources had to be used where they did the most to protect
China's threatened autonomy from direct intervention or the consequences of foreign debt or both."[86]

In the late 1870s the Qing government did appropriate and borrow
sufficient funds to recover and keep Xinjiang. This impressive accom-
plishment laid the foundation for twentieth-century successors of the
Qing empire to reconstitute a sovereign state that continues to control
the vast majority of the former empire's territory even today.[87] The Xinjiang campaign demonstrates that the late-Qing state did possess the ca-
pability, however attenuated by financial and military pressures, to carry
out expensive and complex policy initiatives on an empire-wide stage.

The Incredible Famine did not attract the resources allocated to defense projects in the late 1870s. This exercise of real agency on the part
of the Qing state suggests the extent to which statecraft had changed for
the Qing since the eighteenth century and demonstrates how much the
mid-century rebellions and the threat of imperialism had transformed
Qing governance over the course of the nineteenth century. Despite the
Confucian priority of mitigating disasters in order to retain the Mandate
of Heaven (particularly important for a conquest dynasty facing the starvation of millions of Han Chinese in North China), and despite the fear
that the famine might provoke additional internal rebellions, relieving
the famine could not compete with the self-strengthening projects and
military campaigns aimed at securing the territory of the Qing empire
from foreign aggression.[88]

THE DROUGHT

The combination of internal rebellions, foreign aggression, fiscal problems, deterioration of the granary system, and weakness and division in
the top echelons of power left both the Qing state as a whole and Shanxi
Province in particular unprepared for a drought of the magnitude of the
one that struck North China between 1876 and 1879. Mike Davis

demonstrates convincingly that the cause of the severe droughts that struck northern China, India, southern Africa, and northeastern Brazil in the late 1870s was a particularly powerful "El Niño event," or a rapid warming of the eastern tropical Pacific that led to the prolonged and virtually complete failure of the monsoons that normally provide rainfall for the affected areas.[89]

In North China a failure of the spring rains generally meant that the wheat and barley planted the winter before would fail to ripen. It also jeopardized the sowing of the autumn millet crop, since the loess soil dried and hardened quickly. A drought that lasted through the summer would doom whatever crops farmers had planted in the spring, resulting in the total failure of both the winter and autumn crops for that year. If rain still failed to arrive during the autumn months, the winter wheat could not be sown and the populace faced the prospect of a hungry spring following on the heels of a brutal winter.[90] This was the general pattern all across North China in the late 1870s. As the drought spread over, not one or two, but *five* major provinces, the normal interaction of grain markets across the entire region was thrown into increasing chaos.

To prevent disaster it was imperative that the state take measures to stabilize prices and transport grain from South China, Manchuria, and Mongolia into the stricken northern provinces. The late-Qing state, however, was poorer, weaker, and more beleaguered than its high-Qing predecessor, and also less committed to using government intervention to shore up the food supply of North China. Thus reports of serious droughts in Shandong, Zhili, Shanxi, Henan, and Shaanxi were not met with early intervention as they would have been a century earlier.

The imperial court did begin prescribing relief measures for famine areas in June 1876, but due to the dismal condition of state and local granaries by the 1870s, relief was often given in cash rather than in grain, and the amounts distributed were not enough to stave off disaster. With the court's attention focused on drought areas closer to the capital and on the Xinjiang campaign, even when the situation in Shanxi took a turn for the worse after the entire autumn millet crop was doomed by the severe summer drought in 1876, no preventive action was taken.

Rain and snow were scarce during the autumn and winter of 1876–77, and the Wei River valley grain surplus so vital to Shanxi's well-being was also stricken by drought. By the spring of 1877 grain prices in Shanxi had skyrocketed, and the poor were surviving on grass roots and tree bark. Early in 1877 the Board of Revenue finally allocated relief money for Shanxi, but not until November was an official relief program formulated, including grain transfers from Manchuria and the sale of grain at reduced prices.[91] By that point, it was simply too late to stem the course of the disaster. Shanxi's mountainous geography made the belated official relief efforts even more ineffective there than in the other stricken provinces. When both the spring and summer rains failed to materialize in 1877, the crops failed for a second year in a row, and the people of Shanxi starved en masse.[92]

CHAPTER 2

Experiencing the Famine

The Hierarchy of Suffering in a Famine Song from Xiezhou

Two decades after the North China Famine, an educated man from Xie Department in southern Shanxi wrote a vivid account of the disaster titled *Huangnian ge* (Song of the famine years). This man, whose pen name was Liu Xing, experienced the famine firsthand and felt compelled to record the events of those years in detail so that later generations would not forget the horror of Guangxu 3. Through Liu Xing's famine song and other local sources, one may examine the famine as experienced by literate survivors who daily witnessed the famine's effects for three years. Although *Huangnian ge* is a personal account of the famine's impact on one small corner of southwestern Shanxi, it foreshadows many of the themes that loom large in a wide range of local, official, treaty-port, and foreign famine accounts from the 1870s. Observers from different levels of late-Qing society interpreted the famine in strikingly diverse ways, but their accounts often echoed Liu Xing's concern over the hierarchy of suffering created by the disaster, the relationship between human misdeeds and the "wrath of Heaven," the responsibility of the emperor and Qing officialdom, the impossible choices the famine forced on family members, the sale of starving women, and famine-related cannibalism.[1]

This song of famine tells us nothing about its author's education or occupation; we do not even know Liu Xing's formal name. The fact that Liu had the resources necessary to survive the catastrophe, however, distinguishes him from the roughly 68 percent of the population of Xie Department that either fled Xie during the famine or perished from starvation or disease.[2] Since Liu Xing was literate and knew which officials were in charge of relief efforts in Xie Department (Xiezhou), he was likely a member of the local elite, perhaps a tutor or a student at a local Confucian school.[3] At the same time, the author of *Huangnian ge* emphatically distanced himself from the rich and powerful in his locale and associated himself instead with the middle-class (*zhongdeng*) families that had to struggle to survive the disaster years. The horrors he describes demonstrate that the famine was traumatic for people of Liu's social standing and for his poorer neighbors who starved or fled.

I became aware of this extraordinary text thanks to Nan Xianghai, a manuscript collector in Gaotou Village, just north of Xie Department. According to Nan Xianghai, the yellowed handwritten manuscript he shared with me had belonged to Nan Haiqing, the grandfather of a fellow villager. In Gaotou, as in much of southwestern Shanxi, stories of the Incredible Famine continued to circulate well into the second half of the twentieth century. Elderly villagers remember how "Grandfather Nan" (Haiqing) used to read the manuscript aloud to village children to encourage them to save grain and avoid wasting food. Xianghai purchased the manuscript from Haiqing's grandson in order to preserve it and to learn more about the disaster of which his grandfather and mother told chilling tales during his youth. He finds today's children uninterested in such stories. "Those who have full bellies don't want to hear about such circumstances," he sighed.[4]

Liu Xing's famine account reveals different levels of suffering during the disaster. Some elements in Liu's narrative are self-serving. In the rare instances where he describes his own actions, he portrays himself as a positive model of compassion and order. Several of the horrors that Liu describes, such as wolf and rat attacks, originate in tropes of famine reportage that emphasize the hungry, verminous face of "disaster upon disaster." But despite its drawbacks, Liu Xing's famine song remains a remarkable source. A local view of the disaster from one social position, it records a survivor's emotional, physical, and spiritual turmoil. It is important to hear Liu's voice so that imperial, treaty-port, and foreign descriptions of the disaster do not drown out the ground-level experience of the famine.

It is no accident that Liu Xing's famine memoir was written and preserved in the Xie area of southern Shanxi. Xie Department was located in the wealthy Yuncheng basin in far southwestern Shanxi. Li Sui, the diarist who spent two years traveling through Shanxi as secretary to the provincial education commissioner, praised Xiezhou's well-watered

Map 3. Southwestern Shanxi (Graphic Services, Indiana University)

terrain and jade-colored pools when he visited the area in 1795. The land held no treasure back, he wrote, so people prospered. Trade was also vital to the local economy. The southernmost counties in Xiezhou bordered on the Yellow River and carried on a brisk trade with neighboring Henan Province. Li Sui described crowds of merchants assembled to display goods of all kinds at the local Guandi temple.[5] Liu Xing's centrally lo-

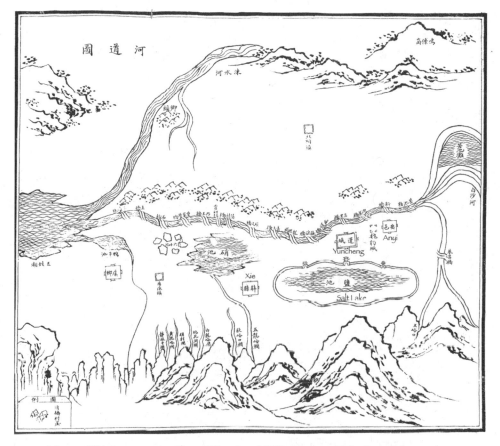

Map 4. Xie Department (from *Xie xianzhi* [Gazetteer of Xie County], 1920)

cated Xie County and the adjacent Anyi County were also home to the
salt lake so vital to Shanxi's famed Hedong saltworks.[6] Probably due to
the wealth and transportation network of this area, when Yan Jingming
was appointed the special high commissioner for famine relief in Shanxi
in October 1877, he established the main relief office for all of southern
Shanxi in Yuncheng, a large city just across the salt lake from Liu's home
in Xiezhou City.

The extreme severity of the famine in this region and the location of
the main relief office and its records in Yuncheng have kept the level of
interest in the famine high in this part of the province. A considerable
number of famine-related sources have been preserved. The Republican-
era Xie County gazetteer published in 1920 covered the famine in unusual detail, and thus provides a useful companion volume to Liu Xing's

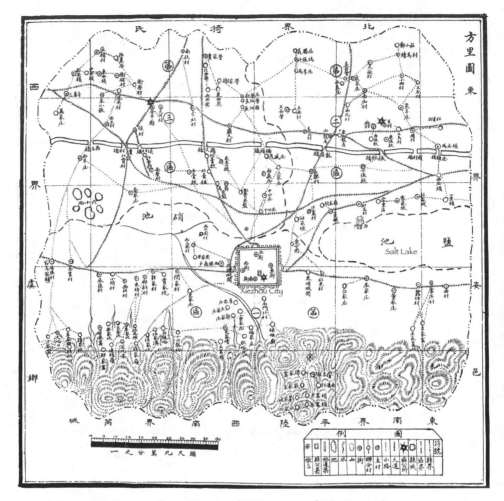

Map 5. Xie County (from *Xie xianzhi* [Gazetteer of Xie County], 1920)

more subjective account of events and persons. I also draw on a second famine lament from Hongdong County in Pingyang Prefecture and on gazetteer essays from other counties in southern Shanxi. Finally, a rich array of folk stories about the famine and about Yan Jingming's relief efforts have survived in the Xie area. Several of these stories, along with additional written accounts and stele inscriptions collected by local historians based in Yuncheng, were published in the late 1980s by the city's gazetteer office and by its *wenshi ziliao* (literary and historical materials) office.[7] This combination of sources makes it possible to explore how local observers who witnessed the famine experienced the horror of mass starvation.

THE COURSE OF THE DISASTER

While *Huangnian ge* is far from a straightforward chronology of the disaster, Liu Xing provides readers with time markers by which the course of the disaster in Xie Department can be reconstructed. Liu dates the beginning of the dearth to the second year of the Guangxu emperor's reign (1876), when Heaven sent a great summer drought. By autumn the fields were desiccated. Late-Qing Shanxi's staple crops were millet and wheat. Sorghum, maize, oats, barley, and soybeans were also important food crops, though cultivation of cotton, opium, and other cash crops increased in the nineteenth century.[8] Millet and sorghum were planted in the late spring (between the third and the fifth month of the Chinese lunar calendar) and harvested in the autumn (between the fifth and the eight month). These grains ripened only if it rained in late summer. After gathering their fall crops, Shanxi farmers planted their winter wheat in late autumn. Assuming spring rains came on time, the winter wheat was harvested in the late spring (May or June) of the following year.[9]

The summer drought of 1876 ruined the autumn crops, and the dried, hardened soil made it difficult for farmers to sow winter wheat. Grain prices rose as the harvest was threatened. A limited amount of rain fell during the ninth and tenth months of 1876, and Liu Xing reports that wheat was planted in spite of the dry fields in hopes that the situation would improve by the following spring. But in 1877 the vital spring rains also failed, and the land became so dry that even hardy sesame and cotton crops grew poorly. When the people harvested their wheat in the fifth month of Guangxu 3, their "eyes opened wide" with shock at the pitiful yield.

After harvesting the wheat, farmers hoped to plant their autumn crop of millet or sorghum. Liu Xing writes that people looked for rain until they had exhausted their eyes. Each day they gathered together and searched the heavens for signs of rain. Often there were clouds in the sky, but after a short while the west wind blew and the clouds disappeared, crushing people's hopes. Throughout the summer the scorching sun continued to beat down, rain failed to arrive, and everyone grew increasingly anxious. The autumn crops were a total loss, and by the ninth month of 1877 the streets were filled with women begging for food. "With my own eyes I saw people taking jujube skins (*zao hu*) as food," Liu states. As the time for sowing the winter wheat crop arrived but the fields still lay parched, some people said that if the wheat crop failed to take root, their lives would be cut short. Others hoped that since the ground was not yet frozen, rain would fall and the wheat could take root. But during the long winter of 1877, no rain or snow was seen. Recalls Liu, "The masses opened their mouths, each and every one of them, and cried out to the empty skies."[10]

Liu Xing's descriptions of the endless waiting and increasing anxiety experienced by people desperate for rain are hallmarks of a famine caused by drought rather than by flood or blight. The suffering occasioned by drought, notes historian Paul Cohen, is generally "slow-moving, incre-mental, and of indeterminate duration." Liu's portrayal of the people who gathered day after day to stare up at the empty sky and exchange fearful conjectures about what might occur if the rains did not arrive epit-omizes the combination of anxiety, hope, and uncertainty about the fu-ture that makes droughts psychologically difficult.[11]

The people of Xie had reason to worry. Grain prices continued to rise as the lack of rainfall guaranteed another failed crop. Liu Xing writes that by the end of 1877, the price of wheat had risen far beyond what ordinary people could pay. By that point a serious famine had developed. The pitiful cries of people out on the roads did not cease, states Liu. Worse still, the corpses of those who had starved to death were left exposed, and crows and magpies pecked out the eyes of the unburied dead.[12]

With serious famine came increasing social disintegration. Liu de-scribes how hungry people gathered in crowds that refused to disperse. During the day, they begged, but at night they plotted rebellion. In the countryside, some "evil people" formed gangs armed with guns and rope whips. Entering villages in the dark of night, they stole valuables and grain and tore the clothing off of women. Any man who tried to protect a woman from the bandits saw his life pass before his eyes, recalls Liu Xing. The provincial governor posted regulations in order to control such offenses. Criminals were no longer sent up to the county level for judg-ment, but were instead killed on the spot, regardless of gender. While night belonged to the robber bands, during the day people feared each other. Women stole food while carrying their children with them, and those who had noodle soup to eat consumed it fearfully with their doors tightly closed. A person who purchased a steamed dumpling, Liu re-counts, would take one bite, then look around in terror and hide the food lest someone steal it. Other starving people gathered at the market, where they were beaten for grabbing beans and eating them raw.[13]

As it became more difficult to purchase normal food like noodles or dumplings, people began to consume "famine foods" to survive. Liu Xing reports that people first took their cats and dogs and chopped them up to eat, and then sought leaves, roots, and tree bark that could be steamed into buns and eaten. Others began to eat white clay as if it were white flour, proclaiming it special earth sent down by Heaven. Liu claims that after consuming everything else, people even resorted to eating human flesh. People first consumed the dead, he writes, then killed and ate the living, including finally their own family members.[14]

Liu Xing then details what appears to have been the total economic collapse of Xie Department. Over the course of the fall and winter of Guangxu 3, he states, all businesses closed due to lack of trade. For the starving people left at home, it was "like sitting in a fire." Everyone tried to sell or pawn whatever he or she owned. Women sold their hair ornaments and earrings; many tried to sell themselves as well. Beautiful embroidered cloth sold for almost nothing, and lacquered furniture could be sold only if broken into pieces to be used as firewood. Good houses were torn down and sold piece by piece as well, but one hundred pounds (*jin*) of firewood sold for only fifty copper coins (*wen*). In spite of the pittance that luxury goods brought, owners had no choice but to sell. If they did not, their bellies were empty, their heads dizzy, and their eyes blurred. People could hardly move their legs to walk, recalls Liu. Their bodies were sore, their faces swollen. So many people starved to death that their corpses were buried in "ten-thousand-person pits" (*wan ren keng*), but still the bodies piled up "like a mountain."[15]

Liu Xing's description of the New Year's holiday that marked the beginning of Guangxu 4 (1878) demonstrates how the famine affected religious and clan observances. That year there were no offerings placed in ancestral halls, and no family or shop hanged the couplets customarily placed on one's main door to ward off evil and bring good fortune in the new year. People set off no firecrackers to welcome in the new year, mourns Liu, nor did they sing the traditional folksongs or perform dramas. By that point in the disaster, people in Liu's extended family, and perhaps Liu as well, were struggling. Families normally celebrated the Chinese New Year by cooking multiple dishes and enjoying meat. In 1878 all Liu could do to mark the holiday was procure two pounds of noodles and divide them with three elderly aunts in his clan. Even that was clearly a sacrifice, for he explains that he chose the three to share with because their families lived together in one courtyard and because, when he had been a boy, the three aunts had treated him generously. "People living in this world must preserve a little good conscience," he states. "As the saying goes: 'If someone does you the favor of giving you a little water, you should repay them with a flowing spring.'"[16]

Early in 1878 the situation got even worse. In the second month of the new year the price of grain increased radically again, and the "middle-class families" with whom Liu Xing associated himself now found it increasingly difficult to obtain food. Many tried to sell their houses and clothing in exchange for food but found no buyer. In great families, writes Liu, over half the people starved to death, while in small families the family line was broken (all starved). In large towns tens of thousands starved, while in smaller villages only three persons out of ten survived.[17]

In the spring of 1878 the situation looked as if it might finally improve. Halfway through the third month, rain fell and those who had survived the winter prepared to sow their autumn crops. But many farmers lacked the draft animals and seeds to plant a sufficient amount. After recording the price per pint (*sheng*) of maize, millet, sorghum, and mung bean seeds, Liu comments that those who could obtain seeds planted them with great hope, while those who lacked seeds felt as if they were being "fried in oil." People pawned or sold anything they had left in order to buy a few seeds. After the spring rains, grass began to sprout and people searched everywhere for it. The weeds and grass they gathered then became "pills of immortality" for the starving. In the fourth month of 1878 the rain came in the proper amount. Everyone scanned the fields constantly, wishing the crops would ripen in one day so they could eat. People were "as anxious as if they had been pierced by arrows," and the instant the mung bean crop (*lu dou*) was ready, they picked the beans and cooked them as a meal. The rains continued in the fourth and fifth months, and the fall harvest looked promising. "Crowds of people, old and young, rejoiced in their hearts," writes Liu.[18]

The disaster was still far from over, however. People had hoped to reap a picul of grain per *mu* of land that autumn, reports Liu Xing, but Heaven changed course and sent additional trouble. During the hottest summer months of 1878 the rains failed yet again, endangering the autumn harvest. Worse still, in the seventh and eighth months a great pestilence (*wenyi*) arrived to decimate the weakened population. Liu does not specify what the epidemic was, but foreign relief workers identified it as typhus. According to the report R. J. Forrest wrote for the China Famine Relief Committee, when the fever broke out in the winter of 1877, it "slew thousands and thousands that the famine had spared," including an American missionary relief worker named Albert Whiting.[19] Liu Xing also claimed that pestilence and a throat disease killed and injured tens of thousands. "Only wood shops [presumably coffin makers] profited," he states. Walking through villages, one could see only empty courtyards overgrown with weeds, and broken-down houses with corpses piled up inside.[20]

The fall harvest of 1878 provided little comfort. Since it was meager due to the summer drought, the price of corn and millet remained high. When it came time to sow the wheat crop halfway through the eighth month, the price of wheat seed was prohibitive. "People with money planted wheat seedlings with happy smiles covering their faces, but people without money were short on seeds and had difficulty right and left," writes Liu bitterly. They had no choice but to wait until later to plant peas and hope to survive until the next year.[21] He claims that at that point the emperor distributed seeds and plough oxen to the suffering people, but they were not grateful. "The Guangxu emperor loves the common people and sympathizes with them," Liu Xing asserts. "He looks at the common people just like a father looks at his son, but there is not one person who takes his favor with thanks."[22]

The disaster continued in the form of wolf and rat attacks even after the threat of outright starvation decreased. "Those who had not starved to death and who had escaped the pestilence never expected yet another calamity—wolves coming down from the mountains!" laments Liu. In the winter of 1878–79 hungry wolves roamed the streets in packs, he recounts, eating people both young and old. People were afraid to walk outside at night, and those who left the village took knives with them. One woman was holding her baby and spinning in her courtyard at home when a wolf lunged at her, took her baby, and ate it. "She saw it with her own eyes but, having never seen a wolf, took it as a dog," writes Liu. "When the baby cried, she saw the wolf was right in front of her." In addition to the wolves, over the course of 1878 the number and size of rats greatly increased. The rats gnawed and ruined everyone's clothing and possessions. As some people had their noses and ears bitten off by the rats at night, no one slept in peace. "Encountering the wolf disaster, encountering the rat disaster, disaster followed disaster!" exclaims Liu.[23]

Liu Xing concludes his chronicle by urging people to store a copy of his famine song in their houses so that they can read it often to their families and prepare for future disasters. "I feared people would not remember the famine years, so I wrote this song to exhort the world," he explains. "When women and children hear it, it's easy for them to understand that the five grains cannot be lightly discarded. Preserving life depends entirely on this [saving the five grains]; if only the people of the world will carefully remember."[24]

WINNERS AND LOSERS IN FAMINE-STRICKEN SHANXI

According to Liu Xing's famine song and other local accounts, the hideous disaster brought some degree of suffering upon everyone in southern Shanxi. There is a noticeable tension in these sources, however, between the common claim that all classes in Shanxi society suffered and died during the famine, and the equally pervasive assertion that some wealthy households and unscrupulous low-level officials benefited from the crisis. Such claims point to the key role that socioeconomic class plays in determining the level of suffering experienced by different groups during a major famine as distinguished from other traumatic events. Before the advent of modern hygiene and medicine, disasters such as epidemics affected the upper classes and the poorer classes in a society. Even in the twenty-first century, traumatic events such as earthquakes, tsunamis, or massive terrorist attacks can kill people from different classes in roughly equal numbers. Rising food prices and declining food supplies, on the other hand, affect people living close to the margin of survival first. In some cases certain groups in a famine-stricken society may actually increase their food intake during the disaster even as other groups starve to death. In late-Qing Shanxi, people's famine experiences differed according to their social class and occupation.

At the same time, accounts written by contemporary observers agree that the Incredible Famine was so prolonged and so acute that everyone in Shanxi was afflicted to some degree regardless of where he or she fit in the social hierarchy. Scholars of the Great Irish Famine of the 1840s have made similar claims about the broad reach of that catastrophe. In his meticulous search for "winners" and "losers" during the Irish famine, for example, economic historian Cormac Ó Gráda finds that while many survivors profited after the disaster, "in the end it is difficult to pinpoint any major group of economic agents who benefited from the Irish famine while it lasted." Individual laborers, emigrants, landlords, farmers, traders, and moneylenders all found ways of taking advantage of the crisis, concludes Ó Gráda, "but none of those categories, taken as a whole, escaped unscathed."[25]

Local, provincial, and foreign descriptions of Shanxi's plight during the late 1870s emphasize the universal suffering brought by the Incredible Famine. Many survivors were reticent about identifying families or social groups that had profited during the disaster. In a lengthy report published in the *North China Herald* and in *China's Millions,* Walter C. Hillier, a member of the British Consular Service in Shanghai, recorded a conversation he had with "a crowd of wretched people" in a small mountain town on the road leading north from Henan into Shanxi during his inspection tour of the famine districts. The villagers surrounded Hillier, asked him for help, and told him chilling stories of the terrible ordeal they had survived the previous year. When they informed him that nine-tenths of their prefamine number had disappeared, Hillier asked: "How is it that you are here to tell me of all these things? Why is it that you are alive, then, when so many others have died?" The villagers replied that "all had shared alike; the fact of their survival was due only to the possession of a stronger physique at the outset, which enabled them to stand a strain to which the weaker members had to succumb."[26]

Chinese tradition divided society into four classes, with scholar-officials at the top followed by farmers, artisans, and merchants. Following this tradition, Liu Xing upheld the claim that all classes suffered alike during the disaster. "The scorching sun beat down; the rain did not fall; people's hearts were frightened. Scholars and farmers, artisans and merchants were all in torment," he wrote near the beginning of his account. He also described how people of different social standings all had to sell their homes in order to purchase food as conditions worsened during the winter of 1877. "At this time, it didn't matter who was noble [*gui*] and who was base [*jian*]," he claimed; "good land and good houses were all pawned or sold." Liu also characterized the rat infestation that followed the famine as a plague that affected people regardless of their morality or wealth. "When Heaven sent down calamity," he wrote, "at this time it did not distinguish between evil and good; it also did not care [whether] families were poor or rich—all were the same."[27]

A famine lament entitled "Shanxi Miliang wen" (A Shanxi essay on grain) and attributed to Liang Peicai, a man who lived north of Xie Department in Hongdong County, echoes Liu Xing's observation that all social groups grew anxious as the drought continued month after month. Scholars used up all their books and brushes, wrote Liang, while farmers and artisans exhausted all the tools of their trade, and the employees of merchant family firms were cast out without pay when business ground to a halt. Liang's striking description of those who actually starved also highlights the famine's wide net:

Of those who starved to death, many were heroes. Of those who starved
to death, many were talented *shengyuan* [licentiates]. Of those who starved
to death, many had accumulated blessings and done good works. Of those
who starved to death, many were well-skilled artisans. Of those who starved
to death, many were old and crippled. Of those who starved to death, many
were young girls and boys. . . . Middle-aged people starved to death by the
thousands and ten thousands; it was even more difficult to protect eighty-
year-old men and three-year-old children.[28]

The emphasis Liu Xing and Liang Peicai placed on the universal suffering brought by the famine hints that, like most who have directly experienced a difficult event, they felt compelled to fashion "a past that is
psychologically tolerable."[29] Anthropologist Jun Jing noted a similar unwillingness to discuss the divisive aspects of China's 1959–61 famine
when he attempted to carry out a household survey among the 3,300
residents of Dachuan Village in Gansu Province. The village cadres opposed Jing's plan to determine how the Mao-era famine had affected the
village, because they feared his survey would "cause the community as
much pain as tearing open an old wound."[30] Instead, Jing was allowed
to discuss the famine privately with six literate villagers. Their stories,
which were "fraught with guilt, humiliation, and lingering disbelief,"
made it clear to him why the village cadres regarded the famine as "too
painful a subject to be discussed openly." Thirty years after the famine,
the respondents Jing interviewed continued to feel guilty over having survived while other family members had died, and still expressed resentment against former cooks and cadres who were believed to have favored
their own immediate relatives in the distribution of food during the crisis. No one wanted to risk tearing the village apart by reopening the issue
of whether villagers had suffered or died due to the actions of their neighbors or kinsmen.[31]

Liang and Liu, as survivors of a disaster that meant death or emigration for more than half of the people in their home counties, may have
experienced a strong sense of "survivor guilt," a type of self-blame common among survivors of disasters in which many others die. Often
haunted by the question "Why have I lived while others have not?" survivors may fear that they did not do enough to help those who perished.[32]
Liang and Liu may also have worried about the harm that opening old
wounds might cause in their communities if they wrote about the famine
in detail. In what was perhaps an attempt to make their own survival
less morally suspect, they repeatedly claimed that everyone in their locale had suffered terribly during the disaster or that, as the people in the

mountain village explained to Hillier, "all had shared alike" and those who survived did so only because of their stronger physiques.

Although Liang Peicai and Liu Xing almost certainly overemphasized the indiscriminate nature of the suffering brought by the famine, their claim that all groups in Shanxi society were adversely affected is not without some basis in fact. The epidemic of "famine fever" that raged during the summer of 1878, for example, killed members from all classes of local society as well as privileged Chinese and foreign relief distributors.[33] Rat infestations and wolf attacks also affected both rich and poor households. The claim that few people in southern Shanxi escaped the disaster unscathed is also upheld by Liu Rentuan's estimate that population loss in Liu's Xie Department and Liang's Pingyang Prefecture averaged between 60 and 68 percent.[34]

Reports written by provincial officials and foreign observers suggest that the famine's extent and duration harmed most social groups, particularly those in southern Shanxi who lost access to Wei River valley grain and were farther away from Inner Mongolian surpluses and from the tribute grain imported from Tianjin. Shanxi's governor, Zeng Guoquan, and the imperial famine commissioner, Yan Jingming, repeatedly petitioned the imperial court to transport additional tribute grain into the province to save the five to six million people who had become dependent on government aid by 1878.[35] In a memorial submitted early that year, they claimed that "the distinctions drawn a short time ago in respect of the degree of impoverishment in individual cases have now disappeared. All are equally reduced to utter starvation."[36] In another memorial, Zeng argued that although Shanxi's wealthy and gentry families had contributed as much as they could, depending on their help to deal with such a massive disaster was akin to "gouging out a piece of flesh in order to cure a boil." It was a stopgap that would actually increase the province's desperation by pushing the few remaining stable families and counties toward ruin.[37]

Eyewitness accounts of missionary relief workers based in Liang Peicai's native Pingyang Prefecture demonstrate that the famine was a devastating experience for wealthy and poor families alike in southern Shanxi. When distributing relief to villages in the Pingyang area in the spring of 1878, the Methodist missionary David Hill asked the village headmen whether there were any "well-to-do people" in their villages: "Not one," replied the village leaders. "I found it was only too true," wrote Hill, "for on entering some of the best houses in the village, I was greeted by country gentlemen, the squires of the parish, reduced to pinch-

ing want." He found the large houses of the local elite "empty and des-
olate," their once wealthy inhabitants subsisting on husks and roots. As
one elderly gentleman explained to Hill, "You see property is no use what-
soever now; no one will buy it, and one can't eat bricks and mortar."[38]

Walter Hillier was also struck by the plight of formerly wealthy families when he inspected Pingyang Prefecture in February 1879. Unlike Chinese observers, Hillier described the physical appearance of famine victims in terms of class and skin color. "A little experience soon enables
one to judge pretty fairly of the condition of each family from an inspection of the faces alone," he wrote. "A dark, almost black complex-
ion . . . was a sure indication of distress, while a clearness of the skin almost amounting to transparency, which was more frequently to be
observed amongst those who had once been in better circumstances, was
equally a sign of suffering." Hillier also encountered remnants of houses.
"The most distressing instances were those of the occupants of what once
had been large and substantial houses," he wrote. "One enclosure I entered contained the ruins of a house composed of several courtyards, each
of which had been pulled down as the distress of the family grew more
keen." In the farthest and smallest courtyard of that house he found the
three surviving members of the family. The woman and her two boys
were "all cleanly and neatly dressed, but so wan and white that it was
piteous to see them." The bodies of the woman's husband and several
other children were lying in coffins in an inner room.[39]

The above accounts hint that the Incredible Famine, like Ireland's
Great Hunger, produced many losers and very few winners. At the same
time, although Shanxi residents from many walks of life experienced pri-
vation during the famine, not all of them starved to death. Similarly, Ó
Gráda points out that although few groups in Irish society escaped the
disaster unscathed, the negative impact of the Irish famine was unequal
and divisive and "the suffering was by no means evenly shared." Even
in the extreme cases of nineteenth-century Ireland and Shanxi, famine
still produced a "hierarchy of suffering."[40]

Economist Amartya Sen analyzes how such inequalities played out in
twentieth-century South Asian and African famines. According to Sen's
influential entitlement approach, famines often result from maldistribution of food rather than an absolute scarcity of food. "Starvation is the
characteristic of some people not *having* enough food to eat," he cau-
tions; "it is not the characteristic of there *being* not enough food to eat.
While the latter can be the cause of the former, it is but one of many *possible* causes."[41] Sen asserts that during most famines a person starves be-

cause his or her "entitlement set,"—the goods he or she can produce or trade as well as his or her labor power, property rights, inheritance, and state social security provisions—can no longer procure enough food to ensure survival.[42] Government intervention made possible by democracy, political independence, and a critical news media, states Sen, plays an important role in protecting the vulnerable when, for whatever reason, a large number of people in a given society can no longer command sufficient food. "Famines are, in fact, extremely easy to prevent," he concludes. "It is amazing that they actually take place, because they require a severe indifference on the part of the government."[43]

Sen's pathbreaking writings are not wholly applicable to all famines in Qing China. The eighteenth-century Qing state, for instance, provides an intriguing example of an autocratic state that carried out massive and highly effective famine relief campaigns in spite of a complete lack of democracy or a free press. Sen's focus on maldistribution rather than an absolute scarcity of food does work for the Qing empire as a whole during the Incredible Famine. Certainly the food shortages during the late 1870s did not affect the entire country, and the shift of state resources from inland North China to the Yangzi valley hampered the drought-stricken provinces in getting sufficient aid. In Shanxi's case, however, the drought-induced reduction in the grain supply not only in that province but also in the neighboring areas it depended on for grain imports, coupled with serious transportation problems that were not a major factor in the modern famines studied by Sen, also played important explanatory roles.[44] China's late-Qing rulers can be faulted for prioritizing coastal defense and the Xinjiang campaign over famine relief during the 1870s, but charging the state with "severe indifference" would give short shrift to the belated but considerable efforts the government did make to transport grain into Shanxi. Moreover, even a radical redistribution of funds earmarked for military needs would not have made it "easy" for the weakened and beleaguered Qing state to prevent starvation from occurring on some scale during such an acute and widespread drought.

Those reservations aside, Sen's entitlement approach raises valid questions about the Incredible Famine as well as about famines in the modern world. "*Who* died, *where,* and *why*," Sen asks repeatedly in his case studies. "From which occupation categories did the destitutes come?" Why did some groups in a given society have to starve while others could continue to feed themselves?[45] Some sense of the disaster's impact on different groups in Shanxi society may be gained by reading Liu Xing's *Huangnian ge* with an ear attuned to class and occupation. Liu

frequently undercut his own claim that all classes of society were devastated by the famine by providing searing examples of how certain
groups of people in the Xiezhou area attempted to benefit from the disaster. Folk stories about the famine published in the 1980s also identify
persons and groups said to have either died in great numbers during the
disaster or profited in some way from it.

According to Liu Xing's song, as the drought continued through the
long hot summer of 1877, people from all walks of life grew more ap-
prehensive. When beggars began to fill the streets in the autumn of 1877,
local rich people initially distributed buns, grain, and cash to them in order to accumulate merit. When the drought extended through the winter and the price of grain rose sharply, however, the collective anxiety
and suffering described by Liu gave way to sharp divisions. Some grain
sellers rejoiced at the opportunity to sell at higher prices. "There were
many grain-hoarding people who laughed incessantly," wrote Liu disapprovingly. "These kind of people took good conscience and completely
ruined it."[46]

Grain hoarders were not alone in benefiting from the initial distress
in Shanxi. As Pierre-Etienne Will has suggested, in Qing China, famine
often "exacerbated the differences between rich and poor because the
poor were forced to pawn and sell what little they had to avoid starvation."[47] According to Liu Xing's account, those villagers in Xie Department with almost no surplus began to suffer when faced with the poor
autumn harvest of 1876 and the rising grain prices that followed. Presumably, farmers who grew food crops experienced what Sen terms a
"direct entitlement failure" when the drought destroyed the crops they
depended on for food, whereas those who grew cash crops such as opium
poppies ran into trouble when they no longer had anything to exchange
for cash with which to purchase the ever more expensive grain.[48] When
poorer villagers eventually tried to sell their possessions to buy food, it
was people from what Liu referred to as "middle class" or "middle level"
families (*zhongdeng jia*) like his own who profited. Liu describes how
they eagerly purchased the land and goods of their poorer neighbors at
low prices. The further rise in food prices early in 1878, however, exhausted the reserves of middle-class families as well, forcing those households to sell or pawn their possessions in a far less friendly market.

Liu Xing drew a moral lesson from the pain of witnessing eager buyers transformed into desperate sellers. "Take a careful look at those middle-
class families that suffered all kinds of difficulties," he urged his readers.
"The previous year when the calamity arrived, [they were] insatiably

greedy. [They] bought land and houses and men's and women's clothing. But when the fourth year [1878] arrived, they took those things and pawned them all. The inability to sell worried them; their hearts were anxious and not at ease." By that point, continued Liu, what had been happily purchased for one silver tael the previous year could not even be sold for two hundred copper cash. He then voiced the sentiments of a person tormented by the moral conundrum brought about by his covetous behavior earlier in the disaster: "If [I] don't sell, the family cannot obtain food to eat; if [I] sell what was purchased, it rots the conscience. Last year I should not have taken unearned gains. As the saying goes: 'Profiting at other people's expense surely brings disaster.'"[49]

Liu Xing disapproved of people from any level of society who profited from the famine. Nevertheless, perhaps because theirs was the famine experience he knew best, he described with great sympathy the plight of middle-class families desperate to sell their property. Trying to sell their clothing during the disaster broke people's hearts, he commented, and attempting to sell land was worse. Members of one household who had not eaten for three days asked a middleman to sell their fields and houses to a rich family, recalled Liu. The middleman implored rich families to buy, assuring them the land and houses in question would bring them profit after the famine. Moreover, buying the property of their starving neighbors would allow them to accumulate merit by showing compassion for famine victims. But far too many people were trying to sell property, so in the end the rich families refused all offers and sent the middleman away.[50]

Foreign observers also highlighted the predicament of those wealthy enough to profit from the distress of others early in the famine but not rich enough to buy sufficient food as prices continued to rise. Charles P. Scott, a missionary who arrived in Shanxi in late 1878 to distribute relief, even speculated that the wealthy may have suffered more than the poor. "The people relate that more well-to-do families than very poor ones have perished in the famine," reported Scott. "The poor felt the pinch very soon, sold houses, lands, etc., at a loss to the rich, and fled while they had the time and strength," he explained. The wealthy, in contrast, "bought up all the land, houses, and furniture of the poor, waited on, hoping matters would improve; exhausted their supplies, and finally, when too ill or too impoverished as regards money to move, died in the midst of their possessions."[51]

Scott's account is flawed in that it ignores the fate of truly poor families who had no houses or lands to sell and lacked the resources necessary to survive the long journey out of the enormous famine area. It does, however, uphold Liu's claim that some moderately wealthy people who might have profited from a shorter disaster ended up dead when the drought persisted beyond all expectations.

While families of moderate means were able to stave off starvation well into 1878 by selling their land and possessions, landless families whose livelihood depended on trade or handicraft work suffered what Sen refers to as "trade entitlement failure" once the firms that employed them closed due to lack of business and they no longer had cash wages or goods to exchange for food.[52] "When Heaven sent down these famine years each business firm came to a stop," wrote Liu Xing. As the silver shops in each county closed, he noted, women desperate to buy food for their children had no place to sell their jewelry.[53] David Hill, the English missionary who distributed relief in southern Shanxi's Pingyang Prefecture during the disaster, asserted that industries harmed or ruined by the famine ranged from saltworks and paper manufactories to straw-hat manufacturers and shops that plaited women's hair to make head ornaments. "Iron works are closed, earthenware kilns extinguished, coal mines except in a few instances unworked," he wrote.[54] Both Hill and Liang Peicai reported that eventually even pawnshops failed to escape the ever expanding disaster. So many people attempted to sell or pawn their clothing and utensils, wrote Liang, that before long the pawnshops were overwhelmed and had to close their doors.[55]

Unemployed laborers had no food crops to rely on and no land to sell. When they could not even pawn what little they had in order to buy food, there were few recourses left open to them. Henrietta Harrison offers a stark example of the famine's impact on one type of nonagricultural laborer in her study of the diarist Liu Dapeng and his village in central Shanxi. Because Liu Dapeng's home village of Chiqiao was irrigated by the Jin River, which did not dry up during the famine, district officials assumed that villagers could survive without government relief. As in many villages in late-Qing Shanxi, however, the majority of families in Chiqiao depended on nonagricultural labor to make a living: up to 70 percent of the population there was primarily employed in the village paper industry. As grain prices rose due to the drought, the market for paper collapsed, and the papermakers were left unemployed. With no way to pay for food at famine prices, some of these jobless laborers fled and others perished of hunger or disease. By the end of the summer of 1878, "almost 70 percent of the population of Chiqiao village was dead."[56]

Liu Xing's description of the agony suffered by an artisan nicknamed

Zhang San throws the plight of unemployed artisans into vivid relief. "Listen to me describe a true gentleman (*junzi*) in detail," writes Liu. Described by Liu as "a remarkable man in the world," this handicraft worker repaired musical instruments. "I don't know where he was from, from which department or county," Liu writes. "But upon encountering the disaster, he lived in our district [Xiezhou] in front of Taibao Street."[57]

Toward the end of the winter of Guangxu 3, recalls Liu Xing, more than half the people in Xiezhou had already died. Realizing the situation had reached a crisis point, Zhang San took all the tools of his trade and sold them to buy some grain and noodles for his family to eat. Then in the middle of the night on the third day of the twelfth month, Zhang started a fire and burned down his own house while he and three remaining family members were still inside. Zhang himself barred the door until everything had burned. No one in the crowd watching the conflagration knew there were still people in the house. Liu claims that when Zhang's actions were reported to a local official, he wept and praised Zhang for his willingness to die rather than survive by committing wanton acts.[58]

Liu Xing then describes himself standing in front of Zhang San's burning house and weeping:

> My own eyes saw him use fire to burn [everything] up. He who burned up his family became ashes with them. Several days before I had heard the miserable sound of his family's cries, but only at that time did I understand his plan. At the time when I saw him, it made my heart ache. . . .
> There was also a no-good thief observing this. Taking advantage of the fire, he stole a beam from the middle [of the house]. When I saw the thief, my anger exploded into courage. By the house I beat the thief with a brick.[59]

Watching a man he knew bar the door of his own house and burn himself and his family to death rather than face starvation was one of Liu Xing's most traumatic experiences during the famine. The events of that night forced Liu into a close personal encounter with violence and death. His description of Zhang barring the door, of the crowds of people watching the flames, and of his own tears and initial inability to tell anyone of the incident retain the "compelling, precise, and often visceral detail" and the "underlying imagistic and emotional core" characteristic of traumatic memories.[60] Liu's account of the fire also displays "the tension that any survivor has to endure between witnessing (in the third person) and suffering (in the first)."[61] His decision to record standing before Zhang's burning house and weeping as he remembered hearing the

miserable cries that Zhang's family members had made a few days before their death but whose import he had failed to understand demonstrates that even twenty years after the famine, Liu still felt guilt and re-
morse as he recalled the disaster.

Moreover, the violent rage Liu Xing experienced when he saw a thief
stealing wood from a house transformed into a funeral pyre empowered
him to act to redeem the situation. Liu's description of how he beat the
thief with a brick is one of only a few instances in which he records his
own actions during the disaster. Both there and in the passage detailing
his sharing food with three elderly aunts to mark the New Year, Liu portrays himself as one who tried to preserve a basic sense of moral behavior even in the midst of mass starvation and death. Throughout his song,
Liu saved his harshest moral censure for people of any class who used
the famine for personal gain. Watching a thief try to profit from an unemployed artisan's decision to die a fiery death rather than turn to crime
in response to the famine compelled Liu to act. By assaulting the thief,
Liu took one small step toward abolishing the kind of immoral behavior he believed had angered Heaven and brought down the drought.

Liu Xing and Liang Peicai offer few specifics about how people's oc-
cupations shaped their famine experiences and in some cases determined
whether they survived. A modern famine folktale titled "Jisha yanmin"
(A plan to kill the salt people), in contrast, identifies one important group
of laborers in Xie society that was especially hard-hit during the famine.
This story is part of a lengthy essay titled "Dingchou zhenhuang ji"
(Record of relieving famine in 1877) that was published by the Yuncheng
literature and history materials office in 1988.[62] Wang Yongnian, the article's primary author, drew on local legend, his grandmother's depictions of the famine, and textual sources. Although he terms the essay he
compiled with Jie Fuping "historical fiction" rather than fact, and does
not claim that the stories recounted are fully accurate,[63] late-Qing textual accounts of the famine verify some of the events recorded in the essay. More important, like the Irish famine folklore examined by Cathal
Poirteir, these stories provide a tantalizing glimpse of how the disaster
may have been experienced and remembered by illiterate laborers who
left no written accounts of their suffering.

According to Wang and Jie's account of the salt workers, in the 1870s
some two thousand salt laborers were employed by the Hedong saltworks
just south of Yuncheng. Many of them came from Shandong and Henan,
while others were local people who had turned to the saltworks after going bankrupt as farmers.[64] The saltworks were thriving when Alexander

Williamson visited them in 1866. The main salt lake was some eighteen miles long and three miles wide, he reported, and it belonged to the imperial government's salt monopoly. "No fewer than three hundred firms are engaged in the production of the salt," he wrote with enthusiasm. "They employ numerous workmen, who are paid at the rate of forty cash . . . per day, in addition to their food." Williamson described teams of men pouring the lake's brine into narrow waterways where it evaporated in the sun, while other work teams swept the dry salt into heaps or packed it into carts for transportation. "The salt produced here supplies the greater part of the provinces of Shanxi, Shaanxi, and Henan," he stated. "The revenue derived from it is very great."[65]

The famine had a serious impact on Shanxi's Hedong saltworks. As He Hanwei explains, in spite of renewed competition from other provinces after the suppression of the mid-century rebellions, Shanxi's saltworks remained stable until the famine because labor was cheap and the transportation costs for salt remained manageable. During the famine, it became more and more difficult to transport Hedong salt to central and northern Shanxi and to other provinces. Many horses and camels were killed and eaten by starving people, and the remaining draft animals and able humans were needed to transport grain along Shanxi's mountain roads. Facing higher transport costs, salt merchants were forced to raise the price of salt.[66]

As food supplies dwindled, people in Shanxi's famine districts purchased less and less salt. Some tried to gather salt themselves, though that was illegal. As people died in large numbers, the local market for salt collapsed. In Yicheng County, for example, salt sales fell to less than a third of their prefamine norm. At some points during the famine salt's production cost exceeded its selling price. Shanxi's salt merchants had huge overstocks of salt they could not sell, and many of them ran out of money.[67]

While He Hanwei emphasizes the damage the famine inflicted on salt merchants and manufacturers, the famine folk story in Wang and Jie's essay focuses on the difficulties faced by the laid-off salt workers. According to the story, the leader of the two thousand salt workers in the Yuncheng area was a well-liked Shandong native named Ding Qishan. After the salt workers lost their jobs due to the reduced demand for salt, they found it harder and harder to survive. Finally they asked Ding to act as their representative to approach the salt merchants for relief.[68]

The leader of the salt monopoly merchants refused Ding's request, telling the workers that since a natural disaster (*tianzai*) had stopped production at the salt lake, they would have to find a way to survive by themselves. Ding then collected about ten other salt workers and said: "My brothers and I lack family and employment. We cannot sit waiting for death. The salt merchants are not benevolent, so seeking [aid] from other people is not as good as asking it from oneself." He then proposed that they produce salt themselves and sell it in order to live.[69]

When Ding and his group began mining the next day in the "Bianhexing" salt yard, the rest of the two thousand desperate salt workers joined them, as did famished people from the surrounding area. After the salt merchants discovered the plan to violate the state monopoly, they reported to the *daotai* (circuit intendant) that a band of "lawbreaking evil people" was pilfering salt. The *daotai* ordered armed police led by constable Ma Rufei to hurry to the salt lake to warn the workers that they would be killed if they continued to steal government salt. When the laborers would not back down, Constable Ma fired on the crowd in the salt yard, killing one person and wounding several others. Ding Qishan and other salt workers fought back with the shoulder poles they used for carrying salt. In the ensuing battle thirteen salt workers died and over one hundred suffered wounds, while Constable Ma and two other policemen were surrounded and beaten to death by the crowd. The rest of the police escaped and returned to the *daotai*'s office to report what had occurred. Ding Qishan and several other salt workers also decided to go there to explain their side of the story.

The *daotai*, however, had already reported the outbreak of violence to imperial famine commissioner Yan Jingming, who had devised a cruel but clever plan to crush the salt workers without causing more social unrest. Yan could not allow the famished workers to defy their superiors and rebel, but he also realized that since they no longer feared death, the situation was indeed grave. Aware that oppressing the salt workers directly might lead to a full-fledged uprising of strong and rootless men, he advised the *daotai* to order the salt merchants to give the laborers some relief money, and then to invite the leader of the salt workers to his office and slay him so that the others could be dispersed more easily.

When Ding and his men arrived at the *daotai*'s office, Ding explained that the two thousand salt workers could not simply sit waiting for death, so they had broken the law in order to survive. The *daotai* said that he understood the reasons behind the workers' actions, and assured them that his office had already commanded the salt merchants to provide relief. He urged the laborers to drink some tea while they waited for merchant representatives to arrive to discuss the details of the relief plan.

The tea was poisoned, however, and Ding and the others were soon gripped with terrible stomach pains. Realizing they had walked into a trap, Ding and his men tried to flee, but it was too late. Soldiers armed with sharp swords burst into the office and killed them all. Left leaderless, several hundred more salt workers were killed by soldiers or police in the days that followed, and most of those who initially managed to escape soon starved to death along the roads.[70]

The Republican-era Xie County gazetteer confirms the general outline of this story, albeit in a less colorful fashion. The gazetteer states that during the famine illegal salt sellers provoked turbulence, and the situation nearly became serious. Luckily, Ma Piyao, the official in charge of managing relief, arrested the leaders of the illegal salt sellers, thus averting a riot.[71]

A close reading of local famine songs such as Liu Xing's and Liang Peicai's, combined with modern-day famine folklore, allows us to get a sense of how people from different levels of Shanxi society experienced the Incredible Famine. Although almost everyone in southern Shanxi was adversely affected by the severe and lengthy disaster, the onset and degree of suffering differed greatly. People with no reserves began to beg on the streets of Xiezhou City in the summer of 1877. Others sold what little they had and fled the famine area. Nonagricultural laborers such as the salt workers of famine folklore, the paper makers of Chiqiao, and the artisan Zhang San suffered greatly because once the market for their products collapsed, they had no cash, land, or grain reserves to fall back on. They were also less likely to receive government aid than farmers. By the end of 1878, hundreds of thousands of unemployed laborers and poor farmers whose crops had failed multiple times had starved to death or succumbed to disease, leaving piles of corpses within city walls and along country roads.

"Middle class" families like Liu Xing's profited early in the disaster by purchasing the goods of poorer families at low prices. But by 1878 they too began to struggle as their grain and cash reserves were exhausted. They were more likely to lose property and possessions, however, than their lives. Wealthy landowners with large grain reserves, and rich merchants and bankers with easy access to cash, probably suffered least during the famine. Nevertheless, even those fortunate families that had sufficient reserves to feed themselves through the disaster faced considerable economic loss due to the ruin of many of the province's industries, and few escaped the epidemics of 1878 or the rat and wolf plagues of 1878–79 unscathed.

When Liu Xing looked back on his own famine experience two decades later, he continued to be appalled and bewildered by the scope of the devastation he had witnessed. Simply raising the topic of the famine made him turn cold with fear. "Those disaster years—bringing them up makes one tremble inside," he wrote. Liu reported that many who experienced "those fierce years" tried their best to forget them. He, on the contrary, was terrified that people would indeed forget and thereby allow such horrors to recur. He thus insisted on describing the famine's most terrible aspects and implored his audience to listen to his words. "Wolves eating people—it's really strange," he admitted before relating the story of the wolf snatching a woman's baby from her arms. But he begged his readers to stay with him in spite of the horror. "Listen to me tell of it. If I don't speak of it, people won't know." Liu's determination to record the hideous events of the famine in vivid detail and force people to take heed of them was an important part of his effort to make the experience of the famine coherent and meaningful. In addition to describing the experience of the famine, Liu Xing and other Chinese and foreign observers who tried to make sense of the devastation continually wrestled with the question of why such an unimaginable calamity had fallen on Shanxi. It is to the famine's causation that I turn next.

PART II

Praise and Blame

Interpretive Frameworks of Famine Causation

WHEN A SERIOUS DROUGHT AND massive famine kill millions of people, one question that haunts survivors and later scholars is *why* a disaster of such magnitude occurred. Recent studies of human responses to traumatic events demonstrate that both individual and public tragedies commonly provoke a furious search for causal precursors and explanations. Traumatized individuals and groups repeatedly review their past behavior, searching for acts or omissions that might have predicted or altered the terrible outcome, and seeking ways to prevent the traumatic event from recurring.[1]

This horrific famine, which occurred during a period of deepening national crisis, elicited divergent responses from different levels of Chinese society. During and after the disaster, surviving Shanxi villagers, Chinese officials and foreign relief workers, and journalists and philanthropists in the treaty port of Shanghai all struggled to explain why the massive famine had occurred and what could be done to prevent another such strange disaster. The dissension over famine causation foreshadowed the more radical breakdown in consensus in coming decades over what good governance entailed and over how much and what kind of foreign influence should be permitted.

In the following examination of the "language of moral anxiety" and the "rhetoric of dismay" put forth in local, foreign, official, and treaty-port discussions of the famine, I employ a method suggested by historian Paul Greenough. I "read participants' statements literally to discover their own explanatory categories, their culturally given 'definition of the situation.'"[2] I then locate these contending interpretations of famine causation in their broader ideological frameworks. The chapters that follow address such questions as, What different theories of famine causation were put forth by those who witnessed the disaster of the late 1870s? Who were the culturally defined heroes and villains they praised or blamed for either mitigating or exacerbating the catastrophe? What signs and key words did witnesses and commentators employ to make their readings of the disaster convincing and meaningful to their respective audiences? Finally, what measures did Chinese and British observers believe would effectively check the disaster and prevent future famines?

CHAPTER 3

The Wrath of Heaven versus Human Greed

Local literati who struggled to understand why the Incredible Famine had befallen Shanxi expressed a set of concerns different from those put forth in official memorials, treaty-port newspapers, or missionary journals. Their discussions of the human and cosmic forces that interacted to bring about the famine's horrors demonstrate the complexity of late-Qing understandings of famine causation. During and after the famine, a key concern among authors of county gazetteers and local famine songs was providing a cosmic and moralistic framework and defining the famine's heroes and villains.

Liu Xing's narrative is repeatedly interrupted by his struggles to explain why disaster fell upon disaster in Shanxi. He responded to the trauma of the famine by searching for some meaning or lesson in the hideous events he had witnessed. Liu's first attempt to explain the arrival of the drought comes early in the song, after he describes how the people of his locale prayed fervently for rain but were disappointed day after day. He surmises that Heaven's refusal to send rain stemmed from people's inability to admit they were at fault. "How can they not know that during the last several years they were guilty of too much evil to escape punishment?" he demands. Because sons were not filial and daughters-in-law were not well behaved, Liu charges, they had reaped hardship from Heaven.[1] The connection between human misdeeds and Heaven's retribution is a major theme in Liu Xing's essay. "Heaven sent down calamity because people's vice and wickedness accumulated," he states bluntly after describing the rampant trade in women during the famine. "Men smoked [opium] and women dressed extravagantly."[2]

Liu Xing's basic assumption that a natural disaster could be attributed to a supernatural power's anger at human wrongdoing is not unique to late-imperial China. In the 1870s, foreign missionaries as well as Chinese observers looked to Heaven to explain the drought and ensuing famine. The Welsh missionary Timothy Richard, for example, encouraged Chinese villagers to "turn from dead idols to the living God and pray unto Him and obey his laws" so that they might receive rain.[3]

Roughly thirty years before the North China Famine, many of the Irish commoners who witnessed the wholesale destruction of their potato crops also explained the famine they endured as divine punishment. According to the children and grandchildren of Irish famine survivors who were interviewed by the Irish Folklore Commission in 1945, people who experienced the famine firsthand traced the arrival of the potato blight to God's anger at wasteful behavior. "Afterwards it was said that the Famine was a just retribution from God for the great waste of food," stated a farmer interviewed by the Commission. "Most people think it was a punishment from God for the careless manner in which they treated the crops the years previous when there was a very plentiful supply of potatoes," explained another respondent. "They were left in the ground by some people and not dug out, and they threw them on the headlands or in the ditches and left them to rot." Mused a third interviewee born in 1878: "They were too well-to-do before the Famine an auld man told me. Every day was a holiday during that time and plenty of poteen drunk. They were too well off. . . . The year of the Famine the potatoes rotted in the ground when they were growing. . . . It looked like the hand of God."[4]

The inclination to find religious or cosmological reasons for the arrival of a calamity crosses temporal as well as cultural boundaries. Even in the twenty-first century, the president of the United States and countless other Americans responded to the sudden destruction of the World Trade Center with calls for public prayer. A few religious leaders, like earlier observers of nineteenth-century famines in China and Ireland, suggested that the root cause of the disaster might be God's anger over what they considered to be the immoral behavior of certain segments of American society. Pastor Jerry Falwell said on *The 700 Club* two days after the September 11 attack, "The abortionists have got to bear some burden for this because God will not be mocked. . . . I really believe that the pagans, and the abortionists, and the feminists, and the gays and the lesbians, . . . all of them who have tried to secularize America, I point the finger in their face and say 'you helped this happen.'"[5]

Recent scholarship on psychological responses to trauma helps to explain the seemingly universal proclivity to trace the arrival of a disaster to human misdeeds. The belief in a meaningful world is at the core of people's fundamental assumptions, posits psychologist Ronnie Janoff-Bulman. People in many different cultures appear to need to believe in "a just world, one in which people get what they deserve and deserve what they get." The possibility that negative events occur at random is deeply threatening to most people, writes Janoff-Bulman. "We generally believe in an action-outcome contingency, that we can control what happens to us, and such a belief provides us with one means of maintaining a view of the world as a meaningful place," she writes. "In fact, we tend to perceive a contingency between what we do and what happens to us, even in situations when this is clearly inappropriate."[6] Developmental psychologist David Pillemer, noting that tragic events are almost always followed by a search for underlying causes, hypothesizes that both individuals and societies that have undergone traumatic experiences seek causal explanations so that they can regain feelings of control and predictability.[7] In both the Chinese and the Irish famines, persons who directly experienced the horror of famine, like present-day observers of traumatic events, anxiously reviewed predisaster behaviors in an attempt to render the experience more predictable and understandable by answering haunting "why" questions raised by the drought's arrival.[8]

ONSET OF DISASTER: OFFENDING HEAVEN

The attempt to make sense of calamity by drawing causal connections between a supernatural power's anger at human wickedness and the arrival of disaster was not peculiar to late-Qing China. On the other hand, the "precise formulations that link together divine purpose, natural forces, and human conduct" in local famine texts from Shanxi Province were shaped by the "special cultural forms and historical experience" of that society.[9] Local interpretations drew on the belief that the world inevitably moves through cycles of dearth and plenty. Those seeking to assess blame often focused more on human than heavenly agency. They highlighted the wasteful, unfilial, and unchaste conduct believed to have initially provoked the wrath of Heaven, as well as the subsequent mismanagement of relief efforts that they held responsible for allowing the drought to result in such a terrible famine.

After describing the famine's horrors in excruciating detail in his "Essay on Grain," Liang Peicai, the literate observer from Hongdong County, concluded his account by transforming the famine into a powerful moral lesson for the next generation. Liang claimed that the disaster had been Heaven's warning against extravagance and waste and that the only way to avoid future calamities was to live frugally. "I sincerely hoped that after encountering the disaster, people's hearts would turn. Who could have expected that it would be even more unspeakable than before?" he wrote. "They take the five grains [unrefined cereals] and rice and flour [refined cereals] and casually throw them away. They take cooking oil, salt, firewood, and charcoal and wantonly waste them," he lamented.[10] Liang explicitly attributed Heaven's anger to such wasteful behavior:

> Encountering calamity is all because human evil overflowed. As the saying goes: "Human life concerns earth and concerns Heaven." For a long time [people were] guilty of too many crimes to escape punishment, so Heaven sent down the drought disaster. The people who harvested evil got many good and worthy people into trouble. [I] exhort the people to quickly change their hearts, accumulate merit, and do good. Good is requited with good, evil is requited with evil; retribution lacks bias. No longer dare to throw away the five grains and scatter rice and flour. No longer dare to complain that a meal lacks enough variety or flavor.[11]

Liang's line of thinking was clear. Because farmers depended on rainfall as well as their own labor to get a harvest, human life depended on Heaven's good will. For too long the people of the locale had wasted food and demanded delicacies instead of staples. Once human evil reached a certain point, Heaven's retribution was inescapable, and even good people suffered the consequences. Liang hoped that people would learn from the experience of 1877 that the only way to avoid future disasters was to accumulate merit and avoid wasteful behavior. He concluded his song by asking readers, "for the thousandth and ten thousandth time, never forget Guangxu 3!"[12]

In their discussions of the behavior they believed had drawn down the wrath of Heaven, Liang Peicai, Liu Xing, and other local observers of the Incredible Famine selected vices that resonated with the moral universe of their late-Qing audiences. The belief that frugality could help ward off calamity had deep roots in late imperial Chinese culture. Emphasis on economy, a basic Confucian virtue, tended to increase during hard times. William Rowe, for example, locates the increasingly impassioned discourse on frugality found in eighteenth-century China within Qing approaches to its provisioning crisis, a crisis that had grown far worse by the 1870s. Rowe observes that Chen Hongmou and other eighteenth-century Chinese elites embedded their calls for frugality in the language of morality and virtue, as did Liang Peicai and other survivors of the North China Famine a century later. Frugality, explains Rowe, represented stewardship of the resources Heaven gave humans, a denial of personal indulgence in the interests of family and community, and a means of realizing one's innate moral essence. Yielding to extravagance and frivolity, on the other hand, was believed to be morally corrupting and wasteful of Heaven's gifts.[13]

Liu Xing echoed Liang Peicai's critiques of extravagance, but also identified opium smoking, beef eating, and lack of filial piety or female chastity as certain to bring the wrath of Heaven. Halfway through his famine song, following his lament that tens of thousands of people starved to death, Liu writes, "At that time, I thought vainly about who to resent and blame. I thought it was that families did evil and reaped retribution from Heaven." He then lists a series of offensive actions:

> Most men were unfilial; they secretly took opium. Women wore lewd clothing and gossiped about hair-pins and earrings. [People] ran distilleries and exchanged [grain] for liquor to drink, casting away grain. There were many daughters-in-law who were not careful; they misused oil and salt. Friends were not faithful and merchants were not righteous; they cheated and deceived naïve people. The rich were not benevolent and teachers were not strict; they spoke only of food and clothing. The evil doing that brings retribution weighed heavily and wickedness overflowed, so Heaven sent down the calamitous drought.[14]

Liu's reasoning is a vivid local example of what historian Mark Elvin has termed "moral meteorology," or the view, "linked to the ethical rationality of the Confucian miracles that rewarded filial sons and daughters and faithful widows," that moral and immoral human behavior could influence the weather.[15] Liu Xing defined moral and immoral conduct along orthodox Confucian lines. His concern about opium was specific to nineteenth-century China, but the decision to place unfilial behavior at the top of his list of offenses reflected basic Confucian teachings.[16] The *Classic of Filial Piety* (*Xiaojing*), a Han-era text that maintained "quasi-canonical status" into the twentieth century and that schoolchildren memorized at an early age, described filial piety as "the root of virtue and the wellspring of instruction." Unfilial behavior was believed to bring dire consequences. "From the Son of Heaven down to the common people," warns the *Xiaojing*, "if filiality is not followed from beginning to end, disaster is sure to follow."[17] In late-Qing Shanxi, people frequently attributed personal or familial misfortunes as well as major societal crises to a lack of filial piety. As Henrietta Harrison demonstrates in her analysis of Liu Dapeng, whenever problems ranging from a personal illness to a wife dying in childbirth struck Liu or his family, "Liu was convinced that he was being punished by Heaven for his lack of filial piety."[18]

Liu Xing also categorized evil behavior according to gender and status in society. Men of any social group could anger Heaven through unfilial behavior or by taking opium, but men of particular trades offended Heaven in class-specific ways. Merchants cheated their customers, the rich failed to practice benevolence, and scholars lacked discipline. Women, on the other hand, were consigned to a single group that offended Heaven through extravagant or unchaste behavior. As discussed in depth in chapter 7, the list of sins that literate observers like Liu and Liang believed had angered Heaven were often gendered. Chinese historians in imperial times frequently traced a dynasty's collapse to a woman who brought about disaster by gaining too much power through her cunning or beauty. Thus it is little surprise that local famine texts also viewed female misdeeds—ranging from engaging in unchaste or unfilial behavior to making extravagant purchases or failing to spin and weave— as offenses that angered Heaven and brought on the drought.[19]

Toward the end of his famine song, Liu Xing also explains why people who had survived the worst months of the famine were then struck by the epidemic that raged during the summer of 1878. "In the seventh and eight months the pestilence made thousands and tens of thousands of people sick, all because people ate beef and offended Heaven," he writes. "It looked as if Old Man Heaven's [laotian] eyes were still wide open, wanting to take all the evil people in the world back [wanting to finish them off]. The number of people killed by the pestilence in each village increased continuously. Only those with carpentry shops made a big profit [by making coffins]," laments Liu. He then offers people simple advice for avoiding such a pitiful fate: "The ancients said giving up the eating of beef can avert pestilence. By escaping calamity and averting pestilence, the population will be at peace."[20]

Liu Xing's suggestion that abstaining from certain foods could help move the heart of Heaven also stemmed from a set of beliefs common in late imperial China. While engaging in relief work in Shandong in 1876, Timothy Richard noted that the city magistrate in Qingzhou Prefecture issued a proclamation calling on the people to abstain from eating meat, especially beef.[21] Such proclamations were common during nineteenth-century droughts. In his research on official rainmaking in late-imperial

China, historian Jeffrey Snyder-Reinke finds that when local officials were ordered to commence rainmaking activities in response to a drought, "one of the first steps officials took was to prohibit the slaughter of animals and institute a community-wide fast." Such compliance with prohibitions was supposed to demonstrate the sincerity of official and popular prayers for rain. The slaughter of cattle was forbidden even during normal times, explains Snyder-Reinke, and during serious droughts the state often banned the slaughter, sale, and consumption of pork, duck, chicken, and fish, as well as other "strong-smelling" foods such as garlic and alcohol, in stricken locales. He traces the content of Qing dietary prohibitions to an amalgamation of Buddhist, Daoist, and state traditions of fasting. All three traditions encouraged people to forego animal flesh, at least at specified times.[22]

The Shanxi poet Wang Xilun provides another example of local interpretations of famine causation. Wang, who conducted relief work in the Pingyang area during the disaster, demonstrates the abnormal severity of the famine by describing in an essay how children whose starving parents had abandoned them in ditches were slaughtered and eaten by other famine victims as though they were sheep or pigs. He then asks, "How did it reach this point?" Wang starts his attempt to explain why this horrible disaster befell Shanxi by detailing the inauspicious movements that Mars, Jupiter, and Saturn made across the night sky during the first nine months of 1877. He then echoes Liang and Liu by arguing that Heavenly and human forces interacted to bring about the disaster. "The severe drought's duration and extent is very unusual," he writes. "If it's like this, it is from Heaven, not humans. However, there are causes not wholly from this [Heaven]." His list of human behaviors that helped bring about the disaster include the following:

> Today people do not fear officials, sons do not fear fathers, and wives do not fear husbands. The three cardinal guides have been inverted, and everyone only looks at profit. They hardly understand what propriety, righteousness, and a sense of shame are. In this situation, can they enjoy Heaven's protection?[23]

After tracing Heaven's anger to human disregard of such basic Confucian moral principles as obedience to those above one in the accepted hierarchy, Wang Xilun goes on to focus on factors specific to Shanxi itself. When the southern bandits (the Taiping rebels) brought chaos to the country, he writes, only Shanxi avoided it. Although Shanxi's Pingyang Prefecture and Jiang County were disturbed by the rebels, he admits, compared to the heavy destruction in other provinces, Shanxi fared quite well. The people of Shanxi should have understood that their escape was due to Heaven's favor, and should have responded quickly by "getting rid of stinginess, revering loyalty, expelling wasteful and licentious customs, and returning to pure and virtuous customs such as emphasizing agriculture, collecting grain, and planting nine [rows of crops] but saving [the harvest from] three." This kind of behavior would have vouchsafed Heaven's favor, Wang explains, and ensured that even if small disasters had occurred, conditions would never have become so severe.

But, according to Wang, the people of Shanxi failed to quickly repent of bad conduct after escaping the destruction wrought by the Taiping rebels. Instead, people indulged in "clever writing," abandoned good conduct and integrity, squandered their wealth, and wasted time. Cycles of profit and loss were inevitable, explains Wang. Such cycles depended on both human affairs and Heaven's timing. In this case, bad human conduct evolved and eventually invited dearth. This resulted in Shanxi's unlucky fate—a strange disaster the likes of which had not been seen for a hundred years.[24]

Local observers did not assume that Heaven's anger was the only cause of droughts. Instead, famine accounts often echo Wang Xilun's claim that the drought of 1877–78, while unusual in its length and ferocity, was part of a natural cycle in which times of good harvest inevitably gave way to years of dearth, which then were followed by years of plenty again. Such claims are rooted in a traditional Chinese mode of thinking about disaster causality that historian Lynn Struve analyzes in her study of seventeenth-century memoirs written during the Qing conquest. This way of thinking posited that "the world goes through alternating phases of peace-order-prosperity and discord-chaos-adversity" and that "whether one's lifetime intersects with a negative phase is a matter of fate."[25]

Local famine accounts frequently began with brief descriptions of disasters in ancient times, suggesting that none of their authors expected the 1877 disaster to be the last natural disaster to strike their locale. For instance, licentiate Wang Doukui began his lament inscribed on a stone stele erected in Xie Department's Ruicheng County in 1884: "We have heard of the nine years of flood under Yao and the seven years of drought under Tang. Natural disasters are prevalent; what dynasty lacks them?"[26] The author of a Yicheng County gazetteer piece echoed this sentiment: "The heavenly way has that which is exalted and that which is not; human affairs have that which is flourishing and that which is declining;

yearly harvests have those that are abundant and those that are deficient; this follows the principle of cycles [*xun huan zhi li*]."[27]

A belief in the inevitable cycle between eras of dearth and plenty distinguished local observers of the famine in Shanxi from Timothy Richard and other Western relief workers. Richard's famine proposals were "rooted in the conviction that the fundamental causes of famine could be eradicated altogether." He urged the construction of railroads, the opening of mines, and the furthering of Western scientific education in the belief that such innovations would help China progress to the point that famines would no longer exist.[28] Believing that the world operated according to alternating phases of prosperity and want, local observers in Shanxi made no mention of ending dearth altogether. However, they did not espouse fatalistic passivity in the face of whatever Heaven might bring. On the contrary, these observers insisted that human action and preparation could prevent floods and droughts from resulting in a major famine.

ESCALATION: HUMAN HEROES AND VILLAINS

Literate survivors of the Incredible Famine, although often tracing the onset of the drought to Heaven's anger, went on to assert that it was people's failure to prepare for disaster beforehand, combined with human greed and official mismanagement of relief supplies during the disaster, that allowed the absence of rain to escalate into such a severe and horrific famine. Their conviction that famines could be prevented even though floods and droughts were inevitable was a culturally distinctive view of disasters. Paul Greenough, viewing imperial Chinese discussions of food and famine from a South Asian perspective, notes that whereas Sanskritic thought recognized no essential distinction between famines and floods, in Chinese thought, "famines are distinguished from floods and droughts, the former being a 'result of the interaction of human and natural forces,' the latter belonging to a category of 'heavenly calamities.'"[29]

Local observers were adamant that disasters as devastating as the Incredible Famine could be prevented if only the common people could be persuaded to live frugally and save grain so that they would have something to rely on during times of dearth. The author of the famine essay in the Yicheng County gazetteer, for example, urged readers to guard against future famines by following the example of the ancients, who prepared for heavenly calamities by filling their cupboards in times of plenty.[30] Liang Peicai also emphasized that preparation could help people survive hard times. "Heaven sends down each kind of disaster in turn. Doing good brings good luck, doing evil brings calamity; from antiquity it has been so," he warned. "From today on, never again scatter rice and flour. When there are clear skies guard against clouds, at night protect from robbers, in abundant times guard against famine years."[31]

While they criticized ordinary people for failing to prepare for disaster, literate survivors also blamed rich families and low-level officials for allowing the drought to become a full-blown famine. They carefully recorded for posterity the actions taken by officials and local leaders who either ameliorated the situation by rushing grain to famine victims or angered Heaven anew by unscrupulously profiting from the desperation bred by mass starvation.

Heroes are few and far between in local-level famine texts. Many accounts praise the emperor for having compassion on the people and sending relief, but the almost obligatory statements about official relief efforts are far outweighed by critiques of the corrupt clerks and runners who worked in the county *yamen* and by horrific descriptions of the people's suffering. In addition, discussions of government relief work conclude that transportation difficulties rendered official relief too little, too late. The stele inscription from Ruicheng County, for example, states that out of compassion for the people the empress dowager appointed Yan Jingming to manage relief work and allowed the people to delay payment of their taxes. Perhaps intending to damn with faint praise, the author of the inscription then observes that the court's relief came too late to rescue those famine victims who had already died, and that although the court greatly favored the people, they were not rescued from their trouble.[32]

Liang Peicai left a more positive account of government relief efforts. His depiction of imperial kindness frustrated is representative of the tenor of stele inscriptions and county gazetteer essays about this subject. After the disaster reached the point that parents were killing and eating their children and over half the homes in a village were empty, Liang writes, the officials of each department and county sent memorials asking for aid, and in the capital a crowd of ministers petitioned the throne. The empress dowager took each report and investigated it in detail, according to Liang. Only then did the court understand that Shanxi was experiencing a great calamity. On that day the granaries were opened and imperial grace was unstinting. Anxious to rescue Taiyuan, the court ordered envoys to transport imperial grain there.[33]

According to Liang, the court sent 480,000 silver taels and 180,000 bushels (*shi*) of Jiangsu tribute rice to Shanxi. The masses of people accepted this generosity, believing that, now that imperial grain had arrived, they could eat their fill. But though the total amount was great, when divided up, each person received just a little. It was difficult to save even 20 or 30 percent of those people who depended on relief grain alone for survival. High government officials, upon investigating the situation in Shanxi, clamped down on corrupt officials and underlings who abused their power. They dispatched official envoys to buy grain and send it to Shanxi through Henan. The masses waited for the official grain expectantly, writes Liang, but how could they know that the road was long and the journey was difficult? In a village of ten households, he concludes, over half were expected to starve.[34]

Liang's claim that the imperial court was genuinely eager to help the starving people of Shanxi but was stymied by delayed reports, transportation difficulties, and the corruption of lower-level officials is repeated over and over again in local accounts of the famine in Shanxi. Historian Andrea Janku suggests that voicing appreciation for imperial kindness helped local literati rebuild the integrative framework of their society after the disaster. The emperor was often portrayed, Janku finds, as "the port of last resort" to whom Shanxi's governor and famished populace could appeal when all else failed. "The emperor—as an emblem, being in fact in 1877 an infant of six years—appears as the ultimate integrative figure, accepted by everybody, uncontested," she writes.[35]

Belief in imperial good will during the famine outlasted the Qing dynasty itself. Despite five decades of propaganda aimed at them about the evils of the old feudal government, most of the fifty-one local historians and elderly villagers I interviewed in southern Shanxi in 2001 upheld a positive view of imperial relief efforts. In response to questions about why the disaster had reached such extremes in Shanxi, for instance, Xi Yunpeng, a seventy-nine-year-old man from Xiangfen County in Pingyang Prefecture, said that the emperor did send relief during the Guangxu 3 famine, but little of it got to his grandfather's village. As a child he was told that originally the emperor sent fifty taels of silver for each person (an enormous sum), but due to transportation problems and corrupt local officials, by the time the money reached the common people, only two cents (*ma quanr*) per person were left.[36] Several other respondents repeated the same general story.

Second only to the idealized emperor, the figure who appears most often in both late-Qing and contemporary famine narratives from the

Yuncheng area is the imperial famine relief commissioner, Yan Jingming. A former vice president of the Board of Works, Yan was appointed special high commissioner of famine relief efforts in Shanxi in October 1877. He was ordered to travel throughout the province to investigate local conditions, oversee relief efforts, and report any cases of corruption among local relief officials.[37] Although Qing and Republican-era texts praised Yan for his famine relief work in Shanxi, during his term of duty hundreds of thousands of people starved to death. While Shanxi's governor, Zeng Guoquan, and in some cases even the empress dowager and Guangxu emperor have faded from modern-day famine folklore, Yan Jingming remains a well-remembered and controversial "hero."

Yan's biography in the Republican-era Xie County gazetteer depicts him as a model of Confucian frugality and uprightness. Yan was originally from Shaanxi, explains his biographer. But because his native place was devastated by the Muslim uprising, when he retired from service as governor of Shandong, he settled in the Yuncheng area instead, where he taught in the Xieliang Academy in Xie County. There Yan lived very simply, wore ordinary clothing, ate only vegetables, and nearly forgot that he had been a high official. Indeed, it was apparently because of his reputation for frugality that Empress Dowager Cixi appointed Yan to serve as the imperial famine commissioner in Shanxi.[38] Liu Xing's famine song also praises Yan Jingming as a "pure official rare in this world" who "exhausted his loyal heart to manage relief work and rescue the people from hardship."[39]

While Governor Zeng Guoquan was based in Taiyuan and oversaw the relief affairs in central Shanxi, Yan's office was in Yuncheng, and he continued to live in Xie County during the disaster. In Yuncheng he and Ma Piyao, the department official for Xie Department, worked together to improve conditions in southern Shanxi. According to a biographical sketch of Yan published in 1926, Yan insisted that nothing could be wasted while doing relief work, to the extent that many local people resented his stinginess. The Xie County gazetteer states that Yan used some 300,000 taels of relief money to distribute aid. Cixi's expectation that Yan would use relief money frugally was not disappointed, for after the relief office was closed, a fair amount of money remained unspent. Although his biographies do not specify the amount, modern folk stories put it at a full 100,000 taels. The Xie County gazetteer states that he used the remainder of the relief money to open a silk-spinning and -weaving office, to build charitable granaries that encouraged people to store grain for future times of dearth, and to hire someone to publish statecraft writings.[40] According to late-Qing and early-Republican sources, then, Yan was a model relief inspector who combined frugality and hard work to help the people of southern Shanxi during and after the disaster.

The famine poems and folk stories cited in local compilations published in Yuncheng in 1986 and 1988, on the other hand, focus on the negative aspects of Yan's relief management. A famine poem written by Chai Zesan from Anyi County in Xie Department and cited in the *Yuncheng wenshi ziliao*, for example, states that during the famine years the officials gave out relief but half of it went to the rural gentry and the other half to lower level officials. Officials and runners descended on the countryside "like tigers," wrote Chai, while the rural gentry were as greedy as wolves. Famine victims waited expectantly for relief just as they waited for the harvest, he continued, but they did not live long enough to meet the relief officials Yan [Jingming] and Luo. According to the *Yuncheng wenshi ziliao*, the common people nicknamed Yan Jingming "Yanluo wang," or Yama the Buddhist King of Hell.[41]

Several of the famine folktales recorded in the essay written by Wang Yongnian and Jie Fuping and published in the 1988 issue of the *Yuncheng wenshi ziliao* also demonstrate how even well-meaning Qing officials like Yan Jingming could be tricked into supporting the misuse of power by local bullies during famine relief distribution. According to one story, as the famine situation grew more desperate, Yan Jingming called the officials and gentry of the Hedong area together to discuss how to handle the situation. The gentry convinced Yan that rather than establishing a few government-run gruel kitchens for famine victims, he should allow each village to set up its own soup center run by a "just and upright" member of the local gentry (*duanzheng xiangshen*). By supporting this plan rather than depending on government relief officials, argue Wang and Jie, Yan Jingming fell into the trap set by the rich and powerful gentry. He inadvertently enabled local bullies to abuse official authority to extort money from the poor, take revenge on their local enemies, and embezzle relief funds.[42]

Contested characterizations of Yan Jingming's effectiveness as a famine relief inspector also came to light in the words of elderly villagers who live in the Yuncheng area today. When I interviewed seven members of the Old Person's Association in a village outside Yuncheng, four of them, all well-educated men ranging in age from sixty-eight to eighty-three years, got into a heated debate over Yan's handling of the 1877 crisis. Three of the respondents charged that while Yan had been an admirable official in most respects, he managed the Incredible Famine very badly.

They faulted him for failing to care for people's lives during the famine, for delaying the distribution of relief, and worst of all, for managing the already inadequate official relief fund so tightly that a substantial amount of money actually remained unspent at the end of the famine. According to Li Tong, Yan was so unpopular after the famine that a local opera was written to poke fun at him, though his grandson paid ten thousand yuan to stop it from being performed.[43]

Liu Xueji, in contrast, offered a spirited defense of Yan Jingming. Mr. Liu's father had taught him that by the time the Qing government sent Yan to inspect the relief effort in southern Shanxi, it was already far too late to stop the crisis. Because Yan had a reputation for frugality and strictness, the local officials feared that he might usurp their power, and refused to cooperate with him. Thus it was not at all Yan's fault that relief efforts failed, argued Mr. Liu. He identified transportation problems and opium as the main causes of the disaster.[44]

In sum, although the amount of government relief grain that reached the villages of southern Shanxi was woefully insufficient to keep people alive, many there were inclined to believe that the emperor and high officials did care about their distress and had sent aid as soon as they were properly informed of the real situation in Shanxi. Emperors and high officials were too distant from village-level Shanxi to leave a strong impression, however. Ordinary people remained unsure whether to view those officials who were close at hand, such as Yan Jingming, as heroes or villains. Instead, local accounts consistently highlight the long roads and legions of corrupt *yamen* underlings who separated the supposedly compassionate Qing court from the starving people of southern Shanxi.

While the "heroes" described in local famine accounts are often vague figures far removed from the everyday life of famine victims, the cast of villains depicted by Liu Xing and modern famine folk tales are vivid and memorable. According to Liu Xing, an already dire situation was made far worse when the failure to prepare for the drought was compounded by the greedy, corrupt behavior of local rich families and low-level officials who were expected to organize relief efforts.

The most obvious villains in Liu Xing's account were the local rich families who refused to contribute to relief campaigns and the low-level officials who stole relief grain from the starving. Liu's critiques of rich households (*fuhu*) in his locale are far harsher than his relatively sympathetic depiction of the middle-class families that took advantage of poorer neighbors early in the famine but suffered as the drought dragged on. This can be seen in his description of a heated exchange between

Ma Piyao, the official in charge of relief in Xie Department, and the wealthy households in the area. Ma, Liu Xing thought, pitied the people and exhausted his heart trying to take care of them. By the time the economic situation in Xie became desperate during the winter of 1877–78, relief donations collected earlier had already been exhausted. Ma Piyao therefore invited wealthy families in the area to the Xiezhou City *yamen* and told them how dire the situation had become.[45] "It is all because human hearts are bad that Heaven sent down disaster," he said. "Look at the rural villages—the poor people are starving to death by the tens of thousands." Informing them that he had received an official order to raise more relief, Ma pleaded with the wealthy to donate grain a second time.

Every one of the rich households, however, kept silent. Only a man named Li Xiude, who had already contributed six hundred taels of silver in response to an earlier call, offered to donate again. Ma Piyao praised Li effusively for his willingness to rescue the poor. When he saw Li's generous contribution, Ma realized that the people could readily be rescued if all the rich families followed Li's example. He once again turned to the assembled rich households and implored them to grasp the extent of the disaster and donate according to their hearts. At this point a few families agreed to give very small amounts, while others still refused to contribute anything.[46]

According to Liu Xing's account, Ma Piyao finally lost patience with the selfishness of rich families. His anger exploding, he summoned three underlings to the *yamen* hall: "Go quickly and bring a wooden cangue (*mujia*) and a bamboo stick," he ordered. "I will take this gang [of rich families] and let them donate their lives." Ma then warned the rich, saying: "Cutting short your lives still can't be counted [as enough]. Even if you become ghosts, you must still come and contribute grain! Look at you—you'd all die rather than pay attention to shame. If in order to rescue the people, I kill you, it won't be taken as going against Heaven!" After being beaten and in some cases jailed, Liu concludes, many of the wicked and crafty rich finally donated to relief efforts.[47]

Liu Xing's account of this confrontation should not necessarily be taken at face value, as it may present an idealized picture of the righteous official in times of famine. The story does express Liu's strong sense that rich households had a moral duty to help the poor and that they should reap official or supernatural punishment if they ignored their responsibility. Moreover, Liu's depiction of the tension between Ma Piyao and Xie Department's wealthy families offers a memorable example of

the important but "essentially ambivalent" position of the local elite regarding government relief efforts.

As Lillian Li and Pierre-Étienne Will emphasize in their research on
state famine relief structures in late imperial China, the local elite played
a crucial role in enabling the government to carry out relief activities in
rural areas. The regular imperial bureaucracy never had sufficient personnel to enable it to reach every county and village, and especially in
the post-Taiping era, the subbureaucracy and the rural gentry held de
facto control of the Chinese countryside. The county bureaucracy had
no choice but to depend on a combination of local gentry, *yamen* secretaries, and village chiefs to compile relief registers and carry out the day-
to-day distribution of food. Officials thus used moral suasion rather than
force to motivate wealthy families to donate. Like Ma Piyao, they constantly reminded the rich that they were the "fathers and mothers" of
the poor and had an obligation toward them.[48]

While Liu Xing positively assessed members of the regular bureaucracy such as Ma Piyao and Yan Jingming, he unequivocally criticized
the *yamen* clerks, official underlings, and village chiefs who made up the
subbureaucracy in Xiezhou. As soon as Yan Jingming arrived at his office
in Yuncheng, wrote Liu approvingly, he sent envoys to Zhoujiakou in
Henan to buy as much relief grain as possible. The distance between Zhoujiakou and southern Shanxi was great, however, and the commissioners
and gentry who managed the grain relief ignored their consciences and
deducted relief cash for private gain. During the lengthy journey the
official underlings guarding the grain and the cart families and boat families who transported it all stole grain. Then, when the grain finally arrived at the Hedong Inspection Office in Yuncheng, the officials responsible for receiving it and those overseeing distribution colluded to make
off with as much grain as possible. They were akin to "cats and mice
who sleep together," charged Liu.[49]

Even after the relief grain that had not been stolen along the way finally
arrived in Yuncheng, problems were far from over. According to Liu Xing,
relief distributors, who were generally village headmen and members of
the local gentry, engaged in every possible kind of corrupt behavior.
Rather than removing the names of relief recipients who had died from
their registers, distributors simply changed the names and collected the
rations of the dead for their own families. They secretly took official grain
and sold it on the streets. Grain distributors in rural areas deducted some
of it at each level, Liu declared, as if they were unaware that Heaven was
above them and saw their deeds. "The cheating and cunning of the grain

dispensing office cannot be told in detail," he lamented. "I can only tell roughly 20 or 30 percent of it."[50] Shi Jiashao, the author of a famine-related essay in Shanxi's Yicheng County gazetteer, vividly illustrates the corruption that so disturbed Liu Xing. *Yamen* underlings, Shi charged, made the famine victims they were supposed to be helping ill by secretly putting saltpeter in the cooking pots in gruel kitchens so that the gruel would cook more quickly and the underlings could steal the unused firewood.[51]

Liu Xing also chastised relief distributors who used their position to settle old scores with fellow villagers. "If during normal times you had a conflict with him [the grain distributor], today when he dispenses grain, you cannot eat," wrote Liu. He rued the fact that after high provincial officials ordered distributors to classify needy households as either "less poor" [*cipin*] or "extremely poor" [*jipin*] and post people's status on the front gate of their homes, some of the corrupt headmen in charge of village-level distribution falsely categorized extremely poor families as those with money to spare.[52] "How pitiful! Those poor people had no place to bring their grievance," exclaimed Liu. "At that time those 'dog people' took power," he continued. "Taking advantage of official affairs to pursue private grudges, they harmed the people endlessly."[53]

The image of corrupt village leaders offering extra relief food to friends and family and withholding it from old enemies or from those who lacked "connections" is alive and well today in local legends concerning the Incredible Famine. According to a story by Wang Yongnian and Jie Fuping titled "Disturbance at the Gruel Kitchen," during the famine years a wealthy member of the local gentry named Hou Ruren lived in Nanzhuang Village. As Hou Ruren had good relations with local officials, during the disaster he and his two brothers received orders to supervise relief work and the gruel kitchen in their village. Hou Ruren's family had long sought to purchase the land of another villager, Hou Youde, but Youde had repeatedly refused to sell.[54]

After the famine struck, the three people in Hou Youde's family ran out of grain half a month before the gruel kitchen was opened, and their lives became extremely difficult. Hou Ruren then took advantage of his position as village relief supervisor in order to obtain Youde's land. He changed Hou Youde's classification from "extremely poor" to "less poor" and required Youde's already struggling family to supply three hundred *jin* of firewood for the relief effort. When Youde still refused to sell his land, Ruren and his brothers used their power in the gruel kitchen to settle old scores. Ruren oversaw the kitchen while his brothers read names off the list of "extremely poor" and "less poor" recipients and ladled out large portions of gruel for the first group and small portions for the second group. When Youde's name was called, he approached to receive his small ladleful of gruel, but Ruren's brother deliberately jostled the ladle so that Youde received only half his allotted ration. The two men began to argue, and Youde's bowl fell to the ground and broke.

A scuffle broke out between the two families, and Youde was kicked in the chest and killed. Hou Ruren accused the people of starting a rebellion, at which point the other relief recipients became so disgusted by Ruren's behavior that they beat him and his brothers with pieces of wood.

Ruren's family fled, and Ruren went to the central relief office to report the incident to Ma Piyao and Yan Jingming and to claim that the people were rebelling. Rather than investigating closely, Ma and Yan immediately had Hou Youde's son and several other people arrested. Youde's son then committed suicide in jail. When Yan heard that news, he smiled coldly and declared that Youde and his son were stupid men who did not understand the court's kindness in providing relief, but just grabbed things for themselves.[55]

Wang and Jie used this story to criticize Yan Jingming for placing powerful village bullies in charge of relief in each village, thereby exacerbating famine conditions by allowing the rich and powerful of each village to rob poorer neighbors of already inadequate government relief allotments. Like Liu Xing's and Liang Peicai's late-Qing texts, these modern famine folktales reveal how the famine increased pre-existing tensions in village-level Shanxi.

EXPECTATIONS DASHED

While local famine accounts excoriate the greediness of local rich families and the corruption of official underlings, the texts also demonstrate that as late as the 1870s, Chinese villagers continued to hold government officials and rich households responsible for taking ameliorative action during a major famine. In his article on food riots in Qing China, R. Bin Wong points out that eighteenth-century Chinese officials raised popular expectations of government action during food crises to new levels through the expansion of the granary system. This high-Qing expansion of state grain distribution was then followed by a sharp contraction in the nineteenth century, particularly after the Taiping Rebellion began in 1850.[56] Popular expectations, however, did not decline as rapidly as state granary reserves.

On the contrary, although the late-Qing state lacked the resources and to some extent the will to intervene in subsistence crises as successfully as the high-Qing state had a century earlier, famine accounts such as Liang Peicai's and Liu Xing's demonstrate that popular expectations concerning government relief remained quite high. The claim that officials were the "fathers and mothers of the people" was not empty rhetoric, but instead expressed the idea that officials were responsible for "nourishing the people."

Even when the Qing state could no longer fulfill the people's expectations, villagers who owned land looked to the government to send aid when the drought prevented them from planting their crops. Both villagers and officials expected local wealthy families to make repeated donations to relief efforts. Likewise famished salt workers still assumed that officials would help them negotiate with the salt merchants when those merchants failed to show proper benevolence. Villagers in late-Qing Shanxi were aware that state and local granaries existed. They appear to have believed that the emperor and his high officials had grain and wanted to send it to famine victims in Shanxi. They also knew, however, that they were not receiving the relief grain they expected. The gap between expectations and reality led to a narrative of blame in which the emperor and, more ambiguously, high officials like Yan Jingming were praised, while local salt merchants, *yamen* clerks, and rich households were accused of keeping the emperor's favor from reaching the people.

According to local observers such as Liu Xing, Liang Peicai, Wang Xilun, and the authors of several stele inscriptions, when common people failed to practice thrift and filial piety and when officials and wealthy households failed to act benevolently, they called down the wrath of Heaven in the form of a terrible drought. While it was Heaven that withheld rain, commoners had an obligation to prepare for lean years. Their failure to prepare, combined with the failure of low-level officials and wealthy families to live up to popular expectations of how they should behave during a time of dearth, caused the drought to result in an extraordinarily severe famine. Literate survivors concluded that if ordinary people followed the example of the ancients by living frugally, and if state officials and wealthy families followed the example of the ancients by acting benevolently, then no matter which way the "principle of cyclicality" moved during their lifetimes, there would never again be a catastrophe so severe as the Incredible Famine of 1876–79.

CHAPTER 4

Qing Officialdom and the Politics of Famine

During the North China Famine the Qing court and officialdom repeatedly proclaimed the necessity of rescuing famine victims regardless of cost, thus upholding the faith that local observers had in the Qing government's good intentions. In practice if not in rhetoric, however, Qing officials were deeply divided over the importance of famine relief relative to other crises faced by the embattled state. In the capital the famine intensified an ongoing debate about whether to strengthen China by using Western military and transport technology. High-level officials stationed in the famine-stricken northern provinces, on the other hand, focused less on the benefits or drawbacks of Western technology than on debates about the state's role in stabilizing the price of grain and prohibiting the cultivation of opium.

UNIFIED RHETORIC: NOURISH THE PEOPLE

Throughout the disaster, rulers and officials presented themselves as benevolent "fathers and mothers of the people." The Qing court ordered its officials to bear in mind, "as the first essential, that relief is to be placed equally within the reach of all, and that not a single person be left deprived of the means of subsistence."[1] The officials praised for heroism during the disaster were those who "regarded a public matter as they would their domestic concerns" and who treated the suffering of famine victims as they would the misery of their own children.[2] Shanxi's governor, Zeng Guoquan, for example, described in familial terms the pain officials felt when they saw people dying of hunger. Because they were unable to help their "children" and could only look at each other and weep, reported Zeng soon after his arrival in Shanxi, "the local officials feel ashamed to be the father and mother of the people."[3]

There were important political and cosmological reasons for the Qing state's focus on its role as a provider and protector. Qing rulers were well aware that natural disasters disrupted the already precarious lives of China's peasantry and could lead to revolts like those at mid-century that had nearly toppled the dynasty. Moreover, a peasant-based polity could ensure adequate tax revenue by bolstering people's livelihoods.[4] Finally, as a conquest dynasty, the Qing state had particularly good reasons for promoting civilian granaries and popular welfare. "The legitimation of rule in native Chinese terms, Will and Wong explain, "meant a concern for properly Confucian signs of benevolent rule."[5]

The idea that a righteous ruler is responsible for feeding the people came from the Confucian classics. In the book of *Mencius,* for example, King Hui of Liang visited Mencius to ask advice of the sage. The king complained that although whenever crops failed north of the river he conscientiously moved the population to the east, and whenever crops failed in the east he reversed the process, still the population of his small state did not increase. Mencius offered the king very strict advice:

> Now when food meant for human beings is so plentiful as to be thrown to dogs and pigs, you fail to realize that it is time for garnering, and when men drop dead from starvation by the wayside, you fail to realize that it is time for distribution. When people die, you simply say, "It is none of my doing. It is the fault of the harvest." In what way is that different from killing a man by running him through, while saying all the time, "It is none of my doing. It is the fault of the weapon." Stop putting the blame on the harvest and the people of the whole Empire will come to you.[6]

It was also Mencius who popularized the idea that a ruler's Mandate of Heaven, or Heaven-granted right to rule, was not immutable and could be revoked if the ruler strayed from the path of virtue and failed to act with the good of the people at heart. Just as local survivors such as Liu Xing and Liang Peicai viewed the lack of rain as a sign of Heaven's wrath over human misdeeds, Chinese rulers regarded major disasters as dangerous disorders in the cosmic scheme and as warning signs that a dynasty had displeased Heaven and was in danger of losing its mandate to rule.[7] This line of thinking was still common during the Qing period. "Rainfall and sunshine were thought to be seasonal or unseasonal, appropriate or excessive, according to whether human behavior was moral or immoral," Mark Elvin asserts in his article on moral meteorology in late imperial China. Moreover, "some [individuals] counted for more than others. The emperor's conduct was of preeminent importance; bureaucrats came in second place; and the common people ranked last." Recourse to moral meteorological language was particularly common during droughts, since withholding rain was believed to be Heaven's "distinctive way of showing Its displeasure," while abundant rainfall was "the distinctive mark of Its response to sincerity."[8]

During the Incredible Famine, imperial edicts and official memorials about the disaster were characterized by a distinctive rhetoric of dismay that assumed the connection between the conduct of rulers and Heaven's willingness to send rain. A memorial written by Shanxi's governor, Bao Yuanshen, in the spring of 1877, shortly before he resigned his post in despair, typifies the language officials used to describe their grief over the misery of the starving commoners. "I am anxious to the core and can neither rest nor eat in peace," wrote Bao. "The only way is to lead my staff to engage in penitential fasts and pray sincerely from morning to evening."[9] Imperial edicts highlighted the distress the court felt. "In the anxious regard which the Sovereign cherishes for the interests of the people, no case of suffering from natural calamity ever occurs without filling his mind by day and night with grief and care, and causing him to reflect without ceasing upon the better discharge of his duty," stated one decree.[10] To demonstrate their concern, the child emperor and other members of the imperial family prayed for rain at five state temples, and the dowager empresses and young emperor were praised for practicing frugality and reducing the number of delicacies they ate. When rain finally did fall in drought-stricken areas, it was seen as a sign that the child emperor and his high officials had succeeded in moving the heart of Heaven.[11]

DIVISIONS AT THE CENTER:
SELF-STRENGTHENERS VERSUS THE QINGLIU

In the century preceding the Incredible Famine, the generous fiscal reserves and well-supplied granary system of the high-Qing state enabled official famine relief efforts to match the state's paternalistic rhetoric about nourishing the people. As shown in chapter 1, however, by the late 1870s the fiscal impact of fending off foreign pressure and suppressing the mid-century rebellions had depleted national and provincial resources and left the Qing granary system in shambles. The following imperial edict describes the court's concern about the wide array of problems that faced the country as the drought began in the summer of 1876:

> At the present moment, when the state of affairs is involved in so many difficulties, when peace has not ensued upon the military operations undertaken on the western frontier, when the public revenue is the reverse of abundant, and the people at large are straitened in their means of livelihood, the season of drought which afflicts the population this year . . . has affected Us by day and night, in the recesses of Our palace, with feelings of the profoundest grief and anxiety.[12]

Because the throne itself was weak during the late 1870s due to nagging questions of legitimacy, the kind of imperial oversight and activism that might have advanced the decision-making process was not forthcoming. Although neither the Qing court nor its high officials abandoned the rhetoric of state responsibility for nourishing the people, the most influential officials in the realm disagreed over how to divide financial resources between famine relief and military spending. A fascinating collection of famine-related memorials and edicts gathered for use by the Zongli Yamen outlines a serious dispute, between the Yamen and Li Hongzhang on one side and a group of lower-ranking metropolitan officials known as the Qingliu (Pure Current) on the other, over which of the many problems facing the empire was most deserving of the government's attention and aid.[13]

Both the Zongli Yamen and Li played important roles during the famine. As the coordinating bureau in charge of dealing with the Western powers, the Zongli Yamen had administrative authority over the crucial revenue from the Imperial Maritime Customs Service. It thus wielded significant influence over how customs revenues and loans guaranteed with those revenues were used.[14] Following the disastrous Arrow War (1856–60) against the British and the French, the Tianjin Massacre of 1870, and Japan's bold foray into Taiwan in 1874, Prince Gong and other powerful statesmen on the Yamen were anxious to improve China's coastal defenses. They viewed as their top priority the establishment of modern arsenals and shipyards and the purchase of Western weapons.

Li Hongzhang, who during the 1870s was superintendent of trade for North China, governor-general of Zhili, and grand secretary, was a leading proponent of self-strengthening policies, an ally of the Yamen, and a crucial figure in China's negotiations with foreign powers.[15] In the early 1870s Li exercised his considerable influence with the court and with the provincial bureaucracy in South China to divert tribute grain to Zhili for famine relief and to command resources for river conservancy work there. During the Incredible Famine he encouraged officials, merchants, and gentry in the wealthy Jiangnan region to contribute to relief campaigns for the starving northern provinces.[16] After he failed during the policy debate of 1874–75, however, to persuade the court to increase funding for coastal defense by abandoning the costly Xinjiang campaign, in the late 1870s Li did all he could to block proposals that aimed to fund famine relief efforts by appropriating money originally designated for coastal defense.

In contrast to the Zongli Yamen and Li, metropolitan officials who were advocates of the current of thought known as *qingyi* (pure discussion) insisted that the ever worsening famine in North China was the most urgent crisis facing the country in the late 1870s. *Qingyi* referred to expression of critical but supposedly disinterested opinion on government affairs.[17] It generally denoted the putting forth of views by low- and middle-ranking officials who aimed to improve or preserve the moral integrity of the state by criticizing governmental policies or attacking officials whose conduct was viewed as corrupt or immoral. *Qingyi* had a long though discontinuous history in China. It tended to appear sporadically, "especially during crises when anxiety among literati officials combined with weakness or uncertainty in the upper bureaucracy or at court."[18] Not surprisingly, then, *qingyi* opposition reemerged in the late 1860s and the 1870s, when the Qing court was relatively weak.

During the North China Famine, expressions of *qingyi* came predominantly from an outspoken coterie of metropolitan officials known as the Qingliu. Historian Marianne Bastid argues that the Qingliu, which was most active between 1875 and 1884, emerged from the bitter controversy over settlement of the Tianjin Massacre of 1870 and the struggle in the Grand Council between *qingyi* advocate Li Hongzao and self-strengthening advocate Shen Guifen.[19] Although the Qingliu was an "amorphous group," most of its members were relatively young, had passed the metropolitan examination, and were or had been members of the Hanlin Academy. Qingliu proponents who played an active role in lobbying the court for greater state intervention during the famine include Zhang Guanzhun, Xia Tongshan, Huang Tifang, Bao Ting, Zhang Peilun, and Wu Guanli.[20]

The Incredible Famine was the most serious natural disaster to occur during the decade of Qingliu activism. It spurred Qingliu officials into action, in part because they feared that such widespread misery could lead to domestic uprisings like the mid-century rebellions. Qingliu advocates believed that the promotion of able men (*ren cai*) and the opening of additional lines of communication between the court and lower-level officials would convince the court to place greater emphasis on implementing effective relief policies. They argued that "popular well being, and hence political harmony, depended on honest administration by able officials," and saw themselves as those able officials.[21] During a period of crisis for the Qing state, Qingliu officials emphasized the Confucian idea that the people were the foundation of the state. Just as Mencius had promised King Hui of Liang the people's allegiance if he fed them with grain from his storehouses, Qingliu officials asserted that "regarding the people's lives as important" would enable the dynasty to "win the hearts of the people" (*zhong min ming, shou min xin*). Failure to sympathize with and relieve the people, on the other hand, would lead to a loss of popular support and possibly the dynasty's fall. It was precisely a ruler's ability to assist disaster victims, they warned, that demonstrated his benevolence or lack thereof.[22]

The high-level struggle between supporters and opponents of self-strengthening policies shaped the way different groups of officials responded to the famine. Qingliu advocates believed that the government's attention to self-strengthening projects such as shipyards and arsenals had squandered money that should have gone to feed the starving. Memorials they submitted regarding the famine were filled with harsh critiques of the self-strengthening or "foreign affairs" movement (*ziqiang* or *yangwu yundong*) and the supposedly misguided priorities of those officials who supported it.

In August 1877, for example, a librarian in the Editorial Service of the heir apparent (*xianma*) named Wen Zhonghan submitted a memorial that described the suffering of famine victims in Shanxi and warned that if the famine refugees were not helped quickly, the country would be adversely affected overall. Funds needed to be raised from a broader area than Shanxi alone, he explained. Wen noted that since Li Hongzhang had requested that transit tax (*lijin*) money from Jiangsu and Zhejiang be allocated to southern and northern coastal defense, a great deal of money entered the coastal defense fund each year. Although he acknowledged that defending the maritime borders required money, he did not see it as the country's top priority. "Originally it was not fitting to appropriate [coastal defense funds] for other uses," he wrote, "but I think the plan for relieving the famine is really that which will guard against calamity. The coastal defense worry is remote, but the calamity of the starving people is before our eyes."[23] Wen then requested that the court order Li Hongzhang to move 300,000 taels from the coastal defense fund in order to relieve the crisis in Shanxi. The court approved of Wen's memorial and issued an imperial edict ordering Li Hongzhang to consider the situation and allocate relief funds for Shanxi.[24]

A memorial submitted by Zhang Guanzhun, the investigating censor of the Henan circuit and a member of the Qingliu group, proposed a more drastic measure that placed self-strengthening projects in sharp competition with famine relief. After pondering the famine situation day and night, explained Zhang, he had come to the conclusion that there was only one way out. The court, he wrote, should order the provinces of Zhili, Jiangsu, Fujian, Guangdong, and Jiangxi to temporarily stop the work of their machinery and ship-building bureaus. The government could then use the money saved to quickly relieve the people's suffering. Machinery and ship-building bureaus cost hundreds of thousands of taels per year, he complained. Coastal defense was urgent only at certain times, and the number of new vessels had already been doubled. Because famine policy, in contrast, concerned the people's lives, raising funds could not be delayed for even a day. Concluded Zhang, "Compare manufacturing weapons to protecting the people: which one is unimportant and which is important? Which can be delayed and which is urgent? This has long been that which the imperial wisdom sees clearly."[25]

A third memorial, submitted by the censor Ouyang Yun in the spring of 1878, went a step further by directly connecting the increasing reliance on foreign technology with the arrival of famine and other natural disasters. Ouyang joined local observers in tracing the drought to Heaven's wrath. "Why have calamities been added successively like this?" he asked. "I fear that recently human affairs must have offended and angered Heaven; I quietly seek the cause." Ouyang reasoned that during the chaotic years of the Taiping Rebellion, the Xianfeng emperor had had no choice but to negotiate peace with the foreigners in order to deal with the bleak domestic situation. Some high provincial officials, however, failed to understand that treating the foreigners with favor was only a temporary measure necessary for defending the country, and proved overly willing to be controlled by the foreigners. In recent years, complained Ouyang, the Shanghai Polytechnic Institution and Reading Room (*gezhi shuyuan*) had been established to promote Western science and technology. Common sense had been abandoned and machinery bureaus, ship-building offices, and the China Merchant Steamship Navigation Company had been established. Such bureaus then built or bought steamships and ironclad vessels that cost several million taels, he lamented. Recently, even a railroad had been discussed, whose construction would cost another several hundred thousand taels.[26]

Ouyang opposed the acquisition of Western machinery, steamships, and railroads because he believed it wasted large sums of money, impoverished the people by causing unemployment among those who depended on traditional forms of land and water transportation, and angered Heaven.[27] He voiced particular concern over the moral implications of allowing foreign imports to spread. Foreign religion was used to mislead the people, he argued, while foreign techniques and machines were used to seduce them. Ouyang warned that if preventive measures were not taken soon, everyone would come to follow foreign religions, practice foreign techniques, and use foreign machines. "Then the way of the sages and men of virtue will be henceforth abandoned, and our ancestors' methods henceforth destroyed," he lamented.[28]

Ouyang then explicitly connected flawed self-strengthening policies with the arrival of the famine and other natural disasters plaguing the country that year. He prefaced his argument by quoting the Han-dynasty Confucian scholar Dong Zhongshu: "When the state has faults, Heaven first sends disasters in order to censure and inform it. If [the rulers] still do not know to examine themselves critically, [Heaven] again sends strange phenomena to warn and frighten them." Ouyang went on to argue that "today, as Heaven has already clearly indicated with the hardship of famine, it is not foreign religion and foreign machines that can save us." On the contrary, he pointed out, successive years of geomantic (*fengshui*) disasters had occurred in Jiangsu, Zhejiang, Fujian, and Guangdong, all provinces where foreign religion and foreign machines were particularly popular. Clearly, reliance on alien technology and concepts angered Heaven and brought down calamity.[29]

Like other Qingliu proponents, Ouyang Yun insisted that pleasing Heaven by championing the people's well-being was the best way to deal with the famine and with the country's problems as a whole. He urged that the government forever ban the building of railroads, reduce the funds allocated for self-strengthening projects already in existence, and use the money saved to fund famine relief. Moreover, he petitioned the court to recall the costly and troublesome envoys China had sent to foreign countries. "Why not stop this nonurgent affair and retain this large sum of money to save the poor masses?" he wrote. Concluded Ouyang, "Prioritize the people's affairs in order to foster the life of the country; consolidate popular feeling in order to be in agreement with the will of Heaven."[30]

Wen Zhonghan, Zhang Guanzhun, and Ouyang Yun all argued from the position that nourishing the people was more crucial to the empire's welfare than pursuing self-strengthening projects. Li Hongzhang and the Zongli Yamen clearly disagreed, but did not dare to claim that their coastal defense projects were more vital than rescuing famine victims. Instead, they generally argued that although disaster relief was important, strengthening China against foreign aggression was so urgent that siphoning off coastal defense money to fund famine relief would endanger the whole country.

Li Hongzhang's response to Wen Zhonghan's proposal that Li allocate 300,000 taels of coastal defense money for famine relief demonstrates Li's commitment to protecting the coastal defense fund under his supervision. Li asserted that contrary to Wen's claims, Jiangsu and Zhejiang had not in fact forwarded much *lijin* money to the coastal defense fund, and little was left in the fund. Moreover, what money remained had been allocated for coastal defense, he wrote, and should not be transferred elsewhere. The country needed to order and purchase foreign ships and weapons, but they were expensive. If the government appropriated coastal defense money to fund famine relief, warned Li, "I deeply fear that it will interfere with urgent needs."[31]

Li then proposed a solution that he hoped would allow him both to obey the imperial edict ordering him to find money for relief and to preserve money for coastal defense. He had loaned *lianxiang* cash (money from a special fund established to pay for modern military training) to Jiangsu and Zhejiang pawnbrokers at interest, he explained. Now he planned to have the equivalent of 100,000 taels of that money forwarded to his Tianjin office to be used for Shanxi famine relief. In that manner, Shanxi could get its relief funds while coastal defense purchases could continue without interruption.[32]

Li was eventually ordered to use some coastal defense money for famine relief. However, the Zongli Yamen stepped in to ensure that Zhang Guanzhun's more radical recommendation that the government shut down all machinery and ship-building bureaus was never carried out. Those bureaus did urgent work for coastal defense, wrote the Yamen in response to Zhang's suggestion. Moreover, it said, Li had already been ordered to allocate 300,000 taels of coastal defense money for famine relief. Additional transfers would interfere with important work and lead to serious consequences. The Yamen asked that the court discount Zhang Guanzhun's proposition and stop deliberations on it. Zhang's proposal was rejected.[33]

The Zongli Yamen offered an even sharper critique of censor Ouyang Yun's attacks on self-strengthening projects and the practice of sending envoys to foreign countries. The Yamen's response to Ouyang's memorial said as little as possible about the famine. Instead, it defended to the court the self-strengthening projects that Ouyang had dismissed as harmful to the "way of the sages," and demonstrated that such ventures had received less funding than the censor had claimed. The Shanghai Polytechnic Institution and Reading Room was established to help people acquire foreign skills, stated the Yamen, while Tianjin and Shanghai established machinery bureaus to make foreign weapons. Zuo Zongtang's initiative to build steamships would prevent future trouble at every port, and the China Merchant Steamship Navigation Company aimed to use merchant power to further China's economic rights. Sending envoys abroad was also critical, argued the Yamen, because doing so allowed China to open trade relations with foreign countries and handle sensitive matters via negotiation. There was no reason to recall them as Ouyang had suggested. The court signaled its tacit approval of the Zongli Yamen's rejection of Ouyang's radical proposals in a brief rescript: "Let it be as recommended."[34]

Qingliu proponents clearly used the famine to attack the self-strengthening projects they opposed. Their concern about the disaster's scope and its potential for kindling internal rebellions went beyond mere political expediency, however. In spite of their heated opposition to the import and manufacture of western weapons and railroads, during the famine some Qingliu officials actually encouraged the government to purchase foreign rice to help feed the starving and to borrow money from the hated foreigners to fund relief efforts. In a March 1878 memorial, for example, Bao Ting, a Qingliu official who held a high position in the central government's Directorate of Education, expressed the fear that if the famine provinces in the north transported large quantities of rice from the southern provinces, the price of rice would rise in the south as well. He suggested that the government purchase foreign rice from the French-controlled port of Saigon in order to help stabilize the price of grain.[35]

In April 1878 a second Qingliu official, Huang Tifang, submitted a lengthy memorial that enumerated ways to collect funds to relieve the people in famine areas and meet emergency needs. Huang's first proposal encouraged the government to borrow five or six million taels from foreign merchants and use it to purchase foreign rice. All other fund-raising measures had been exhausted, he wrote, and what money remained was insufficient to deal with the disaster.[36] Huang was even willing to use much-maligned foreign technology to save the starving. He suggested that the government quickly send telegrams from Shanghai to notify foreign countries that China would purchase any kind of rice. This method would allow the country to collect a good deal of grain within two months and use it to relieve Shanxi, Henan, and Zhili. Huang bolstered his argument by reminding readers that during past famines it had been normal for one province to borrow grain or money from a neighboring province. "Begging from neighbors to avert calamity is what the ancients did," he concluded.[37]

Huang Tifang's proposal to borrow foreign funds echoes a more detailed memorial submitted in December 1877 by Li Qing'ao, who served as the governor of famine-stricken Henan until he was replaced at the end of the year. After describing the terrible situation in Henan and suggesting that serious unrest might break out if more relief was not forthcoming, Li proposed arranging a foreign loan to fund relief efforts. Although fully aware that arranging foreign loans was difficult and interest rates were high, he simply saw no other way of relieving the crisis. Li Qing'ao cited recent precedent to strengthen his case. Zuo Zongtang had arranged for foreign loans when the government lacked funds for the Xinjiang campaign, he pointed out; Shen Baozhen had borrowed from foreigners to purchase ships and armaments, and Li Henian had done so when funds for the defense of Taiwan proved insufficient. Since these officials had borrowed and used several million taels of silver from Western merchants, Li hoped for the court's permission to arrange a two-million-tael loan to relieve the urgent crisis in Henan.[38]

Prior to and during the famine, the Qing court sought foreign loans to fund military campaigns. It not only permitted Zuo Zongtang to borrow five million taels in spring 1876 to bolster his efforts in Xinjiang, but also allowed him to obtain another five-million-taels from Shanghai-based foreign bankers as the famine worsened in summer 1877.[39] In contrast, neither the court nor the Zongli Yamen was willing to incur debt to foreigners to pay for relieving the famine-stricken population in North China. The imperial edict issued in response to Huang Tifang's memorial rejected his proposal on the grounds that foreigners charged high interest rates and that it took so long to arrange loans via foreign merchants that this was a poor method for funding relief.[40]

Similarly, when asked by the court to respond to Li Qing'ao's request for permission to arrange foreign loans to fund famine relief work in Henan, the Zongli Yamen stated quite bluntly that there "was no need even to discuss" Li's proposal. The Yamen's line of argument illustrates how the embattled late-Qing state categorized different kinds of crisis. The Yamen's memorial first countered Li's citation of precedents for permitting high officials to arrange foreign loans by providing examples of the state's unwillingness to become dependent on such a strategy. It then distinguished military emergencies from other, less critical needs. Relief work, explained the Yamen, could be conducted at all times and places. Like river conservancy and army rations, it was part of the regular budget and could not be compared to urgent military needs. The memorial noted that not only Henan but also Shanxi and Shaanxi had many disaster-stricken areas waiting for relief. "If [they] one after the other cite precedent and ask to borrow [foreign money]," the Yamen ministers argued, "we fear that all of the funds China has will be consumed by [paying] the insatiable interest of the foreigners. The impoverishment of the common people will not be removed, and the country's treasury reserves will already be exhausted."[41] Ironically, then, it was virulently anti-foreign Qingliu officials rather than foreign-affairs experts in the Zongli Yamen who were willing to borrow foreign money and buy foreign rice to help save the starving.

The Qing court wavered between the Qingliu perspective that nourishing the people should be a benevolent state's top priority and Li Hongzhang's and the Zongli Yamen's insistence that defending Qing territory from foreign invasion was even more critical. The court generally sided with the Zongli Yamen in protecting self-strengthening projects from Qingliu attacks and resisting pressure to recall the envoys sent abroad. At the same time, Empress Dowager Cixi steadfastly refused to stem the flow of Qingliu critiques.[42] Moreover, Qingliu memorials played a role in convincing the court to order Li Hongzhang and Shen Baozhen, the superintendent of trade for South China, to spend considerable coastal defense money on famine relief. In the fall of 1877, for example, Xia Tongshan, a Qingliu member and vice president of the Board of War, requested that the Board of Revenue give 400,000 taels of customs money to famine relief efforts and that the Tianjin Coastal Defense Fund under Li Hongzhang's jurisdiction provide another 300,000 taels. In response, Li agreed to divert 200,000 taels from the Tianjin fund to Shanxi and Henan relief work.[43]

As the famine worsened during the winter of 1877–78, Li Hongzhang and Shen Baozhen were ordered to consider the proposals put forth in the steady stream of memorials submitted by Qingliu officials urging the government to use coastal defense money to relieve the crisis in Shanxi and Henan.[44] Shen replied that he thought it proper to temporarily transfer coastal defense money from what could be delayed to what was truly urgent. The court then decreed that the customhouse of each province unaffected by the drought (except for Jiangxi's) should forward 50 percent of the money it was expected to contribute to southern coastal defense in 1878 to pay for famine relief in Shanxi and Henan. This order was not carried out in full, but had it been, it would have reduced by half one year's revenue for the special coastal defense fund established for the defense of Taiwan.[45] Due in part to Qingliu pressure, then, the Qing court expressed some willingness to reduce coastal defense spending in order to address the situation in the famished north.

Qingliu officials depicted self-strengthening projects as "villains" that usurped money better spent on famine relief. Ironically, twentieth-century historians have often portrayed Qingliu officials themselves as ultraconservative villains who impeded the reform necessary to strengthen China. Marianne Bastid, for example, states that *qingyi* debate "resulted in a stifling influence," while Lloyd Eastman surmises that *qingyi*, via the use of "intimidation," "abuse," and "bullying," "contributed significantly to the failure of the Chinese state in the nineteenth century to respond successfully to the challenge of the Western powers."[46] It is not difficult to find fault with the intransigent stance that Qingliu spokesmen took against building railroads and steamships or sending envoys abroad. On the other hand, there is something to be said for their rejection of policies that valued "manufacturing weapons" over "protecting the people's livelihood." The Qingliu insistence that "winning the people's hearts" should be the state's top priority during a crisis was a classic expression of deeply rooted Confucian ideals about benevolent rule. The call for activist officials to act as fathers and mothers of the people signified late-Qing concerns that such a severe famine signaled both dynastic decline and a dangerous disconnect between the rulers and their people.

PARENTING THE PEOPLE: DEBATES IN THE PROVINCES

Like Qingliu spokesmen in the capital, officials in charge of governing Shanxi province viewed active state intervention as by far the most effective way to deal with a massive famine. They captured the moral high ground by calling on the government to stabilize the price of grain by rushing official grain into famine districts, to distribute free relief to the poorest famine victims, and to guard the people's food supply by prohibiting opium cultivation and alcohol distillation. Self-strengtheners with a clearer picture of China's insecure position vis-à-vis the Western powers, on the other hand, were less willing to push the already overburdened state to intervene in every situation.

Unlike their British counterparts in nineteenth-century Ireland and India, Qing officials across the political spectrum generally agreed that the state should intervene to stabilize the price of grain during a severe crisis. This consensus did not mean that the late-Qing state ignored market mechanisms. Recent research demonstrates that from the eighteenth century on, Qing rulers and officials viewed the merchants' role in the circulation of food as necessary in general and recommended a mix of public and private grain purchases and sales as the best way to keep prices stable. Determining the precise balance between reliance on the market and state intervention in the purchase, transport, and sale of grain, however, produced tension and controversy in late imperial China.[47] During the Incredible Famine serious disagreements emerged among Qing officials over where, when, and to what degree the state should step in to stabilize grain prices.

Li Hongzhang, for instance, joined his Qingliu opponents in accepting the time-tested assumption that when the state sold grain at prices below market in disaster districts, the inflated market price would be forced down due to increased supplies and the added competition the state posed to local retailers.[48] At the same time, believing that merchants also had a role to play in transporting grain into famine areas, Li argued that whether the state should send grain or cash to a drought-stricken province depended on local conditions. In response to a proposal submitted by one of Li Hongzhang's Qingliu enemies, in the fall of 1877 the court ordered Li to find a way to stabilize grain prices in the famine districts of Shanxi, Henan, and Zhili. In November, Li explained that in carrying out the court's order, he had purchased grain from Manchuria and Shanghai and established price-stabilizing offices in four cities in the three stricken provinces. Such offices were expected to protect the people's food supply by selling government grain at reduced prices (pingtiao), thus lowering the market price of grain in famine areas.[49]

Li's November memorial makes clear that he evaluated requests to transport government grain into famine districts case by case. He agreed with Qingliu proponents that active state intervention in the grain trade was necessary in Shanxi. The price of grain there had risen far higher than the price in Manchuria or Zhili, he informed the court. Thus, in spite of the difficulty and cost, he supported transporting grain into the mountainous province as the only way to stabilize prices there. On the other hand, Li did not favor rushing government grain into famine areas in every situation. Based on his investigation of local conditions, he explained, the price of grain in Henan was only slightly higher than that in southern Manchuria (Fengtian). After taking transport fees into consideration, he argued, purchasing more Manchurian grain and transporting it into Henan was not the most effective way to reduce grain prices there. Instead, Li suggested granting the Henan provincial government 200,000 taels to restock its granaries by purchasing the somewhat more expensive private grain still available within that province.[50]

Li Hongzhang and Shen Baozhen appreciated the importance of merchants in transporting grain into famine districts. In the memorial they wrote to oppose Bao Ting's proposal that the government import rice from Saigon, Li and Shen argued that if it were genuinely more economical to import foreign rice than to transport domestic rice to the northern provinces, grain merchants would have long since begun importing Saigon rice. "As merchants are in a position to obtain intelligence as to the state of the market more rapidly than officials," wrote Li and Shen, "they are sure to take advantage of the slightest margin of profit, and never fail to rush into any market where comparatively low prices rule and transport is cheap." That most Guangdong rice dealers were still purchasing their rice in the Jiangnan region, they concluded, "proves conclusively that the Saigon prices are not actually lower than elsewhere."[51] Li in particular believed that merchants could aid relief efforts by donating money as well as transporting grain. During the disaster he relied on directors of the China Merchant Steamship Navigation Company and prominent merchants in Jiangnan to help gather relief contributions in that prosperous region and forward them to the coordinating bureau he had established in Tianjin.[52]

High officials in famine-stricken Shanxi explicitly rejected the idea of relying on profit-hungry merchants to rush grain into famine areas. A joint memorial submitted early in 1878 by Imperial Famine Commissioner Yan Jingming and Governor Zeng Guoquan emphasized the dangers of entrusting this all-important task to merchants and highlighted the need for government intervention to stabilize grain prices in Shanxi. In their memorial, Yan and Zeng asked that the Board of Revenue grant Shanxi 60,000 bushels of tribute grain due to be transported to the capital from Jiangxi and Hubei provinces in 1878. A total of eighty counties in Shanxi had been declared disaster areas, they explained, and between five and six million people had become dependent on government assistance.[53]

The memorialists refuted the argument, made by unnamed opponents, that since the government had remitted the transit tax (*lijin*) on grain coming into Shanxi, grain merchants from other areas would hurry to the province to sell at a profit and would presumably supply enough grain that prices would decrease without further government grain imports. In fact, Yan and Zeng protested, the roads were so difficult that even in ordinary times only merchants from neighboring Shaanxi and Henan brought grain into Shanxi, and those provinces had also been stricken by the drought. They had already issued notices encouraging merchants to engage in business, continued the memorialists, but had not received a single answer.[54]

Yan and Zeng also challenged the claim (also made by unspecified opponents) that the amount of grain that could be transported to famine districts by the government was more limited than the amount merchants could bring in. This was true, they charged, only for middle-class (*zhong-deng*) families, who could afford to pay the market price for grain. It did not take into account poorer families. Even stabilizing food prices by selling government grain at reduced prices was not sufficient to stem such a severe crisis, insisted Yan and Zeng. Selling grain at a below-market price could help the "less poor" famine victims (*cipin*), but to save the "extremely poor" victims (*jipin*) from starvation, distribution of free relief was imperative. Yan and Zeng ended their memorial by repeating their request for the 60,000 bushels of tribute grain on the grounds that it would rescue the people, demonstrate the dynasty's benevolence, and prevent future unrest.[55] Their memorial testifies to the deep commitment to famine relief intervention that many Qing officials retained even as the dynasty was falling apart in the late nineteenth century.

All of the leading Chinese officials who served in Shanxi during and directly after the famine—Bao Yuanshen, Zeng Guoquan, Yan Jingming, and Zhang Zhidong—urged the state to protect the people's food supply not only by stabilizing grain prices but also by prohibiting the cultivation of the opium poppy in Shanxi. As early as the 1830s, Shanxi-based observers had argued that locally cultivated opium exhausted the soil and "deprived the state of taxes because its production remained secret."[56] Poppy cultivation remained a politically charged issue in the 1870s because it was part of broader late-Qing debates about opium.[57] The imperial prohibition against native opium production, issued in 1831, remained in effect until just three years before the famine. Then, beginning in 1874, due to a controversial policy shift brought about by Li Hongzhang and the Zongli Yamen, the prohibition was relaxed. Li's and the Yamen's position stemmed from their intimate involvement in Sino-foreign relations. They argued that the cultivation of native opium would stop the drain of silver out of the country and would allow China rather than England to take control of the opium supply.[58] The officials whose primary concern was stabilizing the food supply in inland North China, on the other hand, asserted that cultivating opium had left the people of Shanxi wholly unprepared for the drought, and that people must guard against future disasters by planting food crops instead.[59] Once again, disagreements over how to deal with the disaster both reflected and exacerbated larger fault lines in the late-Qing government.

Whereas local literati such as Liu Xing focused on the smoking of opium as an immoral behavior that contributed to the drought by angering Heaven, high provincial officials were more concerned with opium's cultivation. In September 1876, for example, Shanxi's governor, Bao Yuanshen, requested the court's permission to secure the people's food supply by strictly prohibiting the cultivation of poppies in Shanxi. When several northern provinces had encountered a drought the previous spring and summer, he explained, the price of grain had immediately risen to prohibitive heights, and the people had lacked sufficient stored grain to fall back on. Because growing opium poppies was several times more profitable than growing grain, he wrote, Shanxi's farmers failed to realize the harm brought by opium, and more and more of them were abandoning the cultivation of food crops in favor of opium.[60] "I fear that in about a decade, out of ten families eight or nine will plant opium poppies, and only two or three will plant the five grains," he lamented. "Where will the people's food come from then?"[61]

After Bao Yuanshen retired due to illness and his inability to deal effectively with the disaster, Zeng Guoquan replaced him as governor of Shanxi in June of 1877. Zeng, a native of Hunan and the younger brother of the famous self-strengthening official Zeng Guofan, was renowned for having assisted his brother in organizing the anti-Taiping "Hunan Braves," and particularly for recovering Nanjing from the rebels in 1864. After spending the post-Taiping decade fighting the Nian rebels and acting as the director-general of the Yellow River and Grand Canal Conservancy, he was sent to Shanxi to fight an equally destructive foe, the North China Famine.[62] Zeng first witnessed the famine's horrors as he passed through Shanxi en route to Taiyuan in May 1877. He was an energetic relief administrator from the moment he arrived until he was transferred to another post in August 1880, after the drought ended. During his time in Shanxi, Zeng wrote a steady stream of memorials seeking ways to mitigate the growing disaster in that province. Although he identified numerous causes of the famine, including transportation difficulties, Shanxi's financial troubles, and official corruption, he denounced the cultivation of opium with particular vehemence.

Early in 1878 Zeng Guoquan urged that the existing prohibition against poppy cultivation be strengthened so as to increase the people's food supply and prepare against future famines. Zeng's 1878 memorial, which is widely quoted in modern Chinese scholarship concerning the famine's cause, laid out a clear argument that the increased cultivation of opium contributed to the severity of the Incredible Famine in Shanxi.[63] Like local observers, Zeng believed that while natural disasters were inevitable, severe famines were not. Because the ancients guarded against famine by putting aside a third of their annual harvest for bad times, he explained, even when droughts and floods occurred, people had grain to fall back on and did not become famished. Moreover, claimed Zeng, in the past it was unheard of for people to "plant substances that harm humans and exert a pernicious influence throughout one's native place." But in recent years the cultivation of opium in place of grain had increased until people lacked even half a year's grain reserves. Suddenly confronted with the fierce disaster, they had no way to deal with it. Zeng was adamant that the famine was not simply a natural disaster. "Although the present famine in Shanxi is called a natural disaster [*tianzai*], in fact it stems from human affairs," he asserted.[64]

Zeng then analyzed how opium adversely affected two of the three factors he believed were crucial for the people's livelihood: weather, land productivity, and labor power. Shanxi's total amount of cultivable land—about 530,000 *qing*—was already quite limited, he argued, and every *mu* of land devoted to the cultivation of the opium poppy resulted in one less *mu* for growing the five grains. Worse still, because the common people could make more money by growing opium, all too often fertile and well-watered lands were devoted to the opium poppy, while food crops were shunted off to barren areas. Land productivity was thus declining.[65]

Although Shanxi farmers who grew opium as a cash crop presumably expected to make enough money to purchase food imported from other provinces, Zeng warned that opium cultivation had also reduced the grain surplus in Shaanxi's Wei River valley and other areas that Shanxi depended on for grain. It thus became increasingly difficult for Shanxi to import sufficient grain from its neighbors.[66] In a similar argument published in an early-Republican edition of the Xie County gazetteer, the author claimed that during the 1870s most of the fertile land in southern Shanxi was planted with the opium poppy, while grain crops were planted only in the border areas between Shanxi, Shaanxi, and Henan. Thus when the famine struck, people had to buy grain from several thousand *li* away. By the time the grain arrived in southern Shanxi, the people had already starved to death.[67]

Besides monopolizing fertile land that should have been used to grow grain, Zeng argued, cultivating opium impaired Shanxi's labor power. Because the harvest period for poppies was also the busiest agricultural season, he explained, farmers devoted their energies to their more profitable poppy crops and neglected their cereal crops. Moreover, Zeng claimed that before people began cultivating native opium, hardworking farmers could never afford foreign opium, so "those who smoked opium came only from idle and rascally or rich and powerful families." But once farmers began to plant opium as a cash crop, they also began to smoke it. "Formerly industrious farmers have degenerated into lazy farmers," he wrote. Those who became lazy then turned into beggars, and finally even became robbers.[68] Zeng concluded that because opium cultivation harmed both land productivity and labor power, it left Shanxi particularly vulnerable to the third factor that determined the people's livelihood, the weather. He was determined to guard against future famines by turning farmers away from poppy cultivation.[69]

Zhang Zhidong, the reform-minded official who served as governor of Shanxi from 1882 to 1884, also identified opium, along with excessive corvée labor and official corruption, as one of the chief villains that led to the famine's unusual severity. Zhang was appalled by the ravaged condition of the province when he arrived there early in 1882. After investigating the postfamine situation, he noted that the area of Shanxi that produced the most opium, Yuanqu County, had also suffered the greatest number of starvation deaths during the famine. He further observed that areas of the province with the highest opium profits also had the highest grain prices. Disturbed by such correlations, Zhang wrote yet another memorial attempting to strengthen the prohibition against poppy cultivation in Shanxi.[70]

Many of the arguments that Bao Yuanshen, Zeng Guoquan, and Zhang Zhidong employed to call for the prohibition of poppy cultivation drew on the traditional Confucian belief that agriculture was the mainstay of the people's livelihood and the basis of state legitimacy. Their reasoning often had more in common with eighteenth-century efforts to return lands planted in nongrain crops to grain production than with twentieth-century anti-imperialist framings of the opium issue. During the eighteenth century, concern over food shortages had prompted Qing emperors and officials to launch campaigns against various cash crops. In 1727, for example, the Yongzheng emperor attacked the planting of sugarcane on any land suitable for grain, and during empirewide grain shortages in 1748 officials went so far as to propose that profitable cotton lands be returned to grain.[71]

The attempts that Shanxi's famine-era governors made to prohibit opium cultivation can also be traced back to the common Qing practice of enacting rules during times of dearth that prohibited wasting grain on "useless" things such as the distillation and sale of liquor. In 1737, for example, the Qianlong emperor issued a prohibition edict condemning liquor distillation as responsible for much wasting of grain in the five northern provinces (the same five provinces stricken by famine in 1877). He asserted that banning distillation would save more than ten million bushels of grain per year for household grain reserves.[72] Such prohibitions resurfaced during the North China Famine. In the fall of 1877, a censor submitted a memorial urging that the distillation of spirits be prohibited in Shanxi during the disaster.[73] In a rare instance of cooperation between Li Hongzhang and his Qingliu opponents, early in 1878 Li proposed that the throne suspend distillation in Zhili until good harvests returned. He calculated that the thousand distilleries in Zhili consumed some 20,000 bushels of millet or sorghum per day, thus robbing between two and three million people of their daily food. Qingliu officials were impressed by the "sincerity" of Li's proposal and expressed surprise and outrage when it was rejected by the Board of Revenue.[74]

Official attacks on alcohol and tobacco production stemmed from the belief that such products were of no use to humanity, and that their consumption dissipated the population's wealth and squandered the earth's productive capacity.[75] Zeng frequently used this rationale to further his calls for the prohibition of poppy cultivation in Shanxi. When he complained that every acre of land devoted to poppy cultivation equaled an acre lost for growing food crops, for instance, he could easily have been writing about wine distillation or tobacco cultivation in the 1730s instead of poppy cultivation in 1877.[76]

During the 1870s, however, the assertion that opium cultivation led to famine and ruin was by no means the only view that late-Qing farmers and officials held on the subject. On the contrary, advocates of native opium cultivation "argued that Shanxi was a barren land, and that rice, wheat, and coarse cereals grown there would not be sufficient for local use after taxes." Cultivating opium, they claimed, would "actually help to supply food and other necessities."[77] The prohibition against poppy cultivation had to be reissued by successive provincial governors during and after the famine, reflecting the unwillingness of many farmers in Shanxi to return to food crops or less lucrative cash crops after they had become accustomed to the opium poppy's high profits. Indeed, poppy cultivation continued long after the famine had passed. When the late-Qing state finally began a major opium eradication campaign in 1906, soldiers were sent to Shanxi to suppress the crowds of villagers who resisted official enforcement of the prohibition edict.[78]

Other supporters of opium cultivation, in particular Li Hongzhang and the Zongli Yamen, advocated native opium production primarily as a check on foreign control of the opium trade and on the outflow of China's silver. Li Hongzhang's willingness to side with Qingliu officials in temporarily suspending alcohol distillation in Zhili during the famine demonstrates that he was not opposed in principle to using state power to prevent people from wasting grain on "useless" products. Opium, however, had far more serious foreign policy implications than alcohol. After China's defeat in the Arrow War, the Qing government was forced to legalize opium imports in 1858. The amount of opium coming into China from India increased throughout the 1860s and 1870s, both in numbers of chests and as a share of China's total imports. The number of chests per annum peaked at 80,000 in 1880, shortly after the famine ended. Bereft of any other effective means of preventing foreign opium from entering China, Li and his allies hoped to gradually replace foreign with native opium, which sold at roughly half the price of the imported product.[79] "We can thereby resist foreign opium, and once it earns no profits and has gradually disappeared we can then prohibit opium again," he wrote in defense of the 1874 decision to relax the prohibition of domestic cultivation.[80]

Li did not actively oppose Zeng Guoquan's efforts to prohibit the cultivation of opium in Shanxi during the disaster. But just a few years before, he had written a sharp critique of the contention, so crucial to Zeng's understanding of the situation in Shanxi, that poppy cultivation threatened China's food security. "Some people argue that the legalization of opium cultivation would harm the growth of food crops," he had written. "This theory, high-sounding though it is, is tiresome. Opium is cultivated everywhere in Yunnan, Guizhou, Sichuan, and Shaanxi, but there has never been any serious shortage of food."[81] While acknowledging that opium was in general "a harmful substance for people," Li asserted that native opium was "only slightly addictive and less harmful than foreign opium."[82] He agreed with his opponents that China must aim ultimately to root out the habit of opium smoking and forbid both foreign imports and domestic production. Since he knew that the Qing state was then too weak to stop the importation of foreign opium, however, he believed that allowing native opium to compete with foreign imports was the state's best short-term policy.

The foreigners who loomed so large in Li Hongzhang's understanding of the opium problem gave little credence to the argument that opium kept Shanxi or other parts of the country from preparing for a major drought.[83] In contrast, members of Shanxi's elite continued to draw causal connections between opium and the famine decades after the disaster, as did PRC scholars writing over a century later. Understandings of exactly how opium contributed to the disaster changed significantly over time. The author of the Xie County gazetteer article published during the early Republican era, for example, placed far more emphasis on the drug's foreign origin and "poisonous" or addictive quality than did Shanxi's governors during and shortly after the disaster. Opium was brought to China by Westerners, stated the Xie County author, though its seed came from India. In the late Ming period it was used mainly for medicinal purposes, but during the Jiaqing era (1796–1820) people began to smoke it and it exerted a pernicious influence (*liu du*) in China. As more Chinese farmers began to plant opium, he continued, more and more of them smoked it and could not stop, until by the time of the famine, people ate food only every other day but consumed opium daily.[84]

The Xie County author sharply rejected the theory, similar to the one espoused by Li Hongzhang during the 1870s, that planting opium profited the people while prohibiting it would only benefit foreigners and further impoverish China. That argument, he asserted, "shows no understanding of what is essential." After all, for centuries China had been wealthy and its people prosperous even though it had not known of opium. China's sage rulers had always advocated agriculture and silk production. Silk production brought profit rather than injury to farmers, but opium harmed farmers and also left behind a legacy of trouble. "Which brings gain and which brings loss is self-evident," he claimed. Unfortunately, people in Shanxi had not realized the danger posed by opium until too late. "Having abandoned the natural profit given by heaven and earth and planted a poisonous drug that could not appease hunger, even on the brink of death [they] did not awaken," he lamented.[85]

The claim that the opium trade and poppy cultivation exacerbated the famine in North China also has great resonance for modern mainland Chinese scholarship on the disaster, which traces the rise of native opium cultivation to foreign capitalism.[86] In their analysis of the Incredible Famine published in 1994, for example, Li Wenhai and three colleagues state that opium was the most important and most destructive influence that foreign capitalism brought to the agricultural economy of North China before cheap foreign products flooded its markets after the famine. Because the opium trade drained silver out of the country, they explain, the Qing government was forced to encourage domestic poppy cultivation in order to curtail opium imports. The government collected an opium tax, and in some cases officials actually encouraged farmers to plant opium in order to bolster revenues and peasant incomes. Thus opium cultivation expanded rapidly in northwestern China in the early 1870s, particularly in Gansu, Shaanxi, and Shanxi. By the time the Incredible Famine arrived, Li and his colleagues show, one-ninth of Shanxi's total agricultural area was used to cultivate opium. The expansion of opium cultivation in North China aggravated grain shortages in areas prone to scarcity and contributed to their inability to grow or import sufficient grain during the drought.[87]

Li Wenhai and his colleagues quote Zeng Guoquan's assertion that the 1877 famine stemmed from human affairs. Their perspective on the role played by opium is different from Zeng's in important ways, however. They focus not on the ignorant and profit-hungry Shanxi farmers whom Zeng chided for unwisely replacing food crops with opium poppies, but instead on the British gunboats that forced opium on China in the first place. "It is necessary to emphasize that the chief offender who created this disaster is not this insensate plant itself," conclude Li and his coauthors, "but is in fact the preposterous and unscrupulous foreign capitalist economic invasion concealed behind it."[88]

A HOUSE DIVIDED

While Qing officials across the political spectrum retained a commitment to paternalistic government during the famine, the crisis exposed serious conflicts over how best to fulfill the state's obligations to the populace. In the late 1870s, metropolitan officials who supported self-strengthening policies understood Western and Japanese military aggression and economic strength to be the greatest menace to both the dynasty and the Chinese people. Although Li Hongzhang and members of the Zongli Yamen did not deny the pressing nature of the famine or repudiate the state's responsibility to nourish the people, they assigned a lower priority to famine relief than to coastal defense. The self-strengtheners were repeatedly put on the defensive by Qingliu spokesmen who called on the court to rescue famine victims by ordering an immediate and massive shift in resources from coastal defense projects to famine relief. Again and again it was Qingliu proponents, often dismissed in scholarly literature as power-hungry and myopic antiquarians, who championed the cause of the famished people of North China by insisting that harmony between the people and the rulers was more vital to ensuring the survival of the dynasty than Western weaponry. The proper mode of benevolent rule was contested as well on the provincial level, where officials in charge of procuring famine relief for the people of their provinces contributed to broader national debates over grain distribution and opium policy.

Disagreements between powerful groups of officials hampered the state's ability to respond to the famine quickly and effectively. Moreover, these bitter debates illustrate a broader collapse of consensus over how to contextualize a major famine. In late-Qing China the framework in which praise and blame were negotiated was gradually shifting from one in which the key issue for rulers was keeping the Mandate of Heaven, to one that highlighted protecting the empire from the onslaught of foreign powers.

CHAPTER 5

Views from the Outside

Science, Railroads, and Laissez-Faire Economics

Western observers also witnessed the devastation in North China first-hand. Vivid descriptions of the famine written by Anglo-American missionary relief workers stationed in Shanxi and other stricken provinces were published in the Shanghai-based *North China Herald* as well as in missionary journals in England and the United States.[1] Unlike earlier famines in China, the Incredible Famine was thus transformed from a wholly Chinese concern to an internationally recognized disaster that motivated people from Europe, North America, and several countries in Asia to send aid.

Western observers who sought to make sense of the disaster were just as quick as local survivors and Qingliu spokesmen to transform the famine into a moral lesson for their readers. Their interpretations of both famine causation and the Qing government's relief efforts, however, were grounded in perceptual and ideological frameworks that differed significantly from those that informed the views of late-Qing officials and commoners. Rather than placing the famine in morality plays about the need for thrift or imperial benevolence, the British editors of the *North China Herald* viewed the catastrophe as justifying the nineteenth-century British faith in science, railroads, and laissez-faire economics. Missionaries in the field, on the other hand, often saw the disaster as an opportunity to reach more of "China's millions" with the Gospel.

Founded in 1850 by the British auctioneer Henry Shearman, the *North China Herald* was the first foreign-language newspaper established in

China. It aimed to cover Shanghai business, events in England, and important world events. Remaining in the hands of British residents of Shanghai throughout its century of publication, the newspaper generally represented the commercial interests of its treaty-port readers.[2] During the second half of the nineteenth century the *North China Herald* ranked as the chief foreign newspaper in China. Missionaries distributing relief in famine areas in the 1870s regularly sent their reports to the *Herald* for publication, and in 1877 and 1878 the paper printed frequent front-page editorials concerning the disaster.[3] The *Herald*'s take on the Incredible Famine both reflected nineteenth-century British assumptions about famine and influenced how English-speaking residents of China—whether missionaries, merchants, or statesmen—came to view the disaster in the North.

VILLAINS

The editors of the *North China Herald* did not mince words when it came to assigning blame for the famine. "For the absence of rain the Chinese Government is not responsible, but for the effects of famine and desert it has only its own utter worthlessness to thank," they asserted in a front page editorial published in July 1877.[4] Neither the famine's heroes nor its archvillains as identified by the *North China Herald* were hard to miss. The prime villains were undoubtedly the "dominating Mandarins," who one *Herald* editor termed "locusts in human shape." The much longed-for hero, on the other hand, was the "patriotic engineer," the man of science who simultaneously explains the cause of the drought and builds mile upon mile of glistening railway on which to rush grain to the starving.[5]

An overview of the *Herald*'s coverage of the famine from 1877 to 1879 shows that it was less an absence of relief efforts on the part of the Qing state that raised the ire of British observers than it was the *manner* in which official relief was administered. The newspaper repeatedly blamed the transformation of dearth into full-blown famine on three factors: the Qing state's interference in free trade, the distribution of relief without requiring work in return, and the government's reluctance to build railroads and other "modern" forms of transportation.

During the famine the *North China Herald* mounted an unceasing attack on what it viewed as the Chinese government's excessive interference in matters of trade. An editorial comparing famine relief in India and China, for example, accused the Chinese government of being "ignorant of the first rudiments of political economy" because local officials in famine districts fixed the price of grain and forced some purchasers of land from famished villagers to return it without compensation. "By its unwise interference, indeed, with the natural laws of supply and demand," stated the editorial, "the Government has hindered the import of food by private enterprise."[6] The consequences of such interference were dire. Because the Qing government had "entered on a policy of isolation and repressions," claimed a spring 1879 editorial, it had brought about "the aggravation of a serious dearth into a famine, the like of which is not recorded elsewhere in the annals of humanity."[7]

Another editorial writer, moreover, claimed that the famine was simply one awful manifestation of the "insidious decay" that occurred "wherever governments, forgetting their proper sphere of action, have entered into competition with their own people."[8] Yet another complained that the Chinese government had repeatedly ignored the advice of foreign observers that the best means of alleviating the famine was to encourage private enterprise. Rice from South China was carried north to Tianjin in government vessels and then had to await government enterprises to transport it to famine districts, fumed the editorialist. "Instead of trusting to the natural instincts of trade, the Government interfered with the whole system of traffic—embargoed the boats and impressed the coolies—with the result that no one willingly assisted in the work and all who could betook themselves away," he concluded.[9] The *Herald*'s claims about the Qing government's unwillingness to use private enterprise during the disaster were exaggerated. As shown in chapter 4, important officials such as Li Hongzhang and Shen Baozhen actively encouraged merchant involvement in transporting grain into famine areas. The newspaper's scornful denial that imperial benevolence could rescue famine victims as effectively as private enterprise, however, demonstrates the gulf that separated late-Qing and nineteenth-century British assumptions about the state's responsibility during times of dearth.

British definitions of legitimate and illegitimate methods of dealing with famine stemmed in part from a broader European context in which, even in the eighteenth century, the church rather than the state was held responsible for the welfare of the poor. In his essay "Qing Granaries and World History," R. Bin Wong demonstrates that western European states generally relied on commercial exchange to supply needed grain imports, rather than establishing public grain reserves as did the Qing government. "Food supply concerns form part of a larger contrast between European and Chinese states," he explains. "European states often lacked both the capacity and the commitment necessary to establish and sustain granary reserves. Their state-making agenda did not include the kind of paternalistic concern that repeatedly motivated the Chinese."[10]

Wong notes that the European state's traditional failure to aid rural laborers later became part of "a larger set of ideological changes in which the primacy of private market exchange was increasingly affirmed by central governments at the expense of local political control over markets." When English laborers protested high prices and supply shortages during bad times, for example, the eighteenth-century British government increasingly defended the interests of merchants and allowed them to buy and sell according to market conditions regardless of the impact their sales might have on people in exporting areas. In contrast, notes Wong, "when faced with similar struggles, the Chinese state mounted efforts to meet the claims of both local consumers and those in remote areas awaiting grain imports."[11]

The *North China Herald*'s contention that Chinese government intervention helped turn the drought into a major famine also reflected the paper's strong ideological commitment to nineteenth-century free-trade liberalism. Such claims would have sounded searingly familiar to any nineteenth-century Irish or Indian citizen who suffered through a famine under British rule. British relief officials in the nineteenth century, unlike their late-Qing counterparts, rejected the idea that the state bore a paternalistic responsibility to feed its people. During the first two years of the famine that ravaged Ireland in the late 1840s, for instance, the Liberal government in power in Britain was so "resolutely committed to free trade" that it strongly opposed importing cheap foodstuffs into Ireland or preventing the export of food from Ireland as improper government interference with normal commerce. As Britain's head of treasury Charles Trevelyan stated in 1846: "It forms no part of the functions of government to provide supplies of food or to increase the productive powers of the land."[12]

British policy makers in late-nineteenth-century India adhered to similar noninterventionist policies. As famine ravaged both India and China in 1877, the government of British India instructed its new famine commissioner that "the task of saving life, irrespective of the cost, is one which is beyond our power to undertake."[13] In his account of the 1876–78 famine in southern India, William Digby, honorary secretary of the Indian Famine Relief Fund, insisted that "when means of communication are open to a district[,] free trade enters, and all Government competition with that trade is only and wholly evil."[14]

Those who dared to question the usefulness of free-trade rhetoric during famines went unheeded. In November 1876, for instance, the provincial government of Madras informed the government of India that it had arranged to purchase and hold a state reserve of 30,000 tons of grain. Because food prices had risen so quickly due to the shortage of food, explained the Madras government, "merchants and dealers, hopeful of enormous future gains, appeared determined to hold their stocks for some indefinite time and not to part with the article which was becoming of such unwonted value."[15] The reserve of government grain, stated the secretary to the Madras government, "is intended to be held as an insurance, so far as it will go, against the possible catastrophe of failure of supply to the local market, by ordinary trade and private enterprise, or such an entire temporary withholding of stores by grain merchants as has already led to very serious inconvenience." The government of India overturned the Madras government's plan on the ground that it interfered with private trade.[16] The attempt to store government grain was portrayed as a blot on the British government's otherwise perfect record of nonintervention. In spite of British claims that "the energies of private trade were in no case unequal to the task that was thus laid upon them," the famine commission itself estimated that 3.5 million lives were lost in the Madras Presidency during the disaster. Estimates of famine mortality in India as a whole during the 1876–79 catastrophe range from 6.1 to 10.3 million deaths.[17]

Faith in laissez-faire economics curtailed Britain's famine-relief efforts in Ireland to such an extent that as early as the 1850s Irish nationalists like John Mitchel equated the famine with genocide and claimed that "Ireland died of political economy" rather than from a preventable food shortage. Indian nationalists also denounced the inadequacy of British relief policies in the late 1870s.[18] The *Herald* editors were unaware of or unconvinced by such critiques, however. Throughout the North China Famine they lambasted the Qing state for rejecting the same noninterventionist philosophy that had failed so miserably in British-ruled Ireland and India.

A second facet of Chinese official relief efforts that British observers found utterly incomprehensible was the Qing government's distribution of free food and cash. A "prudent" government, argued the author of a summer 1878 editorial, would give relief as wages in return for useful work, instead of distributing gruel for free as the Chinese government was doing. "The people, in place of being taught to labour for their sustenance, have been turned into vagabonds and tramps." They "fester in masses around the large towns, and form hotbeds of crime and disease," warned the journalist.[19]

The *Herald* did not oppose all forms of famine relief. It regularly printed missionary letters and reports from the Famine Relief Fund Committee that urged readers to donate to relief efforts. It was, however, intensely critical of the relief work carried out by Qing officials. The *Herald* frequently called on the Chinese government to follow the example of British India by establishing public works. "It is *work* not *food* which it is the duty of the Government to supply," insisted an editorialist who painted a rosy picture of British efforts to fight famine in India by employing famine victims to build roads, canals, and railroads.[20] "How utterly unsatisfactory is that kind of charity which maintains large bodies of people in a state of almost complete idleness," commented the author of a letter to the editor. Only by utilizing the labor of famine victims as was done in British India, he asserted, could it be guaranteed that "charitable gifts are in no case wasted upon unworthy recipients, nor are the poor pauperized by being allowed to live in idleness instead of living by honest industry."[21]

The *Herald*'s charge that the distribution of free relief resulted in idleness and the formation of "hotbeds of crime and disease" reflected ideology or what historian Peter Gray describes as "the framework of ideas—the worldview—that molded how individuals and groups perceived the problems that faced them" in nineteenth-century Britain.[22] While British Liberals advocated charity for the *deserving* poor, they valued self-reliance above all and regarded the Irish (and Indian) poor as lazy and overly dependant. As Charles Trevelyan asserted in 1846, "the greatest improvement of all which could take place in Ireland would be to teach the people to depend on themselves . . . instead of having recourse to the assistance of the government on every occasion."[23] Instructions provided by the government of British India to its newly appointed special famine delegate on his arrival in the Bombay famine districts in 1877 expressed a similar line of thinking: "Everyone admits the evils of indiscriminate private charity, but the indiscriminate charity of a Government is far worse."[24]

The basic assumption that people would prefer to "eat the bread of idleness" if given a chance, and that they would take advantage of government relief unless closely monitored, shaped nineteenth-century British relief efforts in important ways. Famine victims in Ireland and India were expected to labor on public works projects in exchange for food or subsistence wages. But to gain admittance to the works, appli-

cants first had to convince relief officials that they were genuinely destitute. "To prevent demoralization of the people, and to save the public
treasury from excessive payments, it is absolutely necessary that tests
of some kind should be applied to the great majority of those who seek
assistance," explained the Public Works Department of the government
of India in May 1878. During the Indian famine, those desperate
enough to dig ditches or build roads in exchange for relief first had to
pass the "Distance Test," the "Wage Test," and the "Labour Test." All
three tests sought to ascertain whether or not applicants were truly in-
digent by testing their willingness to work in camps far from their homes
and sleep at the works each night, to accept a wage that was "little more
than a bare subsistence," and to prove their willingness to do "a fair
day's work."[25]

Scholars of the Irish famine trace nineteenth-century British assumptions about famine and its victims to an amalgamation of the writings
of influential classical economists like Adam Smith, Jeremy Bentham,
Thomas Malthus, and John Stuart Mill. Historians Patrick O'Sullivan
and Richard Lucking note that in the eighteenth century, British East India Company officials continued the interventionist famine policies of
the Indian states they replaced. In the nineteenth century, however, company officials increasingly turned a deaf ear to Indian cries for price con-
trols during hard times. They justified their new policy by referring to
truncated versions of Adam Smith's theories of market forces, laissez-
faire, and the invisible hand.[26] Classical political economy, argues Peter
Gray, produced a climate of public opinion in Britain that "prioritized
economic development over the relief of suffering, even in conditions of
social catastrophe." During the Irish famine, classical political economists used this climate of public opinion to argue that even if noninterventionist policies did result in more starvation in the short term, in the
long term, strict adherence to free trade would free Ireland from its economic backwardness as well as from famine.[27]

As further justification for doing as little as possible during a food crisis, British noninterventionists also relied on the Malthusian theory that
famine was God's or Nature's way of solving overpopulation. Why harm
the British economy to save lives if the people who were saved from
hunger today would simply suffer more later on if overpopulation were
not stemmed?[28] In addition, Providentialism, a religious creed which
taught that human affairs are regulated by a divine agency for human
good, served to validate the widespread belief that the potato blight had
been sent by God for an ascertainable purpose. Under this assumption,

states Gray, even many church leaders in England urged the government to remove all restrictions on free trade in order to "subject individuals to the moral discipline of the 'natural economic laws' instituted by God."[29] Such ideas reappeared in the pages of the *North China Herald* thirty years later. The famine would "not have come in vain," a spring 1878 editorial asserted, if it convinced the Chinese government to cease its "suppression of all private enterprise" and embark on modernizing reforms.[30]

Qingliu proponents such as Ouyang Yun argued that the construction of railroads and steamships contributed to the scale of the drought disaster by wasting scarce government resources and offending Heaven. In contrast, editors of the *North China Herald* identified China's lack of modern transportation networks as a third major "villain" responsible for transforming the drought into a famine. The Qing government's distrust of railroads became an obsession for *Herald* editors. Article after article written ostensibly about the famine ended up as an attack on the government's unwillingness to build railways. One editorialist charged that although China was prone to droughts and should have prepared for them, "on the contrary, the policy of the Imperial Government seems to have been inspired by a desire to shut up each province in itself as carefully as its predecessors desired by the Great Wall to shut out the external world." Railroads and canals, argued the journalist, "might have broken through the mountain barrier which divides the starving residue of a prosperous population [in Shanxi] from lands of plenty." But since the repeated offers of Western engineers to build railroads had been "scornfully rejected" by the Qing government, when the drought struck, the country had only "camels and carts" that took weeks to transport grain to the starving.[31]

British observers frequently implied that the famine was the natural consequence of the Chinese government's rejection of foreign technology and refusal to open the country to the West. For instance, in his 1879 report, R. J. Forrest, chairman of Tianjin's Famine Relief Committee, assumed that it was the lack of modern science and engineering that led to Shanxi's transportation problems. "The want . . . of engineering art, the powerlessness of the natives to deal with the caprices of the Yellow River, or the existence of such a trivial observance as a broken bridge, which was observed by a scientific foreign traveler, has thrown Shanxi into compulsory commercial relations with Chihli [Zhili], notwithstanding the enormous difficulties of access over the mountains with that province," wrote Forrest.[32]

That railroads might have enabled the government to transport relief grain into Shanxi more quickly is a valid point. The difficulty and expense of transporting grain over the Taihang mountains, which separated Shanxi from Zhili, was repeatedly mentioned by Shanxi governor Zeng Guoquan and numerous other Chinese observers. But railroads unaccompanied by adequate relief policies were no cure for famine. Even if railroads had existed to ship grain into the province, without state relief, there was no guarantee that farmers and nonagricultural workers left cropless or jobless by the drought would have had enough money to purchase the imported food. Furthermore, while some scholars have argued that railroads helped to lower famine mortality rates in India after 1900, the roughly 6,000 miles of railway operational in India by 1872 did not prevent millions of people there from starving during the 1876–78 famine.[33] On the contrary, in an explanation of its controversial decision to stockpile an emergency reserve of 30,000 tons of grain in 1876, the Madras Presidency stated in a letter to the government of India: "It was apparent to the [Madras] government that facilities for moving grain by rail were rapidly raising prices everywhere and that the activity of apparent importation and railway transit did not indicate any addition to food stocks of the Presidency."[34]

Moreover, by harping on railroads as a panacea that would bring China into the modern age, foreign observers allowed themselves to turn a blind eye to more complex reasons for the famine. The *Herald* never acknowledged that the Guguan Pass was not a route into Shanxi normally relied on by grain merchants and officials, but was instead an emergency route that Qing officials also deemed inadequate. More important, the newspaper did not admit that foreign aggression had helped drain the Qing treasury, thus limiting the government's ability to maintain the granary system and water works so vital to the northern provinces. Considering many treaty-port readers' involvement in the opium trade and the paper's regular reports listing the Shanghai opium returns for each season, it is not surprising that the *Herald*'s editorials about the famine also scrupulously avoided dealing with the opium issue. Nor did the connections that Shanxi's governors drew between poppy cultivation and grain shortages receive serious consideration.[35]

Blaming the severity of the famine on China's lack of railroads enabled the *Herald* editors to avoid uncomfortable topics and turn articles about the disaster into critiques of China as "static" or "backward" and in need of "modernization" along Western lines. An editorial published in October 1877, for example, began by describing the "sad monotony" of Chinese records of past famines. "It never seems to get much worse. It never seems to get much better," the author wrote. "Dynasties pass away. Kings and Ministers change, but the people are periodically decimated by the recurring scourge with a regularity that makes a careless reader fling aside the record in utter disgust." The journalist then proposed "quick and efficient means of transit" as the key to breaking China's monotonous cycle of disasters. "If there were any adequate means of carrying food from the places where it abounds to the starving districts, all might be righted," he proclaimed confidently. "Food and money would be forthcoming if only there was any chance of the supplies reaching the famine-stricken people."[36] The *Herald* editor concluded with a claim similar to those made by British officials who had viewed the Irish famine as a chance to free Ireland from economic backwardness: "These later years of famine might really be the beginning of a better day for China if they taught the rulers that such calamities would be vastly mitigated in severity by the introduction of Railways."[37]

The *Herald's* insistence that famines and railroads were connected stemmed from some of the bedrock assumptions of nineteenth-century British famine narratives. Chris Morash, a scholar of the Irish famine, argues that Britain's hostile view of the Irish famine and its victims was due to the perceived assault that the death and disease brought by famine made on the idea of progress, an idea often symbolized by miles and miles of glistening railroad track. By the mid-nineteenth century, argues Morash, progress was sacred to many Westerners. When British citizens traveled to famine Ireland and saw a land of mass graves, dirt, and destitution, it constituted an affront to their deeply held belief that progress was universal. "With the disappearance of the visible signifiers of material progress—railways, sanitation, the rituals of civil society," he writes, "the idea of progress itself begins to unravel." To British observers, famine Ireland was a frightening and disorienting "enemy of progress."[38] As an article published in the *Saturday Review* in 1866 makes clear, the view of famine as an attack on advancement continued to appear in the British press decades after the Irish famine:

> In the bare idea of famine there is something of a peculiarly painful and shocking character. An epidemic may be considered beyond the prevention of human science—at least of human science in its present stage. . . . But with famine it is altogether different. It gives the lie to some of our most essential conceptions of modern civilization to find, in the same community, some members enjoying every luxury that wealth can procure, while others are dying for want of bread.[39]

In the eyes of British residents of China, who had long considered Qing China a foe of modernization, the arrival of the famine provided more evidence of the dire consequences of standing still. By constantly blurring the discussion of famine with calls for the construction of railroads, then, British observers were able to place the famine into a familiar and reassuring narrative of progress.

HEROES

The British elite as represented by the *North China Herald* upheld science, technology, and practical action as means to ending the famine. A September 1877 editorial described the sort of hero whom British observers most admired. The author had no praise for the compassionate officials whom Chinese sources lauded for serving as the "fathers and mothers of the people" during the disaster. Instead he criticized the "antiquated learning" required of Chinese who hoped to pass the civil service examinations, and predicted that although the famine was growing more severe, "it seems almost certain that nothing intelligent or practical will be done." The editorial then introduced the sort of hero who could pull China out of her misery: "The power wanted is a man of commanding energy and resolution. . . . The man wanted in China now, as in its early days, is a patriotic engineer."[40] This "single-minded and energetic" engineer, explained the *Herald,* would fight the famine by establishing public works programs and constructing roads and railroads. Throughout the newspaper's coverage of the famine, this pragmatic and much longed-for "patriotic engineer" was contrasted with China's tradition-bound officials, accused of acting like "locusts in human shape" by "clinging blindly to their old policy of ousting the foreigner at all costs" and "throttling commerce" so that the people starved.[41]

Nineteenth-century British observers had abundant faith in what could be accomplished by energetic men of science. Quoting an article printed in the *Edinburgh Review,* for example, a writer for the *Herald* proudly proclaimed in 1879 that with regard to the Indian famine, "fresh information is being annually collected and published. On every part of the horizon, the veil of ignorance of fact . . . is being lifted . . . and year by year the questions of measures for the improvement of India are passing from the regions of opinion . . . to those illumined by science." According to the journalist, China fared poorly by comparison. "Of the famine in China, no such statements as these can be made," he chided. "No scientific inquiries have been set on foot, no means taken to mitigate the severity of the scourge should it occur again."[42]

R. J. Forrest echoed the *Herald*'s assertion that Western technology could prevent future droughts, particularly on the plain of Zhili Province. "A few canals, and the necessary flood gates, weirs, and pumping machinery, would place the inhabitants of the South of Chihli beyond the reach of the misery they have endured since 1871," wrote Forrest in 1879. He added that Li Hongzhang, the governor-general of Zhili, was willing to hire hydraulic engineers, but "his progressive ideas . . . are generally strangled by the system which surrounds him; and a useful work of imperative necessity would be vetoed from Peking where the anti-foreign party is supreme, not because the scheme is doubtful, but because foreign machinery and foreigners would have to be employed."[43] Like many Western observers, Forrest had high hopes that the energetic foreign response to the famine would help change the anti-foreign sentiments he bemoaned. "The distribution of the funds your committee have so kindly sent by the brave and judicious band of missionaries now engaged in the work will do more to really open China to us than a dozen wars," he asserted in a letter to the Committee of the Famine Relief Fund in Shanghai.[44]

The "patriotic engineer" so dear to British observers and the activist official heralded by Chinese elites serve as reminders of each group's nineteenth-century priorities. Praise of such heroes helped elites define and uphold sets of values perceived to be at risk during the famine. The *Herald*'s calls for engineers and men of science hinted that a famine of such magnitude did indeed threaten nineteenth-century British assumptions about progress. Likewise, the emphasis that Qingliu supporters placed on rulers and officials who could shore up popular support signified their fear that if left unaddressed, the growing disconnect between the people and the rulers could lead to yet more rebellions and possibly the collapse of the Qing state.

MISSIONARY VOICES

The *North China Herald* was an influential English-language voice on the famine, but it did not represent the whole range of British perspectives on the crisis. Missionary relief workers who viewed firsthand the suffering caused by the famine did not typically employ the *Herald*'s contemptuous tone toward Chinese culture and officialdom. They were more willing to acknowledge the extensive relief efforts carried out by the Qing government, to view the famine as a lesson for England as well as for China, and to criticize some of Britain's policies in China. In a letter published in the Baptist Missionary Society's journal, the *Missionary Herald,* for example, Timothy Richard, the Welsh Baptist missionary who led the foreign famine relief efforts in Shandong and Shanxi, praised Qing relief efforts. "Great as the efforts of foreigners were, they were a mere drop in the bucket compared with what the Chinese Government itself did," wrote Richard. "It gave at least two millions of pounds between the remission of the taxes and the direct relief it gave to Shanxi alone."[45]

During the famine, David Hill, the English missionary who worked with Richard to distribute relief in Shanxi, wrote a letter to the general secretaries of the Wesleyan-Methodist Missionary Society asserting that the famine carried a warning for England as well as for China. "To us as a nation I cannot but think that God is speaking in these Eastern famines," wrote Hill. "The superfluities of a middle class English household would save the lives of half a score of Chinese, . . . and it is only by regarding these responsibilities of wealth, that the ruin which luxury entails can be averted from the British people."[46] In a letter addressed to the youths in the Manchester Sunday school he had taught before traveling to China, A. J. Parrott, a missionary who distributed relief in Shanxi with the China Inland Mission, drew moral lessons from the famine that sound surprisingly similar to those put forth by local observers such as Liu Xing and Liang Peicai. After describing the plight of a young boy whose father, mother, brothers, and sisters had all died during the famine, Parrott wrote: "Boys, never waste a morsel of bread, nor eat more than you want when your kind teachers give you a good Christmas dinner, or a tea-meeting, etc., but always remember the poor heathen here, who have nothing to eat."[47]

Missionary observers were far more willing than *Herald* editors to discuss the opium problem, though they emphasized the drug's harmful impact on the missionary endeavor rather than the causal connections that Shanxi's governors and other Qing officials drew between poppy cultivation and famine. Christian relief workers were shocked by the prevalence of opium smoking in the famine-ravaged provinces they visited. Parrott noted the large number of men he saw taking opium as he traveled through Henan early in 1880: "Until lately I have estimated the number of opium-smokers in this part of the country at one-half of the men, but from observation and further information, I am persuaded that the proportion is considerably greater than this. . . . I was frequently asked if I could cure the dreadful habit, or would recommend some effectual medicine."[48]

Missionary publications argued that Britain's trafficking in opium fostered Chinese mistrust of foreigners and hampered efforts to preach the Gospel. An article in the *Missionary Herald,* for example, decried Britain's role in the opium trade. The Chinese were unanimous, it stated, in their denunciation of the damage caused by opium: "They have a saying that the surest way to ruin an enemy is to make him an opium-smoker. They attribute the late famine to heaven's displeasure for their cultivation of the poppy." Because of Chinese hatred of the drug, continued the article, when "Christian England" foisted opium upon "heathen China" by warfare and diplomacy, it did great harm to missionary efforts. Although some English citizens made justifications for the opium trade, the *Missionary Herald* admitted, English missionaries joined their American counterparts in asserting that the traffic "bars the hearts of a third of the human race against the Gospel," and that "the Chinese meet them with the taunt that they offer them the Gospel with one hand and force the opium on them with the other."[49] The editors of *China's Millions,* the London-based publication of the China Inland Mission, also tried to shame British Christians into action by bringing home to them the massive scale of Britain's opium trade in China. "Is it not humbling to think," asked the journal in 1878, "that the entire amount raised for the famine relief during this year, though it has called forth such grateful acknowledgment from many in China, . . . is actually exceeded by the amount we through our Indian government receive in three days from the sale of opium in China?"[50]

Unlike the *North China Herald* editors, who viewed all types of government intervention as suspect, missionary observers praised the Chinese government's efforts to ban poppy cultivation in famine areas.[51] David Hill admired the campaign against opium in Shanxi. "The officials here under the inspiration of the Famine Commissioner have been very diligent in suppressing the growth of the poppy," he wrote from his relief station in Pingyang. "This is certainly a triumph of moral principle over pecuniary policy, seeing that the poppy would yield a crop about double the value of any ordinary cereal."[52]

An article in *The Friend of China,* a publication of the Anglo-Oriental Society for the Suppression of the Opium Trade, took issue in 1879 with the *North China Herald*'s critiques of Qing attempts to deal with the opium problem. The defenders of the opium trade sometimes denied the existence of the Chinese protest against opium, stated the author, and some even claimed that Protestant missionaries in China were using the opium issue to cover up their failure to convert the Chinese to Christianity. In response to such accusations, the author provided examples of the concrete steps that Zeng Guoquan in Shanxi and Zuo Zongtang in Xinjiang had taken to prohibit opium poppy cultivation in their jurisdictions. Because even the *North China Herald* could no longer ignore such clear evidence of the anti-opium sentiment among high-ranking Chinese officials, he wrote, the *Herald* had changed tactics and accused Zuo Zuotang of "fighting against the laws of nature" with his prohibitions. The author of the article responded sharply to the newspaper's assertion:

> But in China vicious propensities are not regarded as natural laws. Even in this enlightened land [England] we do not regard all such propensities as absolutely beyond government interference. We have our laws against gambling, drunkenness and prostitution, and we do not allow the sale of opium except by duly qualified druggists. The Chinese have much to learn from us, no doubt, but we trust they will never learn that it is the duty of a government not to interfere whenever vice is rampant, and threatens national ruin.[53]

Clearly, then, not every British resident in China agreed with the *North China Herald*'s mantra that all types of government interference were unwise and unnatural.

Missionary relief workers like Hill and Richard employed a more sympathetic tone than the *Herald* editors when writing about the famine, and disagreed with the newspaper on the opium question. At the same time, they shared the *Herald*'s faith in Western science and transportation technology as effective guards against famine, as well as the newspaper's assumption that China needed to open itself to the West. David Hill viewed railroads as both a way to improve transportation and as a means of bringing the Gospel to China more quickly. In the same letter in which he discussed the famine's lessons for England, he also speculated about what "wholesome lessons" disaster might teach the Chinese government and people: "To them the first lesson which it [the famine] will bring home will doubtless be the need of Western means of communication, the lack of which is felt here perhaps tenfold more than in India. And if the lesson be only taken to heart, the old barriers of exclusivism will be broken down and many rough places be made plain for the coming of the Kingdom of God."[54] Hill wrote even more enthusiastically about railroads in his personal notes about the famine. After describing the slow progress of relief transports into Shanxi that depended on camels and mules, he envisioned how a railway would change the situation:

> Now it requires no very profound reasoning to show that if from the jetty at Tientsin to the town of P.Y. [Pingyang] there ran over the plains and through the hills one long line of railway communications, how grain might have been poured in and thousands, millions even of precious lives been saved. And thus the astute Chinaman, careless as he be of human life, is slowly wakening up to see and with a view to this future possibility, shall I say? Nay, this coming certainty. Governor Tseng had just before I left the Province despatched two subordinate officers to survey the land. And doubt-less the transport of grain to save the living as well as the transport of troops to slay them is still silently influencing the official mind and heralds the dawn of a brighter day with regard to the facilities for travel and transport in the interior of China.[55]

The extensive reform proposals put forth during and after the famine by Timothy Richard were also filled with references to the importance of both scientific education and railroads. In his autobiographical work *Forty-Five Years in China,* Richard described how the famine's horrors moved him to consider the root causes of China's poverty and of vary-ing degrees of human suffering all over the world. "In pondering West-ern civilization, I felt that its advantage over Chinese civilization was due to the fact that it sought to discover the workings of God in Nature, and to apply the laws in Nature for the service of mankind," he wrote. "In applying the laws of science to the needs of man, Western nations had made marvelous inventions that were little less than miracles."[56]

During the famine, Richard met with the governor of Shandong and later the governor of Shanxi to propose reform measures such as the con-struction of railways, mines, and other public works. In the more de-tailed proposals he made to Chinese officials after the disaster, he em-phasized the control of nature; development of new techniques to foster agriculture, industry, and mining; construction of an extensive railway system; expansion of free trade and modern banking; and establishment of scientific education and technological expertise in China.[57]

FAMINE AND IDEOLOGY

Unmistakably, the disparate interpretations of famine causation and pre-vention offered by British observers and Qing officials were shaped by their distinctive worldviews. Although both groups of observers described the same miserable situation, they diagnosed the underlying causes of and remedies for the famine quite differently. The heroes and villains they identified in their attempts to make sense of the catastrophe revealed hitherto unquestioned cultural assumptions and priorities.

To both *North China Herald* editors and missionary relief workers, the arrival of such a serious famine proved that China was in desperate need of economic reform and religious salvation. Famine was the antithesis of progress. It began when a combination of official corruption, conservatism, and government interference in commerce exacerbated drought conditions, then spun out of control due to the lack of modern transportation networks. According to this line of thinking, a major famine was undeniably horrific. However, such a disaster might also be "the beginning of a better day for China" if only it convinced the country's rulers to build railroads, usher in free trade, and fall in line with Britain's march to modernity. This ideology of famine was clearly influenced by the "classical famine policy" Britain employed in Ireland and India. That policy was in turn developed out of distinctive nineteenth-century British assumptions about Providence, human nature, and economic behavior.

The Qing officials maligned by foreign observers, though divided over how best to deal with the famine, were unanimous in rejecting the broad laissez-faire policy espoused by the *Herald* and by British relief officials in Ireland and India. Such a policy, in the words of William Rowe, would have represented "a morally repellent abrogation of the basic concept of benevolent rule."[58] Qingliu proponents championed greater direct government involvement in relief efforts. Just as the British obsession with railroads as a talisman against famine emerged from nineteenth-century British faith in scientific progress, so the Qingliu assertion that maintaining popular support was more crucial to the dynasty than arming itself against foreign attack stemmed from long-held Confucian ideals. In both cases, the shock of famine motivated important groups of elite observers to reaffirm, rather than attack or question, cherished assumptions.

CHAPTER 6

Hybrid Voices

The Famine and Jiangnan Activism

Among all the observers of the Incredible Famine, it was Chinese philanthropists and journalists in Shanghai and other cities in the wealthy
Jiangnan region whose perspectives on the disaster were most significantly
shaped by cross-cultural conversation. Local observers in Shanxi made
no mention of missionary relief efforts or the foreign presence in China
in their discussions of the disaster. Relying on Confucian definitions of
moral and immoral behavior, they viewed imperial benevolence and filiality, chasteness, and thrift rather than railroads or free trade as the most
effective guards against famine. By the 1870s, Qing officials in the capital could no longer join local literati in ignoring the Western powers.
Both self-strengtheners and Qingliu proponents viewed the West as primarily a threat to be defended against. As demonstrated in chapter 5,
many British observers in China expressed only contempt for the Qing
state and its relief policies. Although the editors of the *North China
Herald* spent the famine years living and working in a country with a
rich heritage of carrying out successful relief campaigns, they remained
locked within their own cultural framework when discussing famine causation and prevention. In sum, British journalists and Chinese observers
in Shanxi and the Qing capital responded to the Incredible Famine with
the cultural resources they had at hand. They saw the massive death and
destruction wrought by famine as a threat to values crucial to their respective cultures, and they reacted to protect and reaffirm those values.

Jiangnan responses to the disaster, on the other hand, were comparatively hybrid. Southern relief organizers viewed foreigners as a source of new technologies and relief methods that could help strengthen China and prevent future disasters. When the leading Chinese-language newspaper in late-nineteenth-century China, the Shanghai-based *Shenbao,* began to cover the famine on an almost daily basis in 1877 and 1878, the disaster caught the attention of Chinese reformers and gentry-philanthropists throughout the Lower Yangzi region. As recent scholarship has demonstrated, the extragovernmental famine relief effort that resulted was unprecedented in scope and style. By the summer of 1878, gentry and merchant organizers had established relief offices in Shanghai, Hangzhou, Suzhou, and Yangzhou. Over the next three years these centers cooperated to raise over a million taels for disaster relief. Such elite-run efforts cooperated with, but remained separate from, the official relief-coordinating bureau in Tianjin established by Li Hongzhang early in 1878, which also targeted Shanghai as a center of official fund-raising.[1] Some southern philanthropists even traveled north to distribute relief money, bury the dead, and care for orphaned children and for women who had been sold by their starving families.

In their concerted effort to limit the famine's pernicious effects, influential members of the Jiangnan elite drew ideas not only from Chinese texts and philanthropic traditions but also from foreign discussions of relief campaigns overseas and of the benefits of Western technology. Relief activities in the Lower Yangzi region were spearheaded by philanthropists in inland cities like Suzhou, as well as by members of Shanghai's treaty-port elite. Shanghai, however, was the locus of China's first Western-style press, and the place most influenced by foreign critiques of Qing relief efforts and by the foreign presence itself.[2] In Shanghai more than anywhere else in the empire, the famine gave rise to loud cries for reform.

PICTURES TO DRAW TEARS FROM IRON: FROM SUZHOU TO LONDON VIA SHANGHAI

As the famine grew ever more severe during the spring of 1878, Chinese philanthropists from the Taohuawu gongsuo (public hall) in Suzhou designed and printed the brief volume titled *Henan qihuang tieleitu* (The Incredible Famine in Henan: Pictures to draw tears from iron). Xie Jiafu, who directed the Taohuawu public hall and led the Suzhou relief effort, was primarily responsible for compiling and distributing the booklet. The volume's twelve woodblock prints and the accompanying poetic descriptions sought to persuade viewers to have pity on and send aid to the suffering people in North China.[3] The text next to the first illustration in the *tieleitu* set, for example, describes how famine victims were forced to kill their plough oxen, pawn their farming tools and their clothing, and finally sell their houses and fields in a desperate effort to survive. The last sentence begged readers to have compassion: "Think of this, you who live in high halls and fine houses, and let your hearts be moved."[4]

Both the style and subject matter of the booklet drew heavily on China's long tradition of describing disasters. The poetic laments, for instance, use descriptive phrases strikingly similar to those found in the *Qingshiduo,* an anthology of poems from the Qing period compiled by a Zhejiangese scholar just a decade before the famine.[5] The horrors depicted by the illustrations—from starved corpses being devoured by dogs and birds to famine victims throwing themselves into wells or selling their children—all were stock images used repeatedly in local gazetteers from Shanxi and other famine provinces.

In his work on the origins of private charitable relief in late-Qing China, historian Zhu Hu demonstrates that the decision to depict the suffering of disaster victims visually as well as in writing stemmed from Jiangnan's regional philanthropic tradition. A few decades before the Incredible Famine, he explains, a Jiangnan philanthropist named Yu Zhi designed two volumes of "pictures to draw tears from iron" in order to raise relief funds for victims of the Jiangnan flood of 1850 and the Taiping wars of the 1850s and early 1860s. The unmistakable similarities between the style and content of the illustrations in Xie Jiafu's *Henan qihuang tieleitu* and those of Yu Zhi's *Jiangnan tieleitu* show that Xie was deeply influenced by the earlier work.[6]

To motivate people to donate to relief efforts, Xie Jiafu and his Taohuawu colleagues also called on belief systems and fund-raising methods that had deep roots in late-imperial Chinese society. China's tradition of famine relief comprised diverse strands of thought, ranging from the basic Confucian ideal of humaneness and the concern for the well-being of the common people, to Legalist principles that emphasized the manipulation of rewards and punishments, to popular Buddhist teachings about the oneness of all creatures.[7] The Suzhou gentry borrowed from all of these traditions during the Incredible Famine. For instance, before they began printing disaster illustrations in 1878, members of the Taohuawu public hall used a fund-raising method that Xie's father had tried a few decades earlier during the Daoguang-era flood. They designed woodblock prints of a seven-story Buddhist pagoda and encouraged donors to accumulate merit by giving enough to get their name written on the pagoda. The first illustration in the Taohuawu's comprehensive collection of disaster prints is titled "To Save One Person's Life Is Better Than Building a Seven-Story Pagoda" and depicts the "Wild Goose Pagoda for Shandong Relief." Those who contributed one hundred *wen* to the relief effort would have their names written on a level of the pagoda illustration.[8]

Xie and his coworkers also drew on the belief, popularized by morality books (*shanshu*) and shared by local observers like Liu Xing, that Heaven distributed rewards and retributions for good and bad deeds.[9] While local survivors desperate to understand why the famine struck Shanxi tended to emphasize Heaven's wrath at human misconduct, Jiangnan philanthropists focused instead on the rewards that generous donors could accrue by donating to relief. The morality books that circulated widely in late imperial China provided detailed advice on what people should do to earn rewards and escape punishments in this life and the afterlife. Such books specifically addressed the religious ramifications of engaging in famine relief activities. One seventeenth-century ledger, for example, allotted one hundred merit points to a person who saved the life of another but deducted one hundred points from the account of one who "hoards rice rather than distributing it to the needy in times of famine."[10] The Taohuawu famine illustrations echoed such claims. The final print in the *Henan qihuang tieleitu* shows heavenly beings descending to shower rewards of wealth and filial sons on those who contributed to relief. The illustration is titled "On the Good Who Open Their Purses All the Spiritual Powers Bestow Blessing," and the text below assures readers that the accumulation of good actions never fails to result in "superabundant blessing."[11]

Zheng Guanying, a reformer-entrepreneur from Guangdong, also highlighted the rewards Heaven would grant those who aided disaster victims. In 1877 Zheng worked with Xie Jiafu and the Zhejiangese merchant-philanthropist Jing Yuanshan to form a relief bureau in Shanghai to help famine victims in Shanxi. When the government became more involved in relief the following year, Zheng, Xie, and Jing cooperated with Qing officials, particularly Sheng Xuanhuai and Li Hongzhang, to broaden the relief effort to include Henan, Zhili, and Shaanxi.[12] In a letter to the public posted by the Shanghai Relief Managing Office early in 1878, Zheng Guanying reminded "those fortunate people who live in Shanghai and have enough food and warm clothing" that "saving neighbors from disaster brings many good effects." Great wealth and high rank, he explained,

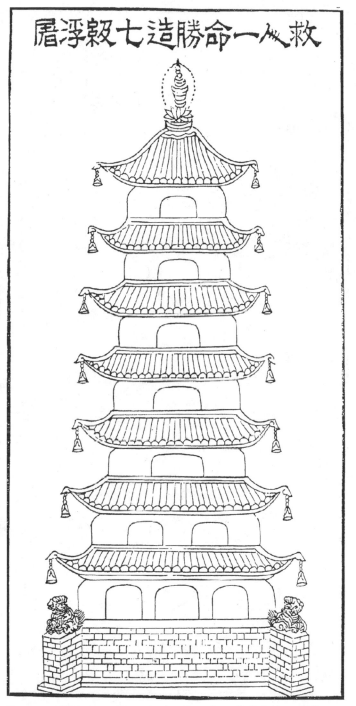

Figure 1. Wild Goose Pagoda for Shandong Relief. From "Si sheng gao zai tu qi," shou juan (Pictures reporting the disaster in the four provinces, opening volume), in *Qi Yu Jin Zhi zhenjuan zhengxin lu* (Statement of accounts for relief contributions for Shandong, Henan, Shanxi, and Zhili) (n.p., 1881), 3a.

Figure 2. Philanthropists Rewarded. From "Si sheng gao zai tu qi,"
19a.

both stemmed from good deeds performed in secret. He implored his Shanghai audience to relieve others as readily as if it were they who were starving and drowning, and assured them that doing so would bring them filial sons and wealthy grandsons. "You can know that following the Way brings blessing, and that you hold your own fortune in your hands," concluded Zheng.[13]

Faced with an epic disaster, members of the Jiangnan elite turned to China's long and multifaceted tradition of philanthropic action and poetic lament. At the same time, much also distinguished their interpretation of and reaction to the famine from late-Ming or hinterland responses. Both Xie Jiafu himself and the volume of famine illustrations he and his Taohuawu colleagues compiled reflect the hybrid character of Jiangnan responses to the famine. Xie and many others who organized the drive to raise relief funds in the Jiangnan region were reformist in outlook and committed to strengthening China by borrowing Western practices. In the 1870s and 1880s, for example, Xie Jiafu, Zheng Guanying, Jing Yuanshan, and Sheng Xuanhuai were involved not only in relief organizing but also in self-strengthening enterprises such as the China Merchant Steamship Navigation Company and the Shanghai Telegraph Office.[14]

While Sheng Xuanhuai and Zheng Guanying are well-known treaty-port reformers, Xie Jiafu offers an instructive profile of the less famous post-Taiping Jiangnan elites who responded to the famine with alacrity. Xie came from a family with a venerable record of philanthropic activity. His father, Xie Huiting, who participated in various local charitable campaigns, has been called "one of the most famous philanthropists in Jiangnan during the Daoguang and Xianfeng periods" (1821–61).[15] According to his biography in the Beizhuan jibu, Xie Jiafu was no stranger to disaster. Born into a scholar-gentry family in 1846, he was only fourteen when the Taiping Army took over his village in Jiangsu's Wu County near Suzhou. Xie was captured by the rebels, and more than twenty members of his family were killed. When his father died shortly after his son's escape from the Taipings, Xie temporarily moved to Shanghai with his mother in 1861.[16]

Xie and his mother were two of thousands of elite refugees who fled to Shanghai during the 1860s as leading Jiangnan cities including Suzhou, Nanjing, and Hangzhou fell to the Taipings. The Shanghai they arrived in had already changed a great deal since China's defeat in the first Opium War (1839–42), which forced the Qing government to open the city to foreign trade and allow British, American, and French authorities to establish foreign concessions there. As it became a major hub for overseas trade as well as north-south coastal shipping and east-west Yangzi commerce, Shanghai developed a distinctive Sino-Western character. The Western-style architecture of the imposing stone buildings that housed the major Western banking corporations and trading firms made the Bund area of the city look more like London than Beijing. By the 1870s, Shanghai boasted several journals and newspapers—most important among them the *Shenbao*—managed by foreigners but written in Chinese for a Chinese audience.[17]

The foreign enclave established in 1843 contributed to Shanghai's emergence as China's "trade, industrial, media, cultural, innovation and crime capital," argues Sinologist Rudolf Wagner. Foreigners were always a small minority among the concessions' predominantly Chinese population, but both the International Settlement, which united the British and North American sectors, and the French Concession enjoyed a high degree of extraterritoriality. Chinese political authority governed the adjacent walled city of Shanghai but not the rapidly growing foreign enclave; the Chinese military was also kept out. The International Settlement was governed by a municipal council made up of wealthy foreigners. "Describing itself as a Model Settlement because of the peaceful cohabitation of people from many different nations, races, cultures and languages," states Wagner, "the Settlement was fiercely proud of its own wealth and achievements, and stressed its independence from both the Qing court and the foreign consulates."[18]

The Chinese population of Shanghai changed dramatically between 1843 and the famine years. "From the 1850s on, each new social disturbance in the interior sent tens of thousands of Chinese refugees to Shanghai, seeking protection under the English and French flags," explain historians Frederic Wakeman Jr. and Wen-hsin Yeh. Indeed, between 1855 and 1865 the population of the International Settlement grew from 20,000 to 90,000, and the French Concession gained 40,000 new residents. Most of the new arrivals were Chinese.[19] Elite refugees like Xie Jiafu brought their wealth and cultural tastes with them to Shanghai. Even after the Taiping Rebellion was suppressed, more traders, artisans, and gentry moved into Shanghai. By the time the famine spread across North China in the 1870s, Shanghai had become the leading metropolis of the wealthy Jiangnan region and was thus in a prime position to raise relief contributions to aid the starving.

When Xie Jiafu arrived in Shanghai, he was determined to study hard and pass the civil service examinations so that he could follow in the footsteps of a late-Ming ancestor who had become a government official. Like a growing number of literati in the well-educated Jiangnan region, how-ever, he took the examinations several times but failed at each attempt. Instead, Xie joined the many Jiangnan literati who made full use of Shang-hai's open and mixed Sino-foreign character to make their living outside the government circuit as educators, journalists, translators, compradors, clerks, merchants, and entrepreneurs.[20]

Through his contact with foreigners, Xie became interested in current and foreign affairs. At one point he encountered a Japanese official from whom he learned about the new policies put in place by Japan's reform-minded Meiji government. Impressed, Xie resolved to pay close atten-tion to world affairs. He familiarized himself with world geography and studied foreign languages with a German teacher. After completing his studies, he did his best to publicize Western ideas about national defense and treaty negotiation. He compiled and edited books on topics ranging from trade relations and peace treaties to military affairs and post-Tai-ping reconstruction.[21]

Before the famine struck, Xie returned to Suzhou and resided at the Taohuawu public hall. There he began to expand the reach of his father's charitable activities. In the spring of 1877, while returning from con-ducting relief work among disaster victims in northern Jiangsu Province (Jiangbei), he heard the disturbing news that foreign missionaries in Shan-dong were adopting orphaned children from famine districts. Rumors had circulated widely in China since the 1860s that Catholic orphanages that took in abandoned Chinese children severed their limbs and gouged out their hearts. Possibly because of such tales, when Xie and many of his compatriots heard *Shenbao* reports detailing Timothy Richard's work with famine orphans in Shandong, they responded with suspicion.[22] Moved by the plight of the orphans and unwilling to see more of them handed over to foreigners, Xie began to raise relief contributions for famine-stricken Shandong. Other members of the Jiangnan elite re-sponded to his call by donating large sums. In June 1877 Xie traveled to Shandong, where he used the money he had raised to establish a shelter and charitable school for famine orphans. After returning from Shandong once the crisis there had eased, early in 1878 Xie mobilized gentry-philanthropists in several Jiangnan cities to start a relief campaign for Henan.[23]

From then on, claims Xie's celebratory biography, people from six dif-ferent provinces begged Xie for assistance when faced with famine. In re-sponse, he worked "from morning to night" to prepare woodblock prints [presumably the *tieleitu*] that publicized the plight of disaster victims. Because many were moved by Xie's work, he was able to collect over 2,500,000 taels for relief, thus saving the lives of countless people. He was highly praised by the *Shenbao* and did not go unrewarded after the famine. In one of many similar examples of private relief campaigns garnering official rewards, Li Hongzhang was so impressed by Xie's extensive famine relief efforts that he wanted to give Xie an official post even though he had never passed the civil service exams. Xie eventually accepted a position at the Shanghai Telegraph Office, which was headed by two of his famine-relief colleagues, Sheng Xuanhuai and Jing Yuanshang.[24]

Xie Jiafu's personal experience with disaster during the Taiping invasion of his hometown, his temporary relocation to Shanghai, the growing appreciation of Western technology and methods he gained from his contact with foreigners there, the positive example of his father's local philanthropic work, his ability to combine traditional motivations and methods of philanthropic giving with a new will not to be outdone in generosity by missionary relief workers, and his postfamine connections with Li Hongzhang's official self-strengthening projects, all make Xie representative of the many Jiangnan elites who responded to the North China Famine with energy and creativity.

The famine illustrations Xie disseminated also mirror the hybrid character of Jiangnan responses to the famine. While the illustrations and accompanying laments borrowed from Qing poetry and traditional art forms such as New Year prints, they also informed new and broader audiences of the horrific situation in North China.[25] The front-page *Shenbao* editorial that introduced and endorsed the *Henan qihuang tieleitu* highlighted the work's innovative character. After outlining the subject matter of each of the twelve illustrations, the *Shenbao* editor compared the *Henan qihuang tieleitu* to a famous Song dynasty (960–1279 C.E.) work, *Liumintu* (Pictures of refugees), by Zheng Lanmin. The journalist declared the new disaster booklet even more admirable than the Song-period volume because it could rouse a wider audience to action.[26] The *Liumintu*, he wrote, was shared only with the emperor Shenzong, but the new *tieleitu* must "become known to all the masses." The *Shenbao* editor chose to print a front-page editorial recommending the illustrations specifically because they could reach a new audience. "Why use them to encourage donations for each province afflicted with flood and drought?" he asked rhetorically at the end of his essay. "Because, though there have been many articles written to encourage relief, only the literate can understand them. But today when these illustrations go forth, even husbands, wives, and children in remote villages will all be able to understand them." Since more people would grasp the extent of the disaster after viewing the illustrations, he concluded, more people would contribute to relief efforts.[27]

Xie Jiafu and other Suzhou gentry may have begun printing famine illustrations with a traditional audience of wealthy scholars, officials, and merchants in mind. The content and style of the poetic laments in their illustration booklets were familiar and perhaps appealing to elite donors. In Shanghai, however, the *Shenbao* advertised Xie's booklet as a creative method of drawing a broader, nonelite audience into the campaign to rescue Chinese famine victims in the northern provinces. Moreover, thanks to the foreign presence in Shanghai and possibly to Xie Jiafu's prior contacts with foreigners there, less than a year after the volume appeared in Chinese an English edition was published in London, where it reached a wholly new foreign audience. Translated by James Legge and issued by the Committee of the China Famine Relief Fund in 1878, excerpts from "Pictures to Draw Tears from Iron" also appeared in the China Inland Mission's London-based journal, *China's Millions,* where they almost certainly played a role in convincing British citizens to send donations to China.

A hint of the English reaction to the volume can be detected in an article published in the *Spectator* shortly after the booklet's appearance:

> We have received from China a grotesque but pathetic little picture book, painting the horrors undergone in the famine districts. . . . A great multiplication of this little book . . . would, we are persuaded, touch more minds and hearts than any mere circular. It brings home what famine means, at once vividly and with that pathos which is all the deeper for its quaint and grotesque character.[28]

The Western, English-language audience, particularly the editors of *China's Millions,* used "Pictures to Draw Tears from Iron" in ways Xie Jiafu could not have imagined. In addition to calling on English Christians to send aid to Chinese famine victims, *China's Millions* also encouraged them to fund mission work that would help prevent future disasters by "shedding light upon the masses now in heathen darkness."[29] Designed in Suzhou but advertised in treaty-port Shanghai and London, the famine illustrations took on new and in some cases quite unexpected meanings as they drew tears and monetary contributions from Jiangnan literati, treaty-port reformers, and English Christians.

SHANGHAI SPEAKS:
THE FAMINE ACCORDING TO THE *SHENBAO*

While Xie Jiafu's famine illustrations moved both Chinese and foreign audiences to donate to relief efforts, it was largely the *Shenbao* newspaper's extensive and critical coverage of the disaster that informed Jiangnan philanthropists like Xie about the horrors of the famine and shaped their responses to the disaster. By the 1870s, Chinese scholars, merchants, and officials based in treaty-port cities had begun to rely on Western-style newspapers that included commercial and international news as well as more traditional discussions of official affairs. The Shanghai-based *Shenbao* was the leading Chinese-language newspaper from its inception in 1872 until at least 1905. By the time the drought reached a crisis point in 1877, the *Shenbao* boasted a circulation of between 8,000 and 9,000 copies a day; had posted sales agents in eleven different cities including Suzhou, Hangzhou, Yangzhou, Tianjin, Beijing, and Hong Kong; and was distributed to some smaller cities as well through the postal system.[30] During the famine years the *Shenbao*'s eight-page daily edition generally consisted of a front-page editorial, three pages of short news reports, price lists, and reprinted excerpts from the *Jingbao* (the official court gazette), and four pages of advertisements.[31]

The *Shenbao* was founded as a commercial venture by Ernest Major, a young British merchant who arrived in Shanghai in 1871. Because it was located in Shanghai's International Settlement, which was neither controlled by the Qing government nor ruled as the colony of a particular foreign power, the newspaper operated relatively independently of both Qing and British authorities. As a purely commercial venture, historian Barbara Mittler explains, it lacked both the "ideological burdens" that hampered missionary papers in China, and the subsidies that kept such publications afloat when they failed to attract sufficient readers. The *Shenbao*'s success thus depended wholly on its acceptance among Chinese readers, particularly its primary audience of gentry, officials, and merchants. Although the paper was foreign owned until 1905, editorial management was largely in Chinese hands. Its editorials were geared to Chinese audiences and "maintained throughout a stance of defending Chinese interests."[32] Exactly what "Chinese interests" entailed, however, was a contentious issue in the 1870s. As historian Bryna Goodman aptly puts it, the *Shenbao* and other early Shanghai-based Chinese newspapers expressed distinctly Chinese viewpoints, but "the ideas and practices of Chinese public opinion at this time must be understood as culturally hybrid, encompassing both Chinese classical language and referents together with newly assimilated Western cultural elements."[33]

The sheer magnitude of the Incredible Famine, as well as the thousands of hungry and diseased refugees who fled to big cities like Shanghai and Tianjin seeking relief, meant that the famine caused disruption far beyond the actual drought-stricken provinces. The *Shenbao,* as well as the *North China Herald,* began to publish articles about the drought in North China as soon as the vital summer rains failed in 1876. Coverage of the crisis increased that autumn, when an influx of hungry refugees from Shandong streamed into major Jiangnan cities. In October 1876 the *Shenbao* reported that in a village in Shandong, of 200 families, 120 had fled their homes. Clearly worried that the arrival of so many refugees would lead to rioting or other disturbances, in November the paper began suggesting ways to keep the refugees calm and orderly.[34]

Particularly in 1877 and 1878, the newspaper energetically advocated famine-relief campaigns sponsored in Shanghai and across the Jiangnan region. Calling the "deliberate support" the *Shenbao* gave to such campaigns "the most striking innovation in social mobilization," Mary Rankin argues that the regular reports, editorials, calls for aid, and lists of charitable donors the paper published during the disaster played a vital role in motivating southern elites to donate time and money to relieve the northern provinces.[35] The Zhejiangese merchant-philanthropist Jing Yuanshan, for instance, traced his decision to raise donations for famine victims to a shocking newspaper article about famine conditions in Henan that he and his friend Li Yushu read in the winter of 1877. Recalled Jing, "In one thousand *li* of scorched earth, people eat each other—how could we fail to regard this with grief?" Jing and Li responded to the article, most likely published in the *Shenbao,* by meeting with other philanthropists in the Guoyutang, one of Shanghai's leading benevolence halls, to discuss ways of raising funds for famine areas. Jing records that he initially collected 1,000 taels from friends in his native village, and he and several of his fellow provincials later raised more.[36]

The *Shenbao*'s commendation of generous donors like Jing demonstrated the symbolic capital that merchants and literati could earn by contributing to famine-relief efforts. The paper thus helped relief organizers capitalize on the social as well as religious ramifications of charitable giving in late-Qing society. In his letters to the public, for instance, Zheng Guangying frequently reminded would-be donors that their names would appear in the *Shenbao* as a public acknowledgement of their benevolence. Several of Shanghai's talented painters and calligraphers were among those who reaped practical rewards by responding to public calls for charitable action. In the summer of 1878, seven artists gathered to paint silk and paper fans, sell them at a discount, and forward the profits to the famished northern provinces. The *Shenbao*'s willingness to publicize such endeavors at its own expense, argues sinologist Roberta Wue, "offered the artist a forum to display his sense of community and activism," and provided painting societies with visibility, social support, and networking opportunities.[37]

In addition to promoting relief campaigns, the *Shenbao*'s coverage of the famine fostered critical examination of the Qing state and Chinese society. The newspaper's discussions of the famine drew close connections between Chinese and Western press coverage of the famine; emphasized employment of new Western methods to reform and strengthen China; reflected a keen interest in contemporaneous famines in foreign countries; and sharply critiqued Qing-government relief efforts.[38]

The *Shenbao*'s Chinese editors were more familiar with and influenced by Western journalists and critics than Xie Jiafu or the self-strengtheners in the Qing government. The paper repeatedly commented on discussions of the famine drawn from unspecified "*xi zi bao*" (Western language newspapers), and like the *North China Herald,* it translated and printed letters written by missionary relief workers distributing aid in famine areas. Rather than accepting Western critiques of Qing policies at face value, though, the paper skillfully selected perspectives that would bolster its own reformist agenda.

The front-page editorial in the 9 March 1877 *Shenbao*, for instance, quoted extensively from a grim letter written by Timothy Richard (Li Timutai), the Baptist missionary who led the initial foreign relief effort in Shandong. Richard's letter also appeared in March issues of the *North China Herald* and the *Celestial Empire*. The *Shenbao* editorial translated Richard's claim that people in Shandong's Qingzhou Prefecture had sold all their possessions and were reduced to eating grass roots, along with his vivid description of birds and dogs devouring corpses left unburied on the roads.[39] It then introduced Chinese readers to critiques that foreigners were leveling against the state relief policies they believed had exacerbated the miserable situation described by Richard. The Western press, reported the *Shenbao,* charged that official regulation of grain prices in Laizhou (a city in famine-stricken Shandong) actually resulted in more grain shortages by discouraging wheat merchants from transporting and selling grain in that area.[40]

The *Shenbao* continued its discussion of grain price regulation the following day. While avoiding the language of free trade and laissez-faire economics employed by the *Herald,* the editorialist agreed with the *Herald* editors that merchants should be allowed to raise grain prices even in famine districts, and he faulted local officials in Laizhou for driving merchants away by prohibiting them from selling grain at high prices. Since selling goods to make a profit is the way of merchants, he explained, whenever merchants learned that a given area was lacking in grain, they would transport it there to sell it. Even if merchants charged a high price for the grain, reasoned the editor, at least those famine victims with money would have grain to purchase. If, on the contrary, local officials continued prohibiting high prices, merchants would simply stop transporting grain to famine areas. Then even people with a lot of money would have no grain to purchase, and could only sit and wait for death. The *Shenbao* editorialist also pointed out that merchants also had to pay a higher price than normal for grain during a famine. Since grain transporting was a business, he concluded, why should it be considered strange that merchants sell grain at a higher price during a bad year?[41]

In this way, the *Shenbao* employed foreign criticism of government relief policies for its own purposes—in this case to defend the commercial interests of its large merchant readership. To some degree the newspaper was simply siding with pragmatic Qing officials, such as Chen Hongmou in the eighteenth-century and Li Hongzhang in the 1870s, who argued that commercial circulation of grain played a vital role in famine relief efforts and that the state should not obstruct such circulation. By arguing so strenuously for a merchant's right to make a profit even during a famine, however, the newspaper went a step further than Li or Chen. It called into question both the Chinese bureaucracy's distrust of unsupervised commercial activity and the deep-seated Confucian contempt for personal profit seeking.[42]

The paper's positive view of commercial activity was rooted in its treaty-port origin. The International Settlement offered a cultural environment for business that "fully accepted the honest pursuit of profit as a legitimate goal and made all provisions for its protection," states Wagner. The *Shenbao* and many of its readers operated "relatively free from the cultural and institutional constraints of the hinterland with its emphasis on the farmer and the literati as the legitimate mainstays of society," he continues.[43] Shanghai's treaty-port environment, then, enabled the *Shenbao* to transform Western critiques of the Qing government's interventionist relief policies into a defense of the "honest pursuit of profit" carried out by the paper's many merchant readers. Ironically, those merchant readers were, as sinologist Natascha Vittinghoff points out, of growing importance to China's national economy, in part because they competed so fiercely with the foreign traders represented by the *North China Herald*.[44]

The *Shenbao* printed several additional translations of missionary letters and Western newspaper articles about the famine in the spring of 1877. A second letter from Timothy Richard, published in April, was addressed to all "philanthropic gentry, merchants, and rich people in Shanghai and other port cities." In a fascinating example of the crossover between Chinese and foreign coverage of the disaster in its early stages, Richard's harrowing depictions of the famine clearly echoed Chinese modes of description. In the letter—originally written in February and, like its predecessor, reprinted also in the *North China Herald* and *Celestial Empire*—Richard stated that after the famished people devoured all their grain, they attempted to survive on grain husks and grass seeds. When those were exhausted, they began subsisting on leaves and the sorghum reeds from their roofs. They then tore down their houses to sell the wood piece by piece, and were at last reduced to selling their clothing and their children.[45]

Richard's description of the famine foods people were eating and the step-by-step progression of the disaster echoes descriptions in Chinese local gazetteers and in the famine illustrations printed by the Taohuawu public hall. Since Richard was working primarily with Chinese Christians and with local officials in Shandong rather than with other foreigners, he frequently would have heard Chinese descriptions of the descent into utter destitution. Although he wrote the first drafts of his letters in English and addressed them primarily to a foreign audience, his depictions reflected Chinese conventions.[46] During the early period of treaty-port press coverage of the famine, so much cross-pollination occurred between the Chinese- and English-language press in Shanghai that Chinese readers of the *Shenbao* were informed of the plight of Chinese famine victims through translations of a foreign missionary's letters. Those letters, which were also read by thousands of foreigners outside China, were in turn shaped by Chinese ways of describing a famine.

The *Shenbao*'s coverage of the Incredible Famine also provides a compelling example of the newspaper's relatively radical outlook even in its first decade of publication. As Mittler observes, the paper defined its desired identity in a prose poem published in 1873: "The *Shenbao* is a *xinbao* [literally, a 'new paper']. It advocates the new. Whatever is not new, it eliminates." The newspaper's editors were committed to informing Chinese readers about the benefits of modernization. Thirteen of the twenty-four front-page editorials printed in its first month of publication either advocated the adoption of innovations such as railroads, steamships, and Western medicine or criticized vices such as foot binding, prostitution, and opium smoking.[47]

The paper frequently defended itself against the charge of serving foreign interests by insisting that it "relied on a Chinese readership and was thus written in Chinese by Chinese according to Chinese customs to be sold to Chinese." At the same time, the Chinese editors and regular guest writers were members of the treaty-port elite who were profoundly influenced by the presence of Western persons, texts, and institutions in China.[48] For instance Qian Xinbo (Qian Zheng), the *Shenbao*'s chief Chinese editor during the famine years, was trained by his father-in-law, Wang Tao, one of the most radical thinkers in pre-1895 China. Wang was a founder of modern Chinese journalism, so when Ernest Major employed Qian Xinbo to help establish the *Shenbao* in 1872, he asked him to travel to Hong Kong to learn from Wang, who was editing a daily newspaper there at the time. After Qian returned to Shanghai, he, his friend He Guisheng, and a Zhejiang *juren* (provincial examination graduate) named Jiang Zhixiang acted as the *Shenbao*'s main editorial board throughout the famine years.[49]

Qian Xinbo could hardly have found a mentor more reform minded or more intimately familiar with Western history, ideas, public figures, and publication styles than Wang Tao. By 1872 Wang had already spent over twenty years working as the Chinese editor for a mission press in Shanghai and a translation project in Hong Kong, and had recently returned from a two-year trip to Europe with his long-term employer, the missionary-sinologist James Legge.[50] As early as 1862 Wang, frustrated by the government's ineptitude and the lack of progress against the Taiping rebels, began to write a penetrating critique of China's ills. Entitled *Yitan* (Presumptuous talk), Wang's critique scrutinized the Qing government's economic, military, and political policies. Declaring that the government should aim to enrich the state and satisfy the people's basic needs, Wang argued for the development, through Western methods (*xi fa*), of new sources of wealth such as mining, shipbuilding, and machine weaving.[51]

While his emphasis on enriching the state through Western methods was anathema to Qingliu conservatives, Wang Tao both anticipated and agreed with Qingliu critiques of "the great chasm" that had come to separate China's rulers from its people. Using the past to justify far-reaching change, Wang argued that China must learn from antiquity, when the people communicated their grievances to the ruler, and foster a greater sense of solidarity between rulers and ruled. He urged the imperial court to open up the so-called *yanlu*, or "road of speech," through which candid criticism could reach the highest levels of government.[52]

Wang began publishing sections of *Yitan* in his Hong Kong–based newspaper in 1874, about the time Qian Xinbo was training with him. Wang himself did not join the editorial board of the *Shenbao* until his return to Shanghai in 1884.[53] The content of the paper's famine-related articles printed between 1876 and 1879 would indicate, however, that many of his reformist ideas were accepted and actively promoted in the 1870s by his son-in-law, and perhaps by other Chinese editors as well. The *Shenbao* often explained and justified its role by drawing on Wang's use of the classical ideal of an unimpeded flow of information between ruler and ruled (*shang xia tong*) and the open *yanlu*. Moreover, during the Incredible Famine the editors of the *Shenbao* repeatedly used reports about the unchecked suffering and loss of life in North China to strengthen calls for reform. They blamed the severity of the disaster on China's poverty and an unwillingness among many officials to try new methods to strengthen and enrich the country.

A front-page editorial published in November 1877, for example, proposed a range of new methods China could use to strengthen itself. The first half of the article explained that the country had fallen into such dire straits that it was completely unable to deal with the massive disaster attacking so many of its provinces. The editor traced the government's depleted treasury and granaries to the destruction caused by the Taiping Rebellion, to a loss of revenue due to foreign competition in China's tea trade, to the silver imbalance stemming from the opium trade, and to military expenses. He argued that such factors left the Board of Revenue and the provinces unable to provide nearly as much relief as had been possible before the mid-century rebellions.[54]

The journalist then prescribed Western methods for saving China from poverty and famine. According to what he had heard from foreigners, only two hundred years earlier all the countries of Europe had also been very poor. Then European countries began investigating their mineral resources and mining gold, silver, copper, tin, lead, iron, and coal, which made possible a rapid chain of inventions. To save manpower, the Europeans adopted mechanical methods for mining. Hoping to make water transportation easier, they manufactured steamships. To improve land transportation, they invented railroads. To foster communication, they set up telegraph wires. Finally, the Europeans manufactured better guns and cannons in order to strengthen their militaries, and developed industry and commerce in order to enrich their countries.[55]

After tracing Europe's impressive rise, the *Shenbao* editor assured his Chinese readers that China had all the resources necessary to become rich and powerful. England, he observed, was small and lacked resources, so it had to take over India before it could prosper. Likewise the Portuguese grew stronger only by taking over Macao and the French by taking Vietnam, and so forth. China's territory, however, was much larger than Europe's and had far more mines. Why, then, did China continue to suffer from poverty and weakness? The *Shenbao* editor blamed China's high officials. They looked after their own interests rather than those of the whole country, he claimed. If the officials in charge of China's domestic and foreign affairs would instead consent to follow Western methods, how could China fail to become the champion of "the four seas and the five continents?"[56] If, on the other hand, they continued to govern the country according to Chinese methods alone, then despite China's size and abundant mines, it would continue to lack wealth and strength. The editorialist then criticized unnamed opponents—possibly Qingliu officials and their allies—who dismissed Western methods as "not methods at all," and he challenged them to offer solutions of their own rather than simply blocking the use of foreign ideas. Otherwise, he concluded with some bitterness, the Western countries would remain rich and strong, China would remain poor and weak, and the Westerners would laugh.[57] Reform-minded Chinese like this *Shenbao* editor clearly viewed the famine both as a symptom of China's deeper ailments and as a wake-up call for conservative compatriots who they believed had contributed to the country's weakness by refusing to adopt any Western methods.

An editorial published in June 1878 vilified officials and literati who refused to realize that China had to adapt to present realities rather than cling to methods of the past. The author echoed the *North China Herald*'s assertion that the most serious problem hindering famine relief in North China was the difficulty of transporting grain to inland areas. Although many people in the famine districts in Shanxi and Henan still had money, he argued, transportation problems meant that there was no grain for them to purchase. He condemned the proposal to re-establish the old canal transport system that had deteriorated during the Taiping Rebellion. The Grand Canal had been necessary during the Ming dynasty, he stated, but it was slow, expensive, and inefficient, and those who defended it needed to consider innovative methods. The author endorsed as one such method using steamships to transport grain from south to north by sea, but noted that this was of limited use during winter months. His primary recommendation was the construction of a main railway line that would bring relief grain to key locations in inland North China, supplemented by a network of surface roads that would connect the railroad to outlying famine districts.[58]

Aware that many Qing government officials fiercely opposed constructing railroads, the author of this editorial tried to defuse some of the most common objections. In a passage that would have delighted Li Hongzhang and other proponents of coastal defense, the editor flatly dismissed the claim that European foreigners would use railroads to invade inland. Because invaders would have to take China's coasts before they could reach its hinterland, he reasoned, it made more sense to ward off invasions by improving the country's coastal defense system than by refusing to construct railroads. The editorialist also expressed impatience with the government's unwillingness to override public opinion and with delays engineered by high officials. Those who opposed railroad construction for specious reasons failed to understand current affairs, topography, or the country's overall situation, he railed, and he concluded that they, rather than Heaven, should be blamed for allowing disaster victims to starve to death.[59]

The *Shenbao*'s support for railroad construction preceded the famine. The paper championed China's first railroad, the Shanghai-Wusong Railway, from the moment it opened on 3 July 1876. The *Shenbao* journalist who rode the train that day wrote a glowing account of the experience, and the newspaper even sold photographs of the train so that those in distant areas could see it. After a Chinese man was crushed to death by a train that August, however, conservative opposition to the railroad increased. To the relief of conservatives like Ouyang Yun, anti-railroad sentiment won the day, and the Qing government dismantled the Shanghai-Wusong line after repaying its British owner in October 1877. The *Shenbao* responded to its destruction with a series of critical editorials.[60] Although the famine did not initiate the *Shenbao*'s critiques of official reluctance to implement reform along Western lines, it intensified the urgency of such attacks. The paper used the massive disruption caused by the famine as a rallying cry for reform.

The catastrophe in North China also motivated Shanghai-based Chinese to look beyond China, as well as back to China's sage rulers, for examples of how other countries and other times dealt with famine. Unlike their compatriots in rural Shanxi, the *Shenbao*'s editors were well aware that China was not the only country experiencing catastrophic drought during the late 1870s. In particular, they were painfully familiar with the *North China Herald*'s bold claims about Britain's "successful" relief efforts in India. (See chapter 5 for examples of the *North China Herald*'s coverage of the Indian famine.) Although the *Herald*'s positive appraisals of British famine-relief policies were based on imperial arrogance rather than fact, they did suggest novel ideas about state response to famine and provided the *Shenbao*'s Chinese editors with ammunition for criticizing their own government's flawed relief campaign. The *Shenbao*'s coverage of famines abroad also provides a window on information flow in the Victorian colonial world.

In early February 1877 a front-page *Shenbao* editorial ostensibly about famine relief work once again served as a call for the enactment of self-strengthening policies for China. The article began by comparing an unnamed Western newspaper's report on relief money expended in Madras with Chinese government reports on the relief effort in Shandong. Providing famine relief for such large populations was a great financial burden on the governments of both British India and China, stated the journalist. Because Chinese officials were poorer than their foreign counterparts, however, they sometimes used public relief money to supplement their own incomes. The root problem, then, was China's poverty. The second half of the article focused on the need to find ways to enrich the country. Corruption among relief officials was unheard of in Western countries because, the *Shenbao* editor reasoned, the people in those countries were sufficiently wealthy. In China, on the contrary, ever since the Taiping Rebellion, poverty had grown ever more extreme. If the Chinese people could become richer, he concluded, official corruption would be reduced, the upper classes would be capable of offering more relief to the lower classes, and the situation would never reach the point that humans ate each other.[61]

The *Shenbao* drew similar lessons from famines that struck China's East Asian neighbors. A front-page editorial about the serious drought-famine in Korea once again emphasized the relationship between a country's wealth and its ability to cope with famine, and made a direct connection between opening a country to foreigners and enriching it. It also displayed the *Shenbao*'s anxiety about the threat a major famine posed to national stability. This April 1877 editorial began by reporting disconcerting news from Korea. The situation in the famine-afflicted Pusan area had reached the point that the dead were piling up. Because local officials there had not taken action, the people were starting to rebel.

Korea's rulers were willing to aid the starving populace, claimed the author, but both rulers and people were too impoverished to do so. To deal effectively with famine, Korea needed to employ policies to enrich and strengthen (*fuqiang*) the country.[62]

As was common in articles throughout the *Shenbao*'s first decades, the editorialist then used citations from Confucian sages and examples from China's past to confer legitimacy on his reformist ideas.[63] He reasoned that Confucius and Mencius, by asserting that a sage ruler should make the people flourish, teach them, and ensure that the country had enough food and enough soldiers, had in fact advocated strengthening and enriching the country. He then chastised Korea for revering Confucian texts but failing to listen to Confucian teachings about strengthening the country. Because the country had fallen into decline, he continued, neither the rulers nor the people could deal with a famine when it struck. And once many people starved to death, others would begin to cause disturbances.[64]

The editorialist concluded his essay by applying his points to the Chinese case. By first describing something far away—the Korean famine—and then returning to something close at hand—the famine in North China—he introduced controversial content in a popular and familiar form.[65] The drought disaster in China's Zhili and Shandong provinces was as severe as the one in Korea, he wrote, but the people of Zhili and Shandong were relatively fortunate because Westerners in both provinces were diligently raising relief donations. He then boldly claimed that, due in part to the foreigners' efforts, officials and merchants all over China were also motivated to send aid, and local officials had no choice but to report the situation to the government and request relief. If China were to behave like Korea and close its doors, he warned, foreigners would not be able to help. Then the people of Shandong and Zhili would starve to death and grow rebellious like the people in Korea. "How can a country fail to seek wealth?" he concluded.[66] While the advice offered in this editorial was ostensibly for Korea, it was also clearly intended as a warning for Chinese officials who opposed self-strengthening policies and denounced the presence of foreigners in China's interior.

In addition to citing foreign examples and the teachings of the Ancients in order to advocate self-strengthening as a means of famine prevention, *Shenbao* editors also occasionally tried to score points against the Qing state by introducing their own critiques as comments made by foreign observers. In May 1877, for example, the newspaper printed a lengthy front-page editorial that compared famine relief work in India,

China, and Korea. The article's main body consisted of what the Chinese editor claimed was his retelling of what he had heard "English people in Shanghai" say about the disasters in India and North China. The beginning of the editorial echoed points actually made by *Herald* editors. English people in Shanghai, explained the *Shenbao* editor, noted that while Heaven-sent disasters were all the same, human responses to them differed a great deal. The colonial government of British India spent more than thirty million taels to relieve India, the English boasted, while the Qing court spent only forty-five thousand taels to relieve Shandong. The next section of the editorial clearly stemmed from Confucian rather than British ideas about the relationship between food, the people, and the polity. Since it is people who make up the country, how could the Chinese government spend so little money on relief? the British were said to ask. Food is like heaven to the people, they continued. If a country lacks people, it cannot stand firm, and if the people lack food, they cannot live.[67]

Just as eighteenth-century European commentators like Oliver Goldsmith or Voltaire employed fictional Chinese for the purpose of criticizing Western governments and morals, the *Shenbao* author had "the English" lambaste the Qing government's willingness to borrow money from foreigners to fund the Xinjiang campaign but not to pay for famine-relief efforts.[68] The *Shenbao* editors, based in a treaty port far from Central Asia, had backed Li Hongzhang's efforts to avoid hostilities on the northwestern frontier in order to save funds for self-strengthening activities. Not surprisingly, then, the "Englishmen" quoted in this editorial deplored the Qing court's decision to arrange a foreign loan to pay for the recovery of Xinjiang. As for the Chinese government's claim that its treasuries were empty, why, they asked, could the government not simply borrow money from Westerners? Sounding far more like Qingliu officials than British observers, the "English people" in the article then asserted that according to Western thinking, "relieving disaster was better than using weapons." To borrow money to fund military defense of "worthless land" (Xinjiang) but then refuse to borrow in order to relieve the people, they concluded, was a clear case of failing to prioritize correctly.[69]

The *Shenbao* editor spoke with his own voice in the essay's last few lines. He accepted the British claim that China's famine relief effort in Shandong was not as effective at preventing loss of life as Britain's campaign in India had been, but also pointed out that China's relief campaign was far superior to Korea's. He used this three-way comparison to emphasize the necessity of enriching one's country. If China and Korea became as wealthy as England, he concluded, no longer would England alone get all the credit for implementing successful relief policies.[70]

The foreign presence in China loomed large in Jiangnan responses to the famine. The *Shenbao* editors and other treaty-port reformers viewed the famine as proof that something was gravely wrong with China. For them the crisis provided an opportunity to raise serious concerns about China's increasing weakness and poverty vis-à-vis the foreign powers. The *Shenbao*'s take on the famine also provides a provocative example of the interplay between the Chinese and Western press in Shanghai. When faced with famine, the *Shenbao* joined the *North China Herald* in urging the Qing government to relinquish its reliance on tradition and embrace a Western-style reform agenda that would enrich and strengthen the country so that it could deal more effectively with disasters.

To some degree, the *Shenbao*'s coverage of the disaster can be viewed as an example of ideological colonization.[71] When the paper's Chinese editors praised British relief efforts in India and championed railroads as a means of famine prevention, they gave factually problematic British claims far more weight than they deserved. At times the *Shenbao* editors appear to have lost sight of their own government's rich famine-relief tradition and of its record of carrying out effective relief campaigns, only a century earlier, on a scale far beyond anything the nineteenth-century British state could even imagine. They also fell into the trap of assuming that what was new, "modern," or foreign was by definition better or more effective in the face of famine than what the Qing state could offer. As R. Bin Wong has observed, today most people consider it "modern" for states to exhibit concern for popular welfare. In terms of its concern for the material welfare of the poor and the peasantry, the Qing state criticized by the *Shenbao* was profoundly "modern," while there was nothing remotely "modern" about nineteenth-century British attitudes toward famine victims and state intervention during disasters.[72]

On the other hand, the *Shenbao* clearly employed foreign critiques of the Qing government's relief policies in order to foster the paper's own reformist agenda and uphold the interests of its treaty-port readers, not to extol the British empire. As discussed in more detail in chapter 8, its famine coverage also cultivated protonationalist sentiments among members of the Jiangnan elite. Moreover, Jiangnan-based discussions of the disaster are unusually rich because unlike local, official, or British responses, they borrowed extensively from both Chinese and British understandings of famine causation and prevention.

In their efforts to raise relief contributions, both the *Shenbao* editors and southern philanthropists like Xie Jiafu continually drew on the Confucian ideal of humaneness and on popular belief in "accumulating merit" and earning rewards for performing good deeds. They looked not only back to high-Qing predecessors and the Classics, however, but also across the sea to Europe and British India to diagnose what had gone wrong and prescribe remedies. Jiangnan interpretations of the famine were hybrid and, at least in the case of the *Shenbao,* often had as much in common with discussions in Shanghai's English-language newspapers as they did with Qingliu memorials or Liu Xing's famine song. Discussions of official corruption appeared alongside calls for railroads and reform, and local critiques of unfilial and wasteful behavior were replaced by exhortations to strengthen and enrich the country. It was in Shanghai's treaty-port environment rather than in Shanxi, Beijing, or London, then, that the horror of the famine stimulated a critical dialogue and calls for reform.

PART III

Icons of Starvation

Images, Myths, and Illusions

INDIVIDUALS AND SOCIAL GROUPS STRUGGLED to describe the unspeakable misery of the Incredible Famine and to grasp why such a terrible disaster had befallen the northern provinces. Haunting images that Chinese observers repeatedly selected to describe and symbolize the horror of mass starvation include the starving woman sold into prostitution by her desperate family, the woman who sells herself in order to survive, and the famished person who kills and devours a family member. These "icons of starvation" were employed for diverse purposes by Chinese observers from different levels of Qing society, as well as by twentieth-century Chinese educators who revived the images in the 1960s.

My analysis of the "semiotics of starvation" in late-Qing China has been informed by scholars of the Irish famine. In his discussion of literary representations of the "Great Hunger," Chris Morash posits that "the famine as a textual event" is composed of images whose meaning derives primarily from "the strangeness and horror of the images themselves, as dislocated, isolated emblems of suffering." A major famine often upsets people's sense of cause and effect and hampers their attempts to construct sequential narratives, states Morash. Because the atrocity of famine cannot adequately be depicted in words and thus leads to a breakdown of literary convention, famine literature is often constructed as "an archive of free-floating signs, capable of incorporation in any number of sequential semiotic systems." In the Irish case, key images included "stalking skeletons," mothers unable to provide sustenance to their starving children, and corpses whose green mouths bear witness to their futile efforts in life to survive by eating grass.[1] In late-Qing China, accounts of the Incredible Famine abounded with images of intrafamilial cannibalism and the sale of famished women.

I find the semiotic approach useful for explaining the diverse meanings that famine images took on for different groups during and long after the North China Famine. Semiotics can be generally defined as the study of the nature and relationships of signs and symbols in language and society. It also concerns how meanings are made and how reality is represented. Linguist Ferdinand de Saussure, one of the founders of semiotic analysis, stressed the arbitrariness of the link between the signifier and the signified, or between a word or image and the concept it refers to. More recently, the philosopher Umberto Eco and anthropologists such as Clifford Geertz and Victor Turner have demonstrated that signs and keywords are "cultural units" that can take on a multiplicity of meanings according to the social or cultural system within which they are used. Geertz defines signs and symbols as "vehicles of meaning" that play distinctive roles in the particular society that gives them life. Individuals and groups construct and deconstruct symbolic systems as they try to make sense of "the profusion of things that happen to them," he writes. Turner also urges investigators to examine how the meanings of symbols change according to their cultural context. During the Incredible Famine, depictions of cannibalism and the sale of women were ubiquitous in local, treaty-port, and foreign accounts of the disaster. These distinctive icons of starvation, however, took on a fascinating array of meanings and were employed for startlingly diverse purposes according to the social or cultural system in which they were incorporated.[2]

CHAPTER 7

Family and Gender in Famine

A woman wanders east and west on the roads. She puts on a mark to sell herself; her tears do not dry. Ignoring her shame, she opens her mouth and cries out:

"Sirs, listen carefully to this maiden's words. Which one of you kind-hearted men will take pity on me? I'm willing to follow you, and I don't want money. I only want you to receive me—I'm very willing to be your wife. I don't fear any kind of work; I'll be your servant. During the day I will make tea and bring food for you; at night I will make the bed and spread out the blanket for you. Even if you just want a concubine, my heart is willing—even a third or fourth concubine, I don't object. I only need two bowls of thin soup each day. If I can't eat buns, but only soup, I'll be happy."

In the early morning she cries out without ceasing until the sky turns dark, but on the crowded road there is not one person who answers her.

The image of the starving young woman in Liang Peicai's "Essay on Grain" epitomizes the dangers, fears, and the pathos brought by famine.[1] The woman by the roadside cries out to readers as well as to passing gentlemen. Her desperation brings the vast and horrible social phenomenon of famine into bold relief and powerfully symbolizes the destructive effect the famine had on familial and social norms in Shanxi and other drought-stricken northern provinces.[2]

Observers of the North China Famine were not unique in selecting images of women to represent the horror of mass starvation. In her work on literary representations of the Great Irish Famine and the twentieth-century Bengali famine, Margaret Kelleher demonstrates that famine literature represents a very old tradition in which images of women are used as "bearers of meaning" because they have great power to move the reader or spectator. "Again and again, images of women are used to figure moments of breakdown or crisis—in the social body, in political authority, or in representation itself," she writes. Kelleher argues that the feminized images of starvation used repeatedly in Irish famine accounts, such as that of a famished mother offering a dry breast to her already dead baby or a starving child sucking at the breast of its dead mother, signify the failure of "primal shelter" and sustenance, and thus express the famine's deepest horror.[3] Local observers in late-Qing Shanxi employed a different array of feminized images to express the misery brought by famine.

GENDER, GENERATION, AND THE MORAL ECONOMY OF FAMILIES DURING FAMINE

Chinese famine texts from the Incredible Famine abound with images of elderly mothers fed by filial sons, daughters-in-law in danger of being eaten by family members, shameless young women who sell their bodies to survive, self-sacrificing women who commit suicide in order to preserve their chastity or save others, and victimized women who are sold to human traders from South China. These images suggest that Chinese women at different stages of life had radically different options open to them during the disaster. In her work on theorizing Chinese women, Tani Barlow argues that before the twentieth century, no general, social category in China signified "*all* women." *Funü*, the term most commonly used for women in the late imperial period, referred specifically to "women of the patriline." Women were seen as daughters (*nü*), wives (*fu*), and mothers (*mu*) rather than as transcendent agents called "women." They were "gendered by virtue of the protocols specific to their subject positions [within the Chinese family]," she states, "and not necessarily or even in the first case by reference to the physiological ground they may or may not share with people outside the kinship group."[4] In their compilation *Chinese Femininities, Chinese Masculinities*, Jeffrey Wasserstrom and Susan Brownell also present a strong case that in pre–twentieth century China, social gender roles often trumped anatomical sex. "In Chinese gender symbolism, sex-linked symbols are often secondary to other, more fundamental principles of moral and social life," they explain. Anatomical sex was often viewed as simply one principle among many—

including kinship, generation, age, and class—that determined a person's status in the Chinese family and society.[5]

One of the famine illustrations that Xie Jiafu and his Taohuawu colleagues designed to motivate viewers to contribute to relief demonstrates how age and generation were believed to influence a Chinese woman's claim to scarce household resources during the famine. "A Hungry Parent Is Dying: About to Kill the Daughter, the Knife Falls" depicts a small room enclosing two straw beds and three ragged family members. In one bed sits an elderly woman, hand supporting her haggard cheek, hair in a bun, clothing tattered and patched. A frail young girl rests under the ragged canopy of the second bed. Her gaunt father approaches her bed with a knife, but the knife drops from his hand. The rhythmic accompanying text is chilling:

> The old mother is too hungry to get up; the little daughter is too hungry
>   to make a sound. If the daughter dies, it is possible to bear another;
>   if the mother dies, she can never live again. The old mother's life
>   is precious; the daughter's life is light.
> From this sprouted the idea of preserving one life by killing the other.
> Holding the knife straight ahead, his heart pounds.
> His hand trembles, the knife falls and the sound clangs.
> His own flesh, itself in pain; tears of blood fall.
> How could the old woman desire this cup of broth?!
> The father cannot bear to take the child and boil her.
> So, he sends her to the market, to exchange her for one or two pints
>   of grain.[6]

Although the two females in this story belonged to the same family, their respective claims to the family's food supply were so unequal that a filial son could contemplate killing his daughter in order to feed his mother.

Scholars of the Great Irish Famine and of twentieth-century famines in Bangladesh have broadened Amartya Sen's class-based entitlement approach in order to ask how Irish or South Asian family structures influenced which members of a family unit might be more or less likely to be "thrown out of the lifeboat" when it became clear that an equal sharing of the burden of hunger would doom the entire family.[7] As demonstrated by the famine morality play above, Confucian ideals and the Chinese family system during the late imperial period shaped the options available to Chinese women in famine areas.

In late imperial China, most women were part of a joint family system in which women left their natal families, often at a young age, and mar-

Figure 3. An Impossible Choice. From "Si sheng gao zai tu qi," 25a.

ried into their husbands' families. Kinship in Chinese families descended along the male line from a common ancestor, so sons were expected to live with and support their aging parents and provide male heirs to carry on the ancestral line. Daughters, on the other hand, were transient members of their natal families. They were expected to marry into another family, serve their parents-in-law, and bear sons for their husband's family line.[8]

It was not until a young wife bore a son that she could begin to build up what Margery Wolf has termed a "uterine family," or "a small personal circle of security in the midst of the alien world of her husband's family." Only if a woman bore at least one surviving son and succeeded in securing his loyalty could she hope to enjoy a gradual accretion of power and influence in the household. Women thus went to great lengths to foster powerful bonds with their sons.[9]

In Ming and Qing China the *Classic of Filial Piety* was widely used as a primer to teach children reverence for and obedience to their parents while they learned how to read. Although the early-Han text recognized some distinctions in how members of different social groups should practice filial piety, a filial son from any class of society was expected to respect his parents while at home, support them and bring them pleasure, care for them when they were ill, grieve for them when they died, and sacrifice to them after their death. By the 1870s, not only excerpts from the Confucian classics but also daily proverbs, ledgers of merit and demerit, and even the Qing law code preached the accepted norm that to give birth to and rear a child meant pain and exhausting devotion, thus creating a lifelong debt that the son must strive to repay.[10] Liu Xing and other local observers of the disaster frequently identified the failure to practice filial piety as having angered Heaven and called down calamity. Not surprisingly, gazetteer editors eager to restore Shanxi's shattered society after the famine championed the filial behavior that people in their locale had displayed even during the disaster's worst periods.

According to famine narratives recorded in local gazetteers and family handbooks from Shanxi, the prominence of the mother-son relationship in the Chinese family system gave mothers with grown sons an edge during a time of crisis. County gazetteers are rife with detailed stories about sons who sacrificed their wives and children and sometimes even their own lives in order to feed elderly mothers.[11] A gazetteer from southern Shanxi's Yishi County (1880), for example, introduces a filial son named Wu Jiuren who, during the 1877 famine, abandoned his wife but kept his mother alive by carrying her on his back while escaping to another area. People called him extremely filial.[12]

The filial piety section of a Quwo County gazetteer (1880) introduces a grown son who had to choose between his stepmother and his children during the famine. Ma Kongzhao is described as a filial son who was very good to his stepmother after his father died. When the Dingwu famine struck, the family was poor and lacked food, so Ma Kongzhao exchanged his property and sold goods for food in order to take care of his mother. She, however, insisted on sharing her food with Ma's children, which worried Ma. After that, whenever he returned from the market, he left half the food with an old neighbor woman and asked her to invite his mother over to eat the food so that she could eat all of it by herself. Ma and his wife ate nothing but chaff and scraps each day, but his mother was well cared for. In the end Ma grew weak and died.[13]

The final biography in the filial piety section of the Quwo County gazetteer is titled "The Beggar Son." According to this story, during the North China disaster, when starved corpses lay all over the roads, a beggar son and his mother (both unnamed) came and begged for food from the Zhang family. The mother's face was greenish, but the son already had swollen muscles and looked ready to be buried. The master of the Zhang household pitied them and divided a flat cake of wheat for the son to eat. The son picked it up to give to his mother, but his mother returned it to him and asked him to eat first. The son staunchly refused. The mother looked at him and said, "Even unto death, you don't change your character!" Only after she had eaten more than half of the cake was her son finally willing to eat some. Their host was surprised and said: "You are beggars, yet still you have such a filial son!" The mother wept and faced him, saying: "We were not beggars in the beginning. My son is starving, but up until today, when he gets food, he never eats first. Even now, during this time of death, he still persists in this." The master sighed and said, "This is a filial son!" After a few days, he heard that the son had died in the marketplace.[14]

These late-Qing depictions of the way Confucian familial ethics defined moral responses to famine echo an older and more famous morality play introduced in the popular Chinese classic *Ershisi xiao* (Twenty-four examples of filial piety), first compiled during the Yuan dynasty (1279–1368 C.E.) and reprinted in illustrated versions throughout the Ming and Qing dynasties. This story, titled "Guoju Buries His Son and Heaven Blesses Him with Gold," demonstrates once again that generation could take primacy over gender in times of disaster. Readers are introduced to Guoju, who is said to have lived in Henan during the Han period. As Guoju had a very filial heart, after his father died, he treated his mother with respect, fed her well, and made her happy. Guoju's wife was also a model daughter-in-law, and all those who saw the couple proclaimed them a "wonderful son and a wonderful daughter-in-law."[15]

Then famine struck. Prices rose without respite until rice became as precious as pearls. Guoju and his wife were reduced to eating weeds and chaff to assuage their hunger. In spite of this, Guoju continued to give his mother food, drink, and even the delicacies enjoyed by the elderly. At that time, Guoju's only son was three years old. At each meal, Guoju and his wife divided the food between their mother and their little son, but it was not sufficient. Finally, Guoju said to his wife:

> It is a famine year and grain is expensive. My mother is already old. We must do our best to take care of her, but I fear it won't be enough. Now our son takes part of Mother's food, so Mother cannot eat her fill. It is better that we bury our son in order to take care of Mother. If Mother dies, we can never have another Mother. If our son dies, we can bear another. Aside from this, there's no other way.

Guoju's wife agreed, and the couple carried their son outside. Guoju took a shovel in hand and began to dig a hole in the ground. Illustrated versions of the story published in the late-Qing period show Guoju digging a large hole outside his home, while his wife stands behind him anxiously, holding their little boy in her arms and peering over her husband's shoulder as the hole deepens. Fortunately, as Guoju dug the hole he discovered a pan full of gold that had been buried in the earth. On top of the gold were the words, "Heaven rewards the filial son Guoju." Guoju faced the heavens and kowtowed his thanks. Then he and his wife, cradling their spared son, returned to the house.[16]

The apocryphal tale of Guoju's impossible choice and the Taohuawu depiction of a famished son forced to choose between his elderly mother and his young daughter define a quintessential Confucian response to the hideous moral choices raised by a major famine. In both cases, the reverence the grown son felt for his mother was captured by the statement "If my child dies, we can bear another; if mother dies, she can never come back to life." In both scenarios, the filial son proved willing to sacrifice his child in order to fulfill his deep obligation to his starving mother.[17]

The Confucian roots of the moral decisions made by Guoju, Ma Kongzhao, the beggar son, and the grown son in the famine illustration are brought into clear relief by the strikingly different definition of the proper moral response to famine found in a famous famine story set in nineteenth-century Ireland. This morality play, Liam O'Flaherty's novel

Famine, was published fifty years after the North China Famine and is considered the most famous Irish famine text of the twentieth century.[18] *Famine* tells the story of the trials suffered by three generations of the Kilmartin family during the Great Irish Famine of 1845–49. Just as Guoju and his wife and little son lived with and took care of Guoju's elderly mother, Martin and Mary Kilmartin and their baby son lived in a small, dark hut with Martin's elderly parents, surviving mainly on a small potato crop.

O'Flaherty's novel opens with the arrival of the potato blight. When the disease destroys the Kilmartin's harvest for a second consecutive year, the family begins to starve. Mary's young husband, Martin, is forced to flee for his life due to his participation in an anti-landlord riot, and Mary is left to care for her baby son, her own mother, and Martin's aging parents. Toward the end of the novel, the increasingly desperate Mary Kilmartin realizes that not all members of the family can survive on what little food is left. While Guoju and his wife decide to sacrifice their child in order to feed Guoju's mother, Mary decides to abandon her elderly mother and her parents-in-law to their doom in order to flee to America with her fugitive husband and their baby.[19]

When Mary's secret plan to flee to America becomes known, her seventy-one-year-old father-in-law, Brian, confronts her angrily, shouting: "Was that the plan you had? To desert us? Is that what you're up to?" Mary's heated reply destroys any vestige of filial piety, and would therefore be decidedly immoral in the Chinese context. Cries Mary: "You'd rather leave him [Brian's son, her husband] on his keeping until they find him and hang him, I suppose. . . . Is that the kind of father you are? . . . You only think of yourself, and you with only a few years to live. We are young. We have our lives before us." Rather than arguing further, the old man stops speaking and lowers his glance before the fury of his daughter-in-law. "God forgive me," he says. "I didn't think of it that way. You are right, daughter."[20] The novel ends with Mary and her husband and baby reunited on an emigrant ship, while back home, Mary's elderly father-in-law falls while attempting to dig a grave for his starved wife and dies abandoned by all but his howling dog.

The authors of *Famine* and "Guoju Buries his Son" make it clear that their protagonists are basically moral people who have been placed in an impossible situation in which no decision will allow everyone in the family to survive. They show Guoju and Mary struggling to feed both their young child and their elderly parent, but eventually realizing that an agonizing decision must be made before all starve together. The main purpose of these texts is to bring home the horror of famine or to highlight the filial behavior of sons, rather than to sanction the abandonment of either elderly parents or young children. Nevertheless, these morality plays about the impossible choices brought by famine demonstrate that what is defined as the least immoral of several terrible options in one culture may be radically different from the morally sanctioned choice in another.

According to sources about the Incredible Famine, whereas elderly mothers with grown sons had a formidable claim to a household's scarce resources, young daughters and newly married daughters-in-law did not. Famine folklore from contemporary Shanxi province places young daughters in a precarious position during times of famine. Four of the descendents of famine victims whom I interviewed in southern Shanxi in 2001, for example, repeated different versions of what is perhaps the same basic parable about a young woman's powerless position in the family. According to the story, during the 1877 famine a newly married girl discovered that her mother-in-law or father-in-law wanted to eat her. She fled back to her natal family in a panic and begged for help. Upon learning of her plight, her father or mother replied, "If anyone has the right to eat you, *we* do, not they!" The daughter, in danger from both her own parents and her husband's parents, then took to the roads in despair.[21]

Written accounts of the North China Famine also situate young women alone on the dangerous roads, though in the textual sources, young daughters and wives have been abandoned or sold rather than literally consumed. "Fathers abandon their children, and husbands cast away their wives," wrote a student in a Confucian school in Anyi County in his appeal to the emperor. "In a house of eight people, five or six are gone. This one dies at home, another one flees to the outside. A boy eating gruel runs through the land. He treads on the dead, but pays no heed. . . . A girl flees through the wasteland. She breaks her ankle by walking so fast; it is unbearable to listen to her cries."[22] Abandoned women often ended up with human traders from southern provinces. "Young women had no one to take care of them, so finally merchants from other areas came here and collected and sold them," explained an essayist in the Yonghe County gazetteer. "Beautiful women went for less than one thousand cash, and less beautiful ones weren't worth one cent."[23] Other gazetteer essays and stele inscriptions reported that young girls of seventeen or eighteen were worth no more than a string of coins and girls as young as fifteen or sixteen were out on the roads, willingly following whoever would offer them food.[24]

According to famine morality plays from the North China Famine, the Confucian emphasis on filial piety meant that generation trumped gender during times of disaster, as in normal situations. A person's access to household resources was thus determined more by his or her age and status within the family than by his or her anatomical sex. Young women occupied an insecure position during famine, while aged mothers with filial sons possessed a powerful claim to their family's food supply.

TOUCHSTONES OF THE MORAL ORDER: WAYWARD WIVES AND VIRTUOUS WIDOWS

In addition to shedding light on Confucian definitions of how exchange entitlement relations among family members should operate during a famine, images of women signified anxiety about the causes and consequences of the disaster. Chinese observers drew on several different strands of thought about possible connections between women and drought. During the Incredible Famine two imperial censors traced the prolonged drought to the disturbance of Heavenly harmony caused by injustices suffered by women. Similarly, in a drama about the famine written by members of Shanxi's Pingyao County Historical Relics Bureau in 2001, Pingyao's city god initially refuses to intervene to end the three-year-long drought because of a complaint filed in the netherworld on behalf of the wronged ghost of a woman who had died due to a perversion of justice by the county magistrate. "Since women are identified with *yin* (the female principle), which is in turn associated with wetness," explains Paul Cohen, it was not unusual for some Chinese observers to connect wrongs done to a woman with the arrival of a drought.[25]

Because of their association with wetness, women were also believed to be useful for ending a drought. According to the sixteenth-century Arab traveler Ali Akbar, the wives and daughters of distinguished officials who had committed serious crimes were required to pray for rain during times of drought. Such women attempted to move Heaven to send rain by performing rain prayers that included song, dance, special performances, and heartbroken weeping. Moreover, in times of drought *yin* stones (wet "female" stones found in caves) were sometimes beaten with whips in an attempt to bring rain.[26]

Accounts written by male members of the local elite in famine-stricken Shanxi generally portrayed famished women as either defenders or destroyers of the Confucian moral order. Rather than focusing on injustices against women, local observers were inclined to blame unchaste, wasteful, or extravagant women for angering Heaven and bringing the drought upon their locale. In his essay recorded in a Qinyuan County gazetteer, for example, Han Zhonglin outlined a gendered description of the behavior he believed had elicited Heaven's wrath. Qin-area women failed to regard spinning and weaving as fundamental, and even families that owned only a few *mu* of barren land insisted on buying expensive clothing and jewelry for women during weddings. Other local women had added insult to injury by engaging in unfilial behavior such as having inappropriate relations with their fathers-in-law. It was impossible for such people to avoid disaster, he said. Han concluded that if each class of people became industrious and frugal and taught the women in their families to spend time spinning, weaving, and following the way of women, the people would survive future famines.[27]

Han Zhonglin's assertion that female misbehavior was at the root of the drought disaster echoes traditional Chinese attitudes that viewed women, allegedly the weaker and more immoral sex, as "both the cause and the victim of great catastrophes."[28] From Queen Possu, whose refusal to smile was blamed for provoking King Yu to play tricks that eventually resulted in the fall of the Eastern Zhou dynasty, to Yang Guifei, whose legendary beauty is said to have distracted a Tang emperor from issues of governance at a critical time, traditional historical works often held women responsible for dynastic catastrophes. Implicit in many of these stories about women bringing about the fall of a dynasty is the belief that women have great potential power and that their power can affect nature and society in dangerous ways if it is not controlled.[29] After a disaster on the scale of the Incredible Famine, it is thus not surprising that some local literati traced the source of the drought back to women.

Discussions of the role women had played in calling down the disaster were repeated in numerous local sources. Liu Xing, for example, included unfilial sons, opium smokers, and wealthy merchants in his critique of immoral behavior in Xiezhou, but reserved his harshest censure for women. He chastised women for gossiping, wasting oil and salt while preparing food, and wearing lewd or extravagant clothing. "This kind of disaster had not been seen for several hundred years; only women took it as play," wrote Liu. "Women, listen to this song and change your extravagant ways," he warned. "If you don't change, I fear you are cheating Heaven and must suffer punishment. In life you will suffer severe throat problems and be infected by the plague. After death, you will enter the pot of boiling oil and climb a mountain of daggers."[30]

Liu Xing was particularly critical of women who sold their bodies to survive. After the famine years one could not get a wife for a hundred pieces of gold, he observed, but during the disaster, women were cheap. He described young women who, bereft of all propriety, grabbed hold of men as they passed and begged them for help. Others were faulted for going with one man after another in an effort to survive. "I've seen many a young woman make multiple matches," he wrote. "First she's matched with Zhang, then she's matched with Li. She has no shame."[31]

Liu Xing's famine song includes a haunting depiction of an abandoned woman standing along the road begging each passing man to take her in as a wife, concubine, or servant. Strikingly similar to Liang Peicai's, the woman's lament may have stemmed from a famine folksong popular in southwestern Shanxi during the disaster. Cried the woman in Liu's text:

> I lack a husband, and I'm seeking a good match.
> Whichever wealthy household will take pity on me, I'm willing to marry and serve you on the bed.
> I'll be your wife or your servant—I'm fully willing. Even if you make me your scullery maid or slave-girl, I'm not afraid.
> During the day, I'll serve you tea and rice. When night arrives, I'll tidy the bed and make the blankets ready for you.
> . . . I can do both rough and elegant work. If we discuss age, this year I'm twenty-three years old.
> Rising in the morning, I'll weave and sew for you. At night I'll do needle-work; [I'll] rise early and go to sleep late.
> Each day I'll only drink two bowls of noodle-soup broth. I won't eat buns; I'll just drink broth and feel happy.
> I won't eat on the sly, I won't go wandering around; I'll just stay and look after the house. I'll produce a fine child to stand before you.[32]

Certainly the image of the desperate young woman in this account moves the reader. As she cries out to each passing gentleman, readers may glimpse the individual experience of the broad social phenomenon of famine. But there is an unsettling, threatening quality about the woman on the roadside, as well. Since a young woman was expected to remain in the protected domestic sphere of her parents' or husband's home, her mere presence out on the public roads implies the breakdown of families and the traditional moral order. Her determination to arrange a match for herself rather than rely on a matchmaker also would have shocked late-Qing readers. Liu accuses the women on the roadside of shameless-ness and assures his (male) readers that such brazenness would not lead to salvation—the women's pleas "fall on deaf ears." By wandering the public roads calling out to strange men in an effort to survive, the woman by the roadside transgressed the proper boundaries for her sex and thus presented a threat to the Confucian order.[33]

Perhaps most disturbing of all to male gatekeepers of the moral order, although the woman on the roadside has clearly lost all moral value in Liu's eyes, her actions imply that she is acutely aware that she has potential market value during the disaster, more market value, in fact, than her male counterparts. When famished women decided to sell themselves rather than starve to death, they embodied the destructive effect the famine had on female chastity, an all-important virtue in late imperial China. The women selling themselves along the road had clearly rejected the oft-cited assertion, made by the eleventh-century Neo-Confucian philosopher Cheng Yi, that "to starve to death is a small matter; to lose one's chastity is a great matter."[34] In the eyes of local literati like Liu, such women's unchaste behavior signified both familial breakdown and the type of moral degradation that local observers believed had called down cosmic retribution in the first place.

If the image of women leaving their homes and taking to the roads in order to survive epitomized the dangerous and destructive nature of famine, images of virtuous women who starved to death in their homes rather than compromise their chastity provided reassuring evidence that famine could not completely undermine Confucian ethics and the Chinese family structure. After condemning shameless women who sold themselves in exchange for food, Liu Xing proposed a more "virtuous," if deadly, alternative. "There are also those chaste martyr women who keep themselves pure," he wrote. "Willing to starve to death rather than lose their chastity, they hang themselves on a cross beam." Liu assured readers that these virtuous women would both avoid shame in this life and reap rich rewards in the next. "The chaste martyr woman is reborn as a noble official in the next life," he concluded, "but the name of the shameless woman passes on a stench to countless generations."[35]

In the decade following the North China Famine, the editors of several county gazetteers in Shanxi collected and published accounts of women who placed Confucian values such as filial piety, chastity, and self-sacrifice above survival. Such accounts demonstrate how the virtues expected from women in ordinary times shaped and defined moral and immoral responses to the horror of mass starvation. The editor of an 1880 Yishi County gazetteer, for instance, explained that because so many family members had treated each other coldly during the disaster, examples of filial piety, chastity, and loyalty from the famine years must also be recorded.[36]

The "Encountering Famine" (*zaohuang*) section of a Jishan County gazetteer published nearly a decade after the famine contains a rich discussion of virtuous women during the disaster. It records the names and exemplary behavior of twenty-six women who either starved to death or committed suicide in order to preserve their chastity or save another family member. Ma Shichang's widow, Jie Shi, for example, was left widowed and childless at age twenty-six.[37] She was reasonably well off, and others tried to persuade her to marry again, but she only wept in reply. When the 1877 disaster struck, Jie Shi shut her door and did not go out of her house at all. By the time her neighbors went to check on her after several days, she had already starved to death. Likewise, when the famine struck Jishan County, Yang Shanlin's widow, Chen Shi, and her eight-year-old daughter had no way to survive, so they wept and hanged themselves rather than compromise their virtue. Numerous additional women were commended for either hanging or drowning themselves rather than selling their bodies to survive.[38]

The decision to starve or commit suicide during the famine rather than compromise one's chastity was part of a broad "cult of widow chastity" that reached its zenith in the Qing dynasty. The early-Qing emperors launched aggressive "moral education" campaigns that promoted Confucian models of behavior by, among other tactics, locating and honoring chaste commoner widows as well as their counterparts from elite families. During the eighteenth century the number of chaste-widow biographies printed in local gazetteers rose dramatically, as did the number of monumental arches built to honor virtuous women. By the mid-nineteenth century honoring chaste widows had become an important expression of family status for both local gentry and upwardly mobile commoner families.[39]

As historians of Qing China have demonstrated, the rapid economic growth, increasing commercialization, and unsettling geographic and social mobility that characterized the mid-Qing period produced a general anxiety about the blurring of boundaries between literati and merchants, or between "respectable" and "debased" social categories. As that debate extended to concern over the boundaries between "polluted" and "pure" women, the importance of female chastity as a marker of family honor and social position became more pronounced. In the high-Qing context, explains historian Janet Theiss, "the virtue of women—including not only sexual chastity but also modesty, obedience to family superiors and propriety in manners, speech, and dress—became a touchstone of social quality, moral refinement, and cultural identity."[40] When Chinese famine accounts extolled women who starved themselves to death during the 1877 disaster rather than remarry, engage in prostitution, or beg along the roads, they differentiated between moral and immoral responses to the threat of mass starvation, and gave readers hope that even the ravages of the famine had not succeeded in destroying China's moral and cultural norms.

Another popular image found in local famine texts from the 1870s is the self-sacrificing woman who gives up her own life in order to leave more food for other (typically male) family members. Zhao Dazhi's widow, Zhang Shi, for example, another woman praised in the Jishan County gazetteer, raised her only child by herself after her husband died. Her son married and had one son, but then he suddenly died as well. Zhang Shi worked hard to provide for her daughter-in-law and fragile grandson, but when the 1877 disaster struck, it became impossible for all three of them to survive. So she instructed her daughter-in-law, saying: "I'm old and decaying like wood. The only person who can continue the Zhao family line is this little child. You must do your best to protect him." Then she lay down on the bed and waited for death. Her daughter-in-law, holding the baby, knelt down beside her and wept, saying, "If I let you die this way, my offense will be boundless—we should all die together." But Zhang Shi scolded her, saying: "You foolish woman, you don't understand the main point. If I let my grandson die, how can I face my ancestors? . . . If you don't listen to my words, you are not filial!" Her daughter-in-law pleaded again and again, but Zhang Shi still would not eat, and finally she starved to death so that her young grandson might survive. The editor of the gazetteer concludes his depiction of Zhang Shi's actions with high praise: "Who would have thought that among women there are those who see the Way and distinguish it so clearly!"[41]

The confrontation between Zhang Shi and her daughter-in-law brings to light tension between the demands of filial piety, according to which the daughter-in-law should sacrifice herself and her child in order to feed her mother-in-law, and the necessity of preserving the family line to ensure that descendents survive to make sacrifices to the family ancestors. Both women argued along Confucian lines. The daughter-in-law feared that she would be deemed unfilial if she survived while her mother-in-law starved, but Zhang Shi insisted that failing to carry on the family line would be far worse. When the gazetteer editor praised Zhang Shi's decision to starve herself to death, he called into question the message of morality plays that commended filial sons for sacrificing their own lives, or the lives of their young sons or daughters, in order to feed an elderly mother. Zhang Shi's story provocatively suggests how the outcome of a famine morality play may change when agency is placed in the hands of an elderly mother rather than her filial son. It also demonstrates how the ravages of famine exacerbated conflict between different strands of Confucian morality.

Other women were also commended for sacrificing themselves in order that their husband's family line would continue. Lan Runfang's wife, Zhang Shi could not get enough food for both herself and her only child during the disaster. Determined to keep her son alive in order to preserve a descendent for her husband's family line, she stopped eating and died. Qiao Zhikai's second wife, Zheng Shi, made an even greater sacrifice. As a second wife, Zheng Shi was filial to her parents-in-law and kind to her sons and daughters. During the disaster, however, it became impossible to keep the entire family alive. Wanting to continue her husband's family line, Zheng Shi gave extra food to her husband's son by his first wife, and she and her own children starved to death one by one. Two other wives, another Zhang Shi and a Yan Shi, decided to poison themselves because they feared they would become burdens to their husbands as the food supply ran low.[42]

The plight of women driven to commit suicide during the famine is given haunting visual expression in the famine illustrations published by Xie Jiafu and the Taohuawu public hall. A woodblock print titled "Driven by Hunger and Cold, They Hang Themselves from a Beam or Throw Themselves in a River" portrays desperate people committing suicide during the famine. It displays one figure standing on a chair preparing to hang herself, while three others prepare to jump in a river already populated by four floating corpses.[43] The illustration is strongly gendered: while the sex of three of the waterlogged corpses is unclear, all four living figures in the illustration, and at least one of the corpses, are female.

In emphasizing the virtuous behavior of women during the Incredible Famine, local gazetteer essays and Taohuawu illustrations sought to reassure Chinese readers that the Confucian moral order had survived the disaster. In his landmark work on famine in peasant societies, historian David Arnold observes that, "although what happens during the course of a famine will bear many signs of abnormality, it will also continue to some degree to be shaped by pre-existing cultural norms and social relations."[44] The examples of self-sacrifice and obedience to family hierarchy presented by this Jishan County gazetteer are unmistakably influenced by China's Confucian moral order, according to which a virtu-

餓寒交迫懸樑投河

Figure 4. Suicide of Famine Victims. From "Si sheng gao zai tu qi," 12a.

ous daughter-in-law should sacrifice herself to protect her chastity and her husband's family line. To some degree even the most startling famine images, such as a second wife starving herself so that her husband's son by a first wife might survive, shored up cultural norms during a great upheaval, and perhaps offered an anchor to persons attempting to deal with unbearable moral choices.

During the Incredible Famine, fear of familial breakdown and the destruction of social norms was expressed through images of wayward women selling themselves along the roads or bringing down the wrath of Heaven by dressing extravagantly or wasting food. Likewise, local literati eager to preserve prefamine moral norms lavished praise on women who starved or committed suicide rather than compromise their chastity. These didactic local famine texts demonstrate how determined gazetteer editors and other members of Shanxi's Confucian literati were to control the "politics of memory" regarding women.

OUTSIDE CONFUCIAN IDEALS: FAMINE DEMOGRAPHY AND THE TRADE IN WOMEN

The numerous accounts of women who died to preserve their chastity or save another family member while the famine ravaged Shanxi are part of the repertoire of formulaic stories of chaste widows and self-sacrificing daughters that dominated Confucian biography in late imperial China. Because these sources are so thoroughly embedded in the discourse of female chastity, and to a lesser degree in the discourse of filial piety, they cannot be used in any direct way to reconstruct the actual lived experiences of women in famine areas.[45] Confucian rhetoric about filial piety and female chastity undoubtedly influenced the behavior of male and female family members in famine-stricken Shanxi, but the portraits of filial sons and virtuous women offered by local famine accounts are just too orthodox—too predictable—to be left unproblematized.

Demographic research and reports written by foreign observers in famine districts provide useful tools for interrogating the famine morality plays discussed above. Recent demographic research on gender and mortality rates in China's northeastern province of Liaoning upholds the assertion that Confucian norms of family organization left daughters at a disadvantage when it came to the distribution of scarce resources in Chinese families. On the other hand, demographic studies of famished populations in China and many other cultures show that famines often transform rather than reiterate "normal" patterns of sex difference in mortality and that men in fact generally suffer greater increases in mortality during major famines than women.

In late imperial China, female mortality among commoner infants and children was normally much higher than male mortality. In their study of mortality among 12,000 northeastern peasants born between 1774 and 1873, for example, historian James Lee and sociologist Cameron Campbell discovered that in rural Liaoning, girls between age one and five experienced a 20 percent greater mortality than boys.[46] Excess female mortality during infancy and childhood was probably due to discrimination against daughters in the allocation of nutrition and health care. Because families preferred sons—who conducted the rituals of ancestor worship, continued the family name, and remained in the household after marriage—boys generally had a higher claim to food, clothing, and medical care.[47]

The strong preference for sons meant that Chinese girls had to compete for resources within the household far more than their brothers did during normal times. In northeastern China, for instance, the effect that adding another elderly person of either sex to the household had on girls was dramatic. An additional person aged fifty-five or older increased the risk of death for a girl between ages two and fourteen by 30 percent, but did not increase the risk of death for young boys.[48] However, the fact that the addition of an elderly person of either sex to the household—rather than the addition only of an elderly man—significantly increased a young girl's risk of death reinforces the assertion that Chinese females did begin to lay claim more to household resources as they aged.

Scholars of late imperial China generally agree that sex-selective infanticide was not uncommon even during normal times.[49] Moreover, Lillian Li's meticulous research on the age and sex distribution of deaths and births that occurred in officially sponsored shelters for refugees of the 1935 Yellow River flood in Shandong demonstrates convincingly that female infanticide was practiced more extensively during times of adversity.[50] Female infanticide and the treatment of female children and adults during a famine were very different matters, however. As Li points out, "Infanticide was probably not regarded as a form of killing but a form of birth control. Children were generally not considered to be full persons until after their first year of life or at least until they had grown their first set of teeth." She also calls the evidence for higher rates of across-the-board female mortality in China in the 1930s "incomplete or ambiguous."[51]

Chinese females who survived infancy continued to struggle during ordinary times to compete with their brothers' or their elderly relatives' stronger claims to the household food supply. In late-Qing China as in many other cultures, however, famine may have altered rather than replicated the usual patterns of sex differences in mortality. In their research on connections among price fluctuations, family structure, and mortality rates in Qing-era Liaoning, for example, Lee and Campbell found that female mortality was unaffected by rising grain prices, but male mortality at all ages increased with the rise of food prices.[52] According to Kate Macintyre's useful historical review of famine literature, evidence from a wide range of famine studies from different time periods and continents "does indeed indicate an advantage for women in mortality as a consequence of famine." Although women who in normal times often have less access to land, food, and health care might logically be expected to suffer more during a crisis, she writes, "the opposite appears to be the case in relation to the severest of crises—famine." Indeed, research on famine mortality in eighteenth- and nineteenth-century Ireland, Iceland, Japan, India, and Finland finds that males suffered more deaths than females during those famines, though often by a narrow margin. Recent studies of the Donner party in California and of twentieth-century famines in places as diverse as Russia, Holland, and Ethiopia also show that women are more likely than men to survive when famine conditions are at their worst.[53]

Explanations of the consistent sex differential favoring women during famines focus on poor data collection (resulting in a selection bias), biological mechanisms, and socioeconomic and cultural factors. For example, some scholars argue that the perceived female advantage reflects underreporting of female deaths or overreporting of male deaths. Others highlight the physiological advantages of women, such as smaller body size and higher percentage of body fat, a greater ability to survive certain infectious diseases common during famines, or reduced maternal mortality during famines due to decreased fertility. A wide array of cultural factors have also been proposed, including a lower female probability for exposure to epidemic disease since, historically, women were less likely than men to migrate in search of work; better access to food because of women's role as food preparers and their greater familiarity with wild famine foods; a woman's ability or willingness to turn to prostitution to survive or to seek shelter in relief camps; and the enhanced value of primarily female "emotional exchange entitlements," such as providing comfort and nursing to others, during a time of disease and death.[54]

References to several of these factors appear in texts from the Incredible Famine. Moreover, in the case of late-Qing Liaoning, Lee and Campbell also propose a "loss of privilege" hypothesis to explain the high male vulnerability to fluctuations in the price of grain. Since males in Liaoning generally received a greater proportion of a household's surplus in ordinary times, the loss of this privilege struck them more drastically than it did women. Women were more likely to be undernourished in normal years, but suffered a less extreme reduction in food rations than their male counterparts during famine years. Likewise, Lee and Campbell found that mortality differentials between household members of high and low status in Liaoning were also narrower when grain prices were high than when they were low. When times were good, privileged members of a household apparently "appropriated a disproportionate share of the surplus, leaving less privileged members not much better off than when times were bad." When the surplus disappeared during bad times, however, the consumption of high-status members of the household fell and their mortality rates rose, but the already high mortality rates and meager consumption of less privileged family members stayed roughly the same.[55]

Demographic research concerning the North China Famine itself is sketchy. The most detailed work on famine demography in Shanxi, Liu Rentuan's article, uses population records from county gazetteers to estimate the population loss of each county during the famine.[56] But since county gazetteers generally recorded only the total population loss in each village, they reveal little regarding gender and mortality during the famine of 1876–79. Among the thirty-two county gazetteers I collected in southern Shanxi, only one, a Quwo County gazetteer published in 1880, recorded the county's postfamine population by age and gender. According to the census printed in the population (hukou) section, the population of Quwo County's 235 villages and suburbs had fallen from 285,911 in 1841 to only 35,605 in 1880. The editors of the gazetteer explained that in accordance with governor Zeng's wishes, they had carried out a new population census to record the correct postfamine population of the county so that later readers would know the extent of the damage the famine had inflicted. They recorded a total of 9,038 households, 16,264 adult men, 15,665 adult women, 2,474 boys, and 1,202 girls who had survived the famine.[57]

The Quwo gazetteer did not divide the prefamine population by age and gender, so no pre- and postfamine comparison is possible. The postfamine numbers, though, indicate that adult men and women survived the disaster in roughly equal numbers, especially considering that males slightly outnumbered females even in normal times in late imperial China. Not even half of the 235 villages surveyed reported the numbers of male and female children, and those villages that did probably underreported girls. Still, of the children who were reported, the number of boys was more than double that of girls. Girls may have been sold out of the village more often than their male counterparts, or they may have perished in greater numbers.[58]

Although Lee and Campbell examine demographic responses to short-term economic stress rather than to a prolonged disaster like the Incredible Famine, their discovery that Chinese males of all ages were more susceptible to rising grain prices than females, and that Chinese families divided scarce food supplies evenly among family members of low and high status during times of crisis, has interesting implications for the workings of the moral economy of Chinese families during the 1877 famine. Famine morality plays from the 1870s highlighted families that sacrificed low-status members in order to feed more privileged ones. Recent demographic research suggests, on the contrary, that at least in late-Qing Liaoning, Chinese families faced with rising food prices shared their dwindling food supply relatively equally rather than allowing privileged family members to maintain their normal consumption rates while less privileged relatives starved.

Detailed reports written by missionaries and foreign relief workers who visited famine areas during the late 1870s provide a second way to view the famine's impact on Chinese families from outside the Confucian worldview. The famine accounts of these Anglo-American observers are as steeped in "Christian rhetoric" as the gazetteer editors' accounts are in "Confucian rhetoric." They are marked as well by nineteenth-century British assumptions about China itself, the proper roles of men and women, and how a famine should be dealt with. In spite of such qualifications, the foreign observations provide useful alternative first-hand descriptions of the famine's impact on familial and gender relations.

Such reports uphold the possibility that, contrary to the message of Confucian morality plays, adult women fared as well as or in some cases better than their male counterparts during the disaster. In the report he prepared for the China Famine Relief Committee after inspecting the famine districts early in 1879, for example, British consul Walter Hillier noted that although all the people in famine villages looked gaunt and pinched, "the women and children seemed in better condition than the men."[59] David Hill made a similar observation while distributing relief in Shanxi's Pingyang Prefecture in the summer of 1878. He speculated that opium smoking may have played a role in weakening men. "Desolation describes the scene as well as any word," wrote Hill. "I know widows everywhere. The men do not seem to have been able to meet the test of scarcity so well as the women. Opium smoking accounts for a good deal."[60] C. A. Gordon, in *An Epitome of the Reports of the Medical Officers to the Chinese Imperial Maritime Customs Service from 1871 to 1882*, also concluded that women and children were in a better state than men at the end of the famine, apparently because the former possessed stronger constitutions at the beginning.[61] Such opinions echoed that of a British observer of Irish famine victims thirty years earlier: "In the same workhouse, in which you will find the girls and women looking well, you will find the men and boys in a state of the lowest physical depression."[62]

Chinese informants to foreign observers also noted high male mortality rates. When missionary Jonathan Lees of Tianjin traveled into famine districts in June 1878, for example, an innkeeper he interviewed in a village along the way informed him that out of the village's prefamine population of sixty family units or about three hundred people, thirty families had fled to Tianjin during the winter, and fifty people—mostly men—had died, thirty of starvation and twenty of famine fever.[63]

Some foreign observers attributed the possibly better survival rate of women to biological differences, but others concluded that it was the burgeoning market for females, however appalling, that gave women a better chance to survive than men. In 1878 *China's Millions* printed the diary of G. W. Clarke, a missionary who distributed relief in the famine districts of Henan. Clarke wrote that when his party entered Henan, "we passed daily many wheelbarrows loaded with women and girls who had been bought by speculators; they looked to be in good health, and were respectably clothed." He speculated that women might actually have survived the famine better than men because they could be sold. "Women would not suffer so much as men probably, because wives are scarce, and they would be bought up, while the men would be left to suffer or die," he wrote.[64]

Clarke's supposition that women would be purchased before they starved since "wives were scarce" refers to the imbalance in the marriage market in Qing China. During the late imperial period, female infanticide, the discouragement of female remarriage, and the desire of many elite men to possess concubines as well as a legal wife meant that there was a chronic shortage of marriageable women in China. This "insatiable demand for brides" created a market for women that expanded during hard times.[65] "Informal networks for the sale of women always operated in cities and local market centers where there were poor, destitute, or simply unwanted women and children," writes historian Sue Gronewold. "But in times of famine, this normally clandestine operation went public."[66]

In the late 1870s, government attempts to control the sale of women broke down in the face of the famine, and the scale of trafficking in women was enormous. Chinese and missionary sources alike reported cartloads of women being taken south for sale every day, while additional women were transported from Tianjin to Shanghai by boat. In his diary chronicling his journey through Henan, for example, G. W. Clarke often recorded the number of women he passed as they were transported south for sale, as well as the number of corpses he saw on a particular day. On 3 May 1878 Clarke passed some men going north to buy women and girls. The next day he came upon three cartloads of women and children going south and saw a dead man in a field. On 5 May he passed two dead men by the roadside. On the 6th he saw a dead man at the front gate of the *yamen*. The following day he helped two old women who were starving, and saw a dog gnawing the trunk of a dead man. On 8 May he passed three more cartloads of women going south to be resold, and another dead man on the road.[67] Interestingly, throughout his account, Clarke never mentioned seeing a dead woman. All the corpses he saw were male, while most of the women he mentioned were in carts going south.

Clarke's perception of the sex of those who succumbed to starvation or disease may have changed dramatically had he entered the homes of famine victims rather than spending so much time out on the roads. Nevertheless, his account does raise the possibility that the rampant traffic in women may actually have enabled women from famine districts to survive in greater numbers than their male relatives, since so many women were transported out of famine areas to be resold in more affluent cities.

At the same time, it must be remembered that at least younger sons and single men without families were much freer than their female counterparts to escape famine areas by fleeing north into Suiyuan (today's Inner Mongolia) or Manchuria, east to Beijing and Tianjin, or south into the Jiangnan region. Both Chinese and foreign newspapers in Shanghai commented on the massive number of famine refugees who streamed into port cities like Tianjin and Shanghai during the disaster, and observers noted that although refugee groups included women and children, the majority were men.[68] Migration may have provided more men than women the chance of escaping starvation in the famine districts. Famine victims in Shanxi, however, particularly those in the southern half of the province, were surrounded by famine districts that stretched for hundreds of miles in any direction. Walter Hillier emphasized this point in his March 1879 report:

> I have been asked by some, 'If the state of things was as horrible as you say, why did the people stay?' I really do not think they could have got away. When things were at their very worst, not only the whole of Shansi, but large portions of Chihli, Shensi, Shantung and Honan were suffering from the same scourge, so that these unfortunate people were hemmed in by a belt of famine that it would have taken weeks to penetrate.[69]

For people in southern Shanxi, the nearest nonfamished area, Suiyuan, was a long, harsh trek north. The Taihang mountain range and Guguan Pass made it difficult for famine refugees to reach Beijing and Tianjin, and migration to the wealthy Jiangnan region required enough stamina to walk through famine ravaged Henan province. Emigration, then, was a dangerous choice.

Finally, those refugees who did make it to the crowded and squalid urban relief centers often fell prey to epidemic disease, particularly typhus. In 1878, for example, only 10,000 of the roughly 80,000 weak and disease-ridden famine refugees who had arrived in Tianjin the previous year were believed to have survived the winter. Because migration increased the risk of contracting deadly diseases, and because more people died from infectious disease than from starvation alone in most premodern famines, it is possible that male migration increased rather than decreased a man's risk of death.[70]

During the famine, many starving families decided to sell female family members to increase the likelihood that both the young woman and other members of the family would survive the disaster. When Timothy Richard established a shelter for famine orphans in Shandong early in 1877, for instance, a newspaper correspondent observed that of the more than four hundred famine orphans under Richard's care, "nearly all are boys, no girls having been offered, as those whose parents and friends cannot provide for them have been mostly already sold."[71] Richard noted the prices that people paid for women and children. In Pingyao, he observed that a man who stayed in the same inn with him had recently purchased an eighteen-year-old girl for eight hundred cash and three younger children—two sisters and a brother—for a total of nine hundred.[72]

Clearly, the market value of a young woman far exceeded that of either male or female children, thus making it more likely that the sale of a teenage daughter or a young wife would bring enough money for a family to survive.

An experience relayed by American missionary relief worker C. A. Stanley offers a rich example of the survival strategy that the market for women (and to a lesser extent children) provided struggling families. Stanley described the plight of a family that had sold its house and all its possessions and was setting out to beg along the roads. The family consisted of husband, wife, the husband's elderly mother, and two sons. When villagers led Stanley to them, the husband was in the process of selling his wife and youngest son in order to get them food and shelter while at the same time providing something for the remaining three to live on.[73]

Stanley's understanding of this man's decision to sell his wife and younger child contrasts with the previously discussed morality plays about filial sons and their starving mothers. Although the editors of county gazetteers in Shanxi would have clothed the man's decision in the language of filial piety and praised him for sacrificing his wife and son to feed his mother, Stanley described the man's decision as primarily an economic choice. The market value of his elderly mother, not to mention that of the man himself, would have been negligible. Because of the imbalance in the marriage market in Qing China, however, a young or even a middle-aged woman had market value as a prostitute, concubine, maidservant, or second wife who could run the household and care for the children of a widower. By selling his wife and younger son, then, the man offered them an escape route while also keeping himself, his mother, and his eldest son alive.[74]

Some girls and women who had lost their families to death or migration also came to view escaping famine districts by being sold to human traders from wealthier areas as their best chance of survival. The reports of Western observers who worked in famine districts echoed the claim (though not the moral censure) made by local literati that during the disaster, women sometimes chose to sell or give themselves to human traders in exchange for food. Shortly after his arrival in Shanxi, Timothy Richard described the extensive traffic in women that he witnessed on a two-day journey between Taiyuan and Pingyao, a city south of the capital. "On the road we met, daily, about a hundred carts returning, after sending grain southwards, and about half of these had wretched-looking women in them, who were gladly availing themselves of the only means of saving their unhappy lives," wrote Richard. During his stay in Pingyao,

Richard was approached by an inn servant who told him that the main difficulty people faced was finding anybody willing to buy starving women or simply take them for free: "He said if I would take any, a hint was enough, and a score would come in a few seconds, glad to get away for nothing. To stay at home is certain death to so many of them. Some attempt to beg their way northwards, but, unless taken up by somebody, between hunger and cold they soon perish."[75]

An additional report, this one a Chinese translation of an unnamed Western missionary's letter about famine conditions in Shandong, emphasized the extraordinary lengths some famine victims employed to be sold. During his stay at a small inn on Linqu Mountain, explained the missionary, his bedroom happened to be adjacent to a room occupied by seven or eight human traders. Only a wooden partition separated the rooms, so the missionary could hear women being led into the adjacent room one by one. Examining each woman, customers accepted her for purchase or rejected her as too thin, ill, or unrefined. They discussed the women endlessly, lamented the missionary, "as if [they were] looking at merchandise in the market and haggling over the price."[76]

Suddenly, the missionary heard a loud disturbance next door. Getting up to investigate, he learned that the human traders had discovered that one of the "girls" they were examining was actually "a little *boy* with pierced ears and bound feet who had dressed up as a girl so he could be sold!" The females who were purchased by the traders were eager to escape Linqu. When the missionary woke up early the next morning, he heard the women say to their buyers, "When can you take me back with you so I won't have to endure hunger anymore?"[77] Such descriptions demonstrate that women were aware that they could exploit their market value in order to survive the famine, and that many were willing to do so, even at the risk of losing their moral value in the eyes of their local communities.

MORAL OR MARKET VALUE?

Images of the Incredible Famine's female victims were used in extraordinarily complex ways by male observers of the disaster. Local literati in Shanxi expected different behavior from famished women who were at different life stages. They placed daughters in precarious positions during the famine and demanded chastity and self-sacrifice unto death from young wives and widows. Elderly mothers, on the other hand, were in most cases depicted as persons to be sacrificed for, rather than figures who should starve so that others might live. Images of women in local famine morality plays thus delineated Confucian definitions of moral and immoral responses to disaster.

In contrast, demographic studies of famine and gender and observations made by foreign relief workers call into question the assumption that Chinese families discriminated against women when dividing a famished household's dwindling food supply. These sources suggest that the burgeoning trade in women in some cases enabled young women to survive the disaster in greater numbers than their male counterparts. These discussions of the widespread sale of women during the famine raise the possibility that, as demographic studies also hint, a disaster on the scale of the North China Famine reversed normal patterns of mortality within Chinese families and to some extent replaced the moral economy of Chinese families with a market economy. The same young daughters and wives who had the weakest claim to household resources during normal times ultimately had the greatest market value during the famine. In contrast, both elderly mothers and men of all ages, who in ordinary times had higher status than young women and who were often seen as the gatekeepers of the traditional moral order, possessed virtually no market value during a time of crisis.

Moreover, while young women who chose to commit suicide or starve to death rather than use their market value were credited with great moral value after death, women who exploited their market value by allowing family members to sell them or by selling their bodies in exchange for food lost all moral value in the eyes of local literati, but sometimes managed to survive the famine. During the disaster, then, it may have seemed that a person's market value went up as his or her moral value decreased. This turn of events was clearly a threat to Confucian family norms. It helps to explain the vehemence with which male guardians of the moral order denounced the "shameless" women who forsook chastity in order to survive the famine.

CHAPTER 8

The "Feminization of Famine" and the Feminization of Nationalism

During the Incredible Famine not only local literati in Shanxi but also Chinese journalists and philanthropists in treaty-port Shanghai engaged in what Margaret Kelleher calls a "feminization of famine," or "the representation of famine and its effects through images of women."[1] While the sale of starving women was an important trope in all levels of famine-related sources, the nature of the crisis that Chinese observers tried to represent by using female icons of starvation varied dramatically. Provincial officials and local-level observers of the catastrophe in North China viewed the famine as yet another challenge to the Qing Dynasty and, most seriously, as a threat to the Confucian family system. Members of Shanghai's merchant and literati communities took their "feminization of famine" in a radically different direction. Faced with a constant barrage of foreign critiques of the Qing government's relief efforts and with the challenge posed by foreign missionaries who rushed to northern provinces to distribute famine relief, they came to view the famine as primarily a national humiliation.[2]

Both the *Shenbao* editors and Jiangnan philanthropists like Xie Jiafu repeatedly selected images of famished women sold to human traders to represent the crisis and to mobilize others to act on behalf of famine victims. This selection drew public attention to the treatment of women, their oppression, the physical brutality they suffered, and in particular the market in women brought about by the shortage of marriageable women.[3] The scale of the trafficking in women during the famine shocked

Chinese as well as foreign relief workers and highlighted the unstable place women occupied in the Confucian order, according to which women were feared to be the weakest link in the family.[4] The plight of women during the famine rapidly became an issue around which wider debates about Chinese state and society coalesced.

In Jiangnan the crisis brought about by the famine led elite activists to focus on saving starving strangers in distant North China rather than the poor in their own native locales; to compete with the relief activities organized by foreigners; and to question traditional assumptions about the role of women. Treaty-port journalists and reformers used feminized images of the famine to motivate Chinese people from all walks of life to rescue women in order to save China from national disgrace, thus prefiguring the connection between the liberation of women and the salvation of the Chinese nation put forth by Chinese nationalists in the decades after the famine.

"CULTURALISM" AND NATIONALISM IN REPRESENTATIONS OF THE FAMINE

In local famine texts from Shanxi, the extreme stress the famine placed on families was of primary concern. The feminized images chosen to symbolize the famine's horror reflected that focus. Literate survivors desperately tried to shore up cultural and social ideals such as female chastity, frugality, and filial piety. In Shanxi, official as well as local responses to the disaster were characterized by an attempt to restore threatened traditional principles, specifically principles of good governance. Governor Zeng Guoquan and Imperial Famine Commissioner Yan Jingming, for example, tried to lessen the famine's impact and prepare for future disasters by turning people's attention away from cash crops such as opium and back to traditional food crops, by calling on the state to "nourish the people" with shipments of official grain, and by treating the people of Shanxi as compassionately as they treated their own children.

Shaken by the disaster itself but not by external critiques, officials and local observers in the famine-stricken province interpreted the catastrophe according to a traditional form of Chinese identity, often termed "culturalism," that envisioned China not as a country but as "all under Heaven" (*tianxia*) and that assumed the political and moral superiority of Chinese culture over all others. "In the eyes of most of the emperor's subjects the empire was not a country but the country, not a culture but culture itself," explains Henrietta Harrison.[5] "The central cultural dream of traditional Chinese society was that China was the center of world civilization, the only place where life was lived properly, in its full humanity," concludes Mark Elvin.[6] According to this earlier form of Chinese identity, the horrific famine was a crisis in China but not a crisis *of* China. In Shanxi the famine might imperil people's chaste or filial behavior, but it could not cause them to doubt the ultimate value of female chastity or filial piety. Likewise, the massive famine might challenge a particular dynasty's mandate to rule, but it could not humiliate China before other nation-states or call into question China's place as the center and embodiment of civilization.

In Shanghai, on the other hand, the Incredible Famine was one of the major nineteenth-century crises that forced activist members of the treaty-port elite to begin what historian Joseph Levenson called the transition from "culturalism" to nationalism.[7] As it began entering China from the West in the 1860s, modern nationalism differed from earlier forms of Chinese identity "both in its emphasis on the idea of competition between states and in its rejection of much of what previously constituted Chinese identity."[8]

As detailed in chapter 6, treaty-port reformers like the *Shenbao* editors had a positive impression of new transport technologies and relief methods from the West and actively promoted their adoption. They also, however, viewed the Western powers and the foreigners distributing famine relief in North China as alarming sources of competition. Foreign critiques and news about relief efforts overseas and missionary relief campaigns in China forced educated Chinese in Shanghai to wrestle uncomfortably with the possibility that just as China was not "all under Heaven" but simply "one country among many," Chinese famine relief methods were not *the* relief method but only one of many different ways of dealing with disaster.

The rampant trafficking in women from famine areas helped convince Jiangnan reformers to view the famine more as a national crisis than a threat to the Confucian moral order or the Qing empire. As report after report of the miserable fate of women sold into concubinage or prostitution by their starving families appeared in the *Shenbao,* the Taohuawu famine illustrations, and English-language newspapers, some treaty-port reformers began to connect the redemption of famished women with the salvation of China as a whole. Over the course of the disaster, to "save" a famished woman by redeeming her from the clutches of the human traders became one way that elite Chinese men could take action against both the ravages of the famine and the endless foreign condemnations of China.

THE "FEMINIZATION OF FAMINE"

As was the case for many of the themes highlighted by the Shanghai press during the famine, English-language publications led the effort to focus public attention on the widespread sale of women in northern famine districts. British and American observers who sought to convey the unspeakable horror of the famine often did so by describing suffering women, most often those who had been sold as wives, concubines, or prostitutes. They expressed their disapproval of the market for women by drawing connections between the sale of women in China and slavery elsewhere, and by offering vivid depictions of individual young women sold against their will. Anglo-American discussions of the issue assumed that the sale of starving women was only one of the more extreme examples in a long list of objectionable practices stemming from China's unenlightened view of women. By the 1870s Protestant missionaries had already been publishing, for decades, sharp critiques of Chinese practices such as concubinage, female seclusion, widow suicide, and foot binding.[9]

In missionary publications, accounts detailing the plight of young women signified both the horror of the famine and the "heathen darkness" of China as a whole. A report written by W. L. Elliston, a missionary relief worker based in Shanxi during the famine, exemplifies Western suppositions about the fate of Chinese women. Elliston described a fifteen-year-old girl who came to receive relief cash from the missionaries after losing her parents, brothers, and sisters during the famine. Elliston found the girl "quite pretty," with "beautiful dark eyes." He cautioned himself, however, writing, "If I could meet her again in twenty years or less she may be the very reverse. The life these girls are compelled to lead in China soon destroys both beauty of face and character. Who will come and help them?"[10]

The English-language press in China began condemning the sale of women and children in famine districts almost as soon as its coverage of the disaster started, and it laid responsibility for such sales at the feet of the Qing government. In December 1876, for example, a correspondent for the *Celestial Empire*, a Shanghai-based newspaper, submitted a report deploring the sale of children in the famine districts of Shandong Province. "It is equivalent to selling them into slavery," he wrote. The reporter blamed Qing officials for issuing proclamations that allowed people to sell and buy children, mainly girls, without fear.[11] The claim that the Qing government did little to stop the sale of women and children during the famine was reiterated by numerous Chinese and foreign observers. The criticism is supported by research showing that while the Qing government strongly condemned the practice of "forcible sale" of women during ordinary times, during bad times "parents who could show they had sold a daughter under financial duress were treated lightly in the Qing code," as were impoverished husbands who sold their wives.[12]

A letter published in the *North China Herald* that detailed the Reverend J. Lees's journey through the famine areas offered a more pointed critique of Qing employees, in this case soldiers. Lees described how he and his traveling partners encountered a human trader at an inn they had stopped at for the night. "As usual, a soldier was the trader," he observed. The soldier arrived at the inn with a twenty-year-old woman and a "bonny girl of about fifteen" whom he had purchased in Beijing and was transporting south for sale. "It is needless to say that the misery of such poor creatures generally begins at this the first resting place on the road," stated Lees. He explained that many human traders could behave with such impunity precisely *because* of their official uniforms. While "the cries of the girls tell their story too plainly," he wrote, the innkeepers never dared to interfere because "the men are *soldiers*, in uniform, and claim to be traveling with their own families."[13]

Another letter, written by a missionary relief worker named Arnold Foster and published by the *Herald*, made Western beliefs about the low position of Chinese women even clearer. Describing famine conditions in Shanxi's Pingding City in November 1877, Foster stated, "Within twenty miles people were reported to be dying from starvation. Nearer still, that horrid trade in human life which is sure at a time like this to disgrace every nation where the true position and rights of women are not recognized, was actively going on. I heard of parents selling their daughters, and husbands selling their wives, in order to buy food."[14]

In the minds of nineteenth-century Westerners, historian John Fitzgerald has observed, "the female condition served as an indisputable sign of the unredeemed barbarity of the people of Asia."[15] Foreign observers of the sale of famished women during the North China Famine believed that the phenomenon was rooted in China's misunderstanding of the proper position of women rather than in the desperation brought by mass starvation, and they asserted that only a backward and semicivilized country would allow such a practice to occur.

Due to the connections between the Chinese- and English-language press in Shanghai, leading Chinese reformers and philanthropists in Jiangnan were aware of and troubled by the incessant foreign condemnation of the sale of famished women. Proving that the foreigners were wrong about China was part of what motivated them to relieve famine victims and redeem women who had been sold. Most members of the Jiangnan elite who engaged in relief activities in the 1870s rejected the Western claim that the sale of women during the famine stemmed from China's benighted view of women and thus signified a serious flaw in Chinese society and culture. Their confidence in China's Confucian system had not yet been shaken to that extent. Such confidence would collapse in the decades following the famine, however. In the early twentieth century, Chinese nationalists largely came to accept the Western assertion, as Fitzgerald puts it, that "China could redeem itself neither as a civilization nor as a virile young nation until it had addressed the 'women problem.'" The "colonial critique" of the mistreatment of women in China appearing in famine narratives from the 1870s soon became a "formative element of modern Chinese nationalism."[16]

In the spring of 1878 the *Shenbao* began publishing its own denunciations of the trafficking of women in famine areas. The newspaper generally portrayed the famine as a story of victimization in which relatively "backward" hinterlands of China suffered endless misery due to the Qing government's refusal to enact reforms and its consequent inability to provide sufficient relief. The girls and women who were sold during the famine became one of the most haunting symbols of this victimization. Local famine texts from Shanxi Province granted women a certain degree of agency, albeit negative, when they focused on virtuous women who starved to death rather than compromise their chastity and on sexually licentious women who threatened Confucian norms by selling their bodies in order to survive. The *Shenbao* editors, in contrast, portrayed sold women as helpless creatures who bore no responsibility for their fate.[17]

An essay published on 27 June 1878 provides a riveting example of the *Shenbao*'s emotional coverage of the sale of women in famine districts. The article recorded the experiences of Pan Shaoan, a philanthropist from Jiangsu Province, during his journey through famine districts in Henan Province, northwest of Jiangsu. Pan and several other wealthy philanthropists from the Suzhou area traveled north to bury the dead, buy back women who had been sold, and distribute cash, grain, and medicine to the starving. Pan depicted the women he met as tormented and ever weeping victims, and the men who purchased them as archvillains.[18]

Pan's article, titled "Yuxing riji" (Diary of a journey to Henan), provided *Shenbao* readers with a day-by-day account of his experience from 7 April to 9 May 1878.[19] Pan's diary is unremittingly grim. At the end of almost every daily entry, he listed the number of bodies he arranged to have buried that day. On the second day of his journey, Pan and his friends hired people to bury one corpse, but as they entered more deeply into the famine district, the number of corpses increased until on the sixth day, it was necessary to pay for the burials of sixty-six bodies. In spite of the myriad horrors they witnessed, it was the cries of women who had been sold that repeatedly drew Pan and his coworkers to the brink of tears, and that eventually disturbed Pan so deeply that he grew ill and returned home.[20]

Pan Shaoan's record of the seemingly endless stream of women being brought south by human traders began on 14 April, when Pan and his friends, like their missionary counterparts, were forced to share their inn with a human trader who had purchased five girls under age sixteen for a total of only 12,000 *wen*. When he went to distribute cash at the Baiyun temple on 15 April, Pan saw four women who wept without ceasing while the men who had purchased them whipped them into submission. On 18 April he saw a human trader from Fengyang transporting five women south to be sold. The women cried all night. Upon hearing them, Pan's coworker Xiong Chunshu also wept all night, and Pan and his other friends nearly burst into tears as well.[21]

Two days later Pan was walking east of town when he spotted a man who was selling his thirteen-year-old daughter to a human trader. The man explained that there were seven people in his family but that he had already sold his seventeen-year-old daughter, and was now forced to sell the younger one as well. Luckily, Pan and his friend were able to buy the girl back before the trader left. On 23 April Pan saw five large carts arrive from Kaifeng carrying twenty women. "Later the disaster victims north of the river will have no families at all!" he lamented. "What remedy is there?"[22] In early May Pan stopped at a temple and witnessed the transaction that finally broke his will to continue. He saw a crude soldier buy a young woman from Xiuwu in Henan. The woman could write and calculate, and she was sold for 89,000 cash. "Her husband was refined and courteous, probably a scholar," he wrote. "When I saw the circumstances of their parting, my liver and bowels were split." Defeated in body and spirit, Pan left the famine districts and returned home.[23]

In a sharp departure from the writings of local observers in Shanxi, Pan Shaoan never raised the issue of female chastity or virtue in his depictions of the sold women. He also made no reference to the possibility that women who were sold might survive the famine better than they would have if they had remained at home. Instead Pan's diary is a litany of grief, shame, and rage. Pan and his colleagues were moved to tears by the suffering of the women he met, and sickened by the realization that neither their own wealth nor the halfhearted efforts of Qing soldiers succeeded in freeing women from their captors.

The *Shenbao*'s decision to publish Pan's shocking account demonstrates the newspaper's commitment to raising public awareness about the famine and the trade in women. To some degree, the way that Pan Shaoan and other philanthropists and journalists from the Jiangnan region wrote about events in China's famine-stricken north also mirrored the critical tone employed by foreign observers describing China as a whole. Their experiences in famine areas enabled them to establish a moral as well as a geographical distance between their prosperous Jiangnan homes and China's famished northern hinterland.

One of the striking characteristics of the *Shenbao*'s coverage of women during the famine was its focus on the physical torment inflicted on women's bodies by human traders. A letter printed by the newspaper in October 1878 vividly illustrates this emphasis. In the letter a man named Song Jun (Song Shanshi) described the inhumane treatment inflicted on women from famine districts who had been transported south to Qingjiang, a city in northern Jiangsu, and sold to houses of prostitution. Song and several other philanthropists from southern Jiangsu established a bureau in the Guanyin Temple in Qingjiang in order to rescue women who had been sold and escort them back to their homes. In contrast to local observers in Shanxi, Song assumed the innocence of female famine victims sold into brothels. "Those who show a little unwillingness are immediately punished severely. Their suffering is unspeakable!" he exclaimed. "We do not know what wrong famine victims such as these have committed to reach this point."[24]

Song offered graphic descriptions of the terrible fate that awaited women who were sold. When he and his coworkers investigated the situation in Qingjiang, they learned about a family that bought four women from Henan and tried to teach them how to sing theatrical songs. When one of the girls was a little clumsy, the family punished her by burning her with a pipe heated until it was red hot. Eventually she died. Song also detailed how human traders transported women south by cramming as many as possible into boats. The human traders, wrote Song, always took turns raping the suffering women before selling them. Moreover, the traders dealt with any women found even slightly ill by tossing them into the river to drown, lest they infect the other women and lower their market value.[25]

As part of their attempt to "draw tears from iron," Xie Jiafu and his Taohuawu colleagues in Suzhou also highlighted the suffering of famished women. Their famine illustrations offered visual depictions of tormented female bodies that matched the horrific depictions in Song Jun's letter. Several haunting illustrations focused on the misery and pain experienced by women sold by their families. A print titled "Women Are Sold: They Despair of Coming Back Alive" depicts a husband, wife, and child weeping piteously inside their home as the wife prepares to be sold. Outside two well-fed human traders wait with their horse and strings of cash, and in the foreground a ragged father prepares to sell a little daughter who clings to his clothing in despair.

A second illustration, titled "Weeping Bitterly While Thinking of Home; Beaten on the Way," portrays an angry human trader raising a whip to beat a group of ragged girls who cower on the ground before him. The girls lift their arms in futile attempts to fend off his blows. The accompanying text is narrated in the voice of a literate woman from a good family who, unable to stop weeping, asks how she could have sunk to such a state. "The rattan whip strikes three blows; the pain penetrates my bones," she cries. "Alas! May these abductors die ten thousand deaths!"[26] The human traders are the unmistakable villains in these pictures. Invariably depicted as well-fed, greedy, and cruel, such men are harshly condemned for their ambition to grow rich off the misery of their starving compatriots. The women, in contrast, are portrayed as helpless and innocent victims in desperate need of protection.[27]

Xie Jiafu, Song Jun, and the *Shenbao* editors rarely depicted in such detail the suffering of male famine victims. Instead, they selected images of weak, tortured women to convey the famine's horror. These portrayals fit within the category of news items that concerned brutalities committed against women—a news genre that Barbara Mittler's fascinating study of the *Shenbao* identifies as sizable and distinctive. Such reports "invoke an implied reader who is simultaneously fascinated with and disgusted by the pitiable fate of women," argues Mittler. She interprets the *Shenbao*'s decision to print so many articles about suffering women less as a sign of the newspaper's commitment to improving the situation of women than as "bait" to attract its overwhelmingly male readership.[28]

To some extent, images of famished women may have been used to attract male voyeurs. Song Jun's vivid accounts of the abuse of women

Figure 5. A Wife Is Sold. From "Si sheng gao zai tu qi," 30a.

Figure 6. Beaten along the Way. From "Si sheng gao zai tu qi," 32a.

持錢贖命
已受宰烹

Figure 7. Already Killed and Cooked. From "Si sheng gao zai tu qi," 26a.

from famine districts would have appealed to such readers; the unhappy women in his reports were portrayed as weak and suffering but also attractive. At the same time, famine accounts consistently called on men to *act* as well as to gaze and to weep. A macabre illustration in the Taohuawu compilation dramatically portrayed for male readers the consequences of postponing active intervention. In the text accompanying the illustration titled "[He] Brings Money to Redeem Life; [She Has] Already Been Slaughtered and Cooked," a man writing from one of the disaster-stricken provinces describes how he had passed a butcher's gate that displayed different kinds of human meat. Seeing that a young woman was about to be cooked, he rushed home to get money with which to redeem her. But by the time he arrived back at the gate, the woman had already been killed. "Her rosy face could no longer be seen," lamented her would-be rescuer. "All that was left was her wronged ghost hanging in the air." The message to the male reader was clear: horrible things were happening to defenseless young women in the famine districts. A generous donor could save them if he acted quickly, but there was no time to waste.[29]

The *Shenbao*'s stirring depictions of the sale of famished women and the Taohuawu's "Pictures to Draw Tears from Iron" represented more than a means to attract male readers. They were complex forms of cultural representation "in which the moral, the commercial, and the political" were closely intertwined.[30] As explained earlier, the author of the front-page *Shenbao* article that introduced the compilation of illustrations to treaty-port readers went out of his way to praise it because it enabled not only elite men but also illiterate men, women, and children to grasp the extent of the suffering in the north. Moreover, the illustrations were so effective that they enabled Xie and his colleagues to collect an impressive 2.5 million taels for famine relief.[31] Readers who viewed these feminized images of famine clearly found it difficult to gaze without "stepping into the picture" to help the victims portrayed.

THE FEMINIZATION OF NATIONALISM

In Jiangnan calls to rescue famished women rapidly became calls to save China from foreigners' derisive laughter and their gunboats. The use of women during the Incredible Famine thus anticipated the powerful connections that Chinese nationalists writing a few decades later would draw between saving women and saving China. The decision to connect suffering women with a suffering China was not random. Historian Prasenjit Duara argues that women are often selected to embody "the purported authenticity of the nation" because the most effective embodiments of a nation are living beings who produce deep affect but who are denied agency in the public realm. The representation of woman, he continues, has been "a very significant site upon which regimes and elites in China responsible for charting the destiny of the nation have sought to locate the unchanging essence and moral purity of that nation."[32] During the North China Famine, treaty-port elites depicted both starving women and beleaguered China as victims in need of aid.

When the famine worsened early in 1877, the editors of the *Shenbao* repeatedly tried to rouse Chinese readers to participate in relief efforts by appealing to their national pride. A 9 March editorial praised Western merchants in Shanghai for raising contributions for famine-stricken Shandong and called on Chinese gentry and merchants as well to demonstrate their good character.[33] The following day the paper commended Tang Jingxing (Tong King-sing), manager of the China Merchant Steamship Navigation Company, for collecting money and clothing for famine victims in Shandong, and exhorted the gentry and the rich all over China to follow Tang's example lest they be outdone in generosity by foreigners.[34] A sharply worded front-page editorial printed in April 1877 tried to shame readers into acting on behalf of their starving compatriots. The editor claimed that Western officials, scholars, and merchants all "contended to be first to delight in doing good deeds" in famine districts. How could it be, he railed, that Westerners hurried to dispense relief even though they had not been born in the same land as the famine victims, while Chinese people with means showed no sympathy for their fellow Chinese and were willing to fall behind the foreigners in conducting relief work?[35]

Xie Jiafu, though more skeptical than the *Shenbao* editors about the underlying motives of foreign relief workers, was equally incensed by the possibility that the benevolence of Chinese elites might be surpassed by that of foreigners. In a diary entry written in the spring of 1877, Xie recorded his own heated reaction to the news that Timothy Richard and several other well-known Christian missionaries were adopting famine orphans and distributing relief in Shandong. "I deeply fear that the enemy countries are angling for favor," he wrote; "we cannot fail to take action." Like the Qingliu proponents in the capital, Xie worried that the suffering in the northern provinces might cost the Qing government popular support. He declared his determination to compete with the foreigners engaged in relief efforts there. "The relief that the Westerners are

giving to Shandong is on the surface a claim to the reputation of relieving disaster and sympathizing with neighbors," he wrote, "but in secret
it is a tactic to win the people's hearts. I fear if the people's hearts belong to the foreigners, [it will result in] heresy and wantonness, which
will be a great calamity for China." Xie concluded with an urgent call
for action: "We must collect a large sum of money and follow in hot pursuit to bring relief," he wrote. "In the end, by stopping the foreigners
from casting greedy eyes, [we will] strengthen China's borders."[36]

Clearly, the desire to protect China from disgrace and defend the country from the covetous designs of foreigners played an important role in
motivating members of the Jiangnan elite to pour time, money, and energy into famine relief efforts. The deep sense of national crisis brought
about by the severity and length of the Incredible Famine also inspired
them to downplay class and regional differences in discussions of the disaster and to emphasize a broader Chinese identity.

The Shenbao in particular strove to include a multiclass audience in
its appeals for famine-relief contributions. An essay submitted to the
newspaper in June 1877, for example, specifically called on all of Shanghai's residents to contribute to famine relief. The author first specified
the amount of money that members of Shanghai's upper, middle, and
lower classes could be expected to donate. He then included Shanghai's
lowliest residents in his call. In Shanghai not only the rich but even the
poor and mean working-class people such as "shoulder-pole peddlers,
rickshaw pullers, boatmen, maids, and concubines" could get enough
food to fill their stomachs, he wrote, so they too should work together
to give whatever they could to save the starving. Even some foreigners
who lived outside China were sending relief money to Chinese famine
victims, continued the author, and foreign women were selling their own
needlework in order to raise money to donate.[37] Throughout the disaster the Shenbao pointedly called attention to and praised the generosity
of marginalized or unlikely donors ranging from actors to Japanese merchants, overseas Chinese, and foreign women.[38]

It is doubtful that the Shenbao editors, regardless of their optimism
about the paper's appeal to a broad audience, considered foreign women
or Shanghai's underclass of boatmen, rickshaw pullers, actors, and concubines as likely readers. Historian Evelyn Rawski estimates that 30 to
45 percent of Chinese males and only 2 to 10 percent of Chinese females
were literate by the late-Qing period. Certainly peddlers and maids would
not have been among the literate minority. The editors may have hoped,
however, that their descriptions of the disaster and their calls for aid

would be read aloud to illiterate Chinese, or that such news would reach women and lower-class men through oral retellings.[39] In addition, when the *Shenbao* highlighted the altruism of foreigners or marginalized groups, it was clearly trying to goad its primary audience—Chinese gentry, merchants, and officials—into contributing. If it could show that even Chinese laborers, foreign women, and the much despised actors were sending aid to famine victims, surely all members of China's elite would rush to do so as well, to avoid being outdone by their social inferiors.

The crisis posed by the famine also challenged social activists in the Lower Yangzi area to move beyond regional loyalties and adopt a more national vision. Members of the Jiangnan elite had barely finished rebuilding the Lower Yangzi homes and cities that had been destroyed during the Taiping Rebellion when news reached them of the famine ravaging strategically and politically important northern provinces. As Mary Rankin has noted, literati and merchant activists from all over the Jiangnan region feared that the famine, like the Taiping rebels two decades earlier, posed a serious threat to the national fabric. Elites from different parts of Jiangnan worked together to preserve the country's social stability by raising and distributing famine relief in the distant north, thus transforming existing forms of local philanthropic activism into nationally oriented relief efforts.[40] Both Xie Jiafu and Jing Yuanshan, for instance, expanded the focus of the local and regional charitable activities carried out by their philanthropic fathers by mobilizing funds for the northern provinces and, in Xie's case, by traveling to Shandong himself to help famine orphans.[41] The *Shenbao* fostered these broader efforts. In July 1879 the newspaper praised southern philanthropists who had declared it their responsibility to remain in northern famine districts to conduct relief work because, "though the nation is divided into different areas, there is no division of the people" (*guojia you fentu, wu fen ren*).[42]

Bryna Goodman has shown that the public nature of famine relief efforts could in some cases strengthen local identities as well as "reconfigure people's connections to the larger polity." She observes that Zheng Guanying, the reform-minded relief organizer from Guangdong who downplayed regional differences by joining the Zhejiang merchant-philanthropist Jing Yuanshan in establishing a famine relief bureau for Shanxi in 1877, also wrote a letter urging his fellow provincials in Guangzhou to become involved in relief work *so as not to be outdone* by the Jiangsu and Zhejiang natives living in Shanghai. The Jiangnan natives had already donated, wrote Zheng, and he warned that if the Guangdong natives failed to contribute as well, "not only would they lose face, but foreigners would laugh at them."[43] In his letter Zheng clearly distinguished between his fellow provincials from Guangzhou and his Zhejiang and Jiangsu friends like Jing Yuanshan and Xie Jiafu. At the same time, when he chose the mocking laughter of foreigners as the most likely threat to persuade his Guangdong friends to donate, he went beyond provincial loyalty and implied a sense of solidarity with *all* Chinese against the contemptuous outsiders.

The argument that philanthropists from Jiangsu or Guangzhou should focus as much or more attention on rescuing famine victims in distant North China than on the poor in their own native places presents a striking departure from pre–Taiping Rebellion norms for charitable giving. As Joanna Handlin Smith's work on late-Ming and early-Qing philanthropy has demonstrated, benevolent societies traditionally allocated resources according to three main criteria: the morality of the poor, their degree of need, and their geographic proximity. Elite founders "argued for definite territorial boundaries in charitable activities" and believed that the wealthy in one locale should aid the poor of that locale.[44] During the Incredible Famine, however, the *Shenbao* actively rejected such assumptions. It exhorted Chinese people from all over the Jiangnan region to view famine victims in Shanxi as compatriots rather than starving strangers and to rescue the truly desperate people in the north before helping the poor in their more fortunate locales.

Philanthropists from Jiangnan also employed feminized images of famine to galvanize support for nongovernmental relief efforts and to criticize the Qing government's complicity in the sale of women. Stepping into the vacuum left by the decline of Qing officialdom, they used their money, energy, and talent to act as de facto officials who raised people's awareness of the disaster, collected and distributed famine relief funds, promulgated detailed regulations about how to conduct relief work, and redeemed women and children who had been sold. In August 1878, for instance, a *Shenbao* article explained how a group of gentlemen involved in relief efforts petitioned the governor of Jiangsu Province to forbid the transport of women from disaster-stricken Henan and to establish bureaus that would redeem women and send them home.[45] Gentry from the Jiangnan region played an important role in both financing and managing such bureaus. Records of relief contributions collected by Xie Jiafu and his Taohuawu colleagues provide fascinating details about the activities and finances of the "Qingjiang Bureau for Redeeming and Sending [People] Back," which was also discussed in Song Jun's letter published in the *Shenbao*.[46]

The Qingjiang Bureau spent most of the money received from wealthy donors to redeem women; build temporary sheds to house them; give the women clothing, bedding, and food; provide relief for their families; and hire soldiers to escort them home. Those in charge of the Qingjiang Bureau also kept meticulous records listing the name, age, native place, and surviving family members of the forty-three women rescued. Of the nine girls and women given money and escorted back to their native places in March 1879, for example, three were from Shandong and six from Zhili. They ranged in age from eight to seventeen years. Some were returned to family members, while those who lacked any family were sent to a benevolence hall in Tianjin to be cared for.[47]

In his draft of regulations for the Qingjiang Bureau, Xie Jiafu emphasized that officials should be responsible for intercepting human traders, while civilians should be charged with sending redeemed people home. Local officials, the regulations suggested, should carefully investigate anyone who tried to transport women south and should send them to the bureau if they proved to be abductors. The relief bureau would care for the redeemed women and children temporarily and then send them home with relief money as soon as their families could be located. The bureau was also expected to reward Qing soldiers who seized human traders, and to arrange marriages locally for those women who had no family to return to.[48]

Although relief workers from Jiangnan hoped that Qing soldiers and local officials would intercept human traders at checkpoints, they expressed little confidence that the government would or could stop the trafficking in women. In his famine diary published in the *Shenbao*, for example, Pan Shaoan recorded an instance when officials acted to benefit from the sale of women rather than to stop it. When Pan tried to redeem the four women whom he had seen weeping as they were beaten outside the Baiyun Temple, he was informed that two of the women had already been purchased by officials, so there was nothing he could do to help them.[49] Song Jun's letter from the Qingjiang Bureau also accused officials of colluding with smugglers of women. Because the human traders were regularly using gunships to transport women from northern famine districts to the wealthier south, wrote Song, no one dared to intercept them, and even those who loved to do good could only sigh in vain. Song viewed the smugglers as ignorant lower-class people who did not know any better, but was appalled to learn that officials had also gotten involved in the trade in order to enrich themselves. "This class of people is inhuman!" he fumed. He offered the example of the nearby town of

Banzha, where three families were smuggling women without fear due to their connections with officials. Song concluded that if only those in charge of stopping the trafficking would do their work more conscientiously, they could save human life, preserve women's chastity, return people to their native places, and reunite families.[50]

As more members of Jiangnan's merchant elite and literati traveled to famine lands to distribute relief and described their harrowing experiences in letters published by the *Shenbao*, the newspaper became increasingly critical of the traffic in women and the government's inability to stop it. The sharpest denunciation of the practice appeared in a front-page editorial on 11 April 1878. Entitled "Forbid the Trafficking of Girls: Exhort Famine Households Not to Take Lightly and Abandon That Which They Gave Life To," the article prefigures the reform journalism of the late 1890s. The journalist criticized not only the practice of selling daughters during famine but also the underlying assumptions about women that led families to sell their wives and daughters when disaster struck. "Human sensibilities value males and regard females lightly," he wrote. "If [families] often bear girls, they are resentful, and even if they bring forth one daughter after another, they only lament that they have no son."[51]

The author then explained that common custom devalued women because when girls married, they carried their household's property elsewhere and became another family's possession. When a family had a son, on the other hand, family members knew that he would always belong to their household and that if he became influential, he could make the family honorable and rich. The reformist editor bemoaned the results of these common customs, such as unsophisticated parents in mountainous or remote areas drowning girl infants at birth. His harsh rejection of this "backward" thinking, which he carefully located in rural areas far from Shanghai, echoed similar comments that Western observers often made about China as a whole.[52]

Although the *Shenbao* editor understood that some famished couples gave up their children because they could not bear to see them starve, he insisted that only the devaluation of women explained why parents chose to sell their daughters and keep their sons. The situation was made worse by greedy human traders who, unlike Chinese families, valued girls over boys since they were in high demand as servants, concubines, and prostitutes. "All the people in the country are base," he asserted, because during the disaster even good families survived by selling their young daughters into prostitution. "How unfortunate are today's girls!" he lamented.

"How can [parents] endure setting aside their daughters in order to gain a few thousand coins?"[53]

Toward the end of the disaster the *Shenbao* also encouraged Chinese women to contribute to relief campaigns and provided positive coverage of women who did so. Honorary arches or tablets similar to those often erected to recognize chaste women were erected for women who contributed to famine relief efforts. A front-page article printed in August 1879 discussed the honorary arches and praised women in official families who lived frugally so that they could save some of the money given to them to manage the household and contribute it to famine relief. The author urged other women to follow this example, regardless of whether they were from official, gentry, or merchant households.[54] Rather than being honored solely for actions they did *not* take (not remarrying or engaging in extramarital sexual relations), then, women were commemorated during the disaster for taking action to help famished compatriots.

Zheng Guanying also commented favorably on Chinese women who contributed to relief efforts. In his writings about the Shanghai-based relief campaign, he both identified female donors by name and praised women who suggested new methods of fund-raising. Zheng described how, just when he had begun to despair of finding a way to raise additional funds for the continuing disaster in Shanxi and Zhili, four women—Zhu Chen Shi, Chen Yang Shi, Li Shen Shi, and Zheng Liang Shi—came forward and contributed money. The women informed Zheng that, in Suzhou, relief organizers had started to hire a few people to travel to temples and burn incense in place of others, thereby enabling everyone else to donate some of the money they normally spent on pilgrimages to famine-relief work. They asked Zheng if he could arrange a similar plan, and he agreed. "Such sagacity I did not expect to see from women," he commented. "How admirable!"[55]

SAVING WOMEN, SAVING CHINA

During the famine years the spectacle of thousands of young women being sold into prostitution by their starving families, as well as the loud foreign condemnation of this practice, deeply disturbed members of the Jiangnan elite. It also compelled a few reform-minded Chinese to begin asking deeper questions about the low position of women in Chinese families and society. In the four decades after the Incredible Famine, liberation for Chinese women became ever more intimately connected to the propagation of Chinese national identity. As noted by John Fitzgerald, before the arrival of the West, individual members of the Chinese literati had condemned foot binding and other practices affecting women, but such critiques did not become popular until the nation's survival appeared to be at stake after China's devastating loss to Japan in the 1895 Sino-Japanese War. Even after the "woman question" made its way into the mainstream of nationalist debate after the shock of 1895, reformers ranging from Liang Qichao to the *Shenbao* editors called for the emancipation of women less for women's sake than to defend China against Western contempt and to further Chinese nationalism.[56] The determination to restore China's reputation in Western countries was at the heart of the *Shenbao*'s discussions of the treatment of women, writes Mittler. "Footbinding, female illiteracy and concubinage were to be abolished so that the foreigners would no longer regard China as a 'land of savages.'"[57]

By the 1920s Chinese intellectuals active in the May 4th Movement (the decade-long cultural and intellectual upheaval that takes its name from the wave of student demonstrations that started in Beijing on 4 May 1919) had moved from calling for the liberation of women in order to defend China against Western critiques to employing examples of the mistreatment of women in Chinese society as weapons in their attack on China's traditional culture. In her study of prostitution in early-twentieth-century Shanghai, Gail Hershatter shows how Chinese intellectuals increasingly came to view the low position of women signified by prostitution as "paradigmatic of a social decay" and as a contributory factor in China's weakness vis-à-vis the colonizing powers.[58] "Chinese elites of the May Fourth generation argued that China, which mistreated 'its women,' thus figuring China as male, then was treated like a woman by stronger nations: subordinated, humiliated, with pieces of its territory occupied by force," writes Hershatter.[59] Asserting that a social system that permitted the mistreatment of women would inevitably result in a weak nation, May 4th thinkers launched attacks against Confucianism, the patriarchal family, arranged marriages, and other facets of China's traditional culture.

Shanghai-based journalists and Jiangnan philanthropists writing during the Incredible Famine did not use the image of a sold woman explicitly as a marker of *national* decay, as Chinese reformers would do a few decades later. Nor did they view the sale of women into sex work as paradigmatic of a fatal weakness in Chinese culture that had allowed imperialist powers to take over. Nevertheless, late-Qing treaty-port elites viewed the spectacle of young women being taken from their homes by human traders and forced to survive by selling their bodies as an image that could and should rouse both the Qing government and Chinese elites to action. Their appeals for government intervention to stop the traffic in women, for immediate action on the part of educated Chinese, and for a change in old assumptions about the value of women in Chinese society, all anticipated the powerful connections that would soon be formed between the salvation and liberation of Chinese women, and the salvation and survival of the Chinese nation itself.

The Incredible Famine was a major blow in a series of catastrophic events that eventually led to the collapse of confidence in China's Confucian tradition. In both the famine's hinterland epicenter and in culturally hybrid Shanghai, the famine was a catastrophe described largely with feminized images, though these were differently interpreted in Shanxi, for instance, as compared with Shanghai. In Shanghai these feminized icons of starvation helped to construct the language and the imagery that would later be employed to reject traditional Chinese culture and its treatment of women in the name of the Chinese nation. The famine did not create the reformism, emergent national consciousness, and gradual shift in attitudes toward women displayed by members of Shanghai's treaty-port elite. All of these trends were rooted in the hybrid nature of the treaty port, and they both preceded and outlived the famine. Nevertheless, the crisis atmosphere brought about by the disaster accelerated and deepened the sense of impending national doom.

CHAPTER 9

Eating Culture

Cannibalism and the Semiotics of Starvation, 1870–2001

[One's] ears often hear of the eating of human flesh without
seeing it oneself, but truly there were those who took children,
killed them, and ate a meal. Those who died on the street of
the village had no one to bury them. If nobody was looking,
they were dragged away by people and eaten as a meal.

Elder brothers ate younger, younger brothers ate elder;
my own eyes saw it. Wives ate husbands, husbands ate wives;
it makes the heart ache. A small child selling steamed buns
disappeared in an instant; I heard his family say he was killed
and eaten by those who came to buy buns. . . .

When eating dead people, they broke the bones to take a
careful look: If it had any bone marrow, they would certainly
want to eat it as a meal. . . . In the beginning, the eating of
dead people was seldom seen in the cities or villages, but later
on, the eating of living people became simply a tragic thing
to speak of.

At the market, human flesh was sold, and fingernails
became visible [in the meat]. Fathers ate sons; sons ate
fathers, defying principle and destroying Heaven. Many
of those who ate human flesh were reported to the relief
bureau: some were buried alive, some flayed with a knife,
others roasted in a fire.

All levels of famine writings from the Incredible Famine abound with
images of famine-related cannibalism as well as images of suffering
women. The cannibalistic methods of punishment recorded by Liu Xing
in the terrifying passage cited above are unique to his account, as is his
claim to have witnessed instances of intrafamilial cannibalism with his

own eyes.[1] The emotional tone, however, as well as several of the specific images in his depiction, are common to many of the more detailed local descriptions of cannibalism during the famine. The claim that human flesh was sold in shops and markets during the disaster appears in many famine texts, as does Liu's description of the progression from eating the dead to killing family members and consuming them.

Just as depictions of the sale of starving women were interpreted differently in Shanxi and Shanghai, the horrible imagery of "people eating people" also took on a multiplicity of meanings depending on which semiotic system it was incorporated into. To a greater extent than the sale of women, cannibalism continued to serve as the quintessential emblem of the famine well into the twentieth century. Already crucial to local, treaty-port, and foreign descriptions of the disaster in the 1870s, in Mao's China, images of people-eating-people became even more saturated with meaning. Accounts of cannibalism were employed to represent not only the horror of famine but also the rapacity of the "old feudal society" as a whole. Even today, vivid descriptions of starving family members devouring each other continue to dominate the famine folktales that circulate in Shanxi.

COLONIZED CANNIBALISM?

In contemporary Shanxi province, the phrase "the third year of the Guangxu Reign" is almost synonymous with cannibalism. Of the twenty local historians and thirty-one elderly villagers between ages 70 and 101 that I interviewed during my research trip through ten different counties in southern Shanxi in 2001, twenty-nine of them brought up cannibalism when asked if they had heard of the Guangxu 3 (1877) disaster, and several shared two or more specific tales of famine-related cannibalism. By the end of my time in Shanxi, I had been told forty cannibalism stories that went beyond a general mention of people eating people. The number of tales about other facets of the disaster pales in comparison.[2]

A famine folktale told by Chai Fengju, a seventy-year-old woman from Ding Village in the Linfen area of southern Shanxi, demonstrates the vivid and often gruesome nature of the famine stories shared by elderly villagers. Mrs. Chai heard this story from her paternal grandmother, who was a child during the famine:

> In Guangxu 3 there had been three years with no rain. The people were starving. In Caizhuang Village [her grandmother's village], a neighbor

woman sat combing her daughter's hair. Her daughter was five or six years old. The mother was terribly hungry. As she parted her little girl's hair to braid it, she saw the back of her daughter's neck and it looked soft and tender. The mother was so hungry that she became dizzy. She took a knife, sliced off a piece of her daughter's flesh from the back of the neck, and ate it. It tasted good. She then killed the child and boiled her. The starving neighbors all smelled the fragrance of cooking meat. They came and demanded: "What meat did you find?" She would not tell them. But the neighbors insisted. They pushed by the mother, looked into her pot and saw her own five-year-old daughter being cooked.[3]

This story is representative of many of the folk stories told by elderly respondents in that it entails a famine victim who kills and eats a family member rather than one who consumes the flesh of an already dead stranger. Indeed, the majority of the famine stories concerning cannibalism focused on close relatives, such as parents or grandparents who boiled and ate their children, or parents-in-law who tried to eat their grown daughters-in-law. The presence of a knife and the image of a person being boiled in a large pot are two additional motifs that appear again and again in cannibalism-related stories.

Many of the interviewees began their descriptions of the disaster with the same rhythmic phrase: *Guangxu sannian, ren chi ren, quan chi quan* (In the third year of the Guangxu emperor's reign, people ate people and dogs ate dogs). That the phrase is so well known in contemporary Shanxi is probably due to its frequent appearance in a two-volume collection about the 1877 disaster published in 1961 and 1962, some portions of which were introduced to schoolchildren in Shanxi during the Great Leap Famine. As implied by the use of the classical Chinese word for dog, *quan*, instead of its modern equivalent, *gou*, however, the phrase actually originated in stele inscriptions and gazetteer essays written during the 1870s and early 1880s.

The very same phrase is used by both late-Qing and present-day residents of Shanxi in their descriptions of the Incredible Famine. I argue, however, that the chain of associations raised by images of cannibalism was quite different for Chinese writing in the late-Qing period than it has been for Chinese employing such images since the publication in 1918 of Lu Xun's famous story "A Madman's Diary" (*Kuangren riji*).

In Lu Xun's allegory the madman, who is in fact the only person able to grasp what is really going on in China, discovers that the words "eat people" are written between the lines of China's dynastic histories. He comes to believe that everyone around him survives by consuming the flesh of others or destroying them in the name of virtue and morality. "I have only just realized that I have been living all these years in a place where for four thousand years they have been eating human flesh," he laments. The madman's call to "save the children" from China's predatory social system became a rallying cry for May 4th thinkers and their attack on Confucianism and other cornerstones of China's traditional culture.[4]

Ever since Lu Xun's creation of China's twentieth-century national allegory of "the old cannibalistic China," people-eating-people has symbolized not only the 1876–79 famine but imperial China in general. Lu Xun's use of cannibalism as a "powerful trope of negative totality in interpreting traditional Chinese culture and society" stemmed from the writer's incorporation and assimilation of colonial discourse, argues Gang Yue, a scholar of Chinese literature, in his book on cannibalism in modern China. In this sense Lu Xun vividly illustrates what Edward Said views as "the modern Orient" participating in its own "Orientalizing." Starting with Lu Xun, the specter of the cannibalistic old China became modern China's historical Other, just as China and other non-Western societies acted as the Other for the colonizing West. In the grand narrative of the Chinese revolution, writes Gang, "the old China was a monstrous human-eating feast; only through revolution could the oppressed masses free themselves of that devouring system and transform it into egalitarian revelry."[5]

During the Mao era, PRC scholars who wrote about the Incredible Famine often employed images of cannibalism to draw stark contrasts between Qing and revolutionary China. Zhao Shiyuan's article on the 1877 disaster, for instance, clearly depicts late-Qing China as a dark historical other: "The social system of that time was reactionary, the agricultural economy was backward, the production power was weak, the peasant class was poor," writes Zhao. "The reactionary rulers only knew how to plunder and pillage, they did not care about the construction of disaster prevention and control," he continues. "Naturally, a man-eating social system must create a man-eating natural disaster."[6]

Before Lu Xun and other May 4th critics appropriated them early in the twentieth century, the Chinese terms most commonly used for anthropophagy conjured images quite distinct from those raised by the English word "cannibalism."[7] The word "cannibal" first entered European languages when Christopher Columbus used it to refer to the Carib people of the Antilles, described by his Arawak guides as warlike eaters of human flesh. From the moment it passed into Spanish and then into other European languages, the term "cannibalism" was closely connected to colonial encounters between Europeans and peoples they viewed as savage or inferior.[8] Gang Yue argues that because it immediately raises a broad range of grotesque and exotic images "all about the 'other' and unrelated to 'us,'" use of "cannibalism" generally has less to do with actual practice than with the construction of the Other.[9] Indeed, the first time he or she hears the word "cannibalism," an English-speaking child has no way of guessing from the word alone that it refers to people eating other people. A perusal of *Webster's New World Roget's A–Z Thesaurus* (1999) quickly exposes the close links between the English "cannibalism" and images of the uncivilized Other. The thesaurus lists synonyms for the word "cannibal" in this order: "Man-eater, headhunter, savage, native, primitive, aborigine, eater of one's own kind, ogre, ogress, anthropophagus, anthrophagite, anthropophaginian."[10] Fewer than half of the twelve synonyms offered for "cannibalism" actually deal with the practice of eating human flesh; all of the others refer instead to "primitive" or fantastic peoples or groups.

Chinese terms for people-eating-people, on the other hand, came not from colonial encounters but from the Chinese Classics. The Chinese-language phrases commonly used for anthropophagy are blunt three-character expressions that leave so little room for confusion that they do not even appear in standard Chinese dictionaries. Both the modern Chinese phrase for anthropophagy, *chi ren rou* 吃人肉 (to eat human flesh), and the classical expression *ren xiang shi* 人相食 (people eat each other), which was most commonly used by observers of the Incredible Famine, include the character for "people" and a character for the verb "to eat."[11]

Historian Key Ray Chong traces the first textual account of Chinese people eating human flesh for survival purposes back to the *Zuozhuan* (Zuo commentary), one of the Confucian Classics and China's earliest work of sustained narrative history. The *Zuozhuan* recounts a conflict between the warring states of Chu and Song. In 594 B.C.E, the armies of Chu besieged the Song capital for several months. The city ran out of food and the people began to starve. Finally, the Song leaders sent one of their agents to the enemy camp to speak with the Chu general: "My master has sent me to inform you of our distress," stated the agent. "In the city, we are exchanging our children and eating them [*yizi er shi* 易子而食] and splitting up their bones for fuel." The idiom *yizi er shi* is also found in a siege account from the Han Classic the *Shiji* (Historical records). It continued to be used in reports of survival cannibalism during the imperial period and appeared frequently in local gazetteer essays and stone stele inscriptions concerning the 1876–79 famine.[12] A contemporary dictionary of Chinese proverbs places the phrase in the context of extreme food shortages. It refers to "exchanging sons and daughters, killing them, and eating them to assuage extreme hunger," explains the proverb dictionary. "This describes the tragic conditions of a food shortage in the old society."[13] Classical Chinese phrases for anthropophagy generally referred to Han Chinese eating each other during times of desperation, rather than to exotic "head hunters" roasting the meat of unfortunate white captives on semideserted islands. Thus it is not surprising that Chinese and Anglo-American observers of the North China Famine used reports of people eating human flesh in different ways.

Images of cannibalism figured prominently in nineteenth-century Western discussions of the disaster. Since the *North China Herald* routinely portrayed China as an uncivilized Other before, during, and after the famine, it is easy to dismiss its lurid reports of Chinese famine victims feasting on the dead as yet more examples of that newspaper's contempt for China's society and government. The *Herald* was not alone in reporting incidences of cannibalism in Shanxi and Henan, however. In an article printed in April 1878, for instance, the *London Times* correspondent based in Shanghai compared the behavior of Chinese famine victims with that of victims of the contemporaneous famine in India: "The sturdy Chinese peasants do not calmly fold their hands and die, like our poor fellow-subjects, the Madrasses, last year," he wrote. Instead "they eat the dead, and when there are none to take, they kill the living for the same purpose." Insisting that such reports were "no Oriental exaggeration, but the actual state of things in a district not 700 miles from Shanghai," the correspondent provided a letter from the Roman Catholic bishop of Shanxi as supporting evidence. "Up to the present people were satisfied with eating those who were already dead, but now they also kill the living to eat them," wrote Bishop Monsignor Monagatta. "The husband eats his wife, the parents eat their sons and daughters, and in turn the children eat their parents, as one hears said nearly every day."[14]

Whether conscious of it or not, British journalists in the late 1870s drew on images of cannibalism to demonstrate China's cultural and geographical Otherness. As scholar of literature and postcolonial studies Peter Hulme has pointed out, the word "cannibalism," which immediately calls to mind "ferocious consumption of human flesh," has been used most often to mark the boundary between one community and its Others. "'Cannibalism' is a term that has no application outside the discourse of European colonialism," he asserts; "it is never available as a 'neutral' word."[15] Certainly the manner in which cannibalism was presented in the *London Times* article was far from neutral. In one brief sentence, the correspondent manages to portray both Chinese and Indian famine victims as incomprehensible, though pitiable, Others. In this classic example of Orientalist readings of the East as passive or inert, Indian famine victims are depicted as sedately waiting for death. The Chinese peasants who killed and ate their own family members, on the other hand, presented such an extreme Other that the *Times* correspondent feared his British readers would dismiss such reports as "Oriental exaggerations."[16]

Not all Anglo-American discussions of cannibalism during the North China Famine used reports of cannibalism to create a distance between a "civilized" West and "uncivilized" China. The Shanghai-based *Celestial Empire,* founded in 1874 by the English businessman Frederic Henry Balfour as a weekly "journal of native and foreign affairs in the Far East," printed articles that offered a more sympathetic Western reading of famine and cannibalism in China.[17] A lengthy letter written by Timothy Richard and printed in January 1878, for example, reported that a banker in the central Shanxi city of Pingyao had informed him that people were eating children there. Appalled by that information, Richard sought out the banker the following day to clarify the story, hoping to learn that the man had used the expression "eating children" to explain that parents were forced to sell their children in order to live. "No, no," the banker answered Richard, "they lay hold of children, boil them, and eat them!"[18]

During the spring of 1878 the *Celestial Empire* published several additional missionary letters that included reports of cannibalism in Shanxi. Finally, in May 1878 the paper ran a nuanced editorial that attempted to help readers come to terms with the horrific images reported by missionaries. "The terrible truth must be told," stated the editors. "Although the people are not cannibals, and although they love their children as much as other people do theirs, the distress is so great, that they have in many instances . . . actually slain and eaten them; and we are assured of the truth of the statement, that a man actually opened a shop for the sale of human flesh." The editors followed this validation of cannibalism reports with an effort to destigmatize them by reminding readers that Englishmen, too, had committed cannibalism in times of desperation: "It is not, indeed, at all incredible: we well know what our own countrymen have done when driven to extremes in case of shipwreck," they reminded their readers.[19]

The editors of the *Celestial Empire* and some missionaries in famine districts appear to have consciously refrained from using stories of cannibalism to depict China as an uncivilized Other. Nevertheless, even the best-intentioned Western narratives about cannibalism raise questions when examined critically. For example, though Timothy Richard wrote numerous reports about cannibalism in Shanxi, he never saw evidence of cannibalism himself. Instead, in each case, he heard reports or rumors about cannibalism from a Chinese source, often from a low-ranking official. For instance, in one of his many letters printed in the *Celestial Empire,* Richard made this broad statement: "The eating of human flesh is a regular thing, and if the people were really dead before, there is little said about it, but if killed, then litigations arise. Yesterday the *Chehien* [magistrate] here told me he had a case of this kind to try."[20] The only proof Richard offered for his bold claim that consumption of human flesh was a "regular thing" was a local magistrate's statement that someone accused of murder and cannibalism would be tried the next day. Readers had no way of discovering whether the accused was found guilty or whether the case, after further investigation, was instead dismissed as unsubstantiated.

Moreover, neither Richard nor his audience could be sure that the official was telling the truth, rather than exaggerating the situation in the hope of getting more aid from a foreign relief worker. The missionaries themselves also may have focused extra attention on stories of cannibalism in order to motivate foreign readers to send famine relief funds and additional field-workers. Finally, the image of starving Chinese people devouring others in an effort to stay alive fit perfectly within the common missionary portrayal of China as a dark and lost land in desperate need of the light of salvation. Thus missionaries working in famine areas may have been especially quick to accept and repeat rumors of cannibalism at face value, even without careful investigation. Because Western reports of starving Chinese peasants devouring each other were often used to further a "colonial discourse of cannibalism," they must be approached with great caution.

The image of people-eating-people was common in Jiangnan discussions of the famine in North China, as well. The reformist *Shenbao* editors generally referred to cannibalism to signify the famine's severity. They also highlighted the need to strengthen China so that the country would never again reach the point where humans ate each other.[21] Xie Jiafu and his Taohuawu colleagues employed images of cannibalism as part of their effort to draw both tears and donations from even the most impervious audience. They included a particularly graphic print titled "Starved Corpses Fill the Road; [People] Vie to Slice Them Up" in both their first and second set of famine illustrations. This illustration depicts two emaciated men crouching over a corpse with a knife, preparing to slice off flesh and devour it. Famished onlookers watch from behind a tree, while others rush over to join the feast. The figures are barefoot and ragged, the tree has been stripped of all its bark and leaves by the starving populace, and the corpse, which is little more than skin and bones, lies face down in the dust. There is no sense that even one of the living persons in the print has any intention of preventing the man with a knife from stripping the corpse of its flesh. Instead, three of the onlookers hurry to join the knife bearer, while the others are too lost in despair to act.[22]

Another Taohuawu illustration, titled "On the Roads Orphans Are Lured to Their Death in the Dark of Night," shows an adult brandishing a knife at a small child inside a home, while three abandoned children huddle outside on the road. "The grass roots are exhausted, the tree bark is used up. In the beginning they ate corpses; now they eat [living] people," laments the author of the accompanying text. Whether by day or by night, he continues, killing people is as easy as killing pigs. Children cry out for help but no one answers them. They are killed with a knife since meat has become more valuable than human life.[23]

In their depictions of cannibalism in famine districts, the Suzhou gentry drew on a distinctive "literature of the grotesque" found in Chinese vernacular fiction. Incidents of cannibalism appear in the popular Ming novels Sanguo yanyi (Romance of the Three Kingdoms) and Shuihuzhuan (The water margin). Loyalty, filial piety, revenge, or profit rather than outright starvation motivate the characters in these novels to eat human flesh, but some of the themes and images reappear in famine texts from the 1870s. Just as the gaunt father in one of the Taohuawu famine illustrations contemplates (but ultimately rejects) killing his daughter in order to feed her flesh to his starving mother during the famine, in the earlier Sanguo yanyi, the character Liu An kills his wife and serves her flesh to Liu Bei to demonstrate loyalty and filial piety.[24] Images in Shuihuzhuan presage some of the more gruesome rumors about the sale of human flesh during the Incredible Famine. For example, the novel's descriptions of bandit innkeepers who made dried meat out of sleeping travelers, and wine-shop owners who sold steamed dumplings filled with minced human flesh, prefigure the famine illustration that bemoans the fate of a young woman killed and cooked at a slaughterhouse before she could be redeemed.[25]

饿莩載途
争相臠割

Figure 8. People Eating People. From "Si sheng gao zai tu qi," 13a.

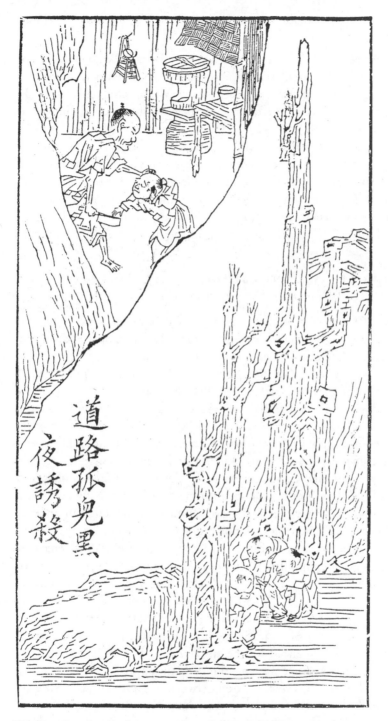

道路孤兒黑
夜誘殺

Figure 9. Famine Orphans Lured to Their Deaths. From "Si sheng
gao zai tu qi," 24a.

To inspire action, Xie Jiafu and his Taohuawu colleagues called on powerful tropes of cannibalism borrowed from popular fiction. In some cases, images of people so desperate that they murdered children or devoured the flesh of dead neighbors convinced people to contribute to relief work. Reports of people consuming one another throughout a thousand *li* of scorched earth, for instance, first motivated Jing Yuanshan and his friend Li Yushu to begin raising relief donations in Shanghai.[26] Because the primary purpose of the famine illustrations was to "draw tears" from a wealthy Jiangnan audience, they should be interpreted more as a means to shock apathetic donors into sending aid than as objective reports of what was actually occurring in the northern famine districts.

WARNINGS CARVED INTO STONE:
THE IMAGE IN LATE-QING SHANXI

Not only Chinese and foreign philanthropists based in distant Jiangnan or London but also local literati who witnessed the famine in Shanxi firsthand repeatedly drew on images of cannibalism in their accounts of the disaster. Twenty-four of the thirty-two late-Qing or early-Republican editions of local gazetteers from southwestern Shanxi that I examined recorded instances of cannibalism during the Incredible Famine. Five of the thirty-two reported instances of cannibalism during the chaos of the late-Ming period, but none cited other occurrences of cannibalism during the Qing dynasty. Nine of ten stone steles erected shortly after the catastrophe reported cannibalism during the 1877 famine, and several described incidents of the practice in some detail.[27] Liu Xing and Liang Peicai also included vivid depictions of cannibalism in their famine songs.

Neither colonialist discourse nor the desire to shock wealthy donors into action explains why literate survivors from Shanxi also selected cannibalism, in particular intra-familial cannibalism, as their primary "icon of starvation" during and after the disaster. Local observers in southern Shanxi lived in a part of China that in the 1870s had very few Western visitors and scant access to the kind of critiques published by the Chinese- or English-language press in Shanghai. Their focus on people-eating-people was not influenced by the discourse of European colonialism. Moreover, since most famine accounts recorded in local gazetteers or stone stele inscriptions were written between one and ten years after the famine had ended, their authors cannot have been motivated by the desire to elicit more imperial or foreign aid by exaggerating the severity of famine conditions. Why, then, was it so important to those who had witnessed the famine firsthand to record such horrific accounts of people devouring each other?

One obvious answer is that cannibalism was what actually happened during the famine. Reports of cannibalism during serious famines are certainly not unique to China. Mike Davis's survey of major late-nineteenth-century famines finds that rumors of cannibalism were reported not only in China but in Brazil, India, and Ethiopia. There are also relatively well-documented cases of cannibalism from the 1932–33 famine in the Soviet Union, the ill-fated Donner party in frontier North America, and the Andes airplane crash in 1972.[28] It is possible, then, that isolated instances of survival cannibalism may have occurred in Shanxi during the severe and prolonged famine. The particular images and phrases used to report widespread cannibalism in Shanxi, however, indicate a metaphorical rather than literal intent of local depictions of people-eating-people.

Many references to cannibalism found in county gazetteers are located in the "Strange Events" (xiangyi) section of the gazetteers and are often brief and highly stylized in placement and phrasing. Gazetteer reports of cannibalism usually appear after descriptions of people eating bark and roots but before discussions of the terrible epidemic that struck Shanxi in 1878 and the plague of rats and wolves that tormented the people in 1879. Certainly part of the function of these references was to highlight the severity of a given disaster. Historians Frederick Mote and Jonathan Spence, for instance, hypothesize that the litany of ren xiang shi (people ate each other) accounts found in local gazetteers from the Song dynasty onward may have been meant to be read symbolically, as a measure of a calamity's severity, rather than literally.[29] About half of the gazetteer references to cannibalism consist of three stock phrases that appear repeatedly: ren xiang shi (people ate each other), yizi er shi (exchanging children and eating them), and several versions of a slightly more elaborate phrase, ren xiang shi, shen you gurou xiangcan zhe (people ate each other to the point that close kin destroyed each other). The first expression specifies no relationship between consumer and consumed, while the yizi er shi idiom highlights an effort to avoid intrafamilial cannibalism. As noted by Lillian Li, it expresses the Confucian principle that even the most desperate parents cannot bear to survive by eating their own children, so they instead exchange their children for children whom they are not related to.[30] In contrast, the most detailed of the three phrases describes family members who consume their own relatives during a disaster.

Descriptions of cannibalism that appear in famine songs, stele inscriptions, and essays about the famine collected in the "Literary Pursuits" (*yiwen*) section of the gazetteers go far beyond the above-mentioned tropes. Such reports are remarkably vivid, specific as to what parts of the body were eaten, and bold in declaring that people were killing and eating the living—both strangers and family members—as well as consuming those already dead. The most common victims are children. A passage in the "Literary Pursuits" section of the Yongji County gazetteer published in 1886 reports that after the people in Yongji devoured all the birds, rats, willow bark, and grass, they began boiling dead bodies and selling the flesh as food. The author recounts a chilling tale of food sellers who caught, killed, roasted, and ate a little boy, and concludes with a report of family members eating other family members.[31] Similarly, a passage in a Republican-era gazetteer from Liang Peicai's native Hongdong County states that during the famine, people ate bird droppings and grass roots, abandoned their infants, and eventually ate human flesh either cooked or raw. Children were lured into the old city temple and killed, and piles of human bones could be sighted outside the town.[32] Liang Peicai himself offers an even more horrifying description of the situation: "[They] used steel knives to cut human flesh, lacking any conscience. [They] dug out the brain, opened the belly, and plucked out the heart and liver. In the beginning, eating dead people was seldom seen, but later eating the living was not uncommon. . . . People ate people, dogs ate dogs; it makes the human heart go cold."[33]

Commemorative steles erected by local elites in southwestern Shanxi often reported intrafamilial cannibalism. "There were those who ate human flesh and roasted the white bones, and even those who ate their own sons and daughters," reads an inscription from Wanrong County.[34] "It reached the point that fathers ate their sons, and daughters ate their mothers," echoes a stele from Wenxi County.[35] The inscription from a Ruicheng County stele erected in 1886 recorded that "in the countryside fathers and sons, elder and younger brothers ate each other. Ignoring human feeling, they paid attention only to eating. Killing the living and eating the dead, they did not fear punishment."[36]

Rather than describing the consumption of already-dead strangers or echoing the classical phrase about parents exchanging their children to avoid eating their own flesh and blood, the more detailed local reports of cannibalism in Shanxi highlighted images of family members who killed and devoured their closest relatives. This emphasis raises serious questions about the message such depictions intended to convey. Other often repeated descriptions of the famine include the bodies of the starved facing each other on the roads, unburied corpses being devoured by wolves, and "ten-thousand-person pits" in which no space was left to bury new bodies. It simply flies in the face of common sense, then, that those forced to survive by eating human flesh would kill and eat their own family members rather than surreptitiously stripping flesh from the multitude of dead or dying strangers. To understand images of intrafamilial cannibalism, it is necessary to explore the cultural force of such dark narratives.

The conspicuous focus on fathers, mothers, sons, and daughters consuming each other demonstrates the figurative nature of local accounts of cannibalism during the famine. These vivid accounts were translated by Catholic and Protestant missionaries in Shanxi and transmitted to Chinese and Western publications in Shanghai as literal fact. Although isolated incidents of survival cannibalism may have occurred during the disaster, I argue that images of cannibalism were primarily metaphorical expressions of the catastrophic destruction of the family unit wrought by the famine. The depiction of such an extreme breakdown in family harmony was also a powerful signifier of severe social crisis. According to Confucian precepts first spelled out in the book of *Mencius,* the five basic relationships of human society existed between ruler and minister, parent and child, husband and wife, elder brother and younger brother, and friend and friend. All but one of these relationships was hierarchical, and in each case the younger or female party was expected to obey and serve the elder or male figure. Local depictions of cannibalism during the Incredible Famine shattered those basic Confucian precepts. Not only were elder or male family members portrayed as surviving off the flesh of younger or female relatives, but sons, daughters, wives, and younger brothers were constantly reported to have killed and devoured their fathers, mothers, husbands, and elder brothers, as well. As the inscription on a stele from Anyi County in Xie Department lamented, "In the eastern part of the village, people ate their sons and daughters; in the western side, they ate their own wives; in the southern side, they ate their fathers and mothers; in the north, elder brothers and younger brothers ate each other . . . the white bones piled up like a mountain."[37]

According to such accounts, the famine had turned proper familial relationships upside down. Familial, societal, and political relations were closely connected in Confucian teachings. As explained in the *Analects,* a person who was a good son and an obedient younger brother at home would become an upright member of society who would never even consider starting a rebellion.[38] By shattering the basic Confucian ideal of love and obedience between elder and younger or male and female family members, then, Chinese images of famine-related cannibalism also shattered the vision of harmony between ruler and ruled, thus invoking fear of a total collapse of familial, social, and political allegiance and morality.

Images of wives who preserved their chastity and sons who continued to behave in a filial manner in spite of their desperation served to reinforce principles shaken by the famine. In contrast, depictions of children who rebelled against filial norms to such an extent that they killed and ate their own parents, as well as images of wayward wives who consumed their husbands or abandoned their chastity in order to survive, expressed the deeply rooted fear that a famine of such magnitude could destroy, or in this case "eat" Confucian culture. In the end, though, Confucian culture in famine-stricken Shanxi proved strikingly resilient. The cannibalistic images so prevalent in late-Qing famine texts indicate that local observers of the famine feared that a disaster of such magnitude might *not* be absorbable, that key Confucian precepts such as filial piety might disintegrate under the weight of death after death after death. But such ideals were not in fact devoured by the famine. No evidence suggests that the people of Shanxi began to question traditional assumptions or call for social change due to the catastrophe, even though the province lost a third of its population during the famine years. Nor did people in Shanxi rebel against the Qing government. It would take another thirty years for the dynasty to fall, and forty years before Confucian precepts such as filial piety and female chastity were shaken to the core by the May 4th Movement of 1919. In neither of those later upheavals did the impetus for change come from Shanxi.

Literate survivors of the Guangxu 3 disaster thus provide a clear example of David Arnold's point that during a major famine, "people may cling all the more resolutely to the cultural and social wreckage of their former lives" in order to sustain themselves during a traumatic time.[39] When faced with famine, Liu Xing, Liang Peicai, and numerous editors of local gazetteers and writers of stele inscriptions neither questioned traditional precepts nor demanded social and political reforms. Instead they desperately tried to shore up cultural and social norms. Liu traced Heaven's wrath to extravagance and to unchaste and unfilial behavior, and gazetteer editors filled postfamine editions of county gazetteers with morality plays about filial sons and chaste wives who starved to death during the famine in order to save other family members. They then used terrifying images of intrafamilial cannibalism to strengthen their plea to later generations to take action to ensure that such a disaster could never be repeated.

Local observers of the North China Famine often stated quite explicitly that they went to the trouble of recording such chilling descriptions of the famine in order to educate and warn future generations. The author of the 1884 stele inscription from Ruicheng County, for example, concluded his description of starvation, disease, and cannibalism during the famine with this stern injunction: "By planting three [rows of grain] but saving one, or planting nine but saving three, even when encountering a famine year, you will be prepared and will suffer no anxiety. We met with this disaster ourselves and tasted its bitterness in person. Fearing people will forget this hardship in future years, [we] record it in stone to serve as a clear warning forever."[40] Liang Peicai ended his "Essay on Grain" with a similar warning. "Although now the harvests are good and grain is very cheap, do not under any circumstances forget Guangxu 3," he wrote.[41] Liu Xing also expressed the desire that his famine song serve as a lesson and a warning to posterity. "Old people's claim that people ate people was something I had heard but not seen, until today my own eyes observed that it was not false talk," he wrote toward the beginning of his account. "I fear taking these disaster years as past and not thinking [of them], he continued; thus I wrote this song to hand down to the generations. Upon obtaining this song, hide it in your home and read it often to your sons and younger brothers. People of the whole household, remember it in your hearts, do not meet with hardship."[42]

Liu Xing's own words demonstrate that he, and perhaps others like him, found meaning and healing in describing the horror of the famine in unsparing detail, because he hoped that doing so would help later generations escape similar torments. This method of finding a purpose for all the suffering one experienced crosses both cultural and temporal borders. Some survivors of Nazi concentration camps, for example, have also "interpreted their suffering in terms of 'bearing witness,' with the ultimate aim of protecting against future evils."[43] By the time Liu completed his song two decades after the disaster, he was confident that what he had written was worth reading and rereading to family members and that remembering the terrible events he bore witness to would help people escape such misery in the future.

CONSTRUCTING A HISTORICAL OTHER: THE MASTER METAPHOR REVISITED IN THE 1960S

The hideous events described by local literati in late-Qing Shanxi were deliberately drawn back into public memory some eighty years later, as

China struggled to cope with the monumental famine brought about by the policies and ideology of Mao's Great Leap Forward and made more lethal by drought and flooding. As explained by economist Carl Riskin, key causal factors of the Great Leap Famine of 1959–61 include "output collapse, irrational methods of cultivation, destruction of work incentives, wasteful consumption of available foodgrain, ignorance of the planning authorities, over-procurement of grain by the government, increased exports in the midst of the crisis, failure to initiate imports in time, [and] bad weather." In the politically charged environment of the early 1960s, it was almost impossible to discuss the human errors that led to the famine. The catastrophe, which resulted in up to thirty million excess deaths, was carefully categorized as a value-free occurrence termed the "three difficult years" or the "three years of natural disaster."[44] As part of their strategy for dealing with the suffering experienced during this "natural disaster," provincial officials in Shanxi sent workers from local history offices out into the villages to collect primary source documents about the 1876–79 famine.[45] Cannibalism loomed large in those documents, and county officials and educators used that fact to downplay the difficulties people were facing in 1960.

In July 1961 and March 1962, some of the famine sources found by local historians were compiled and published in a two-volume work. The prefaces to that compilation clearly illustrate just how desperately the famine-stricken new society needed the construct of a "cannibalistic old China" as a dark contrast to modern troubles. The unnamed editors began the preface to the first volume by noting that during the disaster then afflicting Shanxi, many people were claiming that no one had ever seen such a severe disaster before, while elderly people were drawing direct comparisons between the 1960 disaster and the 1877 famine. Such comparisons presented a dangerous threat to the new government's moral and political legitimacy, since the regime came to power claiming that it, in stark contrast to the predatory officials of the old regime, both embodied and took care of "the masses."[46]

Perhaps because the situation on the ground in 1960 was undeniably grim, rather than launching a direct attack on the hungry villagers making such politically problematic comparisons, officials in Shanxi went to great lengths to prove them wrong. They used "official" or text-based history to question the validity of popular memory. More than eighty years had passed since the 1877 famine, cautioned the editors of the 1961 compilation. Thus even elderly people had not personally experienced the Guangxu 3 disaster and could not say for certain what conditions had been like in 1877. Only by examining primary sources written by those who had actually witnessed the late-Qing famine, they urged, could contemporary residents of Shanxi begin to understand how much worse conditions had been in Guangxu 3.[47]

Famine-related articles published in Shanxi during the 1960s never addressed the cause of the 1959–61 catastrophe. The usually unnamed authors of such pieces appear to have agreed with their late-Qing predecessors that cycles of dearth and plenty were inevitable occurrences that should be expected and planned for. "Our province has continuously received disasters for two years," the editors of the 1961 compilation stated flatly, making no attempt to explain why.[48] While careful to portray the 1959–61 disaster as a value-free incidence, however, the editors laid the blame for the Incredible Famine squarely at the foot of rapacious Qing officials and the cannibalistic "old feudal society."

After enumerating the grim descriptions of intrafamilial cannibalism, stacks of corpses abandoned on the roads, postfamine epidemics, and wolf and rat attacks found in local-level sources from the 1870s, the editors assured their readers that such horrors were characteristic of famines in the old society rather than the new. "The present is totally different," they concluded. "The people are already liberated; the exploiting class has already been overthrown; we already have the leadership of the Party and Chairman Mao, a socialist system, a unified grain purchasing and marketing system."[49] The preface to the compilation's second volume continued in the same vein: "It hasn't been more than eighty-five years from Guangxu 3 to the present," crowed the authors, "but under the leadership of the Party and Chairman Mao, today our society has already given rise to earthshaking change. Although recently we once again faced three years of continuous disaster, the tragic Guangxu 3 conditions of people starving to death and people eating each other did not return."[50]

Some accounts from the Incredible Famine were introduced to schoolchildren and villagers in southern Shanxi even before they were published in the 1961 and 1962 work. One stele inscription, written in 1883 by local gentry from Xia County, was distributed to schoolteachers throughout southern Shanxi in 1960, two years before it appeared in the second volume of the famine compilation. Teachers gave emotional lectures on the content of the inscription, and students were asked to recite and memorize it. In 1960 students and teachers in the Yuncheng area were subsisting on a mixture of government grain rations and substitute foods such as corn-cob paste and wild herbs, but the stele taught them how much worse the situation could be. They learned in terrifying detail how their late-Qing ancestors, when faced with three years of failed harvests, first sold all their possessions and even the roofs of their homes in order to buy a bit of grain; then consumed tree bark, grass roots, and sandy earth in an effort to survive; and finally found themselves in the unthinkable situation of consuming human flesh in a last desperate attempt to prolong life.[51] "Fathers and sons ate each other; mothers and daughters ate each other; this was worse than the parents who exchanged their children to eat them," intoned the inscription.[52] In some regions of southern Shanxi, schools even organized activity nights during which elderly villagers were invited to share stories about conditions during the Incredible Famine. Students and teachers then presented skits, poems, and essays that compared the dismal events of 1877 with the "hopeful" present and encouraged the audience to be thankful for the government's grain rations and to never, ever waste food.[53]

Toward the end of the Great Leap Famine, horrific descriptions of the North China Famine spread beyond the schools and local history offices of southern Shanxi. A copy of the Xia County stele inscription introduced to Shanxi schools was published in a March 1961 issue of the popular nationwide magazine *Zhongguo qingnian* (Chinese youth) and later placed on display at the Socialist Education Exhibition held in Beijing in 1964.[54] Zheng Guosheng, the author of the article published in *Chinese Youth* magazine, used the example of the 1877 famine to bring the chasm between the old and new China to life on a national rather than just a provincial level. After familiarizing Chinese young people with accounts of cannibalism taken from the Xia County stele erected in southern Shanxi's Niu Village in 1883, Zheng informed his readers that the very same Niu Village where the stele had been discovered had once again experienced a severe drought in 1959 and 1960. Thanks to the Party's heroic leadership and its haste in establishing communal kitchens to feed the people, however, the Niu villagers of 1960 were not forced to sell their children or kill and eat each other in order to survive. Instead they managed to produce over six hundred *ting* of grain per person in spite of the drought. "The same Niu Village, the same kind of great disaster," concluded Zheng, "but in the new and old societies conditions were as different as heaven and hell."[55]

When faced with a famine of its own making in 1959–61, China's new government conjured up the hungry ghosts of Guangxu 3 to support its claim that the old society had been cannibalistic, thus downplaying its own total failure to feed the Chinese people. In famine-related articles published in the 1960s, images of the Incredible Famine were used to distance the past from the present and to strengthen the depiction of old China as a dark historical Other. According to these works, natural disasters such as droughts and floods inevitably occur in new China as they did in the old. Only in the old feudal society, however, did corrupt leaders, grasping local elites, and a fundamentally flawed social system allow natural disasters to result in mass starvation and even intrafamilial cannibalism. In the new socialist society, in contrast, good leaders and a just social system enabled people to survive natural disasters without enduring such extreme suffering.

COMMON GROUND: "PLANTING NINE BUT SAVING THREE"

In Mao-era accounts of the 1877 famine, the corruption of the cannibalistic old society replaced the wrath of Heaven as the disaster's main cause. Interestingly, attempts to highlight the famine-relief efforts carried out in Mao's China by blaming corrupt Qing rulers and officials for the horrors of Guangxu 3 fell flat. As discussed in chapter 3, in spite of the concerted campaign to blame the Qing government for the horrors of the Incredible Famine, many Shanxi villagers continued to believe that the Qing emperor and high officials had tried their best to send relief to Shanxi and that premodern transportation networks and corrupt local leaders, rather than the Qing government, had stymied relief efforts. Instead of the official anti-Qing interpretation of the 1877 famine, it was the older message of the disaster as a warning against extravagance and waste that resonated in Shanxi villages during the 1959–61 famine, and this message continues to resonate there to some extent even today.

Most of the details that Liu Xing, Liang Peicai, and other literate survivors of the famine recorded have long since been forgotten by villagers in Shanxi, but their gruesome descriptions of intrafamilial cannibalism and their exhortations to save grain and avoid waste remain. Elderly villagers in southern Shanxi continue to connect their grandparents' obsession with saving grain and avoiding waste to experiences they went through during the Incredible Famine. Li Xingzhong, for example, an eighty-three-year-old retired military man from Yuncheng County, remembered that his grandfather, born in 1870, repeatedly told him stories of how, during the famine, people ate human flesh to the extent that parents kept their children locked inside the house for fear they would be killed and consumed if they went out. Due to his traumatic childhood experience, Mr. Li's grandfather never allowed anyone in the family to waste food. He ate grain so carefully that he never let it drop on the floor or get wasted, and if his grandson accidentally dropped a piece of grain on the ground, his grandfather would force him to pick it up and eat it, saying, "In Guangxu 3 we didn't even have that—*eat it!!*"[56]

Zhang Kaisheng, a fifty-four-year-old middle-school principal, learned similar lessons from both schoolteachers and grandparents. During the 1960 famine, his teacher shocked Zhang and the other students by openly weeping while he told them how young women were sold and family members devoured during the 1877 disaster. The teacher taught Zhang and the other pupils that they must eat less, save more, and prepare for future dearths. He asked them to memorize the proverb, so common in late-Qing famine texts, "Plant three, save one; plant nine, save three" (*geng san yu yi; geng jiu yu san*), and exhorted them to be diligent and thrifty. At home, Zhang heard about his great-grandfather's famine experiences. If Zhang or other children in the family failed to finish their food, their grandparents would scare them, saying, "Do you want to starve like the children in Guangxu 3? If you waste that, we'll sell you like they did back then!"[57] Such stories were recounted by numerous interviewees.

The warnings offered by grandparents, teachers, and local publications in the 1960s were noticeably less complex than those issued in the 1870s. In the 1870s local literati defined along gender and class lines the kinds of behavior they believed had angered Heaven and brought down a disaster so severe that it threatened to consume cultural norms. In contrast, during the early 1960s, traditional class and gender boundaries played no role in the warnings against extravagance and the exhortations to work hard and save grain. The editors of the 1961 compilation, for example, asserted that it was necessary for all Chinese to practice frugality in order to pull through the famine; to economize on human labor and natural resources to avoid running short; and to make long-range plans and preparations against future disasters.[58] In the eighty-three years between 1877 and 1960, then, the basic assumption that natural disasters would occur on a regular basis and must be prepared for had not changed, but maintaining proper class and gender boundaries was no longer considered to be an important aspect of preventing such disasters.

Perhaps because it was so politically inexpedient for anyone writing in 1960 to debate "natural" versus "human" causation of the Great Leap Famine, Mao-era interpretations of the 1877 famine also dissolved complex late-Qing explanations of famine causation and escalation, in which Heaven and humans both played a role and state responses to the famine provided both heroes and villains. Instead, explications of the Incredible

Famine in the 1960s contrasted the Qing "moral famine"—characterized by corrupt rulers, greedy underlings, and a cannibalistic social order—with the 1959–61 "natural disaster," which, they asserted, would soon end thanks to new China's good government and just social system. This simplistic view of history did not resonate with popular memories of the 1877 famine, but the practical moral prescripts put forth by local elites and officials in both famines did.

Late-Qing observers of the Incredible Famine might have been puzzled to hear classroom lectures or read articles in the early 1960s that employed images of cannibalism during the 1877 disaster to construct a frightening historical Other. They would not, on the other hand, have been surprised by the didactic uses to which PRC officials and educators put famine images. By the 1960s the late-Qing use of the famine as a warning for future generations had been partially replaced by a reading of the famine as a master metaphor for the old feudal society. The most durable lessons that local observers in both late-Qing and late-twentieth-century Shanxi drew from the Incredible Famine, however, had fewer national and political implications than personal, family, and moral implications. PRC interpretations of the 1877 catastrophe were most effective when they echoed older, Confucian readings of the famine. Haunting images of famine-related cannibalism survive even today in famine folktales told by elderly villagers who, like their late-Qing predecessors, aim to motivate the next generation to save grain, work hard, and avoid waste.

Epilogue

New Tears for New Times: The Famine Revisited

The Incredible Famine drew tears from all audiences, from local observers in late-Qing Shanxi to high officials in Beijing, philanthropists in the Jiangnan region, nineteenth-century European and American visitors, and twentieth-century Chinese officials, villagers, teachers, and schoolchildren faced with yet another severe famine. As I have shown, the meaning of the famine, as well as the images used to capture its horror, varied tremendously according to the observer. In contemporary Shanxi elderly villagers continue to associate the famine with tales of intrafamilial cannibalism and, to a lesser degree, the sale of women. In the central-Shanxi city of Pingyao, on the other hand, the famine has taken on a new meaning indicative of China's twenty-first-century concerns. Twice each Saturday, tour groups visiting the city may watch a colorful re-enactment of a Qing-era county magistrate's desperate attempt to persuade Pingyao's city god to send rain during the 1877 famine.[1]

In the late-Qing period, Pingyao, a city about sixty miles south of Taiyuan on the eastern bank of the Fen River, was an important center for Shanxi's powerful banking network. The city's high walls, moat, and well-kept temples proclaimed its wealth for all to see. Merchant wealth did not protect Pingyao from the ravages of famine, however. When Timothy Richard visited the city in the winter of 1877–78, he heard that people there had been reduced to eating children and that "a score" of starving women would go with him willingly if he offered them food. Before the famine 40,238 households containing 320,959 individuals lived in the area. By 1881, only 27,920 households and 177,342 individuals remained.[2] The drama performed in twenty-first-century Pingyao's City God Temple every Saturday brings the suffering experienced in the 1870s to life for well-fed tourists. In the play, the Qing-era magistrate bemoans the fact that Pingyao has suffered three years without rain, while the City God laments that people are eating each other and corpses are scattered all over the fields.

Pingyao temporarily regained its prosperity after the North China Famine. Yet like the province as a whole, it fell into decline after the Shanxi banks and the lucrative overland trade with Russia and Mongolia collapsed during the first few decades of the twentieth century.[3] After the 1949 revolution, Pingyao was one of the few cities in Shanxi either too poor or too conservative to tear down the walls that were a defining feature of traditional Chinese cities.[4] That omission turned out to be a blessing in disguise. In 1997 the World Heritage Committee of UNESCO added the "Ancient City of Pingyao" to its list of World Heritage sites worthy of protection. Today Pingyao's imposing city walls, which date back to the early Ming period and are nearly thirty-three feet high and thirty feet wide at the base, are visible from the trains that run over Shanxi's main north-south railroad.[5] Passengers gaze out the coach windows and take photos of the city, while tour groups file off the train to visit Pingyao's walls and temples, as well as its vaunted traditional courtyard-style houses and the site of Shanxi's first banking institution.

In a telling example of a phenomenon seen all over China in recent years due to the rapid expansion of domestic tourism that economic growth has fueled, after Pingyao earned the status of a World Heritage site, enterprising local officials from Pingyao County's Historical Relics Bureau began restoration work to transform the town into a lucrative tourist site.[6] One of the major sites restored was Pingyao's City God Temple (*chenghuang miao*). In 1999 members of the Historical Relics Bureau collected and read everything they could find about the history of Pingyao and its temple. Intrigued by gazetteer accounts of the 1877 famine and the actions of Pingyao's magistrate during the crisis, they then wrote a short play about the famine, the magistrate, and the city god.[7]

City gods, generally identified as the benevolent spirit of a local official or moral exemplar, played important roles in late imperial China, especially during times of natural disaster. "Every major locality had a City God temple inhabited by a god who held a heavenly bureaucratic rank equivalent to his earthly counterpart," writes Angela Zito, a scholar of religious studies and anthropology. As explained by a seventeenth-century magistrate, "The district magistrate governs the visible, or man-ifest, world and the City God the invisible. Generating benefit and ward-ing off harm for the people are the duties of the magistrate. Bringing down blessings and warding off natural disasters are the duties of the City God."[8] According to the Pingyao County gazetteer published soon after the famine, when a new magistrate first took office, he lived in the City God Temple and governed in concert with the god. In Pingyao the mag-istrate, whose office was located very near the temple, was expected to burn incense and worship the god each month.[9] Like earthly magistrates, city gods were viewed as judges who rewarded the virtuous and pun-ished evildoers. But they were objects of intense popular worship as well as "colleagues and allies of human magistrates and prefects." The birth-day of a given area's god was a "quintessentially popular festival," writes historian David Johnson. Some people even kept an image of the god in their homes. Moreover, both magistrates and ordinary people turned to their city god for help during times of drought and flood. To common-ers, states Johnson, the city god was "a savior, who could rescue them from famine, epidemic, warfare, and demons of all kinds."[10] Not sur-prisingly, Pingyao officials interested in transmitting memories of the In-credible Famine to the next generation chose to set their drama about the disaster in the City God Temple.

Pingyao's City God Temple dates back to the Northern Song dynasty (960–1127) but was rebuilt in 1859 after a terrible fire. Before the restora-tion of the city in the 1990s, elderly people in the locale often gathered in the temple courtyard to chat and play chess. In 2001 the temple was opened to the public as a historical site. At first, visitors had to pay ten yuan to enter, but now they pay 120 yuan for a ticket that gives them entry into all of Pingyao's sites. Tourists who visit on Saturdays enjoy the added benefit of viewing the drama about the famine.[11] The play, ti-tled "The County Magistrate Pays Respect to the City God," demon-strates that while the famine has not been forgotten in Shanxi, it is be-ing employed for new purposes by Chinese entrepreneurs whose concerns are quite different from those of either their late-Qing or Mao-era pred-ecessors. One of the most controversial issues raised by the famine—the responsibility and effectiveness of the Qing state during a time of crisis—appears yet again in this play. In a more indirect way, the play also touches on the role of foreigners in various Chinese conceptions of the famine's causation and course.

On a warm Saturday in June 2004 my husband and I, accompanied by an editor from Taiyuan, a Pingyao tour guide, several members of

Pingyao's Historical Relics Bureau, and Zhang Gaiqing, the director of local administration of the Pingyao City God Temple and Wealth God Temple, visited Pingyao's City God Temple to see the drama about the famine. The large blue and yellow sign that greeted us at the entrance to the temple advertised the play in Chinese and awkward English.[12] A beautifully carved wooden archway marked the entrance to the temple, and a large pagoda-shaped incense burner graced the central courtyard. Red lanterns, carved wooden eaves painted in blues and greens, bright flags of red and gold cloth, and wooden signs commanding "awed silence" and "withdrawal in the presence of a superior" decorated the hall of the city god. Inside, tourists burned incense in a large burner emblazoned with dragons and the yin-yang symbol. A few slipped money into a contribution box.

When the play began, a group of twenty or so Chinese tourists gathered to watch, as did my hosts and I. The drama, which lasted about ten minutes, was performed with considerable energy. The human characters in the drama included the famine-era county magistrate—a thin middle-aged man dressed in a long royal-blue silk robe with rich embroidery on the front and back, a conical hat with a red tassel, black boots, a long moustache, and a queue that hung down his back; the magistrate's private assistant in charge of revenue, who was a young man in a blue and burgundy robe; and six *yamen* guards dressed in light blue costumes and conical hats. One of the *yamen* runners signaled the beginning of the play by beating a large gong. The six guards, all carrying long poles, created a path for the magistrate by lining up on either side of the central courtyard, whereupon the magistrate and his assistant marched from the gate of the complex toward the hall of the City God. The guards, playing a role somewhat akin to that of a Greek chorus, loudly announced that the Pingyao County magistrate Wang Zhiping had come to pay respects to the City God.[13]

Inside the hall the celestial counterparts of Magistrate Wang and his assistant were seated behind an incense burner and a table. A very large man with a moustache, a long beard, and a black velvet hat played the City God. He wore a brilliant gold-colored silk robe embroidered with a large dragon. His assistant, introduced as a judge, wore a long black robe and a black hat and maintained a stern and unsmiling demeanor throughout the play. After entering the hall, Wang Zhiping stood to the right of the City God and announced the reason for his visit to both the god and the small crowd of tourists. It was the year Guangxu 3, he explained, and Pingyao had been stricken by a terrible drought. Devoid of even a drop of rain for three long years, the fields were barren and no crops could be harvested. He had thus come to pay a respectful visit to the City God to beg for a large rainfall that would rescue the common people from death.[14]

When Magistrate Wang finished speaking, the City God and the judge emerged from behind the incense burner and faced the audience, along with the magistrate and his assistant. The City God initially refused Wang's plea for rain. Claiming to lack the power to send rain, he refused even to report the request to the Jade Emperor, or *Yuhuang dadi,* the supreme deity of Daoism.[15] Magistrate Wang responded by emphasizing how powerful and respected the City God was in the locale and repeating his plea for rain. The City God then laid the blame for his unwillingness to intervene at the magistrate's feet. "Ever since you took office, you did not think of benefiting the locale, but extorted excessive taxes and levies and cut up the people like fish and meat [savagely oppressed the people]," charged the god. "Cries of discontent rise all around, the fields are littered with corpses, and it has reached the point where people eat people. Now you ask for rainfall, but how can we listen to you!?" After raising the specter of cannibalism, the City God ordered the judge to read aloud his report to the Jade Emperor. The report stated that Pingyao had traditionally been a place of peace and abundance, but that Wang Zhiping had savagely oppressed the people, taken bribes, and perverted justice, all of which had brought unspeakable suffering upon the common people. As punishment for Wang's misrule, the City God had requested that the Jade Emperor withhold rain for five years.[16]

The horrified magistrate and his assistant immediately dropped to the ground and kowtowed before the City God and the judge. Wang Zhiping then gave a long and heartfelt show of repentance. He admitted his wrongdoing, begged for forgiveness, promised that from that moment on he would change his evil actions into good and work to benefit the common people, and implored the god to report him to his superiors and have him removed from office instead of withholding rain. Magistrate Wang's assistant also begged the City God to reconsider. Since the magistrate had admitted his guilt and was willing to be punished, said the assistant, he hoped that the City God would take the people of Pingyao into consideration and use his extensive power to send down a widespread timely rain to save the people from their desperate situation. Even the judge encouraged his superior to think again. "So be it," agreed the City God, and he announced that he would rescue the county from the drought disaster for the sake of the common people.[17]

At this point the City God, the judge, the magistrate, and the assistant all dropped to their knees before the audience and prayed for rain. The judge and the assistant soon moved aside, and the magistrate and his celestial counterpart raised their arms up to Heaven and prayed in loud voices. At one point the City God gazed straight into the audience and ordered people to go home, worship, and pray for rain, thus transforming twenty-first-century tourists into the famished late-Qing villagers who turned to their City God in desperation during the 1877 drought-famine. The god then read aloud from his new report to the Jade Emperor, which described the magistrate's sincere repentance and requested copious rain for the area. Finally, the judge brought a small vase of water with green willow leaves in it to the City God. The god took the leaves out of the vase, raised them to the sky, and shook them to sprinkle water. "Eliminate the drought demon and let fall a widespread welcome rain!" he shouted. Immediately the gong clanged and the *yamen* guards rushed upon the audience from behind and splashed them with "rain" from a large earthenware basin filled with water. The startled crowd laughed and clapped, and the characters in the play lined up and took a bow.[18]

After the drama ended, I had the opportunity to ask Director Zhang Gaiqing and Zhang Kaijin, a member of Pingyao County's Shanxi Opera troupe and the man who played Magistrate Wang, how the drama came into being. Zhang Gaiqing replied that she and others in the Pingyao County Historical Relics Bureau came across descriptions of the famine and Magistrate Wang in the Qing-era Pingyao County gazetteer they read while gathering information about the history of the City God Temple. Before Zhang Gaiqing finished her explanation, Zhang Kaijin interrupted to say that they wanted to perform this play because "we hope that today's officials will do good for the common people (*lao baixing*), just like the magistrate did back in Guangxu 3." Director Zhang seemed a bit taken aback by that reply. She quickly said that the Historical Relics Bureau arranged the drama both as a tourist attraction that would draw people to the City God Temple and as a way to help people today have a better understanding of history. When I asked Zhang Kaijin if he could explain his response a bit more, he stressed the point that the story behind the drama is based on a factual event and is not simply a story. Old people in Pingyao knew this story about the magistrate praying for rain in Guangxu 3, he said. Then people read about it in a gazetteer and decided to alter it somewhat and rewrite it as a drama and perform it to let people know about the temple and about Pingyao's history, and to express the hope that today's officials will also benefit the common people.[19]

In the late-Qing period local observers like Liu Xing and the editors of the many county gazetteers published in the decade after the famine criticized the corrupt behavior of subbureaucratic underlings, but offered a generally positive assessment of the sincere—though often unsuccessful—attempts made by the Qing court and regular bureaucracy to rescue famine victims. In contrast, Chinese discussions of the Incredible Famine published during the first three decades of PRC rule, like *North China Herald* editorials a century earlier, blamed the "reactionary" Qing court and its hopelessly corrupt officials for the famine's severity. In an article published in 1981, for instance, Zhao Shiyuan charged that as the common people starved to death during the famine, the rapacious Qing government refused to reduce its expenditures on frivolous items such as repairing the empress dowager's palace, and high officials who traveled through Shanxi greedily consumed choice foods and demanded that large carts, sedan chairs, and horses be prepared for them. "The people sunk into the grave," he wrote, but still the feudal officials grew rich by oppressing them. "In this dark and corrupt feudal system," concluded Zhao, the officials "completely ignored the disaster victims in the midst of flood and fire and could only add to the disaster!"[20]

The language in the contemporary drama is influenced by critiques found in Mao-era discussions of the Qing government's complicity in the famine. Though the inspiration for the play apparently came from the famine-era Pingyao gazetteer, the City God's charge that Magistrate Wang had taken bribes, perverted justice, and oppressed the people did not. On the contrary, the description of the famine published in the Pingyao gazetteer in 1883, like most late-Qing local accounts, praised the earnest attempts that the Qing court, high provincial authorities, and county magistrates made to rescue famine victims, though the gazetteer editor also acknowledged that the unprecedented severity and scope of the famine made it impossible to save everyone. The section on relief measures states that Pingyao's county magistrate, Wang Shouzheng (Wang Zhiping), paid attention to the people's suffering and unequivocally implemented the relief policies sent by Governor Zeng. Working in concert with the local gentry, Magistrate Wang established a relief bureau in the back courtyard of the City God Temple. Between 1876 and 1879 the bureau distributed relief grain to 113,000 adults and 49,000 children in the extremely poor and less poor categories. Out of compassion for families forced to sell their children in order to survive the lean spring and summer months, Wang oversaw the establishment of adoption bureaus that took care of 1,689 children during the disaster and then returned them to their relatives. He also contributed 2,000 piculs of grain to relief efforts and set up two refugee camps for the homeless poor that served over 140 men and over 2,800 women.[21] The City God's critiques of Magistrate Wang in the present-day drama, then, stemmed from Mao-era depictions of the Qing regime more than from gazetteer accounts of Wang's conduct.

While the play's initial characterization of Magistrate Wang hearkens back to the 1960s, its depiction of Wang's sincere repentance and his admirable persistence in interceding with heavenly powers on behalf of the suffering masses reflects new concerns and a new perspective on China's imperial heritage. In twenty-first-century China the once crucial construct of the cannibalistic "old feudal society" is no longer so needed or compelling. Two and a half decades of phenomenal economic growth have made it possible for Chinese youth to view famine as something from the distant past. As Nan Xianghai discovered when he tried to interest the present generation of village children in Liu Xing's famine song, "Those who have full bellies don't want to hear about such circumstances."[22]

People interested in keeping memories of the famine alive in present-day Shanxi use the famine less as a dark contrast to modern troubles than as entertainment for tourists or as a moral lesson that is the mirror opposite of those drawn by Shanxi officials and educators in the 1960s. The editors of the 1961 and 1962 compilations about the Incredible Famine used terrifying tales from the disaster to create a distance between the corrupt, predatory officials of the old feudal society and the upright officials of the new society. Zhang Kaijin, in a most ironic contrast, sees the sincerely repentant Qing magistrate he depicts in the drama as a model and goad for present-day PRC officials who enrich themselves while ignoring the concerns of ordinary people. The Pingyao famine drama thus serves as a veiled critique of the greedy behavior of contemporary local officials.

The play also indirectly touches on the role of foreigners in various Chinese understandings of the famine. As we have seen, foreigners and their relief efforts were essentially absent from local-level accounts written by late-Qing literati in Shanxi. Timothy Richard, for instance, described his visit to famine-stricken Pingyao in some detail for Anglo-American readers, but the editors of the Pingyao gazetteer made no mention of him or his relief activities in their discussion of the disaster. In contrast, the foreign presence in China loomed large in both central-government and treaty-port debates about the disaster. In the imperial capital, both self-strengtheners and their Qingliu rivals agreed that the

West was a danger to be defended against, but proved unable to reach a consensus on how best to protect the country. In the Shanghai imagination, foreigners were at once competitors in the effort to relieve the starving populace of North China, a disapproving audience whose scornful laughter led *Shenbao* editors to question Qing famine relief policies and commonly held assumptions about the low value of women, and a source of alternative relief methods and technological inventions that could help strengthen and enrich the country.

In twenty-first-century Pingyao, foreigners are welcomed as a lucrative source of tourist dollars rather than ignored or viewed as a threat. An English-language "China Highlights" website, for example, encourages foreign visitors to sign up for a weeklong tour that takes them to Beijing, Datong, Taiyuan, and Pingyao for just $1,165 dollars per person.[23] My husband and I were offered an English-language map of the main Pingyao sites when we arrived at the city, and we noticed a few other European or American tourists exploring the town that day. Since the famine drama was performed only in Chinese, the content of the dialogue would remain a mystery to most foreign tour groups. The fact that the sign at the entrance to the City God Temple advertises the play in English as well as in Chinese, however, demonstrates that the entrepreneurial officials in charge of transforming Pingyao into a major tourist destination hope to attract foreign as well as Chinese tourists. Indeed, the gorgeous costumes, beating of the gong, kowtowing, fervent prayers to Heaven, and surprise showering of the crowd with water at the play's end offer plenty of entertainment even for non–Chinese speakers. The play exemplifies how China's economic growth and rising pre-eminence on the world stage—made real to many Chinese by Beijing's successful bid to host the 2008 Olympics—have made it easier for people to view China's imperial past with pride instead of humiliation. The actor who plays Wang Zhiping portrays a late-Qing magistrate as someone today's local officials should learn from. Moreover, the play in its entirety encourages both Chinese and foreign tourists to learn about popular religious traditions, such as worshipping the City God or calling down rain with a willow branch, rather than dismissing them as "feudal superstition."

A key thread throughout this book has been recognizing and analyzing the tears and laments of different observers who tried to make sense of the Incredible Famine, particularly the varied and complex array of Chinese voices. The famine continues to have power, albeit in a rapidly transforming economic and political context. Multiple meanings of the catastrophe coexist in twenty-first-century Shanxi, both in the famine folktales told by elderly villagers and in the Pingyao play performed for tourists. The successes China has enjoyed over the past two and a half decades, however, have allowed the specter of mass starvation to recede far enough into the past that the Pingyao opera troupe can now perform a drama about the famine that aims to entertain rather than warn, and that ends in laughter and applause rather than tears.

Glossary of
Chinese Characters

This glossary is selective rather than comprehensive. It includes the names, places, and phrases most pertinent to this work.

ANYI 安邑

BAO TING 寶廷
BAO YUANSHEN 鮑源深
BU GU CHI 不顧恥

CHAIYAO 差徭
CHANGPING CANG 常平倉
CHENGHUANG MIAO 城隍廟
CHI REN ROU 吃人肉
CHOUBAN GE SHENG HUANGZHENG AN 籌辦各省荒政案
CHOUZHEN GONGSUO 籌賑公所
CIPIN 次貧
CIXI 慈禧

DAOTAI 道台
DINGCHOU (1877) 丁丑
DINGWU QIHUANG 丁戊奇荒

ERSHISI XIAO 二十四孝

FANGPIAN 坊片
FEN HE 汾河

FUHU 富戶
FUQIANG 富强

GENG SAN YU YI GENG JIU YU SAN 耕三餘一 耕九餘三
GUANGXU CHAO DONGHUALU 光緒朝東華錄
GUANGXU SANNIAN NIANJING LU 光緒三年 年景錄
GUANGXU SANNIAN REN CHI REN QUAN CHI QUAN 光緒三年人吃人犬吃犬
GUGUAN 故關
GUI 貴
GUIHUA 歸化
GUOJU MAIER TIAN CIJIN 郭巨埋兒天賜金

HANLIN YUAN 翰林院
HEDONG YAN 河東鹽
HEJIN XIAN 河津縣
HENAN QIHUANG TIELEITU 河南奇荒鐵淚圖
HONGDONG 洪洞
HUANG TIFANG 黃体芳
HUANGNIAN GE 荒年歌
HUBU 戶部

JIAN 賤
JIANGNAN 江南
JIE GUANSHI XIE SICHOU 借官事挾私仇
JIN 斤
JINDAI MINGREN XIAOZHUAN 近代名人小傳
JING YUANSHAN 經元善
JINGBAO 京報
JINSHI 進士
JINYOU RIJI 晉游日記
JIPIN 極貧
JISHAN 稷山
JUREN 舉人
JUYI CHUJI 居易初集

KUANGREN RIJI 狂人日記

LI HONGZHANG 李鴻章
LI QING'AO 李慶翱
LI SUI 李燧
LI XIUDE 李修德
LIANG PEICAI 梁培才
LIENÜ 烈女
LIJIN 釐金
LINFEN 臨汾
LINYI 臨猗

LIU XING 劉姓 (荒年歌)
LU XUN 魯迅

MA PIYAO 馬丕瑤
MILIANG WEN 米糧文

NÜHUO 女禍

OUYANG YUN 歐陽雲

PAN SHAOAN 潘少安
PINGTIAO 平糶
PINGYANG FU 平陽府
PINGYAO 平遙
PUZHOU FU 蒲州府

QI YU JIN ZHI ZHENJUAN ZHENGXIN LU 齊豫晉直賑捐徵信錄
QIAN XINBO 錢昕伯
QING 頃
QINGJIANG 清江
QINGLIU 清流
QINGSHIDUO 清詩鐸
QINGYI 清議
QINJIAN QINLI QINWEN 親見 親歷 親聞
QINYUAN 沁源
QUWO 曲沃

REN XIANG SHI 人相食
REN XIANG SHI, SHEN YOU GUROU XIANGCAN ZHE 人相食, 甚有骨肉相殘者
RENHUO 人禍
RUICHENG 芮城

SANNIAN KUNNAN SHIQI 三年困難時期
SHANSHU 善書
SHANTANG 善堂
SHANXI PIAOHAO 山西票號
SHECANG 社倉
SHENBAO 申報
SHENG 升
SHENG XUANHUAI 盛宣懷
SHENGYUAN 生員
SHI 石
SI SHENG GAO ZAI TU QI 四省告災圖啟
SONG JUN (SONG SHANSHI) 宋俊 (宋珊室)

TAIPING 太平
TAIYUAN 太原

TAOHUAWU GONGSUO　桃花塢公所
TIANZAI　天災
TONGGUAN　潼關

WANG SHOUZHENG　汪守正
WANG TAO　王韜
WANG XILUN　王錫綸
WANG ZHIPING　汪之平
WEI HE　渭河
WEIYUAN　委員
WEN ZHONGHAN　溫忠翰
WENSHI ZILIAO　文史資料
WENYI　瘟疫
WU XIAN　吳縣
WUGU　五穀
WUJIANG　吳江

XIA TONGSHAN　夏同善
XIA XIAN　夏縣
XIAN TAIYE BAI CHENGHUANG　縣太爺拜城隍
XIANGFEN　襄汾
XIANGYI　祥異
XIAOYI　孝義
XIE JIAFU　謝家福
XIE XIAN　解縣
XIEZHOU　解州
XIFA　西法
XIUCAI　秀才
XUN HUAN ZHI LI　循環之理

YAMEN　衙門
YAN CHI　鹽池
YAN JINGMING　閻敬銘
YANGMIN　養民
YANLUO WANG　閻羅王
YANTA　雁塔
YAPIAN　鴉片
YICANG　義倉
YICHENG　翼城
YINGSU　罌粟
YIQINGTANG WENJI　怡青堂文集
YISHI　猗氏
YITAN　臆譚
YIWEN　藝文
YIZI ER SHI　易子而食
YONGHE　永和
YONGJI　永濟

YUANQU 垣曲
YUNCHENG 運城
YUNCHENG ZAIYI LU 運城災異錄
YUXING RIJI 豫行日記

ZAIZHEN 災賑
ZAOHUANG 遭荒
ZENG GUOQUAN 曾國荃
ZENG ZHONGXIANG GONG (GUOQUAN) ZOUYI 曾忠襄公(國荃)奏議
ZHANG GUANZHUN 張觀準
ZHANG SAN 張三
ZHANG ZHIDONG 張之洞
ZHENG GUANYING 鄭觀應
ZHONG MIN MING SHOU MIN XIN 重民命收民心
ZHONGDENG JIA 中等家
ZHOUCHANG 粥廠
ZHU SHOUPENG 朱壽朋
ZIQIANG 自强
ZONGLI YAMEN 總理衙門
ZUO ZONGTANG 左宗棠

Notes

INTRODUCTION

"Si sheng gao zai tu qi," shou juan (Pictures reporting the disaster in the four provinces, opening volume), in *Qi Yu Jin Zhi zhenjuan zhengxin lu* (Statement of accounts for relief contributions for Shandong, Henan, Shanxi, and Zhili) (n.p., 1881), 4b, 26b.

1. "Report of R. J. Forrest, Esq., H.B.M. Consul at Tien-tsin, and Chairman of the Famine Relief Committee at Tien-tsin," *China's Millions* (November 1879): 139; Peking United International Famine Relief Committee, *The North China Famine of 1920–1921, with Special Reference to the West Chili Area* (1922; repr., Taipei: Ch'eng-wen Publishing Company, 1971), 9; Susan Cotts Watkins and Jane Menken, "Famines in Historical Perspective," *Population and Development Review* 11.4 (1985): 650.

2. Liu Rentuan, "'Dingwu qihuang' dui Shanxi renkou de yingxiang" (The influence of the "Incredible Famine of 1877–78" on Shanxi's population), in *Ziran zaihai yu Zhongguo shehui lishi jiegou* (Natural disasters and social structure in Chinese history), ed. Institute of Chinese Historical Geography, Fudan University (Shanghai: Fudan daxue chuban she, 2001), 122–23.

3. The *Dingwu* phrase refers to the imperial reign dates for 1877 and 1878. *Qihuang* could also be translated as "anomalously severe famine" or "terrible famine." The phrase *Guangxu sannian* refers to 1877, the third year of the Guangxu emperor's reign.

4. Mike Davis, *Late Victorian Holocausts: El Niño Famines and the Making of the Third World* (London: Verso Press, 2001), 6–7, 61–62. Estimates for population losses resulting from the drought-famines of the late 1870s range from

9 to 13 million people in China, 6 to 10 million in India, and 500,000 to 1 million in Brazil.

5. "An Essay Discussing *Henan qihuang tielei tu*," *Shenbao,* 15 March 1878, 1. The *Shenbao* credited Xie Jiafu (also referred to as Xie Suizi) and Tian Zilin with designing and printing the collection. Xie and Tian were based in Suzhou, a wealthy city roughly one hundred kilometers west of Shanghai.

6. Committee of the China Relief Fund, *The Famine in China: Illustrations by a Native Artist with a Translation of the Chinese Text,* trans. James Legge (London: C. Kegan Paul & Co., 1878), 9.

7. Paul R. Greenough, "Comments from a South Asian Perspective: Food, Famine, and the Chinese State," *Journal of Asian Studies* 41.4 (August 1982): 792.

8. The Jiangnan (literally "south of the Yangzi River") region includes much of Jiangsu, Zhejiang, and Anhui provinces, and was the most prosperous and urbanized area of China during the late imperial period. See Linda Cooke Johnson, ed., *Cities of Jiangnan in Late Imperial China* (Albany: State University of New York Press, 1993), preface, 116, 189.

9. Paul Richard Bohr, *Famine in China and the Missionary: Timothy Richard as Relief Administrator and Advocate of National Reform, 1876–1884* (Cambridge, MA: Harvard University Press, 1972); He Hanwei, *Guangxu chunian (1876–79) Huabei de da hanzai* (The great Huabei region drought disaster of the early Guangxu period) (Hong Kong: Zhongwen daxue chubanshe, 1980). For more recent work on this famine, see Li Wenhai et al., "Dingwu qihuang," in *Zhongguo jindai shi da zaihuang* (The ten great disasters of Modern China) (Shanghai: Shanghai renmin chubanshe, 1994); Andrea Janku, "Sowing Happiness: Spiritual Competition in Famine Relief Activities in Late Nineteenth-Century China," *Minsu Quyi* 143 (March 2004): 89–118; and Janku, "The North-China Famine of 1876–1879: Performance and Impact of a Non-event," in *Measuring Historical Heat: Event, Performance, and Impact in China and the West* (Symposium in Honor of Rudolf G. Wagner on His 60th Birthday) (Heidelberg, 3–4 November 2001), www.sino.uni-heidelberg.de/conf/symposium2.pdf.

10. Penny Kane, *Famine in China, 1959–1961: Demographic and Social Implications* (London: Macmillan Press, 1988), chapters 5 and 6.

11. Interview with Wang Shoubang; retired head of the Yangcheng Gazetteer Office in Jincheng Region, Jinnan, 7 April 2001; interview with Liu Chunshu, retired *Wenshi ziliao* editor in Xiangfen county, Linfen Region, 26 March 2001. Wang Shoubang was one of five local historians sent out by the Yangcheng Gazetteer Office from 1960 to 1965 to collect stele inscriptions. The compilation that resulted from the work of local historians is titled *Guangxu sannian nianjing lu* (Annual record of the third year of the Guangxu reign) (Taiyuan: Shanxi sheng remin weiyuanhui bangong ting), 1961.

The 1959–61 famine is now termed "The Great Famine" (*da ji'e* or *da jihuang*), but the people I interviewed still referred to it as the "three difficult years." For more on PRC historiography of the 1959–61 famine, see Susanne Weigelin-Schwiedrzik, "Trauma and Memory: The Case of the Great Famine in the People's Republic of China (1959–1961)," *Historiography East & West* 1.1 (2003): 38–67.

12. Interview with Wang Xinsen, editor of *Hongdong wenshi ziliao,* Hongdong County, Linfen Region, 28 March 2001.

13. Xia Mingfang, "Cong Qingmo zaihai qun faqi kan Zhongguo zaoqi xiandaihua de lishi tiaojian: zaihuang yu Yangwu Yundong yanjiu zhiyi" (The historical conditions of early Chinese modernization as seen from a cluster of natural disasters in the late Qing: Part I of research on disasters and the Westernization Movement) *Qingshi yanjiu* 1 (1998): 70. See also Xia Mingfang, "Zhongguo zaoqi gongyehua jieduan yuanshi jilei guocheng de zaihai shi fenxi" (An analysis of the impact of natural disasters on primitive accumulation during the early stages of industrialization in China), *Qingshi yanjiu* 1 (1999): 62–81.

14. Zhang Kemin, ed., "Zhongguo jindai zaihuang yu shehui wending" (Disasters in modern China and social stability), in *Zhongwai lishi wenti ba ren tan* (An eight-person discussion of questions in Chinese and foreign history) (Beijing: Guojia jiaowei gaojiao shehui kexue fazhang yanjiu zhongxin, 1998), 158.

15. For discussions of famines and famine-relief policies in Qing China, see Pierre-Étienne Will, *Bureaucracy and Famine in Eighteenth-Century China*, trans. Elborg Forster (Stanford, CA: Stanford University Press, 1990); Pierre Étienne Will and R. Bin Wong, with James Lee (contributions by Jean Oi and Peter Perdue), *Nourish the People: The State Civilian Granary System in China, 1650–1850* (Ann Arbor: Center for Chinese Studies, 1991); Lillian Li, *Fighting Famine in North China: State, Market, and Environmental Decline, 1690s–1990s* (Stanford, CA: Stanford University Press, 2007); Li Wenhai, *Jindai Zhongguo zaihuang jinian* (Hunan jiaoyu chubanshe, 1990).

16. John Killen, ed., *The Famine Decade: Contemporary Accounts, 1841–1851* (Belfast: Blackstaff Press, 1995), 1–2; Cormac Ó Gráda, *Black '47 and Beyond: The Great Irish Famine in History, Economy, and Memory* (Princeton: Princeton University Press, 2000), 4, 38–41. Roughly one million people, or almost one-eighth of Ireland's population, died of famine-related diseases and starvation during the famine, and well over a million people emigrated. Public commemorations and popular accounts define the famine as beginning in 1845, when the first potato blight hit, and ending in 1849. Historians, in contrast, often date the beginning of the famine from 1846, when famine-induced deaths began in earnest, and argue that the impact of the famine lasted well into 1851.

17. Colm Tóibín and Diarmaid Ferriter, *The Irish Famine: A Documentary* (London: Profile Books, 2001), 7–11, 30–36; Tom Hayden, ed. *Irish Hunger: Personal Reflections on the Legacy of the Famine* (Boulder, CO: Roberts Rinehart, 1997), 11–16; James S. Donnelly Jr., "The Construction of the Memory of the Famine in Ireland and the Irish Diaspora, 1850–1900," *Eire-Ireland* 31: 1–2 (Spring–Summer 1996): 27.

18. Margaret Kelleher, *The Feminization of Famine: Expressions of the Inexpressible?* (Cork: Cork University Press, 1997); Ó Gráda, *Black '47 and Beyond;* Peter Gray, "Ideology and Famine," in *The Great Irish Famine*, ed. Cathal Poirteir (Dublin: Mercier Press, 1995); Christopher Morash, *The Hungry Voice: The Poetry of the Irish Famine* (Dublin: Irish Academic Press, 1989).

19. Scott Brewster and Virginia Crossman, "Re-writing the Famine: Witnessing in Crisis," in *Ireland in Proximity: History, Gender, Space*, ed. Scott Brewster et al. (New York: Routledge, 1999), 42–58.

20. Liu Xing, "Huangnian ge," in *Yuncheng zaiyi lu* (Record of disasters in Yuncheng), comp. Zhang Bowen and Wang Mancang (Yuncheng: Yuncheng

shizhi ban, 1986), 111; Nan Xianghai's manuscript version, 24. See chapter 2 for an introduction to this source.

21. Mary Daly, "Revisionism and Irish History: The Great Famine," in *The Making of Modern Irish History*, ed. D. George Boyce and Alan O'Day (London: Routledge, 1996), 86.

22. Interview with Tan Ruhua, age eighty-five, 5 April 2001, Shangzhuang Village, Yuanqu County, Shanxi. Mrs. Tan heard this famine folktale and several others from her maternal grandmother, whose husband lived through the famine.

23. Nancy Scheper-Hughes, *Death without Weeping: The Violence of Everyday Life in Brazil* (Berkeley and Los Angeles: University of California Press, 1992).

24. "Chouban ge sheng huangzheng an" (Proposals for preparing famine relief policies for each province), in *Guojia tushuguan cang Qingdai guben neige liubu dangan*, comp. Sun Xuelei and Liu Jiaping (Beijing: Quanguo tushuguan wenxian suowei fuzhi zhongxin, 2003), 38: 18455–963.

25. Arthur and Joan Kleinman, "The Appeal of Experience, the Dismay of Images: Cultural Appropriations of Suffering in Our Times," *Daedalus* 125.1 (1996): 1–24.

1. SHANXI, GREATER CHINA, AND THE FAMINE

1. Alexander Williamson, *Journeys in North China, Manchuria, and Eastern Mongolia; with Some Account of Corea*, vol. 1 (London: Smith, Elder & Co., 1870); Li Sui, *Jinyou riji* (Diary of travels in Shanxi), ed. Huang Jianhui (Taiyuan: Shanxi renmin chubanshe, 1989).

2. Bohr, *Famine in China*, 16; Williamson, *Journeys in North China*, 151–53, 346–50; Barbara Sands, "An Investigation into the Nature and Extent of the Market in Shanxi Province, China: 1928–1945" (PhD diss., University of Washington, 1985), 24; Cao Xinyu, "Qingdai Shanxi de liangshi fanyun luxian" (Routes for the sale of grain in Qing dynasty Shanxi), *Zhongguo lishi dili luncong* 2 (1998): 160.

3. Li Sui, *Jinyou riji*, 13, 20.

4. Williamson, *Journeys in North China*, 250–52, 271–77, 279–302.

5. "Report of R. J. Forrest," 135–36.

6. Li Sui, *Jinyou riji*, 61. A *chih* is one-third of a meter in length.

7. Williamson, *Journeys in North China*, 152–55.

8. Ibid., 65, 18–19.

9. Ibid., 17, 70.

10. Williamson, *Journeys in North China*, 308–10.

11. Ibid., 160–61, 346–50.

12. Li Sui, *Jinyou riji*, 69, 79. According to the editor's notes, the first *zhangju* (accounting office) of this type was established in 1736 by a wealthy merchant from Shanxi's Fenyang County.

13. Ibid., 70.

14. Lianag Peicai, "Shanxi miliang wen" (A Shanxi essay on grain), *Guangxu sannian nianjing lu* (Shanxi sheng renmin weiyuanhui bangong ting, 1961), 78–79.

15. Ibid., 70.

16. Li Fubin, "Qingdai zhonghouqi Zhili Shanxi chuantong nongyequ ken-zhi shulun" (An account of land reclamation in the traditional agricultural areas of Zhili and Shanxi during the mid- and late Qing), *Zhongguo lishi dili luncong* 2 (1994): 153.

17. Henrietta Harrison, *The Man Awakened from Dreams: One Man's Life in a North China Village, 1857–1942* (Stanford: Stanford University Press, 2005), 21–23; Williamson, 152–60, 340–49.

18. Harrison, *Man Awakened*, 22–23; Joseph Fletcher, "Ch'ing Inner Asia c. 1800," in *The Cambridge History of China*, vol. 10., ed. Denis Twitchett and John K. Fairbank (Cambridge: Cambridge University Press, 1978), 56.

19. Zhang Zhengming, *Jinshang xingshuai shi* (A history of the rise and fall of the Shanxi merchants) (Taiyuan: Shanxi guji chubanshe, 1995), 17–29, 64–83.

20. Andrea McElderry, "Guarantors and Guarantees in Qing Government-Business Relations," in *To Achieve Security and Wealth: The Qing Imperial State and the Economy, 1644–1911*, eds. Jane Kate Leonard and John R. Watt (Ithaca, NY: East Asia Program, Cornell University, 1992), 129–30.

21. Harrison, *Man Awakened*, 42–43; Huang Jianhui, *Shanxi piaohao shi* (A history of the Shanxi banks) (Taiyuan: Shanxi jingji chubanshe, 1992), 139–54, 166–70, 182–88.

22. Interview with Chai Fengju, age seventy, 25 March 2001, Dingcun Village, Xiangfen County, Linfen Area. Mrs. Chai heard this famine folktale and several others from her grandmother and mother.

23. "Report of R. J. Forrest," 136–37.

24. *Shenbao*, 1 January 1878 and 12 January 1878.

25. Li Wenhai, *Jindai Zhongguo zaihuang jinian*, 364; Liu Fengxiang "Qianxi 'Dingwu qihuang' de yuanyin" (A brief analysis of the causes of the 'Incredible Famine of 1877–78"), *Jining shizhuan xuebao* 4 (2000): 1.

26. Bohr, *Famine in China*, 16–18; Davis, *Late Victorian Holocausts*, 71.

27. Sands, "Market in Shanxi Province," 27.

28. Harrison, *Man Awakened*, 6–7, 95–96. See also Kenneth Pomeranz, *The Making of a Hinterland: State, Society, and Economy in Inland North China, 1853–1937* (Berkeley: University of California Press, 1993), 1–4.

29. H. M. Morse, *The International Relations of the Chinese Empire*, vol. 2 (London: Longmans, Green, and Co., 1918), 312. For a detailed account of types and amounts of relief money and grain that the central government and non-stricken provinces sent to each of the five famine provinces, see He Hanwei, *Guangxu chunian*, chapter 4.

30. Bohr, *Famine in China*, 22–26; He Hanwei, *Guangxu chunian*, 81, 137–39.

31. Li Wenhai, Cheng Xiao, Liu Yangdong, and Xia Mingfang, "Dingwu qi-huang," in *Zhongguo jindai shi da zaihuang* (The ten great famines of China's modern period) (Shanghai: Shanghai renmin chubanshe, 1994), 102–3; He Hanwei, *Guangxu chunian*, 139–40.

32. Li Wenhai et al., "Dingwu qihuang," 104. For a vivid example of the im-pact that the famine had on the paper-making industry of one Shanxi village, see Harrison, *Man Awakened*, 29–30.

33. He Hanwei, *Guangxu chunian*, 122, 139–41.

34. "Report of R. J. Forrest," 139; Peking United International Famine Relief Committee, *The North China Famine of 1920-1921*, 9; Andrew Nathan, *A History of the China International Famine Relief Commission* (Cambridge, MA: Harvard University Press, 1965), 3; Walter H. Mallory, *China: Land of Famine* (New York: American Geographical Society, 1926), 29; Bohr, *Famine in China*, 113; Watkins and Menken, "Famines in Historical Perspective," 650–51.

35. He Hanwei, *Guangxu chunian*, 123–28.

36. Zeng Guoquan, *Zeng Zhongxiang gong (Guoquan) shuzha* (Zeng Guoquan's correspondence), comp. Xiao Rongjue (1903), 11: 32b. For a chart listing several different estimates of population loss, see He Hanwei, *Guangxu chunian*, 122.

37. "Huangzheng ji" (Record of relief policies), in *Shanxi tongzhi* (Gazetteer of Shanxi Province), comp. Zeng Guoquan, Wang Xuan, et al. (1892), 82: 21b. Neither the *Shanxi tongzhi* nor Zeng's collected works details famine demography. For a discussion of Zeng Guoquan's motives for ordering the compilation of a new provincial gazetteer shortly after the famine, see Andrea Janku, "Integrating the Body Politic: Official Perspectives on the Administration of Relief during the 'Great North-China Famine,'" paper presented at the Association for Asian Studies Annual Meeting, March 4–7, 2004, San Diego.

38. "Report of R. J. Forrest," 134, 139.

39. Liu Rentuan, "'Dingwu qihuang,'" 122–23. Determining famine mortality rates during the North China Famine is difficult. Liu Rentuan, noting that earlier foreign and Chinese estimates were based on little hard evidence, attempts to rectify this problem by relying on the population and land tax sections of Shanxi's local gazetteers to estimate population loss in each of Shanxi's prefectures during the famine. Because the population registers in late-nineteenth-century gazetteers are unreliable, Liu uses the more accurate Qianlong-era (late-eighteenth-century) registers to establish a base population figure for each prefecture. He then estimates average annual population increases between the 1820s and the 1870s to achieve prefamine estimates (91–132). For more on the lack of precise data about the demographic effects of famines in imperial China, see Lillian Li, "Life and Death in a Chinese Famine: Infanticide as a Demographic Consequence of the 1935 Yellow River Flood," *Comparative Studies in Society and History* 33.3 (July 1991), 467–68.

40. Liu Rentuan, "'Dingwu qihuang,'" 122, 128, 130–31.

41. Xia Mingfang, "Cong Qingmo zaihaiqun faqi kan Zhongguo zaoqi xiandaihua de lishi tiaojian," 70–80; Xia Mingfang, "Zhongguo zaoqi gongyehua jieduan yuanshi jilei guocheng de zaihai shi fenxi," 62–77.

42. Davis, 291.

43. Amartya Sen, *Poverty and Famines: An Essay on Entitlement and Deprivation* (Oxford: Clarendon Press, 1981), 123; Will; Will and Wong.

44. William Rowe, *Saving the World: Chen Hongmou and Elite Consciousness in Eighteenth-Century China* (Stanford: Stanford University Press, 2001), 158.

45. Will and Wong, 8–10, 300–307; Will, 182–88.

46. Will, 32, 276–77. For additional examples of large high-Qing relief operations, see Will, 298–99.

47. Ibid., 169–72. See also Davis, 280–85.

48. Cao Xinyu, "Qingdai Shanxi de liangshi fanyun luxian" (Routes for the sale of grain in Qing-dynasty Shanxi), *Zhongguo lishi dili luncong* 2 (1998): 160; Will and Wong, 300–301. The three transportation nodes where grain reserves were held during the eighteenth century were located along the Yellow River at Shanzhou in Henan, just across the Yellow River from Shanxi's Pinglu County; near the Shanxi-Shaanxi border at Puzhou in southwestern Shanxi; and near the Shanxi-Shaanxi border at Tongguan in Shaanxi.

49. Cao, 161–64.

50. Ibid., 161.

51. Ibid., 162–64; Helen Dunstan, *Conflicting Counsels to Confuse the Age: A Documentary Study of Political Economy in Qing China, 1644–1840* (Ann Arbor: Center for Chinese Studies, 1996), 27–29, 48–56. The Guihua Cheng-Tuoketuo region had been part of southern Inner Mongolia, but in Qing times it was administratively incorporated into Shanxi Province. The Hetao region was the fertile agricultural area found along the great bend of the Yellow River in northern Shaanxi and southern Suiyuan.

52. Cao, 164–65.

53. Will, 290–93; Davis, 366–71.

54. Pao Chao Hsieh, *The Government of China, 1644–1911* (Baltimore: Johns Hopkins University Press, 1925), 205–6, 214; Philip A. Kuhn, "The Taiping Rebellion," in *Cambridge History of China*, 10: 264–316.

55. R. Bin Wong, "Food Riots in the Qing Dynasty," *Journal of Asian Studies* 41.4 (1982): 783.

56. Will and Wong, *Nourish the People,* 89–91.

57. Davis, *Late Victorian Holocausts,* 357.

58. Kwang-Ching Liu, "The Ch'ing Restoration," in *Cambridge History of China,* 10: 458–76; Williamson, *Journeys in North China,* 336–39.

59. Li Wenhai et al., *Zhongguo jindai,* 107–8.

60. He Hanwei, *Guangxu chunian,* 7–8.

61. Ibid., 7.

62. Joseph Fletcher, "The Heyday of the Ch'ing Order in Mongolia, Sinkiang and Tibet," in *Cambridge History of China,* 10: 347–50; Harrison, *Man Awakened,* 22, 42; Zhang Zhengming, *Jinshang xingshuai shi,* 79–83.

63. Will, *Bureaucracy and Famine,* 85–86.

64. The Qing throne was occupied mainly by child emperors after the Xianfeng emperor's death in 1861. In the 1860s and 1870s two dowager empresses, the Xianfeng emperor's wife Ci'an (1837–81) and his concubine and the mother of the Tongzhi emperor, Cixi (1835–1908), acted as joint regents for the Tongzhi and Guangxu child emperors. Cixi was the more powerful of the two regents.

65. William Ayers, *Chang Chi-tung and Educational Reform in China* (Cambridge, MA: Harvard University Press, 1971), 70–72; Mary Rankin, "'Public Opinion' and Political Power: *Qingyi* in Late Nineteenth Century China," *Journal of Asian Studies* 41.3 (May 1982): 463; Arthur Hummel, ed., *Eminent Chinese of the Ch'ing Period* (Taipei: SMC Publishing, 1991), 1: 295–97.

66. Richard Horowitz, "Central Power and State-Making: The Zongli Yamen

and Self-Strengthening in China, 1860–1880" (Ph.D. diss., Harvard University, 1998), 105–6.

67. Beatrice S. Bartlett, *Monarchs and Ministers: The Grand Council in Mid-Ch'ing China, 1723–1820* (Berkeley: University of California Press, 1991), 278.

68. Horowitz, 35, 57, 76, 107–9.

69. J. O. P. Bland and E. Backhouse, *China under the Empress Dowager: Being the History of the Life and Times of Tzu Hsi* (London: Heinemann, 1911), 121–27.

70. Lolan Wang Grady, "The Career of I-hsin, Prince Kung, 1858–1880: A Case-Study of the Limits of Reform in the Late Ch'ing" (PhD diss., University of Toronto, 1980), 349.

71. Ibid., 347.

72. Horowitz, "Central Power and State-Making," 195–200, 114.

73. For a discussion of the psychological impact of the burning of the Summer Palace, see Vera Schwarcz, "Circling the Void: Memory in the Life and Poetry of the Manchu Prince Yihuan (1840–1891)," *History & Memory* 16.2 (Fall/Winter 2004): 44–45.

74. Jonathan D. Spence, *The Search for Modern China* (New York: W. W. Norton, 1990), 203–4.

75. Paul A. Cohen, *China and Christianity: The Missionary Movement and the Growth of Chinese Antiforeignism, 1860–1870* (Cambridge, MA: Harvard University Press, 1963), 229–39, 246. Of the 492,000 taels paid in indemnities and reparations, 460,000 went to France, 30,000 to Russia, and 2,500 to Britain.

76. Kwang-Ching Liu and Richard Smith, "The Military Challenge: The North-West and the Coast," in *The Cambridge History of China*, ed. Denis Twitchett and John K. Fairbank, vol. 11, *Late Ch'ing, 1800–1911, Part 2*, ed. John K. Fairbank and Kwang-Ching Liu (Cambridge: Cambridge University Press, 1980), 221–25, 235; Immanuel C. Y. Hsu, "The Great Policy Debate in China, 1874: Maritime Defense vs. Frontier Defense," *Harvard Journal of Asiatic Studies* 25 (1964–65), 220–23; Wen-Djang Chu, *The Moslem Rebellion in Northwest China, 1862–1878* (Paris: Mouton, 1966), chapter 5. For a detailed examination of the Qing conquest of Xinjiang and Mongolia and a discussion of the profound global, regional, and national implications of that conquest, see Peter C. Perdue, *China Marches West: The Qing Conquest of Central Eurasia* (Cambridge, MA: Belknap Press of Harvard University Press, 2005).

77. David Pong, *Shen Pao-chen and China's Modernization in the Nineteenth Century* (New York: Cambridge University Press, 1994), 291–93; Immanuel C. Y. Hsu, *China's Entrance into the Family of Nations: The Diplomatic Phase, 1858–1880* (Cambridge, MA: Harvard University Press, 1960), 172–74; Horowitz, 307–10.

78. Horowitz, "Central Power and State-Making," 311–12; Hsu, "The Great Policy Debate," 213.

79. Kwang-Ching Liu, "Li Hung-chang in Chili: The Emergence of a Policy, 1870–1875," in *Li Hung-chang and China's Early Modernization*, ed. Samuel Chu and Kwang-Ching Liu (Armonk, NY: M. E. Sharpe, 1994), 64.

80. Hsu, "The Great Policy Debate," 216–17. For a full account of Li's proposals, see Kwang-Ching Liu, 64–72.

81. Hsu, "The Great Policy Debate," 219–23.

82. Horowitz, "Central Power and State-Making," 333–34; Hsu, "The Great Policy Debate," 225–27.

83. See examples in chapter 4.

84. Liu and Smith, "The Military Challenge," 238–39.

85. *Shanxi tongzhi,* 82: 18b–19a. The gazetteer states that 3,402,833 people in Shanxi received relief between 1877 and 1879 and that a total of 10,700,315 taels of relief silver and 1,001,657 shi of relief grain were distributed in the province. Of the total amount of money distributed, the Board of Revenue gave 70,000 taels and the Department of the Imperial Household gave 20,000 taels of direct aid. Loans from other provinces were also crucial.

86. Pomeranz, *Making of a Hinterland,* 2–3, 273.

87. R. Bin Wong, *China Transformed: Historical Change and the Limits of European Experience* (Ithaca: Cornell University Press, 1997), 155; Perdue, *China Marches West,* introduction and part 5.

88. The debate over whether the Xinjiang campaign or coastal defense was more urgent occurred in late 1874 and 1875, shortly before the drought in North China began. The Xinjiang campaign was already under way by the time the famine became a major crisis, and it would have been difficult to cancel it at that point. An interesting question is whether the policy debate might have ended differently had the famine struck before or during the debate rather than after it.

89. Davis, *Late Victorian Holocausts,* 6, 13–14, 61–62, 213–17, 230–38, 256–59. The grand El Niño event of 1876–78 disrupted the entire tropical monsoon belt, as well as the East Asian and Arabian monsoons, which provide rainfall for North China and North Africa. Davis draws many of his conclusions from the work of meteorologist Jacob Bjerknes. For more on monsoon systems outside Asia, see Alice M. Grimm, "The El Niño Impact on the Summer Monsoon in Brazil: Regional Processes versus Remote Influences," *Journal of Climate* 16.2 (January 2003): 263.

90. Will, *Bureaucracy and Famine,* 25–26.

91. Bohr, *Famine in China,* 36–47.

92. Li Wenhai, *Jindai Zhongguo,* 347–65.

2. EXPERIENCING THE FAMINE

1. The term "song" or "poem" describes the genre of this text appropriately. It is written in a rhythmic three-character, three-character, four-character pattern. A considerably edited version of this famine song was published in 1986 in a compilation titled *Yuncheng zaiyi lu* (Record of disasters in Yuncheng). The editors of the Yuncheng compilation state that the piece, titled *Huangnian ge,* was written in 1897 by a man called Liu Xing who lived in Xiezhou City.

I also rely on a more complete manuscript version of the famine song owned by Nan Xianghai. The published version includes an introduction and a conclusion that are missing from Nan Xianghai's manuscript copy, but Nan's copy includes several lengthy sections omitted by the Yuncheng editors. With the exception of a few minor discrepancies, the portions of Liu's song that are included in both copies are virtually identical. I thus cite the published text whenever possible, but rely on Nan's unpublished manuscript for several of the more intriguing and personal passages that were edited out of the published version.

Hereafter *Yuncheng zaiyi lu* refers to the published text (*Yuncheng zaiyi lu* [Record of disasters in Yuncheng], comp. Zhang Bowen and Wang Mancang, [Yuncheng shi, 1986]). "Nan" refers to Nan's manuscript. Both texts are cited when there are discrepancies between the two in a passage included in both.

2. Chinese provinces were divided into prefectures (*fu*), departments (*zhou*), and counties (*xian*). Prefectures were generally larger than departments, and both prefectures and departments contained several counties within their borders. The late-Qing Xie Department (Xiezhou) administered Xie, Pinglu, Anyi, Xia, and Ruicheng counties. Xiezhou City, where Liu lived, was the county seat of Xie County in Xie Department. In his study of the famine's long-term impact on Shanxi's demographics, Liu Rentuan estimates that Xie Department suffered a 68.6 percent population loss during the famine. Only about 300,000 people out of its prefamine population of 955,000 people remained after the disaster. (Liu Rentuan, 97.)

3. As Henrietta Harrison has demonstrated, members of the local elite often viewed the world somewhat differently than did metropolitan officials or members of the treaty-port elite. Henrietta Harrison, "Newspaper and Nationalism in Rural China, 1890–1929," *Past and Present*, no. 166 (February 2000): 183–87.

4. Interview with Nan Xianghai, age seventy-three, and Li Li, village leader, 3 April 2001, Gaotou Village, Linyi County. My thanks to Bi Yuan and Bi Xinxin for bringing me to their home village and introducing me to Nan Xianghai.

5. Li Sui, *Jinyou riji*, 71–72.

6. "Da qinji," in *Pinglu xian xuzhi* (1932; repr., Zhongguo fangzhi congshu 426, Taibei: Chengwen chubanshe, 1968), *ce* 4, *juan xia*, 84b–87a; *Xie xianzhi* (1920; repr., Zhongguo fangzhi congshu 84, Taibei: Chengwen chubanshe, 1968), maps.

7. *Yuncheng zaiyi lu*, 37–44, 105–17; Wang Yongnian and Jie Fuping, "Dingchou zhenhuang ji" (Record of famine relief in 1877), in *Yuncheng wenshi ziliao* (Yuncheng literary and historical materials) 2 (1988), 97–125.

8. Sands, "Market in Shanxi Province," 25; He Hanwei, *Guangxu chunian*, 6–9; Will, *Bureaucracy and Famine*, 25–26nn6–8.

9. Will, *Bureaucracy and Famine*, 25, note 6.

10. *Yuncheng zaiyi lu*, 105–6. Jujubes are datelike fruits of the buckthorn family.

11. Paul Cohen, *History in Three Keys: The Boxers as Event, Experience, and Myth* (New York: Columbia University Press, 1997), 72–73.

12. *Yuncheng zaiyi lu*, 107.

13. Ibid., 107–8.

14. Ibid. China has a rich tradition of identifying plants and other substances that can serve as food during famines. A classic example is the *Jiuhuang bencao*, a two-volume treatise compiled in the early fifteenth century by a Henan resident named Zhou Dingwang. The compilation identifies and describes a total of 414 different herbs, trees, cereals, fruits, and vegetables that can be eaten during a famine. (Bernard E. Read, *Famine Foods Listed in the Chiu Huang Ben Ts'ao* [1946; repr., Taipei: SMC Publishing, 1982], 2–3.

15. The published and unpublished manuscripts often list different numbers

when explaining the price of items during the famine. In this case, Nan Xiang-hai's documents says that one hundred *jin* of firewood sold for fifty *wen*, while the published accounts says ten *jin* of firewood sold for twenty copper cash. I am not sure how to account for these discrepancies. Either the original manuscripts were slightly different, or the modern editors adjusted the prices to make them easier for modern readers to grasp. Nan, 19–20; *Yuncheng zaiyi lu,* 108, 110.

16. *Yuncheng zaiyi lu,* 110–11.

17. Ibid., 111; Nan, 21–23.

18. *Yuncheng zaiyi lu,* 111–12. Much of this section is missing from Nan Xiang-hai's manuscript.

19. "Report of R. J. Forrest, 138. David Hill, an English missionary who distributed relief in Pingyang Prefecture (north of Xie Department) in 1878 and 1879, described in some detail the diseases that struck people weakened by famine. They suffered from a swelling or bloating of the face, diarrhea, constipation, continuous low fevers, and typhus or typhoid fever. Others perished from starvation rather than disease. They suffered "a gradual prostration and helplessness" that led to death, wrote Hill. (David Hill, "Lin Fen Hien Famine Notes," box 26, card 1141, David Hill Papers and Letters, Methodist Missionary Society collection, Library Archives, School of Oriental and African Studies [hereafter Hill Papers and Letters]).

20. *Yuncheng zaiyi lu,* 112; Nan, 25, 27.

21. *Yuncheng zaiyi lu,* 112.

22. Nan, 26. This section was edited out of the *Yuncheng zaiyi lu* version.

23. *Yuncheng zaiyi lu,* 112–13. Missionary relief workers also described these wolf attacks in detail. "I think I haven't mentioned to you the ravages which wolves have been making in this district during the last few months," wrote David Hill in a letter he wrote while distributing relief in Pingyang early in 1879. "In another village I was shown the stains on the ground made by the blood of a girl of seventeen that had been dragged out by a wolf on to the village square in the sight of one or more women, who dared not attack the brute but had to stand and watch the girl seized by the throat and devoured—all except the skull and one big bone," he continued. One night Hill even heard a hungry wolf "howling and prowling" outside the Buddhist temple where he and fellow relief workers lived. (W. T. A. Barber, *David Hill: Missionary and Saint* [London: Charles H. Kelly, 1898], 201–2).

24. *Yuncheng zaiyi lu,* 113. Nan's manuscript omits this conclusion, probably because much of the last page has decayed.

25. Ó Gráda, *Black '47 and Beyond,* 125, 156.

26. "Report of Walter Hillier, Esq., of H.M.B Consular Service" (submitted to the chairman of the China Famine Relief Committee in Shanghai), *North China Herald and Supreme Court and Consular Gazette,* 15 April 1879 (hereafter Hillier Report).

27. Nan, 1; *Yuncheng zaiyi lu,* 109, 113. Liu's Confucian definition of the four classes of society (scholars, farmers, artisans, and merchants) clearly differs from, and in fact cuts across, the modern sense of class that stems largely "from the study of the transition from feudalism to capitalism by means of an urban bourgeoisie who gradually won power." (Spence, *Search for Modern China,* 45).

28. Liang Peicai (Qing), "Shanxi miliang wen" (A Shanxi essay on grain), *Guangxu sannian nianjing lu* (Taiyuan: Shanxi sheng remin weiyuan hui bangong ting, 1961), 77, 80, 85. The editors of the 1961 volume provide a short introduction to "Shanxi miliang wen." According to Wang Xinsen, the director of the Hongdong County *wenshi ziliao* office, an ink-brush-copied version of Liang's extraordinary famine song was found at the home of Lan Wenyu in Dongguo cun, Wucun zhuang, in the Linfen area. It was copied down by the Southern Shanxi Work Team when it canvassed villages to collect and publish documents about the 1877 disaster during the 1959–61 famine. A shortened version of this song was reprinted in the *Yuanqu wenshi ziliao* 4 (1988), 150–60.

29. Cohen, *History in Three Keys*, 5–6.

30. Jun Jing, "Male Ancestors and Female Deities: Finding Memories of Trauma in a Chinese Village," in *Disturbing Remains: Memory, History, and Crisis in the Twentieth Century*, ed. Michael S. Roth and Charles G. Salas (Los Angeles: Getty Research Institute, 2001), 209–11.

31. Ibid. See also Weigelin-Schwiedrzik, "Trauma and Memory," 38–67.

32. Ronnie Janoff-Bulman, *Shattered Assumptions: Towards a New Psychology of Trauma* (New York: Free Press, 1992), 130.

33. Recent research demonstrates that excess mortality during the Irish Famine, as well as during Indian and Russian famines that predated the advent of modern medicine, was caused less by literal starvation than by infectious diseases such as typhoid, typhus, dysentery, diarrhea, and dropsy. Joel Mokyr and Cormac Ó Gráda, "Famine Disease and Famine Mortality: Lessons from the Irish Experience, 1845–50," in *Famine Demography: Perspectives from the Past and Present*, ed. Tim Dyson and Cormac Ó Gráda (Oxford: Oxford University Press, 2002), 20, 31, 37–40.

34. Liu Rentuan, "'Dingwu qihuang,'" 97, 106–7. Liu Rentuan estimates that Xie Department experienced a 68.6 percent population loss during the famine. He placed population losses in Liang Peicai's Pingyang Prefecture at 60 percent. Population loss varied considerably in this large prefecture's eleven departments and counties. Liu estimates that Liang's home county of Hongdong suffered a 35 percent loss, considerably lower than the prefecture's average.

35. *Guangxu chao Donghualu* (Guangxu reign period [1875–1908] records from the Eastern Gate), vol. 1, comp. Zhu Shoupeng (1909; repr., Beijing: Zhonghua shuju chuban, 1958), Guangxu 3, 12th month, 6th day (1/8/1878), 514–15.

36. Memorial translated and quoted in *China's Millions* (1879), 137.

37. Zeng Guoquan, *Zeng Zhongxiang gong (Guoquan) zouyi* (Zeng Guoquan's memorials), comp. Xiao Rongjue (1903; repr., *Jindai Zhongguo shiliao congkan* 44, Taipei: Wenhai chubanshe, 1969) (Guangxu 3, 12th month, 16th day), 694. For similar arguments offered by Yan Jingming, see *Guangxu chao Donghualu*, 514.

38. *China's Millions* (1878), 116.

39. Hillier Report.

40. Cormac Ó Gráda, "Famine, Trauma, and Memory," *Béaloideas* 69 (2001), 121–43. The phrase "hierarchy of suffering" is borrowed from Ó Gráda.

41. Sen, *Poverty and Famines*, 1.

42. Ibid., 1–7, 159; Amartya Sen, "Food, Economics, and Entitlements," in

The Political Economy of Hunger: Selected Essays, ed. Jean Dreze, Amartya Sen, and Athar Hussain (Oxford: Clarendon Press, 1995), 52–53. In the Bengal famine of 1943, the Ethiopian famine of 1973, and the Bangladesh famine of 1974, Sen found either no significant decline or even a small increase in food availability per head.

43. Amartya Sen, "Nobody Need Starve," *Granta* 52 (Winter 1995), 219–20.

44. David Arnold, *Famine: Social Crisis and Historical Change* (Oxford: Basil Blackwell, 1988), 45. For Sen's critique of the argument that transport difficulties were a cause of the Ethiopian famine of 1972–74, see Sen, *Poverty and Famines,* 93–96. On Ireland's "more than adequate" communications in the 1840s, see Ó Gráda, *Black '47 and Beyond,* 7, 137.

45. Sen, *Poverty and Famines,* 120, 70, 154.

46. *Yuncheng zaiyi lu,* 106; Nan, 1–2.

47. R. Bin Wong and Peter C. Perdue, "Famine's Foes in Ch'ing China," review of *Bureaucratie et Famine en Chine au 18c Siécle,* by Pierre-Étienne Will, *Harvard Journal of Asiatic Studies* 43.1 (1983): 297; Will, *Bureaucracy and Famine,* 34–36, 53–54.

48. Sen, *Poverty and Famines,* 50–51, 101.

49. *Yuncheng zaiyi lu,* 111; Nan, 21–22. In the late 1870s one tael (*liang*) of silver should have been worth between 1,275 and 1,500 copper coins (*wen*).

50. Nan, 22–23. This section was edited out of the published version.

51. "The Famine in the North," *North China Herald,* 31 January 1879.

52. Sen, *Poverty and Famines,* 50–51.

53. *Yuncheng zaiyi lu,* 109; Nan, 16.

54. David Hill, "Lin Fen Hien Famine Notes" and "Famine Notes Continued, Lin Fen Hien," box 26, card 1141, Hill Papers and Letters.

55. Hill, "Famine Notes"; "Shanxi miliang wen," in *Guangxu sannian nianjing lu,* 78–79. Ó Gráda's discussion of a similar chain of events in famine-stricken Ireland thirty years earlier more clearly explains why even pawnshops and other institutions that specialized in trading with the poor fared badly during disasters as severe as the Irish and Shanxi famines. In prefamine Ireland only about 2 percent of pawned items were forfeited, while by 1848 forfeitures were at about 30 percent. In 1845, in the early stages of the Irish famine, unredeemed goods easily sold at high prices at pawn office auctions. As the crisis worsened, more and more goods remained unredeemed, and the increasing destitution of the population most likely to buy pawned goods meant that pawnbrokers found it difficult to sell the excess goods. Pawnbrokers' premises were filled with clothing, bedding, tools, and other items they could not sell. By 1847 many pawnbrokers had stopped receiving most goods. Pawnbrokers thus experienced a sharp increase in business during the early stages of the famine, but as the proportion of pledges actually redeemed fell drastically, they faced default and responded by accepting fewer pledges and offering fewer loans. (Ó Gráda, *Black '47 and Beyond,* 149–54).

56. Harrison, *Man Awakened,* 28–31.

57. Nan, 13; *Yuncheng zaiyi lu,* 109. The first line quoted is only in Nan's version, but the rest of the account is in both texts.

58. *Yuncheng zaiyi lu,* 109; Nan, 13–14. The section about the local official's response to news of Zhang's actions is only in Nan's account.

59. *Yuncheng zaiyi lu,* 109; Nan, 13–14.

60. David Pillemer, *Momentous Events, Vivid Memories* (Cambridge, MA: Harvard University Press, 1998), 53, 137. According to the *Diagnostic and Statistical Manual of Mental Disorders,* 4th edition (DSM-IV), "Witnessing an event that involves death, injury, or a threat to the physical integrity of another person" is one of the experiences that can lead to post-traumatic stress disorder (DSM-IV, 1994, 424). Liu's general reticence to insert himself into the text or to write in the first person singular makes his description of Zhang San's death all the more unusual. Liu uses the personal pronoun *wo* four times in this short passage, and *yu,* another character for "I," three times.

61. Klaus Muhlhahn, "'Remembering a Bitter Past': The Trauma of China's Labor Camps, 1949–1978," *History & Memory* 16.2 (Fall–Winter 2004): 125.

62. In 1986 scholars from the Yuncheng City Gazetteer Office (Yuncheng shi zhi ban) published the *Yuncheng zaiyi lu,* a volume that records all the natural disasters that occurred in Yuncheng from ancient times through the 1980s. The compilation included several pieces relating to the Incredible Famine. The authors relied primarily on local gazetteers and dynastic histories to write their compilation, and they also drew on some unpublished manuscripts like Liu Xing's *Huangnian ge.* Then in 1988, the *Yuncheng wenshi ziliao* (Yuncheng literature and history materials) office published a twenty-eight-page page essay titled "Dingchou zhenhuang ji" (A record of famine relief in 1877). While the gazetteer office's publication relied on texts written during the Qing Dynasty for its discussion of the 1877 famine, the *wenshi ziliao* piece relies on contemporary famine folklore and literature as well as on local gazetteers.

63. Wang and Jie, "Dingchou zhenhuang ji." Wang Yongnian, a retired principle and novelist, said that his grandmother was born shortly after the famine and was deeply influenced by it. She and other villagers often told him famine stories and legends during his youth. Wang's sources in this essay reflect the nature of *wenshi ziliao* publications, which are required to be based on events that local people either saw, experienced, or heard of firsthand (*qinjian, qinli,* or *qinwen*). (Interview with Wang Yongnian, 22 March 2001, Yuncheng City).

64. Wang and Jie, "Dingchou zhenhuang ji," 115.

65. Williamson, *Journeys in North China,* 346–50.

66. He Hanwei, *Guangxu chunian,* 139–40.

67. Ibid., 139–42.

68. Wang and Jie, "Dingchou zhenhuang ji," 115.

69. Ibid., 115. It was illegal to sell salt by oneself without working through the government's salt monopoly.

70. Ibid., 116–17.

71. "Ming xianzhuan," *Xie xianzhi* (1920), 5: 19b–20a.

PART II. PRAISE AND BLAME

1. Pillemer, *Momentous Events, Vivid Memories,* 84–85; Janoff-Bulman, *Shattered Assumptions,* 130–35.

2. Greenough, "Comments from a South Asian Perspective," 792.

3. THE WRATH OF HEAVEN VERSUS HUMAN GREED

1. Nan, 1. This section is not included in the *Yuncheng zaiyi lu*.

2. Nan, 19.

3. Timothy Richard, *Forty-Five Years in China: Reminiscences* (New York: Frederick A. Stokes Co., 1916), 97–98. See also Paul Cohen's discussion of the religious construction of drought during the Boxer movement. Cohen explains that because droughts are more difficult than other types of disasters to explain strictly in terms of human agency, historically they have "more often been understood as resulting from the action of supernatural forces that need to be propitiated or cosmic imbalances that require correction." Cohen, *History in Three Keys*, 73.

4. Cathal Poirteir, *Famine Echoes* (Dublin: Gil & Macmillan, 1995), 37–40.

5. "Transcript of *The 700 Club* with Pat Robertson and Jerry Falwell," *Speaking of Faith*, September 13, 2001, http://speakingoffaith.publicradio.org/programs/2007/05/19/fundamentalism/falwell.shtml.

6. Janoff-Bulman, 9–10. Janoff-Bulman's discussion of people's need to believe in a just world is influenced by psychologist Melvin Lerner's "just world theory."

7. Pillemer, 83–86.

8. Pillemer, *Momentous Events*, 84–85; Janoff-Bulman, *Shattered Assumptions*, 132–33.

9. Greenough, "Comments from a South Asian Perspective," 795; Cohen, *History in Three Keys*, 88.

10. "Shanxi miliang wen," in *Guangxu sannian nianjing lu*, 97.

11. Ibid., 98. The term "five grains" (*wu gu*) is an ancient classification that refers to cereals or staple foods in general. The list varies, but generally includes two kinds of millet, wheat, beans, and rice, and sometimes barley, hemp, and sesame seed. Deng Yunte, *Zhongguo jiuhuang shi* (The history of famine relief in China) (Taipei: Taiwan shangwu yinshuguan gufen youxian gongsi, 1970), 2.

12. "Shanxi miliang wen," 98–99.

13. William Rowe, *Saving the World*, 195–97. As Rowe observes, certainly, elite overtones may be heard in the assumption that saving grain and practicing thrift were more "moral" than the "burning off" sometimes engaged in by people living on the margin. Nevertheless, Liang Peicai's critiques of extravagance would have been familiar to commoners in late-Qing Shanxi as well as to members of the local elite. The injunction to "prize moderation and economy," after all, was one of the sixteen maxims that constituted the Kang Xi emperor's *Sacred Edict* (1670). From the late seventeenth century onward, these proverbs were rewritten in the vernacular, accompanied by simple explanations and illustrations, and read aloud twice a month in villages. By the nineteenth century, illiterate commoners also heard the Confucian virtues set forth in the *Sacred Edict* from popular entertainers who spoke and sang folktales based on those teachings. (Victor H. Mair, "Language and Ideology in the Written Popularizations of the *Sacred Edict*," in *Popular Culture in Late Imperial China*, ed. David Johnson, Andrew Nathan, and Evelyn Rawski [Berkeley: University of California Press, 1985], 325–29).

14. Nan, 24. This section was edited out of the *Yuncheng zaiyi lu* version.

15. Mark Elvin, "Who Was Responsible for the Weather? Moral Meteorology in Late Imperial China," *Osiris*, 2nd ser., 13 (1998): 213.

16. See chapter 4 for a discussion of the relationship drawn between opium and the famine.

17. *The Classic of Filiality* (*Xiaojing*), in *Sources of Chinese Tradition: From Earliest Times to 1600*, 2nd ed., comp. William Theodore de Bary and Irene Bloom (New York: Columbia University Press, 1999), 325–27.

18. Harrison *Man Awakened*, 52, 65.

19. Nan, 16–17, 24; Lin Yutang, "Feminist Thought in Ancient China," *T'ien Hsia Monthly* 1.2 (1935): 127–28. For specific examples of the gendered nature of the offenses that local observers believed had angered Heaven, see chapter 7.

20. Nan, 25. The sentence about coffin makers is also in the *Yuncheng zaiyi lu* version, 112.

21. Richard, *Forty-five Years in China*, 7.

22. Jeffrey Snyder-Reinke, "Dry Spells: Rainmaking, Power, and the State in Late Imperial China" (Ph.D. diss., University of Michigan, 2006), 128–35. Snyder-Reinke notes that cattle fell into a different category than other livestock because they were used in agricultural work and thus enjoyed special protections as beasts of burden (personal correspondence with Snyder-Reinke).

23. Wang Xilun, *Yiqingtang wenji* (1912), 6: 1b, 20a–20b. The Three Cardinal Guides consist of the ruler guiding the subject, the father guiding the son, and the husband guiding the wife.

24. Ibid., 6: 20b.

25. Lynn Struve, "Chimerical Early Modernity: The Case of 'Conquest-Generation' Memoirs," in *The Qing Formation in World-Historical Time,* ed. Lynn Struve, Harvard East Asian Monographs 234 (Cambridge, MA: Harvard University Asia Center, 2004), 369.

26. Wang Doukui, "Liyu Guangxu chunian huangzai ji wenyi langshu zai shangji" (Sorrowful record narrating the famine, plague, and wolf and rat disasters of the early Guangxu years), stele inscription, Ruicheng County, Da Yudu Village, Guangxu 10 (1884), Wu Jun collection.

27. Zhang Gongduan, "Dingchou Wuyin daqin jiehou wen" (The great disaster of 1877 and 1878: an essay to admonish later generations), *Yicheng xianzhi* (Gazetteer of Yicheng County) (1929; repr., Zhongguo fangzhi congshu 417. Taibei: Chengwen chubanshe, 1968), 38: 24a–24b.

28. Bohr, *Famine in China*, 140–41, 146.

29. Greenough, "Comments from a South Asian Perspective," 795. For further discussion of the distinction between natural disasters (*tianzai*) and famines (*zaihuang*) and between natural and human-caused disasters (*ren huo*), see Deng Yunte, *Zhongguo jiuhuang shi* (The history of famine relief in China) (Taipei: Taiwan shangwu yinshuguan gufen youxian gongsi, 1970); and Li Wenhai and Zhou Yuan, *Zaihuang yu jijin, 1840–1919* (Disaster and famine, 1840–1919) (Beijing, Xinhua shudian, 1991), preface.

30. Zhang, "Dingchou Wuyin," 24a–24b.

31. "Shanxi miliang wen," 96.

32. Wang Doukui, stele inscription (1884).

33. "Shanxi miliang wen," 90.

34. Ibid., 91–93.

35. Andrea Janku, "Documenting the North-China Famine: The Chapter on 'Relief Affairs' in the *Xiangling xianzhi*," paper presented at the Qing Dynasty Natural Disasters and Chinese Society conference, Qing Research Institute of the People's University of China, August 21–24, 2005, Beijing, 6–7. A Chinese translation of the paper appears in Li Wenhai and Xia Mingfang, eds., *Tian you xiongnian: Qingdai zaihuang yu Zhongguo shehui* (Heaven sends bad years: Disasters and Chinese society during the Qing dynasty) (Beijing: SDX Joint Publishing Company, 2007), 479–508.

36. Interview with Xi Yunpeng, Xizhang Village, Xiangfen County, Pingyang Prefecture, 27 March 2001. Mr. Xi's account and several other similar stories reflect famine tales and images still current at the local level. Mr. Xi is the grandson of Xi Shengmo, the first Shanxi native to become a Protestant minister. The pastor of the Three Self Church in Linfen City took me to interview him. Mr. Xi's famous grandfather was the sixth of seven brothers. The third brother tried to eat ground-up stones during the Guangxu 3 famine, and he starved to death. The fourth brother fled to Inner Mongolia. He returned ten years later and found that most of the other villagers had died. Xi Shengmo himself became a Christian after he met David Hill and other Protestant missionaries who came to Shanxi during the famine. He stopped smoking opium once he became a Christian.

37. *Peking Gazette*, 13 October 1877, reprinted in *North China Herald*, 8 November 1877.

38. "Mingxian zhuan," *Xie xianzhi* (1920): 5: 18a–19a; Fei Xingjian, *Jindai mingren xiaozhuan* (Biographical sketches of eminent persons in the Modern era) (1926., repr. in *Jindai Zhongguo shiliao congkan* 8, Taipei: Guangwen shuju, 1980), 78: 113–14.

39. Nan, 3–4, *Yuncheng zaiyi lu*, 106. Some of the phrases about Yan have been edited out of the *Yuncheng zaiyi lu* version.

40. "Mingxian zhuan," 5: 18a–19a; Fei Xingjian, 78: 114.

41. Wang and Jie, 112. According to editors in the gazetteer offices in Yangcheng, Yuncheng, and Hongdong counties, many of the accounts of the 1877 famine that were published in local compilations in the 1980s were originally collected during the 1959–61 famine. The Cultural Revolution (1966–76) put plans to publish those accounts on hold, but as conditions relaxed, local scholars began to publish famine-related compilations based on materials gathered in the early 1960s. (Interview with Wang Shoubang, former head of the Yangcheng Local Gazetteer Office, and Liu Bolun, editor of the Yangcheng County gazetteer, Yangcheng, 8 April 2001).

42. Wang and Jie, "Dingchou zhenhuang ji," 110–12.

43. Group interview with seven members of the Old Person's Association in Xiwang Village, Yuncheng County, 9 April 2001. The persons included in this debate were Li Tong (age 79), Li Shangli (75), Li Heting (83), and Liu Xueji (68).

44. Liu Xueji, in group interview, 9 April 2001.

45. Nan, 10. This entire section was edited out of the *Yuncheng zaiyi lu*.

46. Nan, 10–12. Liu Xing's account of Li Xiude's generosity during the famine is corroborated in the short item devoted to Li in "Biographies of the Fil-

ial and Righteous," a section of the Republican-era Xie County gazetteer. Li was praised for "viewing the affairs of the people as he viewed the affairs of his family" and for supporting efforts to build a bridge and establish a shelter for travelers and a place for students to live while they were taking the civil service exams. During the famine he was one of several wealthy commoners Ma Piyao enlisted to manage the Xie County relief office. ("Xiaoyi juan," and "Jiuwen gao," *Xie xianzhi* (1920), 7: 41b–42a; 13: 15a).

47. Nan, 12.

48. Lillian M. Li, "Introduction: Food, Famine, and the Chinese State," *Journal of Asian Studies* 41.4 (August 1982): 698–99; Will, *Bureaucracy and Famine*, 102–5.

49. *Yuncheng zaiyi lu*, 106; Nan 4.

50. *Yuncheng zaiyi lu*, 106–7; Nan, 5.

51. Shi Jiashao, "Zhenji tiaoyi," in *Yicheng xianzhi* (1929), 38: 1602–9.

52. *Yuncheng zaiyi lu*, 106–7. Qing officials were eager to identify those in greatest need so that they could properly target the limited amount of cash relief. Relief administrators like Yan Jingming followed the well-established precedent of ordering local officials to classify the famine victims into "extremely poor" (*jipin*) and "less poor" (*cipin*) groups and to distribute relief accordingly. (*Guangxu chao Donghualu*, Guangxu 3, 12th month, 514). For additional discussion of the classification system developed by the Qing state, see Will, 97–102.

53. *Yuncheng zaiyi lu*, 107; Nan, 5.

54. Wang and Jie, "Dingchou zhenhuang ji," 112–13.

55. Ibid., 114–15.

56. Wong, "Food Riots in the Qing Dynasty," 782–83.

4. QING OFFICIALDOM AND THE POLITICS OF FAMINE

1. *Peking Gazette,* 30 June 1877, trans. in *North China Herald,* 22 July 1876.

2. These statements were made in a memorial from Ding Richang that requested rewards for officials in Taiwan who "practiced personal economy and retrenchment" in order to raise contributions for famine relief. *Peking Gazette,* 8 October 1878, trans. in *North China Herald,* 28 November 1878.

3. *Jingbao,* Guangxu 3, 6th month, 4th day, repr. in *Shenbao,* 28 July 1877.

4. Arnold, *Famine,*101–2.

5. Will and Wong, *Nourish the People,* 14.

6. *Mencius,* trans. D. C. Lau (London: Penguin Books, 1970), book I, part A, 52.

7. Bohr, *Famine in China,* 27.

8. Elvin, "Who Was Responsible for the Weather," 213, 229–33. Elvin finds that while eighteenth-century Qing rulers such as the Yongzheng emperor suggested that localized disasters might be due to immoral conduct among the common people of that area, the localized character of moral meteorological effects vanished as a major theme after the Jiaqing reign, and by the 1860s "the focus of moral meteorological decrees was on the political center."

9. *Guangxu chao Donghualu,* 1: 409–10 (hereafter cited as DHL). Zhu Shoupeng (*jinshi* 1902) originally published this collection of important Guangxu-era

official memorials and imperial edicts in 1909. A punctuated and corrected edition was published by PRC scholars in 1958. All the citations in this book are taken from volume 1, which covers the famine years.

10. *Peking Gazette,* 1 August 1877, trans. in *North China Herald,* 25 August 1877.

11. DHL, 559; *Peking Gazette,* 8 June 1878, trans. in *North China Herald,* 13 July 1878. See also Bohr, 32–33.

12. *Peking Gazette,* 2 July 1876, trans. in *North China Herald,* 22 July 1876.

13. "Chouban ge sheng huangzheng an," 38: 18455–963. The compilation consists of copies of imperial edicts about the famine, as well as famine-related correspondence that the Zongli Yamen received from and sent to the Grand Council (Junjichu), the Board of Revenue (Hubu), and an array of high officials ranging from Li Hongzhang to metropolitan censors. The documents cover the period Guangxu 3–Guangxu 7 (1877–1881).

14. Horowitz, "Central Power and State-Making," 188–89.

15. Chu and Liu, *Li Hung-chang*; Hummel, 1: 466.

16. Lillian Li, *Fighting Famine in North China,* 268–77.

17. *Qingyi* may be translated as "pure discussion," "pure counsel," "pure talk," or "literati opinion." For discussions of *qingyi,* see Chen Yongqin, "Wan Qing Qingliu pai de xumin sixiang" (The late-Qing Qingliu group's ideology of relieving the people), *Lishi dangan* 2 (2003): 105–12, and Chen, "Guangxu shiqi Qingliu pai dui nongye youguan wenti suo ti jianyi ji qi shiwuxing" (The pragmatic recommendations regarding agricultural problems promoted by the Guangxu-period Qingliu group), *Zhongguo nong shi* 3 (1994): 39–47; Ayers, *Chang Chi-tung*; Marianne Bastid, "Qingyi and the Self-Strengthening Movement," in *Proceedings of the Conference on the Self-Strengthening Movement in Late-Ch'ing China, 1860–1894,* part 2, comp. Institute of Modern History, Academia Sinica (Taipei: 1988), 873–93; Lloyd Eastman, "Ch'ing-i and Chinese Policy Formation during the Nineteenth Century," *Journal of Asian Studies* 24.4 (August 1965): 595–611; Eastman, *Thrones and Mandarins: China's Search for a Policy during the Sino-French Controversy, 1880–1885* (Cambridge, MA: Harvard University Press, 1967); and Rankin, "'Public Opinion' and Political Power," 453–84.

18. Eastman, *Thrones and Mandarins,* 17–18; Rankin, "'Public Opinion' and Political Power," 453–55. Rankin argues that by the closing decades of the nineteenth century, *qingyi* referred specifically to the opinion of men who held low- and middle-rank posts in the metropolitan bureaucracy. Such posts included positions in the Hanlin Academy, the Censorate, and the Imperial Academy, as well as such routine jobs as secretaries of the Grand Secretariat or six boards.

19. Bastid, "Qingyi and the Self-Strengthening Movement," 882–83. For more on how the Tianjin Massacre exacerbated tensions within the Chinese bureaucracy, see Cohen, *China and Christianity,* 234–47.

20. Eastman, "Ch'ing-i and Chinese Policy Formation," 600–601. According to Chen Yongqin, who offers the most comprehensive list of men associated with the Qingliu, the group included roughly twenty people including: Li Hongzao, Zhang Zhidong, Zhang Peilun, Chen Baochen, Bao Ting, Huang Tifang, Deng Chengxiu, Wu Dacheng, He Jinshou, Liu Enpu, Zhang Guanzhun,

Deng Qinglin, Xia Tongshan, Chen Qitai, Zhang Kai, Shao Jicheng, Wu Kedu, and Wu Guanli. (Chen, "Wan Qing Qingliu pai," 111).

21. Rankin, "'Public Opinion' and Political Power," 463–64.

22. Chen, "Wan Qing Qingliu pai," 105; DHL, 532. The quote about winning the people's hearts is taken from a memorial submitted by the Qingliu proponent Zhang Peilun early in 1878. "Relieving the people [*xu min*] is the basis of famine relief policy," wrote Zhang.

23. "Chouban ge sheng huangzheng an," Guangxu 3, 7th month, 5th day, 18480–81.

24. Ibid., 18478. For a brief summary of Wen Zhonghan's memorial, see "Chouban ge sheng huangzheng an chaodang mulu" (Catalogue of proposals for preparing famine relief policies for each province), in *Guojia tushuguan cang Qingdai guben neige liubu dangan*, 37: 18376.

25. "Chouban ge sheng huangzheng an," Guangxu 3, 7th month, 23rd day, 18486–90.

26. "Chouban ge sheng huangzheng an," Guangxu 4, 4th month, 15th day, 18678–81. Ouyang Yun is not one of the officials generally associated with the Qingliu group, but he clearly shared Qingliu perspectives on the relative importance of nourishing the people over funding self-strengthening projects

27. Ibid., 18683. Ouyang Yun harshly denounced railroads. He argued that by destroying the people's property, exposing their ancestral tombs, and depriving them of the benefits of cart transportation, the railway opened by foreigners (but wisely destroyed by the Chinese government) led to an accumulation of resentment and hatred and offended heavenly harmony. If Chinese people themselves opened a railroad, that would be akin to using foreign poison to poison themselves.

28. Ibid., 18685–86.

29. Ibid., 18686–87.

30. Ibid., 18687–90.

31. "Chouban ge sheng huangzheng an," Guangxu 3, 8th month, 10th day, 18507–8.

32. Ibid., 18508–11.

33. "Chouban ge sheng huangzheng an," Guangxu 3, 8th month, 1st day, 18499–503.

34. "Chouban ge sheng huangzheng an," Guangxu 4, 6th month, 5th day, 18781–87.

35. DHL, 551–52; Chen, 106–7. The court asked Li Hongzhang and Shen Baozhen to consider Bao Ting's proposal. Li and Shen rejected the idea of purchasing rice from the treaty port of Saigon. Saigon rice was not well adapted for Chinese consumption, they argued, and the cost of transporting the grain from Saigon to Tianjin via Hong Kong was greater than simply purchasing rice from the Jiangnan region. (*Peking Gazette*, 3 July 1878, trans. in *North China Herald*, 10 August 1878).

36. DHL, 559–60.

37. Ibid.

38. "Chouban ge sheng huangzheng an," Guangxu 3, 11th month, 16th day, 18562–65.

39. Chu, *The Moslem Rebellion*, 120–23. According to the terms of the loan, the government agreed to pay monthly interest of 1.25 percent and to repay the capital within seven years.

40. DHL, 563–64.

41. "Chouban ge sheng huangzheng an," Guangxu 3, 12th month, 11th day, 18579–81. Li Hongzhang also opposed reliance on foreign loans to fund relief efforts on the grounds that foreigners charged excessively high interest rates. See *Jingbao*, Guangxu 3, 10th month, 9th day, repr. in *Shenbao*, 27 November 1877.

42. Ayers argues that Cixi allowed Qingliu attacks on self-strengtheners to continue as an indirect reward for the support that Pure Current members such as Zhang Zhidong had offered her during the Guangxu emperor's succession crisis. Eastman concludes that she deliberately encouraged *qingyi* members to criticize high officials such as Li Hongzhang because *qingyi* as a political force "undoubtedly abetted her efforts to dominate domestic politics" by checking the power of potential rivals. (Ayers, 73–74; Eastman, "Ch'ing-i and Chinese Policy Formation," 606–7.

43. "Chouban ge sheng huangzheng an," Guangxu 3, 8th month, 27th day, 18521–24; 18529.

44. "Chouban ge sheng huangzheng an," Guangxu 4, 3rd month, 4th day, 18616. According to the edict ordering Li and Shen to respond to proposals for using coastal defense money to fund relief, Huang Tifang and Wu Guanli, both Qingliu spokesmen, had sent memorials on this topic, as had a like-minded official named Li Hongmo.

45. *Dezong shilu* (Veritable records of the Guangxu emperor), part 2, in *Qing shilu* (Veritable records of the Qing), vol. 53 (Beijing: Zhonghua shuju, 1987) (Guangxu 4, 3rd month, 21st day), 87–88. As He Hanwei points out, the amount that actually reached Shanxi and Henan often fell short of what the court had asked other provinces to contribute. In this case, Zeng Guoquan claimed that only a few customhouses forwarded half their money earmarked for southern coastal defense to Shanxi, and that the total amount sent to Shanxi under this plan did not even reach ten thousand taels. (He Hanwei, 79–81).

46. Bastid, "Qingyi," 884; Eastman, "Ch'ing-i and Chinese Policy Formation" 604–5, 609.

47. Will, *Bureaucracy and Famine*, 211–15; Dunstan, *Conflicting Counsels*, 7–9. See also Rowe, *Saving the World*. For examples of different kinds of market consciousness displayed by eighteenth-century officials like Chen Hongmou and Qin Huitian, see Dunstan, 293–326.

48. Dunstan, 30–31. Chinese thinkers advanced the idea as early as the fifth century B.C.E. that state intervention was necessary for stabilizing grain prices (Will and Wong, 3).

49. *Jingbao*, Guangxu 3, 10th month, 9th day, repr. in *Shenbao*, 27 November 1877. The proposal submitted by the Qingliu official He Jinshou asked the imperial court to call on Li Hongzhang to raise roughly one million taels, including several hundred thousand taels from foreign loans, with which to purchase grain to stabilize prices in famine areas. For overviews of how "[price-]stabilizing sales" (*pingtiao*) worked, see Dunstan, *Conflicting Counsels*, 30–32, and Will, *Bureaucracy and Famine*, 182–86.

50. *Jingbao,* Guangxu 3, 10th month, 9th day.

51. *Peking Gazette,* 3 July 1878, trans. in *North China Herald,* 10 August 1878.

52. Rankin, *Elite Activism and Political Transformation in China: Zhejiang Province, 1865–1911* (Stanford, CA: Stanford University Press, 1986), 143.

53. DHL 514–15.

54. Ibid., 514.

55. Ibid.

56. David Bello, "Opium in Xinjiang and Beyond," in *Opium Regimes: China, Britain, and Japan, 1839–1952,* ed. Timothy Brook and Bob Tadashi Wakabayashi (Berkeley: University of California Press, 2000), 130.

57. After the British discovered in the late eighteenth century that they could improve their massive trade deficit with China by selling opium to the Chinese, the amount of opium purchased by China steadily increased despite numerous imperial edicts banning the drug. By 1838 the British were selling 40,000 chests of opium to China each year, and roughly nine million taels of silver flowed out of China annually to pay for it. (Spence, *Search for Modern China,* 128–32, 149–50).

In the late 1820s and early 1830s the availability of silver bullion seriously declined, causing the price of silver to rise in relation to copper. The government feared that the rising price of silver would hurt China's peasantry, since commoners normally used copper currency for everyday transactions but had to pay their taxes to the state in silver. Some officials blamed the rise in silver prices on illegal opium imports. After the Daoguang emperor expressed concern over the opium problem, one group of Qing officials suggested in the 1830s that instead of repeating previously ineffective bans on opium imports and sales, the silver drain could instead be prevented by simply legalizing the opium trade and then taxing it in order to increase state revenue. (James Polachek, *The Inner Opium War* [Cambridge, MA: Harvard University Press, 1992], 103–5, 113–19; Frederic Wakeman Jr., "The Canton Trade and the Opium War," in *The Cambridge History of China,* 10: 180–81). Other officials even went so far as to propose that the state follow the precedent of tobacco and allow opium to be cultivated in China. Permitting the domestic cultivation of opium, argued the statecraft activist Jiang Xiangnan, would allow silver to circulate within China and would "put an end to the monopolistic position of the barbarians." (Man-houng Lin, "Two Social Theories Revealed: Statecraft Controversies over China's Monetary Crisis, 1808–1854," *Late Imperial China* 12.2 [December 1991]: 11–13).

Opponents of the opium legalization initiative of 1836, however, put forth a moralist argument similar to positions embraced by Qingliu officials in the 1870s. They contended that opium was an agent of barbarian aggression and a "moral poison" that debased the people's minds and blurred the distinction between Chinese and barbarians. The Daoguang emperor eventually sided with the moralists and ordered his officials to enforce the prohibition against opium more strictly. Efforts to carry out that prohibition eventually resulted in the Opium War of 1839–42. (Wakeman, "The Canton Trade and the Opium War," 180–81). For a detailed discussion of the internal political pressures that led to the first Opium War, see Polachek.

58. Man-houng Lin, "Late-Qing Perceptions of Native Opium," *Harvard Journal of Asiatic Studies* 64.1 (June 2004): 121.

59. Li Hongzhang presents a complex case. During the famine, he served both as an important figure in China's negotiations with Western countries and as the governor-general of Zhili, one of the famine-stricken northern provinces. He thus had to balance his responsibilities to Zhili with national and foreign policy concerns in a way that the governors of Shanxi and Henan did not.

60. In an 1879 letter the Shanxi-based missionary David Hill estimated that the poppy would yield a crop about "double the value of any ordinary cereal." ("Letter to J. R. Hill, Ping Yang Fu, May 1, 1879," in Barber, *David Hill*, 211.) According to a report on opium cultivation in Sichuan in 1909, opium was between two and six times as valuable as alternative crops such as mulberry, tea, wheat, millet, or corn. R. Bin Wong, "Opium and Modern Chinese State-Making," in Brook and Wakabayashi, *Opium Regimes*, 192.

61. DHL (Guangxu 2, 8th month, 9th day; 26 September 1876), 272–73.

62. Hummel, *Eminent Chinese*, 2: 749–51.

63. Zeng Guoquan, *Zeng Zhongxiang gong (Guoquan) zouyi* (Zeng Guoquan's memorials) (Guangxu 4, 1st month, 26th day), 733–37.

64. Ibid., 733.

65. Ibid.

66. Ibid., 735.

67. "Jiu wengao," *Xie xianzhi* (1920), 13: 964–67.

68. Zeng Guoquan, *zouyi*, 734.

69. Ibid., 733, 736–37. Zeng Guoquan and Yan Jingming later submitted additional anti-opium memorials that reiterated Zeng's original arguments against the plant. See, for example, Zeng Guoquan, *zouyi* (Guangxu 4, 7th month, 26th day), 909–10.

70. Hummel, *Eminent Chinese*, 1: 27–28; Chen Cungong, "Zhang Zhidong zai Shanxi, 1882–1884," (Zhang Zhidong in Shanxi), *Zhongyang yanjiuyuan jindaishi yanjiu suo jikan* 17 (1988), 5–8.

71. Rowe, *Saving the World*, 161–62.

72. Dunstan, *Conflicting Counsels*, 203–6.

73. Sun Anbang, comp., *Qing shilu: Shanxi ziliao huibian* (Veritable records of the Qing dynasty: A compilation of materials regarding Shanxi) (Taiyuan: Shanxi gujie chubanshe, 1996), 3: 2179.

74. Chen Yongqin, "Wan Qing Qingliu pai," 107; *Peking Gazette*, 22 January 1878, trans. in *North China Herald*, 21 March 1878; DHL, 560–62. Writing in support of Li's proposal, the Qingliu official Huang Tifang urged the court to disregard the spurious argument that suspending distillation might lead to a loss of jobs or revenue. Huang and other Qingliu officials went so far as to call for the impeachment of Dong Xun, president of the Board of Revenue, in part due to the board's rejection of Li's proposal. Huang claimed that Dong Xun rejected the proposal to suspend distillation out of greed and thus placed his own personal gain above the good of the country. According to Chen, it was intense pressure from Qingliu officials that eventually persuaded the court to suspend distillation in famine areas.

75. Rowe, *Saving the World*, 161–62.

76. Zeng Guoquan, *zouyi, 733.*

77. Man-houng Lin, "Late-Qing Perceptions of Native Opium," 125–26.

78. Ibid., 126.

79. Brook and Wakabayashi, *Opium Regimes,* 7–11, 36; Man-houng Lin, "Late-Qing Perceptions of Native Opium," 120.

80. Man-houng Lin, "Late-Qing Perceptions of Native Opium," 121.

81. Jerome Chen, *State Economic Policies of the Ch'ing Government, 1840–1895* (New York: Garland, 1980), 56–60.

82. Man-houng Lin, "Late-Qing Perceptions of Native Opium," 129. Li Hongzhang also used revenue from opium taxes to pay coastal defense expenses and to pay the interest on foreign loans. (Wong, "Opium and Modern Chinese State-Making," 205).

83. See chapter 5 for a discussion of how missionary relief workers and editors of the *North China Herald* viewed the opium question.

84. "Jiu wengao," *Xie xianzhi* (1920), 13: 965. Although the gazetteer was published in 1920, the unnamed author of this essay refers to the Qing as "my" or "our" dynasty and makes no reference to the major opium eradication campaign that began in 1906. It is thus possible that he wrote the essay before the 1911 Revolution. His claims about when opium arrived in China and when its use as a drug began are problematic. Recent research demonstrates that as early as the eighth century, medicines imported from the Arab world included opium as an ingredient. Discussion of the medicinal use of opium as a curative for diarrhea and male impotence appeared in Chinese medical texts in the sixteenth and seventeenth centuries. The practice of smoking opium for recreation rather than using the pods and flowers of the poppies for medicinal purposes began when Dutch and English traders began lacing tobacco with opium in the seventeenth century. Officials on China's southern coast began expressing concern about opium smoking in the 1720s, which led the Yongzheng emperor to ban the sale and distribution of the drug in 1729. (Man-houng Lin, "Late-Qing Perceptions of Native Opium," 133–34; Brook and Wakabayashi, *Opium Regimes,* 5–6.)

85. "Jiu wengao," *Xie xianzhi* (1920), 13: 964–67.

86. For examples of recent mainland Chinese discussions of opium and excessive demands for corvée labor as causes of the famine, see Li Wenhai et al., 108–10; Wang Jinxiang, "Shanxi 'Dingwu qihuang' luetan (A brief exploration of the "Incredible Famine of 1877–78" in Shanxi), *Zhongguo nongye shi* 3 (1983): 25–27; Zhao Shiyuan, "'Dingwu qihuang' shulue" (An account of the "Incredible Famine of 1877–78"), *Xueshu yuebao* 2 (1981): 66–67; and Liu Fengxiang, "Qianxi 'Dingwu qihuang' de yuanyin" (A brief analysis of the causes of the "Incredible Famine of 1877–78"), *Jining shizhuan xuebao* 2 (2000): 1–2.

87. Li et al., *Zhongguo jindai,* 109–10. Estimates of the quantity of opium grown in Shanxi in the 1870s vary, but foreigners who visited Shanxi expressed surprise over the extent of poppy cultivation there. Takezoe Shin'ichiro, for example, the secretary of the Japanese legation in Beijing, found Shanxi "quite overgrown with poppies" when he traveled through the province in 1876. He made the unlikely estimate that 70 percent of the people in Shanxi smoked opium (Brook and Wakabayashi, *Opium Regimes,* 8–9).

88. Li et al., *Zhongguo jindai,* 110.

5. VIEWS FROM THE OUTSIDE

1. The foreign-run China Famine Relief Fund Committee collected contributions from Great Britain, the United States, Canada, Australia, New Zealand, Tasmania, India, Singapore, Penang, Hong Kong, China, and Japan. It distributed a total of 204,560.37 taels during the disaster. Between 1877 and 1879 eleven British and American Protestant relief workers, all of them men, distributed relief in Shanxi on the committee's behalf. In October 1878 three female missionaries from the China Inland Mission arrived in Taiyuan to work with famine orphans. Bohr notes that roughly forty Roman Catholic missionaries were also involved in distributing relief in the affected province. Bohr, 187–97; "The Orphanage Work—from Mrs. Hudson Taylor," in *China's Millions* (1879): 19. According to the *Chronicle of the London Missionary Society,* in 1878 thirty different Protestant missionary societies were working in China, along with seven Roman Catholic societies. The *Chronicle* claimed that there were 13,035 Protestant Chinese Christians and 404,530 Chinese Roman Catholics. *Chronicle of the London Missionary Society for the year 1878* (London, 1878), 257.

2. Ma Guangren, *Shanghai xinwen shi* (History of the press in Shanghai), *1850–1949* (Shanghai: Fudan daxue chubanshe, 1996), 11–23. In 1864 the newspaper's management board began printing a daily paper called the *North China Daily News* in addition to its weekly Saturday edition. In 1870 the paper was renamed the *North China Herald and Supreme Court and Consular Gazette,* a title that lasted until it closed, after the birth of the People's Republic of China put a permanent end to treaty-port life in China. The *Herald*'s weekly Saturday edition continued after the company began publishing the *North China Daily News,* and I base my discussion of this newspaper's coverage of the famine on the weekly rather than the daily edition.

3. The weekly *Herald* editions published during the famine were about thirty pages long. The first half of an issue normally consisted of news articles and editorial selections, followed by short reports from other treaty-port "outposts" such as Tianjin, Chefoo, and Fuzhou, and three or four pages of "abstracts" translated from Chinese memorials and edicts in the *Peking Gazette (Jingbao).* The second half included law reports from the *Supreme Court News,* export lists, weekly returns for Shanghai's silk and opium trade, commercial intelligence, telegrams and news clips about commercial matters, and advertisements.

4. *North China Herald,* 27 July 1877. Not all British elites discounted the notion that a higher power sent famines in response to human misdeeds. During the Irish famine of 1845–49, for example, Charles Trevelyan, the head of the treasury, asserted that God had sent the famine in order to force poverty-stricken Ireland to reform and modernize. Officials like Trevelyan differed from their Qing counterparts, however, in believing that God's wrath was directed not at unrighteous rulers but at the famine-stricken populations themselves, either as a remedy for overpopulation or a wake-up call for lazy and "backward" groups of people. (Gray, "Ideology and the Famine," 92–93).

5. *North China Herald,* 4 August 1877; 22 September 1877.

6. "Famine Relief in India and China," *North China Herald,* 15 March 1877.

7. *North China Herald,* 6 May 1879; Roswell S. Britton, *The Chinese Peri-*

odical Press, 1800–1912 (Shanghai: Kelly & Walsh, 1933), 48–51. The *Herald* did publish more sympathetic letters written by missionaries in famine districts, but in editorials written by the *Herald*'s staff, blame for the famine was repeatedly directed at the Qing government.

8. "The Government and the Famine," *North China Herald*, 27 April 1878.

9. "Famines and Neglectful Government," *North China Herald*, 6 May 1879.

10. Will and Wong, *Nourish the People*, 517, 522.

11. Ibid., 518–20.

12. Noel Kissane, *The Irish Famine: A Documentary History* (Dublin: National Library of Ireland, 1995), 50.

13. Government of India to Richard Temple, 16 January 1877, cited in B. M. Bhatia, *Famines in India: A Study in Some Aspects of the Economic History of India with Special Reference to Food Problems, 1860–1990* (Bombay: Konark, 1991), 90.

14. William Digby, *The Famine Campaign in Southern India, 1876–1878* (London: Longmans, Green, and Co., 1878), 2: 277. For estimates on mortality during the Indian famine, see Davis, 7.

15. Bhatia, *Famines in India*, 94.

16. "Chief Secretary to the Government of Madras to the Secretary to the Government of India, Financial Department," 13 November 1876; "Viceroy of Delhi Camp to Secretary of State," 5 January 1877, in *The Threatened Famine in Western and Southern India* (1877), Cmnd. 1707, 83–84; Cmnd. 1754, 12. The latter telegram makes the British government's displeasure quite clear: "We consider the policy of making large purchases of grain adopted by Madras Government to be very erroneous, calculated seriously to interfere with operations of trade," wrote the viceroy of Delhi Camp. "We have instructed the Governor to abandon this policy, and shall take pains to make publicly known our intention to leave trade unfettered." See also Bhatia, *Famines in India*, 94.

17. Her Majesty's Secretary of State for India to His Excellency the Right Honourable the Governor General of India in Council, 10 January 1878, in *East India (Report of Famine Commission): Proceedings of the Commission, and Selected Evidence*, Appendix II, (1882), Cmnd. 3086, 2; Bhatia, *Famines in India*, 96; Davis, *Late Victorian Holocausts*, 7.

18. Tóibín and Ferriter, 9; Ó Gráda, *Black '47 and Beyond*, 6; Davis, *Late Victorian Holocausts*, 41–47. Britain's failure to prevent massive loss of life during the famines that wracked India in 1896–97, 1899–1900, and 1943–44 also became "a touchstone for anti-imperialist rhetoric" in India. See Michelle Burge McAlpin, *Subject to Famine: Food Crises and Economic Change in Western India, 1860–1920* (Princeton, NJ: Princeton University Press, 1983), 3; Sen, *Poverty and Famines*, 78–83.

19. *North China Herald*, 27 July 1878.

20. "Famine Relief in India and China," *North China Herald*, 15 March 1877.

21. "Correspondence: The Famine in the North," *North China Herald*, 22 September 1877.

22. Gray, "Ideology and the Famine," 87.

23. Kissane, *The Irish Famine*, 59.

24. Bhatia, *Famines in India*, 90.

25. "Government of India, Public Works Department Resolution," 16 May 1878; "Enquiries of the Commission," 28 June 1878, in *East India (Report of Famine Commission)*, 4, 12. The "bread of idleness" quote comes from Digby, *Famine Campaign in Southern India*, 373.

26. Patrick O'Sullivan and Richard Lucking, "The Famine World Wide: The Irish Famine and the Development of Famine Policy and Famine Theory," in *The Meaning of the Famine*, ed. Patrick O'Sullivan (London: Leicester University Press, 1997), 206–21. For a more detailed discussion of the ideological and personnel links between the British empire in Ireland and India, see C. A. Bayly, "Ireland, India, and the Empire: 1780–1914," *Transactions of the Royal Historical Society*, 6th ser., 10 (2000), 378–80.

27. Gray, "Ideology and the Famine," 89–90.

28. O'Sullivan and Lucking, "The Famine World Wide," 206–8.

29. Gray, "Ideology and the Famine," 91.

30. "The Government and the Famine," *North China Herald*, 27 April 1878.

31. "The Famine in China," *North China Herald* (repr. from *The Times*), 10 August 1878.

32. "Report of R. J. Forrest," 135.

33. In her study of famines and economic change in Western India between 1860 and 1920, South Asianist Michelle McAlpin asserts that after 1880 railroads increasingly helped India to withstand harvest shortfalls. Railroads "brought a staggering reduction in transport costs and an equally startling expansion in capacity" for those parts of India that lacked good water transport, she argues. Railways also allowed the market to penetrate further into rural areas, which raised rural incomes by providing higher prices for farm goods that were sold. McAlpin notes that mortality rates in India remained high during the great famines of the 1890s, but declined significantly after 1900. By that point the combination of railroads and information on crops "made it possible for even rather massive shortfalls in harvest in several regions of the subcontinent to be mitigated by the surpluses of the remaining regions." Despite her positive assessment of the impact of railroads in British India, McAlpin acknowledges that although railways "could perform the crucial task of moving grain from one part of India to another, they could not assure that hungry people would have the money to buy that grain." (McAlpin, *Subject to Famine*, 161, 165, 174–76, 207, 212).

34. Bhatia, *Famines in India*, 94. The statement that India had 6,000 miles of railways by 1872 comes from Charles Blair, *Indian Famines: Their Historical, Financial, and Other Aspects* (London: William Blackwood & Sons, 1874), 125.

35. The Shanghai opium returns for the week of April 20, 1878, for example, reported that a total of 246 chests of opium had been imported into China that week. "Shanghai Silk and Opium Returns," *North China Herald*, 27 April 1878.

36. *North China Herald*, 25 October 1877.

37. Ibid.

38. Chris Morash, *Writing the Irish Famine* (Oxford: Clarendon Press, 1995), 13–16.

39. Quoted in Blair, *Indian Famines*, 119–20. The article was from the 3 November 1866 issue of the *Saturday Review*.

40. "The Prospect of Famine," *North China Herald,* 22 September 1877.
41. Ibid., *North China Herald,* 15 March 1877.
42. *North China Herald,* 3 October 1879.
43. "Report of R. J. Forrest," 139.
44. "Evil Controlled for Good," *Missionary Herald* (August 1, 1878), 211.
45. "Rev. Timothy Richard on the Recent Famine in China," *Missionary Herald* (January 1, 1880), 7. The Protestant relief effort in Shanxi was led by Timothy Richard of the Baptist Missionary Society, Joshua Turner of the China Inland Mission, and David Hill of the Wesleyan-Methodist Missionary Society. They distributed relief mainly in Taiyuan and Pingyang prefectures. "Report of R. J. Forrest," 138–39.
46. David Hill to the General Secretaries of the Wesleyan Missionary Society, 16 May 1878, box 18, card 721, Hill Papers and Letters.
47. "For the Young: A Letter from Shan-si," in *China's Millions* (1879), 145–46.
48. "Bible Colportage in Ho-nan: From the Diary of Mr. A. J. Parrott," in *China's Millions* (1880), 110.
49. "Opium as Affecting Missions in China," *Missionary Herald* (July 1, 1880), 224–26.
50. Preface to *China's Millions* (1878).
51. Man-houng Lin argues that the missionary view of opium as a moral poison influenced Zeng Guoquan's and Zhang Zhidong's critiques of the plant. Timothy Richard, Lin writes, advised Zeng to prevent starvation by eliminating opium cultivation. (Man-houng Lin, "Late-Qing Perceptions of Native Opium," 131). Missionary views of opium may well have influenced Zeng's decision to portray it as a harmful substance that led to social debilitation. Zeng's argument that opium cultivation should be prohibited because poppies took up land that should be reserved for food crops, however, clearly stemmed from the Qing practice of enacting bans on wasting grain. Moreover, I have not found any missionary letters or reports written in Shanxi during the famine that trace Zeng Guoquan's decision to prohibit the cultivation of opium to his communications with Timothy Richard. In *Forty-five Years in China,* Richard himself makes no mention of the opium problem in his descriptions of his meetings with Zeng Guoquan (Richard, *Forty-Five Years in China,* 127–28, 137).
52. "Letter to J. R. Hill, Ping Yang Fu, May 1, 1879," in Barber, *David Hill,* 211.
53. "Anti-opium Action of the Chinese Government," in *The Friend of China* (January 1879), 263, in box 27, card 1172, Methodist Missionary Society collection, Library Archives, School of Oriental and African Studies, London (hereafter SOAS). The Anglo-Oriental Society for the Suppression of the Opium Trade was established by a Quaker entrepreneur in 1874. (Man-houng Lin, "Late-Qing Perceptions of Native Opium," 135.)
54. Hill to the General Secretaries.
55. David Hill, "Personal Experiences," box 27, card 1180, Hill Letters and Papers.
56. Richard, *Forty-five Years in China,* 158.
57. Bohr, *Famine in China,* 148–53.
58. Rowe, *Saving the World,* 204.

6. HYBRID VOICES

1. Mary Rankin, *Elite Activism and Political Transformation in China: Zhe-jiang Province, 1865–1911* (Stanford, CA: Stanford University Press, 1986), 143–45. For more on the origins and motivations of the extragovernmental relief effort based in Jiangnan, see Zhu Hu, *Difangxing liudong ji qi chaoyue: Wan Qing yizhen yu jindai Zhongguo de xinchen daixie* (The fluidity and transcendence of localism: Late-Qing charitable relief and the supercession of the old by the new in modern China) (Beijing: Zhongguo renmin daxue chubanshe, 2006); and Yang Jianli, "Wan Qing shehui zaihuang jiuzhi gongneng de yanbian: yi 'Dingwu qihuang' de liang zhong zhenji fangshi wei li" (Changes in social disaster relief in the late Qing: Taking the two kinds of relief methods during the "Incredible Famine of 1877–78" as examples), *Qingshi yanjiu* 4 (2000): 59–76.

2. For the case that Suzhou rather than Shanghai was the initial center of famine-relief activities, see Zhu, *Difangxing liudong,* 186–200.

3. "An Essay Discussing *Henan qihuang tieleitu,*" *Shenbao* (15 March 1878), 1.

4. Committee of the China Famine Relief Fund, *The Famine in China,* 12–13.

5. For an introduction to the *Qingshiduo,* see Will, *Bureaucracy and Famine,* 55. The roughly nine hundred Qing-era poems in the *Qingshiduo* were compiled in 1869 by the Zhejiangese scholar Zhang Yingchang. The poems in sections (*juan*) 14 and 15 describe the suffering of people stricken by natural disasters, while those in section 17 describe the sale of women and children and the plight of disaster refugees. The poems' emotional language and vivid imagery closely resemble those used in Xie's famine illustrations a decade later. A short poem titled "Traveling through the Shanxi Famine" (Jin ji xing), for example, employs some of the same phrases found in both local gazetteer essays about the 1877 famine and in several of the Taohuawu illustrations. The poet mourned that Shanxi's plains had become "a thousand *li* of scorched earth," that the people were reduced to eating tree leaves and bark, and that officials grew rich off relief money while the common people starved. *Qingshiduo* (Anthology of poems from the Qing period), comp. Zhang Yingchang (1869; repr., Beijing: Zhonghua shuju, 1983), 1: preface, 443; 2: 564–75.

6. Zhu, *Difangxing liudong,* 176–79.

7. Joanna Handlin Smith, "Chinese Philanthropy as Seen through a Case of Famine Relief in the 1640s," *Philanthropy in the World's Traditions,* ed. Warren Ilchman, Stanley N. Katz, and Edward L. Queen, II (Bloomington: Indiana University Press, 1998), 133–68. For discussion of Buddhist faith as a motivation for elite participation in relief work, see Paul R. Katz, "'It is Difficult to Be Indifferent to One's Roots': Taizhou Sojourners and Flood Relief during the 1920s," *Bulletin of the Institute of Modern History, Academia Sinica* 54 (December 2006), 35–37; and Janku, "Sowing Happiness."

8. "Si sheng gao zai tu qi," in *Qi Yu Jin Zhi zhenjuan zhengxin lu,* 2b–3a. The compilation *Qi Yu Jin Zhi zhenjuan zhengxin lu,* which consists of one volume of illustrations and eleven volumes of textual records, is held in the historical documents room (lishi wenxian shi) of the Shanghai Library. See also "Yue Henan qihuang tieleitu shuhou," *Shenbao,* 15 March 1878, 1.

The volume of illustrations includes five separate sets of famine illustrations designed by Xie Jiafu's Taohuawu public hall in Suzhou. The original *Henan qihuang tieleitu* is not among them. The first set, however, has the synonymous title *Yu ji tieleitu* (The Henan famine: Pictures to draw tears from iron). Only one of the sixteen illustrations in the *Yu ji tieleitu* is identical to an illustration in the *Henan qihuang tieleitu,* but four other illustrations found in both works concern the same subject matter (people eating tree bark to survive, people selling their children, famine-related suicides, and cannibalism), share the same accompanying texts, and are similar though not identical in appearance. Some of the poetic laments that accompany each woodblock print are signed and clearly were written by a number of different people. In one of his letters-to-the-public published by the Shanghai relief bureau, Zheng Guanying mentions writing "inscriptions to draw tears from iron" and receiving additional laments from his friends. (*Zheng Guangying ji,* 2: 1074). While Xie and other members of the Taohuawu arranged and printed the sets of woodblock illustrations, then, philanthropists in Shanghai and elsewhere appear to have shared the work of writing the laments. The pagoda method of fund-raising had been used at least since Ming times. (Handlin Smith, "Chinese Philanthropy," 149).

9. For a detailed analysis of the connection drawn by the *Shenbao* and leading relief organizers in the 1870s between famine relief work and the accumulation of merit, see Janku, "Sowing Happiness."

10. Quoted in Cynthia J. Brokaw, *The Ledgers of Merit and Demerit: Social Change and Moral Order in Late Imperial China* (Princeton, NJ: Princeton University Press, 1991), 3–4.

11. Committee of the China Famine Relief Fund, *The Famine in China,* 34; "Si sheng gao zai tu qi," 19a. This illustration is the final one in both the *Henan qihuang tieleitu* and the *Yu ji tieleitu.* It is the only illustration that is exactly the same in both sets of *tieleitu.*

12. Xia Dongyuan, *Zheng Guanying zhuan* (Biography of Zheng Guanying) (Shanghai: Huadong shifan daxue chubanshe, 1985), 277.

13. "Shanghai chouzhen gongsuo quanmu Henan, Shanxi yizhen gong qi" (A public letter posted from the Shanghai Relief Managing Office exhorting people to raise charitable relief for Henan and Shanxi), in *Zheng Guanying ji* (Collected works of Zheng Guanying), ed. Xia Dongyuan (Shanghai: Shanghai renmin chubanshe, 1982), 2: 1071. For further examples of Zheng Guanying's traditional ideas concerning rewards and retribution for good or bad deeds, see his volume *Jiuzai fubao* (Good fortune received as recompense for famine relief), which he compiled in 1878. Xie Jiafu wrote the preface to the 1888 reprint of this volume. In it Xie introduced Zheng as his friend. Zheng and Xie, from Guangdong and Jiangsu, respectively, became friends most likely while working together for disaster relief projects during the North China Famine. Zheng Guangying and Jing Yuanshang also began their partnership during the disaster.

14. For more information on Zheng Guanying, see Paul Cohen, *Between Tradition and Modernity: Wang T'ao and Reform in Late Ch'ing China* (Cambridge: Council on East Asian Studies, 1987); Yen-p'ing Hao, *The Comprador in Nineteenth Century China: Bridge between East and West* (Cambridge, MA: Harvard University Press, 1970); and Bryna Goodman, *Native Place, City, and Nation:*

Regional Networks and Identities in Shanghai, 1853–1937 (Berkeley: University of California Press, 1995). On Zheng's feminist views, see Charlotte Beahan, "The Women's Movement and Nationalism in Late Ch'ing China" (PhD diss., Columbia University, 1976). For a good introduction to Jing Yuanshan, see Rankin, *Elite Activism.*

15. Zhu, *Difangxing liudong,* 156; Janku, "Sowing Happiness," 100–110. Suzhou is about one hundred kilometers west of Shanghai. For further discussion of and lengthy quotations from Xie Jiafu's unpublished diaries (held in the Suzhou Archives), see Zhu, *Difangxing liudong,* chapters 1–3.

16. *Beizhuan jibu* (Supplementary collection of stele biographies), comp. Min Erchang (1923; repr., Qingdai zhuanji congkan 123, Taibei: Mingwen shuju, 1985), 506–7. Xie was back in Suzhou by the time the famine began, but he maintained close connections with merchant-philanthropists in nearby Shanghai.

17. Rudolf Wagner, "The Role of the Foreign Community in the Chinese Public Sphere," *China Quarterly* 142 (June 1995): 426; Frederic Wakeman Jr. and Wen-hsin Yeh, ed., *Shanghai Sojourners,* China Research Monograph 40 (Berkeley: Institute of East Asian Studies, University of California Center for Chinese Studies, 1992), introduction.

18. Wagner, "Role of the Foreign Community," 428–31; Wagner, "The Early Chinese Newspapers and the Chinese Public Sphere," *European Journal of East Asian Studies* 1.1 (March 2001): 3–5.

19. Wakeman and Yeh, *Shanghai Sojourners,* 1–2.

20. *Beizhuan jibu,* 507–8; Wagner, "Role of the Foreign Community," 428–31.

21. *Beizhuan jibu,* 507–8.

22. Zhu, *Difangxing liudong,* 108, 156; Cohen, *History in Three Keys,* 162–67.

23. Zhu, *Difangxing liudong,* 108–13; *Beizhuan jibu,* 508–9.

24. *Beizhuan jibu,* 509–10.

25. *Qingshiduo,* 1: 443, 2: 564–75; Janku, "Sowing Happiness," 95–105. Janku states that the Taohuawu was famous for its New Year prints and drew on that expertise to design the famine illustrations.

26. "Yue Henan qihuang tieleitu shuhou," *Shenbao,* 15 March 1878, 1. The article made no mention of Yu Zhi's disaster illustrations printed in the 1850s and 1860s.

27. *Shenbao,* 15 March, 1878.

28. Committee of the China Famine Relief Fund, *The Famine in China,* 10.

29. *China's Millions* (October 1878), 134. The quotation is from a letter written by the Reverend Joshua Turner from his post in Shanxi's Pingyang Prefecture and published with several of the famine illustrations. Turner wrote: "It will take the province a long time to recover from the effects of this calamity. . . . We feel that some more direct missionary work should be done by us in this place. . . . We are waiting on the Lord for guidance and fitness for the work. When will the time come when there shall be bands of Christians scattered among the cities of this province, shedding light upon the masses now in heathen darkness?"

30. Wagner, "Early Chinese Newspapers," 3; Wagner, "The *Shenbao* in Crisis: The International Environment and the Conflict between Guo Songtao and

the *Shenbao*," *Late Imperial China* 20.1 (June 1999): 108. The circulation number of 8,000 to 9,000 copies per day in 1877 is taken from Natascha Vittinghoff, "Readers, Publishers and Officials in the Contest for a Public Voice and the Rise of a Modern Press in Late Qing China (1860–1880)," *T'oung Pao* 87.4–5 (2001): 398. For more background on the history of the *Shenbao*, see Barbara Mittler, *A Newspaper for China? Power, Identity, and Change in Shanghai's News Media, 1872–1912* (Cambridge, MA: Harvard University Press, 2004); Ma Guangren, *Shanghai xinwen shi*, 57–71; Xu Zaiping and Xu Ruifang, *Qingmo sishinian Shenbao shiliao* (Materials on the *Shenbao* in the last forty years of the Qing) (Beijing: Xinhua chubanshe, 1988); and Britton, *The Chinese Periodical Press*.

31. Madeleine Yue Dong, "Communities and Communication: A Study of the Case of Yang Naiwu, 1873–1877," *Late Imperial China* 16.1 (June 1995): 79, 91–92. In its early period the *Shenbao* reprinted on a daily basis either lengthy excerpts from or entire issues of the *Jingbao* (court gazette or Peking gazette). The *North China Herald* also regularly translated and printed important imperial edicts and official memorials from the *Jingbao*. The *Jingbao*, explains Wagner, "is the collective name for a whole set of private rescripts and reprints, . . . consisting of the set of government-approved public communications posted every day in front of the *liubu*, six boards, in Beijing." Up until the late nineteenth century, Chinese scholars, officials, and urban merchants depended on various versions of the *Jingbao* to keep informed of issues. Each day the imperial court released a large body of state papers for general publication, and various independent publishing houses selected different official communiqués and imperial edicts to publish in many different "Peking gazettes." The larger daily gazettes printed in Peking contained three parts: a daily communiqué about the imperial audiences, edicts and decrees of the emperor, and memorials which officials had presented to the emperor. Shorter gazettes recording imperial edicts were published in the provinces. The gazettes were regularly read throughout the empire by officials, retired officials and those waiting for appointment, scholars, local gentry, and some merchants. Wagner, "Early Chinese Newspapers," 10–11; Mittler, *Newspaper for China?* 16, chapter 3. See also Lin Yutang, *A History of the Press and Public Opinion in China* (Chicago: University of Chicago, 1936), 16–19; and Britton, *The Chinese Periodical Press*, 3–15.

32. Wagner, "Early Chinese Newspapers," 3–5, 15–18; Mittler, 3–4, 208. See also Wagner, "Ernest Major's Shenbaoguan and the Formation of Late Qing Print Culture" (unpublished manuscript). Wagner emphasizes the active role Major took in running the paper during the 1870s and 1880s. Major, his twin brother, and two other British merchants provided the initial capital for the enterprise.

33. Bryna Goodman, "Improvisations on a Semicolonial Theme, or, How to Read a Celebration of Transnational Urban Community," *Journal of Asian Studies* 59.4 (November 2000): 902.

34. *Shenbao*, 13 June 1876; 11 October 1876; and 20 November 1876. For similar English-language reports, see *North China Herald*, 29 July 1876 and 28 December 1876.

35. Rankin, *Elite Activism*, 144–45. In 1878 the publishing house in charge

of the *Shenbao* also raised money for famine relief by publishing *Kuipin liang* (Food for the Starving), a volume of previously unpublished papers by famous men, and donating the profits to the relief campaign. (Wagner, "Ernest Major's Shenbaoguan").

36. Jing Yuanshan, *Juyi chuji* (Dwelling in leisure, first collection) (Shanghai, 1902), 2: 41a–41b.

37. *Zheng Guanying ji*, 2: 1073–74; Roberta Wue, "The Profits of Philanthropy: Relief Aid, *Shenbao*, and the Art World in Later Nineteenth-Century Shanghai," *Late Imperial China* 25.1 (June 2004): 189–96, 199. For a succinct summary of pragmatic factors that motivated elites in the 1920s to engage in charitable activities, see Katz, "'It is Difficult to be Indifferent to One's Roots,'" 24–37. Katz argues that some elites relied on charitable activities to increase their cultural networks of power and to accumulate symbolic capital.

38. See chapter 8 for a discussion of two other themes prominent in the *Shenbao*'s coverage of the famine—the newspaper's critique of the sale of women in famine districts and its protonationalist unwillingness to allow Chinese-led relief efforts to be outdone by foreign campaigns.

39. *Shenbao*, 9 March 1877, 1.

40. Ibid. The *Shenbao* author did not specify which Western-language newspaper (or even which "Western language") he was citing, but he could have been referring to any number of *North China Herald* editorials critical of the Qing government's interventionist policies.

41. "Quanzhen Shandong jimin bing huangnian bu neng pingtiao shuo," *Shenbao*, 10 March 1877, 1.

42. Rowe, *Saving the World*, 162–83; Dunstan, chapter 6; Will, 211–14. See chapter 5 for examples of Li Hongzhang's perspective on merchants and grain circulation.

43. Wagner, "Role of the Foreign Community," 430–31.

44. Vittinghoff, "Readers, Publishers and Officials," 419–21.

45. *Shenbao*, 3 April 1877, 2; *Celestial Empire*, 15 March 1877, 313.

46. Neither Timothy Richard's fluency in Chinese nor his receptivity to and genuine interest in Chinese cultural perspectives were typical of the majority of Protestant missionaries in China in the 1870s.

47. Mittler, *Newspaper for China?* 14–15; Xu and Xu, *Qingmo sishinian Shenbao shiliao*, 10–12.

48. Mittler, *Newspaper for China?* 32. Both Mittler and Madeleine Yue Dong point out that the *Shenbao*'s readers were often its writers as well. Members of the paper's editorial board took turns submitting articles and frequently invited "guest" writers to submit correspondence about events not accessible to the paper's own reporters, as well as articles on contemporary affairs, diary excerpts, and other literary writing that would function as the editorial for that day. See Mittler, *Newspaper for China?* 84; Yue Dong, 91–92.

49. Xu and Xu, *Qingmo sishinian Shenbao shiliao*, 24–25.

50. Hummel, *Eminent Chinese of the Ch'ing Period*, 2: 836–37.

51. Cohen, *Between Tradition and Modernity*, 39–40.

52. Cohen, *Between Tradition and Modernity*, 40–41. On Qingliu discus-

sions of the need to open additional lines of communication between the court and lower-level officials, see Rankin, "'Public Opinion' and Political Power," 463–64.

53. Mittler, *Newspaper for China?* 2–3, 28–29; Wagner, "Early Chinese Newspapers," 6–7, 18; Cohen, *Between Tradition and Modernity,* 39–41, 284.

54. "Lun kuxiang zhichu yichou shanfa yi yu duzhi" (On the treasury's insufficient funds and devising good methods to increase revenue), *Shenbao,* 22 November 1877, 1.

55. Ibid.

56. *Shenbao,* 22 November 1877, 1.

57. Ibid.

58. "Lun zhuanyun mo shan yu zhu huoche malu" (On how water transport is not as good as constructing railroads and roads), *Shenbao,* 29 June 1878, 1. Wang Tao espoused this exact position in the late 1870s. Rejecting calls to reestablish the canal system, he promoted ocean transport. It is possible that Wang himself wrote this editorial as a "guest writer," or he may have simply transmitted his ideas to his son-in-law, Qian. See Cohen, *Between Tradition and Modernity,* 190–91.

59. *Shenbao,* 29 June 1878, 1. For another example of the *Shenbao*'s call for railroad building as a way to prevent future famines, see the front-page article in the 7 June 1877 edition.

60. Ye Xiaoqing, "Shanghai before Nationalism," *East Asian History* 3 (June 1992): 44–47. See also Wagner, "Role of the Foreign Community," 435–37.

61. "Lun zhenwu" (On relief affairs), *Shenbao,* 3 February 1877, 1.

62. "Lun Gaoli zaiqing" (On disaster conditions in Korea), *Shenbao,* 4 April 1877, 1.

63. See examples in Mittler, *Newspaper for China?* 123–35.

64. *Shenbao,* 4 April 1877, 1.

65. By focusing on "first the far and then the near," the editor was employing techniques for persuasive writing advocated by the Tongcheng school. Mittler, *Newspaper for China?* 72–73.

66. *Shenbao,* 4 April 1877, 1.

67. "Ji Yingren lun qusui zaishi," *Shenbao,* 2 May 1877, 1.

68. Jonathan D. Spence, *The Chan's Great Continent: China in Western Minds* (New York: W. W. Norton, 1998), 72–80, 94–100.

69. I am certain that the *Shenbao* editor was voicing his own critique of the government's costly military campaign to recover Xinjiang, rather than repeating a British critique, because the points raised by the "English people" in the May editorial are nearly identical to those raised in another front-page editorial the *Shenbao* published two months earlier, in March 1877. The author of the March editorial, writing in his own voice rather than speaking through an English observer, asserted that the disaster in Shandong had reached such an extreme that the government simply could no longer claim that it had no more money to offer. Instead it must provide the starving people with food even if that meant borrowing money from Western countries. *Shenbao,* 13 March 1877, 1.

70. "Ji Yingren lun qusui zaishi," *Shenbao,* 2 May 1877, 1.

71. My thanks to R. Bin Wong for his helpful comments along these lines,

made in response to my Association for Asian Studies conference paper based on treaty-port responses to the famine.

72. Wong, *China Transformed*, 97–101.

PART III: ICONS OF STARVATION

1. Chris Morash, "Literature, Memory, Atrocity," in *"Fearful Realities": New Perspectives on the Famine*, ed. Chris Morash and Richard Hayes (Dublin: Irish Academic Press, 1996), 112–14, 117; Kelleher, *Feminization of Famine*, 22–23. The phrase "semiotics of starvation" is borrowed from Morash.

2. See Daniel Chandler, *Semiotics: The Basics* (New York: Routledge, 2002); John Lechte, *Fifty Key Contemporary Thinkers: From Structuralism to Postmodernity* (New York: Routledge, 1994), 127–30, 145–51; Clifford Geertz, *Local Knowledge* (New York: Basic Books, 1983), 11–12, 118–20; Victor Turner, *The Forest of Symbols: Aspects of Ndembu Ritual* (Ithaca, NY: Cornell University Press, 1967), 43–46.

7. FAMILY AND GENDER IN FAMINE

1. "Shanxi miliang wen," 86–87. See chapter 2 for an introduction to this source.

2. A shorter, altered version of this chapter was published in the *Journal of Women's History* 16.4 (2004): 119–47. Reprinted with permission of the Johns Hopkins University Press.

3. Kelleher, *Feminization of Famine*, 6–8, 23–24, 29, 60nn44–45. Kelleher follows Julia Kristeva and Marina Warner in positing that because the mother's milk is a "central metaphor of the gift of life," her dry breast is "one of the famine's deepest horrors, expressive of a primal fear, where the 'fountain of life' is now death-giving." See Julia Kristeva, "Stabat Mater," in *The Julia Kristeva Reader*, ed. Toril Moi (Oxford: Basil Blackwell, 1986), 174–82; and Marina Warner, *Alone of All Her Sex: The Myth and Cult of the Virgin Mary* (New York: Vintage Books, 1983), 192–205.

4. Tani Barlow, *The Question of Women in Chinese Feminism* (Durham, NC: Duke University Press, 2004), 39–43.

5. Susan Brownell and Jeffrey N. Wasserstrom, ed. *Chinese Femininities, Chinese Masculinities: A Reader* (Berkeley: University of California Press, 2002), 26.

6. "Si sheng gao zai tu qi," 24b–25a.

7. David Fitzpatrick, "Women and the Great Famine," in *Gender Perspectives in Nineteenth-Century Ireland: Public and Private Spheres*, ed. Margaret Kelleher and James H. Murphy (Dublin: Irish Academic Press, 1997); Ó Gráda, *Black '47 and Beyond*; John Bongaarts and Mead Cain, "Demographic Responses to Famine," in *Famine*, ed. Kevin M. Cahill (New York: Orbis Books, 1982), 54–55. Sen also emphasizes the need for additional research on the question of maldistribution within the family. See Sen, *Poverty and Famines*, 29; and Sen, "Food, Economics, and Entitlements," 57.

8. Susan Mann, *Precious Records: Women in China's Long Eighteenth Century* (Stanford, CA: Stanford University Press, 1997), 10–12.

9. Margery Wolf, *Women and the Family in Rural Taiwan* (Stanford, CA: Stanford University Press, 1972), 32–41.

10. For a detailed discussion of filial piety, see Hsiung Ping-chen, "Sons and Mothers: Demographic Realities and the Chinese Culture of *Hsiao*," in *Women in the New Taiwan: Gender Roles and Gender Consciousness in a Changing Society*, ed. Catherine Farris, Anru Lee, and Murray Rubinstein (Armonk, NY: M. E. Sharpe, 2004), 14–40; Hsiung Ping-chen, "Constructed Emotions: The Bond between Mothers and Sons in Late Imperial China," *Late Imperial China* 15.1 (June 1994): 87–117; *The Classic of Filiality (Xiaojing)*, in de Bary and Bloom, *Sources of Chinese Tradition*, 325–29. The *Classic of Filial Piety* taught that emperors, officials, scholars, and commoners each had their own way to practice filial piety. Scholars were asked to serve their rulers as they served their own fathers, for example, while commoners were expected to be industrious and frugal so that they could take care of their aging parents.

11. There are also a few accounts of sons who sacrificed everything in order to feed their fathers. Li Wenbing of Linjin County, for instance, was praised for ensuring that his elderly father "never experienced hunger" during the famine, even though his wife and children all starved to death. Mother-son examples, however, are more plentiful and richer in descriptive detail. *Xuxiu Linjin xianzhi* (1880), 1: 78b.

12. *Xu Yishi xianzhi* (1880), 1: 85a.

13. *Xuxiu Quwo xianzhi* (1880), 27: 8a. The Chinese text uses the character for stepmother (*jimu*) in the introductory line, but for the rest of the story simply uses the character for mother (*mu*).

14. Ibid., 27: 8b. The example of the beggar son and the Zhang family hints at the class disparities that persisted during the famine, and shows that food was available for purchase in Shanxi for those who had enough cash to pay the high famine prices.

15. "Guoju maier tian cijin" (Guoju buries his son and heaven blesses him with gold), in *Baixiao tushuo* (A hundred filial piety illustrations and sayings), comp. Guo Lianqing (Beijing: Zhongguo shudian, 1996), 13–14.

16. "Guoju," 13–14.

17. While expressions of filial piety certainly changed and developed over time, the fact that the Guoju story and the text accompanying the famine illustration, though six centuries apart, offer a virtually identical message regarding the duty of a truly filial son, demonstrates that examples of filial behavior set down in earlier dynasties continued to resonate in late-Qing China. For more on the dimensions of filial piety in late imperial China, see Hsiung Ping-chen, "Constructed Emotions," and Harrison, *Man Awakened*, chapter 3.

18. Kelleher, *Feminization of Famine*, 135.

19. Liam O'Flaherty, *Famine* (1937; repr., Dublin: Wolfhound Press, 2000).

20. Ibid., 387–89.

21. Versions of this story were told by Li Yingge (age 88) in Hongdong County, Li Tong (79) in Linyi County, Li Yuying (81) in Linyi County, and Tan Wenfeng (45) in Yuanqu County.

22. Unpublished hand-copied petition to the emperor written by Dong Qishu

of Anyi County (undated), collected by Tao Fuhai, head of Ding Village Museum, from the Ding family home in Xiangfen County, Shanxi. Permission to cite given by Tao Fuhai.

23. Jin Jincheng, "Qing Guangxu sannian bei zai shen da lue qingji" (Outline of the circumstances of the big disaster of Guangxu 3), in *Yonghe xianzhi* (1931; repr., Zhongguo fangzhi congshu 88, Taibei: Chengwen chubanshe, 1968), 15: 592.

24. Gazetteers that report the sale of women and children include *Linjin xianzhi* (1923; repr., Zhongguo fangzhi congshu 420, Taipei: Chengwen chubanshe, 1976), 597; *Xu Yishi xianzhi* (1880), preface; *Hongdong xianzhi* (1917; repr., Zhongguo fangzhi congshu 79, Taipei: Chengwen chubanshe, 1968), 1614; *Xiezhou Ruicheng xianzhi* (1880), 3: 26b; and *Xia xianzhi* (1880), 5: 8a.

25. Cohen, *History in Three Keys*, 74, 316n21; Pingyao County Historical Relics Bureau, "Xian taiye bai chenghuang: Xiju xiaopin" (The county magistrate pays respects to the City God: A short drama) (unpublished draft, 2001), 1–6. See the epilogue of the present volume for more on the Pingyao famine drama. Cohen's source for the information about the two censors during the 1870s drought is Jonathan Ocko's not-yet-published manuscript entitled "Righting Wrongs: Concepts of Justice in Late Imperial China." My thanks to the anonymous outside reviewer who brought this topic to my attention.

26. Cohen, *History in Three Keys*, 74, 316n21; Aliakebaer [Ali Akbar], *Zhongguo jixing* (Notes on a trip to China) (Beijing: Sanlian shudian, 1988), 108; Wolfram Eberhard, *A Dictionary of Chinese Symbols: Hidden Symbols in Chinese Life and Thought* (London: Routledge, 1986), 323.

27. Han Zhonglin, "Jiu jie li yang" (Humble advice for rescuing people from disaster), *Qinyuan xianzhi* (1933; repr., Zhongguo fangzhi congshu 404, Taipei: Chengwen chubanshe, 1976), 8: 918–22.

28. Mittler, *Newspaper for China?* 293.

29. Lin Yutang, "Feminist Thought in Ancient China," 127–28; Emily Martin Ahern, "The Power and Pollution of Chinese Women," in *Women in Chinese Society,* ed. Margery Wolf and Roxane Witke (Stanford, CA: Stanford University Press, 1975), 193–214.

30. Nan, 16.

31. *Yuncheng zaiyi lu,* 110.

32. Ibid.; Nan, 17–18. Liu Xing and Liang Peicai also used similar phrases when discussing cannibalism. Depictions of desperate women offering their sexual "services" to men in exchange for food also appear in literature on the Great Leap Famine. See Weigelin-Schwiedrzik, "Trauma and Memory," 53.

33. In imperial China the decision to sell a wife or daughter to increase chances that both she and other members of her family could survive was generally made by family members rather than by the woman herself. Liu Xing's famine song and other local texts, however, present examples of abandoned girls and women who, bereft of any surviving family members, "shamelessly" tried to sell themselves to passing men. The presence of large numbers of abandoned girls and women was also noted by both missionary observers and by Jiangnan philanthropists who set up bureaus that arranged marriages for women who lacked

any family to return to. In such cases, all male family members had likely migrated or died of starvation or infectious disease, leaving surviving women and children to fend for themselves on the public roads.

34. Cheng Yi, *Henan Chengshi yishu* (Transmitted sayings of the Cheng brothers of Henan), in *Sibu beiyao* (Shanghai: Zhonghua shuju, 1927–1937), 22: 3a. See also Marina H. Sung, "The Chinese Lieh-nü Tradition," in *Women in China: Current Directions in Historical Scholarship*, ed. Richard W. Guisso and Stanley Johannesen (Youngstown, NY: Philo Press, 1981), 63, 71–73.

35. Nan, 18.

36. *Xu Yishi xianzhi*, 1: 81a–81b.

37. *Xuxiu Jishan xianzhi* (1885), 2: 72a. It was customary in imperial China for wives to be referred to by their own family name followed by "Shi," a title roughly equivalent to "Mistress."

38. Ibid., 2: 72b–75a.

39. Susan Mann, "Widows in the Kinship, Class, and Community Structures of Qing Dynasty China," *Journal of Asian Studies* 46.1 (1987): 37–56.

40. Janet M. Theiss, "Femininity in Flux: Gendered Virtue and Social Conflict in the Mid-Qing Courtroom," and Susan Mann, "Grooming a Daughter for Marriage: Brides and Wives in the Mid-Qing Period," in Brownell and Wasserstrom, *Chinese Femininities/Chinese Masculinities*, 48, 64, 89–95.

41. *Xuxiu Jishan xianzhi*, 2: 74b. Both Zhang Shi and Brian Kilmartin, the elderly father-in-law in Liam O'Flaherty's novel *Famine*, end up starving to death while their grandsons survive, but their underlying cultural motivations for doing so are different. Zhang Shi starves in order to ensure that her husband's family line will be continued, whereas Brian eventually accepts his daughter-in-law's decision to flee to America because he is old and has only a few years left to live, while his son, daughter-in-law, and grandson are young and still have their whole lives before them.

42. *Xuxiu Jishan xianzhi*, 2: 73b–75a.

43. "Jihan jiaopo, xuanliang touhe" (Driven by hunger and cold, they hang themselves from a beam or throw themselves in a river), in "Si sheng gao zai tu qi," 11b–12a.

44. Arnold, *Famine*, 8.

45. Gail Hershatter, "Modernizing Sex, Sexing Modernity: Prostitution in Early-Twentieth-Century Shanghai," in Brownell and Wasserstrom, *Chinese Femininities/Chinese Masculinities*, 219–20.

46. James Z. Lee and Cameron D. Campbell, *Fate and Fortune in Rural China: Social Organization and Population Behavior in Liaoning, 1774–1873* (Cambridge: Cambridge University Press, 1997), 64; James Z. Lee and Wang Feng, *One Quarter of Humanity: Malthusian Mythology and Chinese Realities* (Cambridge, MA: Harvard University Press, 1999), 47–51.

47. George Alter, Matteo Manfredini, and Paul Nystedt, "Gender and Mortality: A Eurasian Comparison," paper presented at the 24th General Population Conference, Salvador, Brazil, 18–24 August 2001, 7; Lee and Wang, *One Quarter of Humanity*, 47–48.

48. Alter et al., "Gender and Mortality," 17–18, 33–34.

49. Lee and Wang, *One Quarter of Humanity*, 47–51; Arthur P. Wolf, "Is

There Evidence of Birth Control in Late Imperial China?" *Population and Development Review* 27.1 (March 2001): 134–37. Wolf repudiates many of Lee and Wang's conclusions about Chinese demography, but agrees with them that the Chinese used infanticide to regulate family size.

50. Lillian Li, "Life and Death," 478, 487–95. Of the 3,268 births for which the sex of the child was reported that occurred among refugee families between September and December 1935, Li finds that 1,965 were boys and only 1,303 were girls, producing a sex ratio at birth of nearly 151 for the Shandong refugee group ([1,965 ÷ 1,303] × 100).

51. Li, "Life and Death," 475–76, 501–3. For Li's Shandong flood sample as a whole, 47.6 percent of deaths were male and 51.4 percent were female. "This slightly higher proportion of female deaths was maintained at most childhood ages, until ages fifteen to eighteen sui, when there were more male deaths," writes Li. Mortality rates for women were significantly higher than for men in the young adult years and the years after eighty sui, but from age fifty to seventy-nine sui, more men died than women. (Sui refers to the number of calendar years a person lives. According to the Chinese system of counting age, a person is one sui at birth and becomes two sui at the next lunar new year. A person's sui is on average one and a half years higher than his or her age according to Western practice.)

52. Cameron D. Campbell and James Z. Lee, "Price Fluctuations, Family Structure, and Mortality in Two Rural Chinese Populations: Household Responses to Economic Stress in Eighteenth- and Nineteenth-Century Liaoning," in *Population and Economy: From Hunger to Modern Economic Growth*, ed. T. Bengtsson and O. Saito (Oxford: Oxford University Press, 2000): 391, 412–13.

53. Kate Macintyre, "Famine and the Female Mortality Advantage," in Dyson and Ó Gráda, *Famine Demography*, 240–43; Ó Gráda, *Black '47 and Beyond*, 101–3.

54. Macintyre, 247–51; Ó Gráda, *Black '47 and Beyond*, 101–3; Alter et al., "Gender and Mortality," 12–15.

55. Campbell and Lee, "Price Fluctuations," 391, 413.

56. Liu Rentuan, "'Dingwu qihuang' dui Shanxi renkou de yingxiang," 91–132.

57. *Xuxiu Quwo xianzhi*, 13: 8b–14a.

58. Ibid. Although children normally have much higher mortality rates than adults during famines, it is quite improbable that only 3,676 children survived out of a total of 35,605 people. Although they present the most detailed population records I have found in gazetteers from southern Shanxi, the figures in this gazetteer raise more questions than they answer. Many of the villages listed no children at all under their record of the number of adult men and women. It is possible that those villages simply counted and reported the total number of males and females without breaking down the information by age, or it may be that some villages did not include children in their reports. For more on the vulnerability of young children during famines see, Li, "Life and Death," 475, 498–501.

59. *North China Herald*, 15 April 1879, 362.

60. David Hill, personal letter, Pingyang Fu, 19 June 1878, box 26, card 1116, Hill Letters and Papers.

61. C. A. Gordon, *An Epitome of the Reports of the Medical Officers to the Chinese Imperial Maritime Customs Service from 1871 to 1882* (London: Bailliere, Tindall, & Cox, 1884), 386.

62. Ó Gráda, *Black '47 and Beyond,* 101.

63. *North China Herald,* 13 July 1878.

64. G. W. Clarke, "The Famine in Henan," in *China's Millions* (1878), 118–19. For references to modern scholarship on prostitution as a female survival strategy during famines, see Macintyre, 249–50.

65. Lee and Wang, *One Quarter of Humanity,* 7–8; Mann, *Precious Records,* 12.

66. Sue Gronewold, *Beautiful Merchandise: Prostitution in China, 1860–1936* (New York: Institute for Research in History and Haworth Press, 1982), 45.

67. *China's Millions* (1878), 118–19. See also Gronewold, *Beautiful Merchandise,* 45–50.

68. *North China Herald,* 28 December 1876. See also *Shenbao,* 16 April 1877, 2–3.

69. Hillier Report.

70. Gordon, 10; Macintyre, 249–50; Joel Mokyr and Cormac Ó Gráda, "Famine Disease and Famine Mortality," in Dyson and Ó Gráda, *Famine Demography,* 20.

71. "Report on the Famine in the Northern Provinces of China," in Irish University Press Area Studies Series, *British Parliamentary Papers,* China, 42.2 (1878): 9.

72. *Celestial Empire,* 28 December 1877.

73. "The Rev. C. A. Stanley," in *China's Millions* (1878), 116.

74. My discussion of "moral" versus "rational economic" choices is informed by the "moral economy debate" between James Scott and Samuel Popkin over the basis of peasant behavior. For a concise summary of this debate, see Daniel Little, *Understanding Peasant China: Case Studies in the Philosophy of Social Science* (New Haven, CT: Yale University Press, 1989), 29–67.

75. Timothy Richard, "Famine in the North," *Celestial Empire,* 31 January 1878.

76. "Translation of a Western Missionary's Letter about the Famine Relief in Shandong," *Shenbao,* 4 May 1877, 2.

77. Ibid.

8. THE "FEMINIZATION OF FAMINE"
AND THE FEMINIZATION OF NATIONALISM

1. Kelleher, *Feminization of Famine,* 2.

2. An earlier version of this chapter was published in *Social History,* 30.4 (November 2005): 421–43. Reprinted with permission of Taylor & Francis, www.tandf.co.uk/journals.

3. For more on the gender-unbalanced marriage market, see Lee and Wang, *One Quarter of Humanity,* 7–8; Gronewold, *Beautiful Merchandise,* 45–50; and Mann, *Precious Records,* 12–14.

4. Ahern, "The Power and Pollution of Chinese Women," 210–14. Ahern argues that Chinese women were "outsiders" who, through marriage, broke into the male-oriented kinship system and thereby threatened family stability.

5. Henrietta Harrison, *The Making of the Republican Citizen: Political Ceremonies and Symbols in China, 1911–1929* (Oxford: Oxford University Press, 2000), 7; Joseph Levenson, *Confucian China and Its Modern Fate: A Trilogy* (Berkeley: University of California Press, 1968), 1: 98–103.

6. Mark Elvin, "The Inner World of 1830," in *The Living Tree: The Changing Meaning of Being Chinese Today,* ed. Tu Wei-ming (Stanford, CA: Stanford University Press, 1994), 44.

7. Levenson, *Confucian China,* 1: 103–8.

8. Harrison, "Newspapers and Nationalism," 182.

9. Beahan, "The Women's Movement and Nationalism," 51–53.

10. "Distribution of the Famine Relief Fund in Ts-eh-chau Fu, from Mr. W. L. Ellison," *China's Millions* (1880), 49.

11. "The Famine in the North," *Celestial Empire,* 14 December 1876.

12. Mann, *Precious Records,* 41–43.

13. "The Famine in the North," *North China Herald,* 13 July 1878.

14. "The Famine in the North," *North China Herald,* 15 November 1877.

15. John Fitzgerald, *Awakening China: Politics, Culture, and Class in the Nationalist Revolution* (Stanford, CA: Stanford University Press, 1996), 132.

16. Ibid., 9, 132–33.

17. For representative examples of the *Shenbao*'s coverage of the sale of women and children in famine areas, see articles in the 11 April 1878, 30 May 1878, 27 June 1878, 6 August 1878, and 29 October 1878 issues.

18. Pan Shaoan, "Yuxing riji" (Diary of a journey to Henan), *Shenbao,* 27 June 1878, 3. Pan was from Wujiang, just south of Suzhou. A slightly more detailed version of his account is also included in the *Qi Yu Jin Zhi zhenjuan zhengxin lu.* That version identifies seven gentleman who accompanied Pan. See "Suzhou zhuzhenju" (The Suzhou relief bureau) in *Qi Yu Jin Zhi zhenjuan zhengxin lu,* vol. 4, part 1, pp. 66–70.

19. The dates in Pan Shaoan's diary (3/5/78 to 4/8/1878) correspond to the Chinese lunar calendar. I have replaced these dates with their Western equivalents.

20. Pan Shaoan, "Yuxing riji," 3.

21. Ibid.

22. Ibid.

23. Ibid.

24. *Shenbao,* 29 October 1878, 3. The newspaper refers to Song Jun by his courtesy name, Song Shanshi.

25. Ibid.

26. "Si sheng gao zai tu qi," 29b–30a, 31b–32a.

27. Visual images of helpless women have also figured prominently in representations of the Irish famine. A sobering illustration of the ragged "Widow O'Leary" and her two emaciated children has become a ubiquitous emblem of Ireland's misery during the potato blight. Originally published by the *Illustrated London News* during the famine, today the image of the widow and the chil-

dren she cannot feed graces the covers or inside jackets of numerous books on "Black '47." In the museum shop at Ireland's National Famine Museum in Strokestown, the haunting gaze of this suffering mother now stares at tourists from souvenir T-shirts, mugs, magnets, and even Frisbees.

28. Mittler, *Newspaper for China?* 290. For a similar argument, see also Yue Dong, "Communities and Communication," 99.

29. "Si sheng gao zai tu qi," 25b–26a.

30. Kleinman and Kleinman, "The Appeal of Experience," 8.

31. *Shenbao,* 15 March 1878, 1; *Beizhuan jibu,* 508–9.

32. Prasenjit Duara, "The Regime of Authenticity: Timelessness, Gender and National History in Modern China," *History and Theory* 37.3 (October 1998): 296.

33. *Shenbao,* 9 March 1877, 1.

34. "Quanzhen Shandong jimin bing huangnian bu neng pingtiao shuo," *Shenbao,* 10 March 1877, 1.

35. *Shenbao,* 5 April 1877, 1. See also Janku, "The North-China Famine of 1876–1879," 130–33.

36. Zhu Hu, *Difangxing liudong,* 108–9. This excerpt came from the 2 June 1877 (Guangxu 3, 4th month, 21st day) entry of Xie Jiafu's unpublished diary, *Qidong riji.* My sincere thanks to Zhu Hu for pointing me to this source.

37. *Shenbao,* 4 June 1877, 2–3.

38. For examples, see articles printed on 4 June 1877, 12 March 1878, 25 March 1878, and 14 November 1878 (foreign women); 12 March and 25 March 1878 (overseas Chinese and Japanese merchants); 30 April and 25 May 1877 (actors).

39. Evelyn Sakakida Rawski, *Education and Popular Literacy in Ch'ing China* (Ann Arbor: University of Michigan Press, 1979), 1–2; Mittler, *Newspaper for China?* 260–62. Mittler's examination of advertising in the *Shenbao* between 1872 and 1912 demonstrates that, although most advertisers did not openly address women as readers until the turn of the century, in earlier decades they had attempted to appeal to female customers through the mediation of their husbands or other male family members.

40. Rankin, *Elite Activism,* 136–47.

41. *Beizhuan jibu,* 508–9. For background on Jing and his father, see Rankin, *Elite Activism,* 140, 144, 353n17. See also the *Peking Gazette* excerpt reprinted by the *North China Herald* on 28 March 1879.

42. *Shenbao,* 21 July 1879, 3. See also *Shenbao,* 20 July 1879, 1; Rankin, *Elite Activism,* 141–42.

43. Goodman, *Native Place, City, and Nation,* 122–23.

44. Joanna Handlin Smith, "Benevolent Societies: The Reshaping of Charity during the Late Ming and Early Ch'ing," *Journal of Asian Studies* 46.2 (May 1987): 329.

45. *Shenbao,* 6 August 1878, 3.

46. "Qingjiang dai shu zi qian ju" (Qingjiang Bureau for Redeeming and Sending [People] Back), in *Qi Yu Jin Zhi zhenjuan zhengxin lu,* vol. 7, part 8, pp. 2–6.

47. Ibid.

48. "Qingjiang dai shu zi qian ju," vol. 7, part 8, pp. 7–9. For a more ac-

cessible though slightly edited version of these regulations, see Zheng Guanying, "Su, Zhe, Hu, Yang chouzhen tongren ni dai shu zaimin yi mai zinu zhangcheng" (Regulations for redeeming the already sold women and children of disaster victims, planned by the relief colleagues of Jiangsu, Zhejiang, Shanghai and Yangzhou), in *Zheng Guanying ji,* 2: 1081–82.

49. *Shenbao,* 27 June 1878, 3.

50. *Shenbao,* 29 October 1878, 3.

51. *Shenbao,* 11 April 1878, 1.

52. Ibid.

53. Ibid.

54. *Shenbao,* 2 August, 1879, 1.

55. "Dai ke shao xiang qi," in *Zheng Guanying ji,* 2: 1077–78.

56. Fitzgerald, 133–34.

57. Mittler, *Newspaper for China?* 285.

58. Hershatter, "Modernizing Sex," 206–10.

59. Ibid., 211. See also Barlow, *The Question of Women,* 49–55.

9. EATING CULTURE

1. Nan, 8–9; *Yuncheng zaiyi lu,* 108. The version of this passage published in the *Yuncheng zaiyi lu* is missing important lines that are included in the manuscript copy. This translation is of the more complete manuscript version.

2. While Chinese historians and many texts from the 1870s refer to the 1876–79 famine as "Dingwu qihuang" (the Incredible Famine of 1877–78), Shanxi villagers almost always refer to it as "Guangxu sannian," or "the third year of the Guangxu emperor's reign" (1877). Stories about the famine frequently repeated by interviewees include forty stories of cannibalism, thirteen mentions of grandparents telling horror stories from Guangxu 3 to teach children to save grain and never waste food, eleven descriptions of the strange substitute foods eaten during the famine, eleven stories about the good or evil deeds of Imperial Famine Commissioner Yan Jingming, eight tales of women being sold or selling themselves to save their families, seven cases of transportation problems faced by the government during relief efforts, and seven mentions of the percentage of people who died during the famine in the interviewee's home village. (Interviews with twenty local historians and thirty-one elderly villagers in southern Shanxi, March and April 2001.)

3. Story told by Chai Fengju (age 70), 25 March 2001, Dingcun Village, Xiangfen County, Linfen Area. Mrs. Chai heard this famine story and several others from her paternal grandmother, who was a child in Cai Village during the famine.

4. Lu Xun, *Selected Stories of Lu Hsun,* trans. Yang Hsien-yi and Gladys Yang (Peking: Foreign Language Press, 1978), 7–18; Barbara Mittler, "My Brother Is a Man-Eater: Cannibalism before and after May Fourth," in *Festschrift für Wolfgang Kubin,* ed. C. Schwermann (Bonn: Bonn University Press, 2007).

5. Gang Yue, *The Mouth That Begs: Hunger, Cannibalism, and the Politics of Eating in Modern China* (Durham, NC: Duke University Press, 1999), 2, 4, 23–25, 52; Edward Said, *Orientalism* (New York: Pantheon Books, 1978), 321–25.

6. Zhao Shiyuan, "'Dingwu qihuang' shulue,"65–68.

7. Even words in Chinese and English that have identical dictionary defini-tions (let alone terms that have clearly different etymologies) may conjure up very dissimilar chains of association. For more on keywords, sacred symbols, and master narratives in the Chinese Revolution, see Jeffrey N. Wasserstrom and Elizabeth J. Perry, eds., *Popular Protest and Political Culture in Modern China*, 2nd ed. (Boulder, CO: Westview Press, 1994), 269–332.

8. Peter Hulme, *Colonial Encounters: Europe and the Native Caribbean, 1492–1797* (London: Methuen, 1986), 14–17, 34, 41. Columbus never actually visited the "Island of Carib," but by the time he set sail for Spain in January 1493, he equated the term "Caribs" or "cannibals" with "man-eating savages."

9. Gang, *Mouth That Begs,* 4, 23.

10. Charlton Laird and the editors of Webster's New World dictionaries, *Web-ster's New World Roget's A–Z Thesaurus*, ed. Michael Agnes (New York: Mac-millan USA, 1999), 105.

11. The modern character for "to eat," *chi* 吃, is an ideograph that combines a "mouth" character with the character for "to beg," thereby embodying the meaning of craving or starving for something to fill the mouth (Gang Yue, 17). The classical Chinese character for "food" or "to eat," *shi* 食, portrays a vessel with feet and a lid. The lower part of the character by itself means "feast" or "banquet." The full character also mean "eclipse" and indicates the moon "eat-ing up" the sun. (Cecilia Lindqvist, *China: Empire of Living Symbols*, trans. Joan Tate [Reading, MA: Addison-Wesley, 1991], 203.

12. Key Ray Chong, *Cannibalism in China* (Wakefield, NH: Longwood Ac-ademic, 1990), 45–47. Chong's study differentiates between "survival cannibal-ism," motivated by desperation, and "learned cannibalism," motivated by anger, vengeance, or political intrigue.

13. Wang Jianyin, ed. *Zhongguo chengyu da cidian* (Large dictionary of Chi-nese proverbs) (Shanghai: Shanghai cishu chubanshe, 1987), 1599.

14. *London Times,* 27 April 1878, cited in "The Extent of the Famine," *China's Millions* (September 1878), 114–15.

15. Hulme, *Colonial Encounters,* 83–84.

16. See Said, *Orientalism.*

17. Ma, *Shanghai xinwen shi,* 29–30.

18. *Celestial Empire,* 31 January 1878.

19. *Celestial Empire,* 28 March 1878.

20. *Celestial Empire,* 25 May 1878.

21. "Lun zhenwu" (On relief affairs), *Shenbao,* 3 February 1877, 1.

22. "Si sheng gao zai tu qi," 13a; *The Famine in China,* 22; *China's Millions* (September 1878), 115. The content of the cannibalism illustration in both the *Henan qihuang tieleitu* and the *Yu ji tieleitu* is the same, and the accompanying text is identical. The illustrations, however, are slightly different in form. The il-lustration in the *Henan qihuang tieleitu* compilation that was translated into En-glish and published in London, for instance, portrays seven living people, while the version in the *Yu ji tieleitu* pictures only six.

23. "Si sheng gao zai tu qi," 23b–24a.

24. Chong, *Cannibalism in China*, 131–33; Gang, *Mouth That Begs*, 56–57; "Si sheng gao zai tu qi," 24b–25a.

25. Chong, *Cannibalism in China*, 138–41; "Si sheng gao zai tu qi," 25b–26a. Tales about the flesh of young women and children being disguised and sold as food also appear in PRC stories about the Incredible Famine. One of the famine folktales recorded by Wang Yongnian and Jie Fuping, for example, recounts how Yan Jingming discovered an inn that sold human flesh to undiscerning customers. Yan, like many righteous officials, disguised himself as an ordinary person in order to investigate famine conditions more closely. When he stopped at an inn in Wanquan County for a meal, the meat served had a very strange color and could not be identified as chicken, duck, pork, or dog. Yan and his servant called the manager of the inn and demanded to know the truth. When they searched the inn, they found human bones, basins of hearts and livers, and a woman and her daughter who had been bound and gagged after being tricked into entering and who were on the verge of being killed and eaten. (Wang and Jie, "Dingchou zhen-huangji," 104–6).

26. Jing, *Juyi chuji*, 2: 41a.

27. Wu Jun, a retired museum curator who seeks out and makes rubbings of steles throughout the Yuncheng area, located twenty steles concerning the Guangxu 3 famine and made high-quality rubbings of ten of them. The rubbings are kept in Wu Jun's home in Yuncheng, which also serves as the small and informal Yuncheng City Hedong Museum. Several of the actual steles were destroyed during the Cultural Revolution, but I was able to view three that have survived, two in Ruicheng County and one in Wanrong County. My thanks to Mr. Wu for generously allowing me to photograph his rubbings of the steles that no longer exist. For brief descriptions of the general content of eight of the famine-related steles, see Chai Jiguang, "Xuelei banban shi leshi zhu houren: Du Guangxu sannian zaiqing beiwen zhaji" (Blood-tears affairs carved into stone to exhort later people: Commentary on reading stele inscriptions concerning disaster conditions in Guangxu 3), *Hedong shike yanjiu* (Hedong stone inscription research), no. 1 (1994): 33–37.

28. Davis, *Late Victorian Holocausts*, 47, 72, 76, 87, 131; Robert Conquest, *The Harvest of Sorrow: Soviet Collectivization and the Terror-Famine* (Oxford: Oxford University Press, 1986), 257–58, 286; Kristin Johnson, ed., *Unfortunate Emigrants: Narratives of the Donner Party* (Logan: Utah State University Press, 1996); Piers Paul Read, *Alive: The History of the Andes Survivors* (Philadelphia: Lippencott, 1974). My thanks to David Christian and Stephen Wheatcroft for informing me about sources on cannibalism in Russia.

29. Frederick W. Mote, "Yuan and Ming," and Jonathan Spence, "Ch'ing," in *Food in Chinese Culture: Anthropological and Historical Perspectives*, ed. K. C. Chang (New Haven, CT: Yale University Press, 1977), 243, 261.

30. Li, *Fighting Famine*, 35, 274. For examples of the use of these three phrases in local gazetteer essays about the famine, see *Hongdong xianzhi*, 1614–15, 1749; *Xiezhou Ruicheng xianzhi* (1880), 3: 26b; *Xia xianzhi* (1880), 5: 8a; *Xuxiu Jiangzhou zhi* (1879), 17: 17b; *Xuxiu Xizhou zhi* (1898; repr., Zhong-guo fangzhi congshu 428, Taipei: Chengwen chubanshe, 1976), 358.

31. "Dingchou huangnian jishi," in *Yongji xianzhi* (1886), 21: 89b–90a.

32. *Hongdong xianzhi,* 16: 107b–108a.

33. "Shanxi miliang wen," in *Guangxu sannian nianjing lu,* 83.

34. "She cun zaiqing bei," stele inscription, Wanrong County, Guangxu 9 (1883), in *Wanrong xianzhi* (Beijing: Haichao chubanshe, 1995), 669.

35. "Guangxu sannian zaiqing beiwen," stele inscription, Wenxi County, Baishi xiang, Guangxu 5 (1879), Wu Jun collection

36. "Guangxhu Dingchou Wuyin xionghuang beiyan ji," stele inscription, Ruicheng County, Guangxu 12 (1886), Wu Jun collection.

37. *Mencius,* trans. D. C. Lau, book III, part A, 102; "Zaihuang ji bei," stele inscription, Anyi County, Guangxu 6 (1880), in *Yuncheng shi bowuguan bian* (Yuncheng City Museum publication), comp. Wang Zhangbao (Yuncheng, 1989), 182–83.

38. Confucius, *The Analects,* trans. with an introduction by D. C. Lau (London: Penguin Books, 1979), book I.2, 60.

39. Arnold, *Famine,* 8.

40. Wang Doukui, stele inscription (1884), Wu Jun collection.

41. "Shanxi miliang wen," 99.

42. *Yuncheng zaiyi lu,* 105.

43. Janoff-Bulman, *Shattered Assumptions,* 139.

44. Carl Riskin, "Seven Questions about the Chinese Famine of 1959–61," *China Economic Review* 9.2 (1998): 114–15; Weigelin-Schwiedrzik, "Trauma and Memory," 41. For additional background on the Great Leap Famine, see Dali L. Yang, *Calamity and Reform in China: State, Rural Society, and Institutional Change since the Great Leap Famine* (Stanford, CA: Stanford University Press, 1996); Kane, *Famine in China*; and Jasper Becker, *Hungry Ghosts: Mao's Secret Famine* (New York: Free Press, 1996).

45. Interview with Wang Shoubang, retired head of the Yangcheng Gazetteer Office and one of five local historians sent out by that office from 1960 to 1965 to collect stele inscriptions, Yangcheng, 7 April 2001; interview with Liu Chunshu, retired *Wenshi ziliao* editor in Xiangfen County, Linfen Region, 26 March 2001.

46. *Guangxu sannian nianjing lu,* 3–5; Weigelin-Schwiedrzik, "Trauma and Memory," 51. The authors of the 1961 and 1962 compilation are identified only as the editors for the Shanxi Province People's Committee Office.

47. *Guangxu sannian nianjing lu,* 3–5.

48. Ibid., 3, 6.

49. Ibid., 3–5.

50. *Guangxu sannian nianjing lu, xubian,* 2–3.

51. Interviews with Bi Xinxin, editor, and Zhang Kaisheng, middle-school principal, 4 April 2001 and 6 April 2001, Yuncheng. Both men memorized the 1883 stele inscription about Guangxu 3 while in middle school during the Great Leap Famine.

52. *Guangxu sannian nianjing lu, xubian,* 47–49.

53. Interview with Bi Xinxin, 3 April 2001, Yuncheng. In 1960–61 he was a student in Linyi County, Yuncheng Region.

54. Zheng Guosheng, "Yi pian beiwen (One stele inscription)," *Zhongguo*

qingnian (China's youth) 5 (1961): 33; "Xihongmen da dui ju ban," *Beijing Ribao,* 21 April 1964 2; interviews with Shanxi Province local historians and editors who attended school during the 1959–61 famine, March and April, 2001.

55. Zheng, "Yipian beiwen," 33.

56. Interview with Li Xingzhong (age 83), 9 April 2001, one of seven people interviewed during a meeting of the village Old Person's Association, Xiwang Village, Yuncheng County, Jinnan.

57. Interview with Zhang Kaisheng (age 54), Yuanqu County, Yuncheng Area, 5 April 2001.

58. *Guangxu sannian nianjing lu,* 6.

EPILOGUE

1. My sincere thanks to Jeffrey Snyder-Reinke for alerting me to the existence of this play.

2. Timothy Richard, "Famine in the North," *Celestial Empire,* 31 January 1878; *Pingyao xianzhi* (1883), 3: 4b. The household register section of the Pingyao gazetteer lists the Xianfeng-era (1851–61) census as the last one taken before the famine.

3. Harrison, *Man Awakened,* 6–7, 95–96.

4. Interview with Bi Xinxin, editor, 27 June 2004, Taiyuan. According to Mr. Bi, people laughed at Pingyao when city officials failed to tear down the walls believed to symbolize the oppressive and "feudal" mindset of the old society. But now, those who destroyed their own city walls envy the profit that Pingyao is making from the tour groups.

5. World Heritage Center, http://whc.unesco.org; "Ancient City Wall of Pingyao," www.TravelChinaGuide.com. Pingyao's history can be traced back to the reign of King Xuan (827–782 B.C.E.) of the Western Zhou dynasty. The present city walls, made of rammed-earth and bricks, were built in 1370 C.E. They form the shape of a rectangle 3.85 miles around and have six gates. UNESCO stands for the United Nations Educational, Scientific, and Cultural Organization.

6. According to statistics from China's National Tourism Administration, the number of domestic tourists in China increased from 639 million in 1996 to 870 million in 2003, while the number of foreign tourists visiting the country increased from 51.13 million in 1996 to 91.66 million in 2003. *Xinhua News* reported that domestic tourism revenue in 2004 totaled 471.1 billion yuan, or $58 billion. Local officials and entrepreneurs are eager to enrich themselves and their locales by drawing more visitors to local sites. ("China Travel Statistics," www.chinatour.com).

7. Interview with Zhang Gaiqing, director of local administration of the City God Temple and the Wealth God Temple, 26 June 2004, Pingyao, Shanxi.

8. Angela Zito, "City Gods and Their Magistrates," in *Religions of China in Practice,* ed. Donald S. Lopez Jr. (Princeton, NJ: Princeton University Press, 1996), 72, 76; David Johnson, "The City-God Cults of T'ang and Sung China," *Harvard Journal of Asiatic Studies* 45.2 (December 1985): 424.

9. *Pingyao xianzhi,* 3: 4b–5b.

10. Johnson, "City-God Cults," 436, 439, 448–49.

11. *Pingyao xianzhi*; interview with Zhang Gaiqing, 26 June 2004, Pingyao, Shanxi.

12. The Chinese title of the play is "Xian taiye bai chenghuang." The English translation on the sign read "The County Magistrate Offer the City God." The sign also stated that the play is shown every day at 10:30 A.M. and 3:30 P.M., but our guide told us that at present the drama is only performed on Saturdays.

13. In the written and performed version of the drama, the county magistrate (县令) was identified as Wang Zhiping (汪之平), but in the Pingyao gazetteer published in 1883, the magistrate in charge of Pingyao during the famine was identified as Wang Shouzheng (汪守正). According to the gazetteer, Wang Shouzheng came from Qiantang County in Zhejiang and took office in 1873 (Tongzhi 12). *Pingyao xianzhi*, 7: 6b.

14. "Xian taiye bai chenghuang: xiju xiaopin" (The county magistrate pays respects to the city god: A short drama), as performed on 27 June, 2004. In this description I also refer to an unpublished draft copy of the play that was written by Zhang Gaiqing and other members of the Pingyao County Historical Relics Bureau in 2001. Director Zhang provided me with a copy of this six-page hand-written draft during my visit to Pingyao in 2004. The written version from 2001 is longer and more complex than the drama I saw performed in 2004. The written version begins with a wronged female ghost appearing in the City God Temple to file a complaint in the netherworld against the magistrate Wang Zhiping. She accuses the magistrate of taking bribes and perverting justice. Only then does the magistrate arrive to pray for rain. In contrast, the version of the play performed in June 2004 began with the magistrate's visit and did not include the wronged female ghost at all. Director Zhang said that the performers had simplified and modified the play as they performed it over time. She did not have a written copy of the play as it is now performed. (Interview with Zhang Gaiqing, 26 June 2004, Pingyao, Shanxi.)

15. The longer written version of the drama gave a much more negative portrayal of Magistrate Wang than the version actually performed. In the written version from 2001, the City God's angry refusal is a response to what the wronged female ghost has just told him about Magistrate Wang's unrighteous behavior. Magistrate Wang tries to change the City God's mind by bribing him with a gift of gold, and it is not until the wronged ghost is called to repeat her charges against the magistrate that he finally admits his misdeeds and repents. ("Xian taiye bai chenghuang: xiju xiaopin" [unpublished draft, Pingyao County Historical Relics Bureau, 2001], 1–6). In the shortened performed version, the City God still accuses Wang of wrongdoing, but neither the ghost nor the bribe of gold were included.

16. "Xian taiye bai chenghuang" (2001), 4.

17. Ibid., 5.

18. In the written version of the drama the City God draws the willow branch out of a "rain-bringing golden bottle" rather than the blue vase used in the performance. The written version does not include the City God calling on the people to go home and pray, nor does it mention the *yamen* guards spraying the crowd with water. Instead, it states that after the City God brings rain by holding the willow branch to the sky, "golden drums start beating, loud thunder is heard,

and all the people kneel together and give thanks" ("Xian taiye bai chenghuang," 5–6). The Jinci gazetteer compiled by Liu Dapeng describes people in Chiqiao dipping willow branches in bowls of water and waving them as they prayed for rain during the North China Famine. See Harrison, *Man Awakened,* 29. Our tour guide in Pingyao said that Guanyin, the bodhisattva of compassion, is sometimes depicted using a willow branch to call rain.

19. Interview with Zhang Kaijin, member of Pingyao County's Shanxi Opera troupe, and with Zhang Gaiqing, 26 June 2004, Pingyao, Shanxi.

20. Zhao Shiyuan, "Dingwu qihuang shulue," 67.

21. Because Wang Shouzheng of the gazetteer and Wang Zhiping of the drama share the same surname and were both identified as Pingyao's county magistrate during the famine, it is reasonable to assume that they are indeed the same person and that the authors of the modern drama either chose to alter Wang's name as one of their revisions or used a courtesy name or a local nickname for Wang (*Pingyao xianzhi,* 5: 21b–23b, 33b–34b).

22. Interview with Nan Xianghai (age 73), and Li Li, village leader, 3 April 2001, Gaotou Village, Linyi County.

23. CITS Guilin, China Highlights, www.chinahighlights.com/tour/chd-2/.

Bibliography

Ahern, Emily Martin. "The Power and Pollution of Chinese Women." In *Women in Chinese Society*. Edited by Margery Wolf and Roxane Witke, 193–214. Stanford, CA: Stanford University Press, 1975.

Aliakebaer [Ali Akbar]. *Zhongguo jixing* (Notes on a trip to China). Beijing: Sanlian Shudian, 1988.

Alter, George, Matteo Manfredini, and Paul Nystedt. "Gender and Mortality: A Eurasian Comparison." Paper presented at the 24th General Population Conference, Salvador, Brazil, August 2001.

Appelbaum, Paul S., Lisa A. Uyehara, and Mark R. Elin, editors. *Trauma and Memory: Clinical and Legal Controversies*. Oxford: Oxford University Press, 1997.

Arnold, David. *Famine: Social Crisis and Historical Change*. Oxford: Basil Blackwell, 1988.

Ashton, Basil, et al. "Famine in China, 1958–1961." *Population and Development Review* 10.4 (December 1984): 613–45.

Ayers, William. *Chang Chi-tung and Educational Reform in China*. Cambridge, MA: Harvard University Press, 1971.

Barber, W. T. A. *David Hill: Missionary and Saint*. London: Charles H. Kelly, 1898.

Barlow, Tani E. *The Question of Women in Chinese Feminism*. Durham, NC: Duke University Press, 2004.

Bartlett, Beatrice. *Monarchs and Ministers: The Grand Council in Mid-Ch'ing China, 1723–1820*. Berkeley: University of California Press, 1991.

Bastid, Marianne. "Qingyi and the Self-Strengthening Movement." In *Proceedings of the Conference on the Self-Strengthening Movement in Late-Ch'ing China, 1860–1894*, part 2, 873–93. Compiled by Institute of Modern History, Academia Sinica. Taipei: 1988.

Bayly, C. A. "Ireland, India, and the Empire: 1780–1914." *Transactions of the Royal Historical Society,* 6th ser., 10 (2000): 377–97.

Beahan, Charlotte. "The Women's Movement and Nationalism in Late Ch'ing China." Ph.D. diss., Columbia University, 1976.

Becker, Jasper. *Hungry Ghosts: Mao's Secret Famine.* New York: Free Press, 1996.

Beizhuan jibu (Supplementary collection of stele biographies). Compiled by Min Erchang. 1923. Reprint, Qingdai zhuanji congkan 123. Taipei: Mingwen shuju, 1985.

Bhatia, B. M. *Famines in India: A Study in Some Aspects of the Economic History of India with Special Reference to Food Problems, 1860–1990.* Bombay: Konark Publishers, 1991.

Blair, Charles. *Indian Famines: Their Historical, Financial, and Other Aspects.* London: William Blackwood & Sons, 1874.

Bland, J. O. P., and E. Backhouse. *China under the Empress Dowager: Being the History of the Life and Times of Tzu Hsi.* London: Heinemann, 1911.

Bohr, Paul Richard. *Famine in China and the Missionary: Timothy Richard as Relief Administrator and Advocate of National Reform, 1876–1884.* Cambridge, MA: Harvard University Press, 1972.

Brewster, Scott, and Virginia Crossman. "Re-writing the Famine: Witnessing in Crisis." In *Ireland in Proximity: History, Gender, Space.* Edited by Scott Brewster et al., 42–58. New York: Routledge, 1999.

Britton, Roswell S. *The Chinese Periodical Press, 1800–1912.* Shanghai: Kelly & Walsh, 1933.

Brokaw, Cynthia. *The Ledgers of Merit and Demerit: Social Change and Moral Order in Late Imperial China.* Princeton, NJ: Princeton University Press, 1991.

Brook, Timothy, and Bob Tadashi Wakabayashi, editors. *Opium Regimes: China, Britain, and Japan, 1839–1952.* Berkeley: University of California Press, 2000.

Brownell, Susan, and Jeffrey N. Wasserstrom, editors. *Chinese Femininities, Chinese Masculinities: A Reader.* Berkeley: University of California Press, 2002.

Cahill, Kevin M. *Famine.* New York: Orbis Books, 1982.

Campbell, Cameron D., and James Z. Lee. "Price Fluctuations, Family Structure, and Mortality in Two Rural Chinese Populations: Household Responses to Economic Stress in Eighteenth and Nineteenth Century Liaoning." In *Population and Economy: From Hunger to Modern Economic Growth.* Edited by T. Bengtsson and O. Saito, 371–419. Oxford: Oxford University Press, 2000.

Cao Xinyu. "Qingdai Shanxi de liangshi fanyun luxian" (Routes for the sale of grain in Qing dynasty Shanxi). *Zhongguo lishi dili luncong* 2 (1998): 159–67.

Celestial Empire: A Journal of Native and Foreign Affairs in the Far East. Shanghai, 1876–80.

Chai Jiguang. "Xuelei banban shi leshi zhu houren: du Guangxu sannian zaiqing beiwen zhaji" (Blood-tears affairs carved into stone to exhort later people: Commentary on reading stele inscriptions concerning disaster conditions in Guangxu 3). *Hedong shike yanjiu* (Hedong stone inscription research), no. 1 (1994): 33–37.

Chandler, Daniel. *Semiotics: The Basics.* New York: Routledge, 2002.

Chang, K. C. *Food in Chinese Culture: Anthropological and Historical Perspectives.* New Haven, CT: Yale University Press, 1977.

Chen Cungong. "Zhang Zhidong zai Shanxi, 1882–1884" (Zhang Zhidong in Shanxi). *Zhongyang yanjiuyuan jindai shi yanjiu suo jikan* 17 (1988): 1–33.

Chen, Jerome. *State Economic Policies of the Ch'ing Government, 1840–1895.* New York: Garland, 1980.

Chen Yongqin. "Guangxu shiqi Qingliu pai dui nongye youguan wenti suo ti jianyi jiqi shiwuxing" (The pragmatic recommendations regarding agricultural problems promoted by the Guangxu-period Qingliu group). *Zhongguo nong shi* 3 (1994): 39–47.

———. "Wan Qing Qingliu pai de xumin sixiang" (The late-Qing Qingliu group's ideology of relieving the people). *Lishi dangan* 2 (2003): 105–12.

Cheng Yi. *Henan Chengshi yishu* (Transmitted sayings of the Cheng brothers of Henan). In *Sibu beiyao.* Shanghai: Zhonghua shuju, 1927–37.

China's Millions. China Inland Mission. London, 1877–1881.

Chong, Key Ray. *Cannibalism in China.* Wakefield, NH: Longwood Academic, 1990.

"Chouban ge sheng huangzheng an" (Proposals for preparing famine relief policies for each province). In *Guojia tushuguan cang Qingdai guben neige liubu dangan,* 38: 18455–963. Compiled by Sun Xuelei and Liu Jiaping. Beijing: Quanguo tushuguan wenxian suowei fuzhi zhongxin, 2003.

"Chouban ge sheng huangzheng an chaodang mulu" (Catalogue of proposals for preparing famine relief policies for each province). In *Guojia tushuguan cang Qingdai guben neige liubu dangan,* 37: 18375–413. Compiled by Sun Xuelei and Liu Jiaping. Beijing: Quanguo tushuguan wenxian suowei fuzhi zhongxin, 2003.

Chronicle of the London Missionary Society for the Year 1878. (London, 1878).

Chu, Samuel C., and Kwang-Ching Liu, editors. *Li Hung-chang and China's Early Modernization.* London: M. E. Sharpe, 1993.

Chu, Wen-Djang. *The Moslem Rebellion in Northwest China, 1862–1878.* Paris: Mouton, 1966.

Cohen, Paul. *Between Tradition and Modernity: Wang T'ao and Reform in Late Ch'ing China.* Cambridge, MA: Council on East Asian Studies, 1987.

———. *China and Christianity: The Missionary Movement and the Growth of Chinese Antiforeignism, 1860–1870.* Cambridge, MA: Harvard University Press, 1963.

———. *History in Three Keys: The Boxers as Event, Experience, and Myth.* New York: Columbia University Press, 1997.

Committee of the China Famine Relief Fund. *The Famine in China: Illustrations by a Native Artist with a Translation of the Chinese Text.* Translated by James Legge. London: Kegan Paul & Co., 1879.

Confucius. *The Analects.* Translated and with an introduction by D. C. Lau. London: Penguin Books, 1979.

Conquest, Robert. *The Harvest of Sorrow: Soviet Collectivization and the Terror-Famine.* Oxford: Oxford University Press, 1986.

Daly, Mary. "Revisionism and Irish History: The Great Famine." In *The Mak-*

ing of Modern Irish History. Edited by D. George Boyce and Alan O'Day, 71–88. London: Routledge, 1996.

Davis, Mike. *Late Victorian Holocausts: El Niño Famines and the Making of the Third World.* London: Verso, 2001.

de Bary, William Theodore, and Irene Bloom, compilers. *Sources of Chinese Tradition: From Earliest Times to 1600,* 2nd ed. New York: Columbia University Press, 1999.

Deng Yunte. *Zhongguo jiuhuang shi* (The history of famine relief in China). Taipei: Taiwan shangwu yinshuguan gufen youxian gongsi, 1970.

Dezong shilu (Veritable records of the Guangxu emperor), part 2. In *Qing shilu* (Veritable records of the Qing), vol. 53. Beijing: Zhonghua shuju, 1987.

Digby, William. *The Famine Campaign in Southern India, 1876–1878.* 2 vols. London: Longmans, Green, & Co., 1878.

Dong, Madeleine Yue. "Communities and Communication: A Study of the Case of Yang Naiwu, 1873–1877." *Late Imperial China* 16.1 (June 1995): 79–119.

Dongfang zazhi (Far eastern miscellany). Shanghai, 1920.

Donnelly, James S., Jr. "The Construction of the Memory of the Famine in Ireland and the Irish Diaspora, 1850–1900." *Eire-Ireland* 31.1 (Spring 1996): 7–25.

Dreze, Jean, Amartya Sen, and Athar Hussain, editors. *The Political Economy of Hunger: Selected Essays.* Oxford: Oxford University Press, 1995.

Duara, Prasenjit. "The Regime of Authenticity: Timelessness, Gender, and National History in Modern China." *History and Theory* 37.3 (October 1998): 287–308.

Dunstan, Helen. *Conflicting Counsels to Confuse the Age: A Documentary Study of Political Economy in Qing China, 1644–1840.* Ann Arbor, MI: Center for Chinese Studies, 1996.

Dyson, Tim, and Cormac Ó Gráda. *Famine Demography: Perspectives from Past and Present.* Oxford: Oxford University Press, 2002.

East India (Report of Famine Commission): Proceedings of the Commission and Selected Evidence, appendix 2. Cmnd. 3086. 1882.

Eastman, Lloyd. "Ch'ing-i and Chinese Policy Formation during the Nineteenth Century." *Journal of Asian Studies* 24.4 (August 1965): 595–611.

———. *Thrones and Mandarins: China's Search for a Policy during the Sino-French Controversy, 1880–1885.* Cambridge, MA: Harvard University Press, 1967.

Eberhard, Wolfram. *A Dictionary of Chinese Symbols: Hidden Symbols in Chinese Life and Thought.* Translated by G. L. Campbell. London: Routledge, 1986.

Ebrey, Patricia Buckley. *Confucianism and Family Rituals in Imperial China: A Social History of Writing about Rites.* Princeton, NJ: Princeton University Press, 1991.

Edgerton, Kathryn. "The Semiotics of Starvation in Late-Qing China: Cultural Responses to the 'Incredible Famine' of 1876–1879." PhD diss., Indiana University, 2002.

Edgerton-Tarpley, Kathryn. "Family and Gender in Famine: Cultural Responses to Disaster in North China, 1876–1879." *Journal of Women's History* 16.4 (2004): 119–47.

————. "The 'Feminization of Famine,' the Feminization of Nationalism: Famine and Social Activism in Treaty-Port Shanghai, 1876–9." *Social History* 30.4 (November 2005): 421–43.

Elman, Benjamin. "The Relevance of Sung Learning in the Late Ch'ing: Wei Yuan and the Huang-ch'ao ching-shih wen-pien." *Late Imperial China* 9.2 (December 1988): 56–85.

Elvin, Mark. "Who Was Responsible for the Weather? Moral Meteorology in Late Imperial China." *Osiris,* 2nd ser., 12 (1998): 213–37.

————, and G. William Skinner, editors. *The Chinese City between Two Worlds.* Stanford, CA: Stanford University Press, 1974.

Fei Xingjian. *Jindai mingren xiaozhuan* (Biographical sketches of eminent persons in the Modern era). Shanghai: Chongwen shuju, 1926. Reprinted in *Jindai Zhongguo shiliao congkan* 78. Taipei: Guangwen shuju, 1980.

Feng Jinniu. "Sheng Xuanhuai dang'an zhong de Zhongguo jindai zaizhen shiliao" (The Sheng Xuanhuai Archives: Modern China's disaster relief materials). *Qingshi Yanjiu* 3 (2000): 94–100.

Fitzgerald, John. *Awakening China: Politics, Culture, and Class in the Nationalist Revolution.* Stanford, CA: Stanford University Press, 1996.

Fitzpatrick, David. "Women and the Great Famine." In *Gender Perspectives in Nineteenth Century Ireland: Public and Private Spheres.* Edited by Margaret Kelleher and James H. Murphy, 50–69. Dublin: Irish Academic Press, 1997.

Foley, Tadhg, and Sean Ryder, editors. *Ideology and Ireland in the Nineteenth Century.* Dublin: Four Courts Press, 1998.

Forrest, R. J. "Report of R. J. Forrest, Esq., H.B.M. Consul at Tien-tsin, and Chairman of the Famine Relief Committee at Tien-tsin." In *China's Millions* (November 1879): 134–39.

Gang Yue. *The Mouth That Begs: Hunger, Cannibalism, and the Politics of Eating in Modern China.* Durham, NC: Duke University Press, 1999.

Geertz, Clifford. *Local Knowledge: Further Essays in Interpretive Anthropology.* New York: Basic Books, 1983.

Gittings, John. *Real China: From Cannibalism to Karaoke.* London: Simon & Schuster, 1996.

Goodman, Bryna. "Improvisations on a Semicolonial Theme, or, How to Read a Celebration of Transnational Urban Community." *Journal of Asian Studies* 59.4 (November 2000): 889–926.

————. *Native Place, City, and Nation: Regional Networks and Identities in Shanghai, 1853–1937.* Berkeley: University of California Press, 1995.

Gordon, C. A. *An Epitome of the Reports of the Medical Officers to the Chinese Imperial Maritime Customs Service from 1871 to 1882.* London: Bailliere, Tindall, & Cox, 1884.

Grady, Lolan Wang. "The Career of I-Hsin, Prince Kung, 1858–1880: A Case-Study of the Limits of Reform in the Late Ch'ing." PhD diss., University of Toronto, 1980.

Greenough, Paul. "Comments from a South Asian Perspective: Food, Famine, and the Chinese State." *Journal of Asian Studies* 41.4 (August, 1982): 789–97.

————. *Prosperity and Misery in Modern Bengal: The Famine of 1943–1944.* Oxford: Oxford University Press, 1982.

Gray, Peter. "Ideology and the Famine." In *The Great Irish Famine*. Edited by Cathal Poirteir, 86–103. Dublin: Mercier Press, 1995.

Grimm, Alice M. "The El Niño Impact on the Summer Monsoon in Brazil: Regional Processes versus Remote Influences." *Journal of Climate* 16.2 (January 2003): 263.

Gronewold, Sue. *Beautiful Merchandise: Prostitution in China, 1860–1936*. New York: Institute for Research in History and Haworth Press, 1982.

Guangxu chao Donghualu (Guangxu reign period [1875–1908] records from the Eastern Gate), 5 vols. Compiled by Zhu Shoupeng, 1909. Reprint, Beijing: Zhonghua shuju chubanshe, 1958.

Guangxu sannian nianjing lu (Annual record of the third year of the Guangxu reign). Taiyuan: Shanxi sheng renmin weiyuanhui bangong ting, 1961.

Guangxu sannian nianjing lu, xubian (Annual record of the third year of the Guangxu reign, continuation). Taiyuan: Shanxi sheng renmin weiyuanhui bangong ting, 1962.

"Guoju mai er, tian cijin" (Guoju buries his son and heaven blesses him with gold). In *Baixiao tushuo* (A hundred filial piety illustrations and sayings). Compiled by Guo Lianqing. Beijing: Zhongguo shudian, 1996.

Handlin Smith, Joanna. "Benevolent Societies: The Reshaping of Charity during the Late Ming and Early Qing." *Journal of Asian Studies* 46.2 (1987): 309–35.

———. "Chinese Philanthropy as Seen through a Case of Famine Relief in the 1640s." In *Philanthropy in the World's Traditions*. Edited by Warren Ilchman, Stanley N. Katz, and Edward L. Queen, II, 133–68. Bloomington: Indiana University Press, 1998.

Hao, Yen-p'ing. *The Comprador in Nineteenth-Century China: Bridge between East and West*. Cambridge, MA: Harvard University Press, 1970.

Harrison, Henrietta. *The Making of the Republican Citizen: Political Ceremonies and Symbols in China, 1911–1929*. Oxford: Oxford University Press, 2000.

———. *The Man Awakened from Dreams: One Man's Life in a North China Village, 1857–1942*. Stanford, CA: Stanford University Press, 2005.

———. "Newspapers and Nationalism in Rural China, 1890–1929." *Past and Present* 166 (1999): 181–204.

Hayden, Tom, editor. *Irish Hunger: Personal Reflections on the Legacy of the Famine*. Boulder, CO: Roberts Rinehart, 1997.

He Hanwei. *Guangxu chunian (1876–79) Huabei de da hanzai* (The great Huabei region drought disaster of the early Guangxu period). Hong Kong: Zhongwen daxue chubanshe, 1980.

Hejin xianzhi (Gazetteer of Hejin County). 1880.

Herman, Judith Lewis. *Trauma and Recovery*. New York: Basic Books, 1997.

Hershatter, Gail. "Modernizing Sex, Sexing Modernity: Prostitution in Early-Twentieth-Century Shanghai." In Brownell and Wasserstrom, *Chinese Femininities, Chinese Masculinities*, 199–225.

Hill, David. Papers and Letters. Methodist Missionary Society collection. Library Archives and Manuscripts, School of Oriental and African Studies, London.

Hillier, Walter C. "Report of Walter Hillier, Esq., H.M.B Consular Service," submitted to the chairman of the China Famine Relief Committee in Shanghai.

In *North China Herald and Supreme Court and Consular Gazette*, 15 April 1879. Also published in full in *China's Millions* (1880): 4–8, 20–24.

Hongdong xianzhi (Gazetteer of Hongdong County). 1917. Reprint, Zhongguo fangzhi congshu 79. Taipei: Chengwen chubanshe, 1968.

Horowitz, Richard. "Central Power and State-Making: The Zongli Yamen and Self-Strengthening in China, 1860–1880." PhD diss., Harvard University, 1998.

Hsiung Ping-chen. "Constructed Emotions: The Bond Between Mothers and Sons in Late Imperial China. *Late Imperial China* 15, no. 1 (June 1994): 87–111.

———. "Sons and Mothers: Demographic Realities and the Chinese Culture of *Hsiao*." In *Women in the New Taiwan: Gender Roles and Gender Consciousness in a Changing Society*. Edited by Catherine Farris, Anru Lee, and Murray Rubinstein, 14–40. Armonk, NY: M. E. Sharpe, 2004.

Hsu, Immanuel C. Y. . *China's Entrance into the Family of Nations: The Diplomatic Phase, 1858–1880*. Cambridge, MA: Harvard University Press, 1960.

———. "The Great Policy Debate in China, 1874: Maritime Defense vs. Frontier Defense." *Harvard Journal of Asiatic Studies* 25 (1964–65): 212–28.

Huang Jianhui. *Shanxi piaohao shi* (A history of the Shanxi banks). Taiyuan: Shanxi jingji chubanshe, 1992.

Huang, Philip C. *The Peasant Economy and Social Change in North China*. Stanford, CA: Stanford University Press, 1985.

Hulme, Peter. *Colonial Encounters: Europe and the Native Caribbean, 1492–1797*. London: Methuen, 1986.

Hummel, Arthur W. *Eminent Chinese of the Ch'ing Period*, 2 vols. Washington, DC: U.S. Government Print Office, 1943. Reprint, Taipei: SMC Publishing Inc., 1991.

Janku, Andrea. "Documenting the North-China Famine: The Chapter on 'Relief Affairs' in the *Xiangling xianzhi*." Paper prepared for the conference "Qing Dynasty Natural Disasters and Chinese Society," Qing Research Institute of the People's University of China, 21–24 August 2005, Beijing.

———. "Integrating the Body Politic: Official Perspectives on the Administration of Relief during the 'Great North-China Famine.'" Paper presented at the Association for Asian Studies Annual Meeting, 4–7 March 2004, San Diego.

———. "The North-China Famine of 1876–1879: Performance and Impact of a Non-event," in *Measuring Historical Heat: Event, Performance, and Impact in China and the West. Symposium in Honour of Rudolf G. Wagner on His 60th Birthday*. Heidelberg, 3–4 November 2001. www.sino.uni-heidelberg .de/conf/symposium2.pdf.

———. "Sowing Happiness: Spiritual Competition in Famine Relief Activities in Late Nineteenth-Century China. *Minsu Quyi* 143 (March 2004): 89–118.

Janoff-Bulman, Ronnie. *Shattered Assumptions: Towards a New Psychology of Trauma*. New York: Free Press, 1992.

Jing, Jun. "Male Ancestors and Female Deities: Finding Memories of Trauma in a Chinese Village." In *Disturbing Remains: Memory, History, and Crisis in the Twentieth Century*. Edited by Michael S. Roth and Charles G. Salas, 207–26. Los Angeles: Getty Research Institute, 2001.

Jing Yuanshan. *Juyi chuji* (Dwelling in leisure, first collection). 3 vols. Shanghai, 1902.

Johnson, David. "The City-God Cults of T'ang and Sung China." *Harvard Journal of Asiatic Studies* 45.2 (December 1985): 363–457.

Johnson, David, Andrew J. Nathan, and Evelyn S. Rawski, editors. *Popular Culture in Late Imperial China*. Berkeley: University of California Press, 1985.

Johnson, Linda Cook, editor. *Cities of Jiangnan in Late Imperial China*. Albany: State University of New York Press, 1993.

Kane, Penny. *Famine in China, 1959–61: Demographic and Social Implications*. London: Macmillan Press, 1988.

Katz, Paul. "'It is Difficult to Be Indifferent to One's Roots': Taizhou Sojourners and Flood Relief during the 1920s." *Bulletin of the Institute of Modern History, Academia Sinica* 54 (December 2006): 1–58.

Kelleher, Margaret. *The Feminization of Famine: Expressions of the Inexpressible?* Cork, UK: Cork University Press, 1997.

Killen, John. *The Famine Decade: Contemporary Accounts, 1841–1851*. Belfast: Blackstaff Press, 1995.

Kissane, Noel. *The Irish Famine: A Documentary History*. Dublin: National Library of Ireland, 1995.

Kleinman, Arthur, and Joan Kleinman. "The Appeal of Experience; The Dismay of Images: Cultural Appropriations of Suffering in Our Times." *Daedalus* 125.1 (1996): 1–24.

———, et al., editors. *Culture and Healing in Asian Societies: Anthropological, Psychiatric, and Public Health Studies*. Cambridge: Schenkman, 1978.

Kristeva, Julia. "Stabat Mater." 1977. Translated in *The Julia Kristeva Reader*. Edited by Toril Moi. Oxford: Basil Blackwell, 1986.

Laird, Charlton, and the editors of Webster's New World dictionaries. *Webster's New World Roget's A–Z Thesaurus*. Edited by Michael Agnes. New York: Macmillan USA, 1999.

Lechte, John. *Fifty Key Contemporary Thinkers: From Structuralism to Postmodernity*. London: Routledge, 1994.

Lee, James Z., and Cameron D. Campbell. *Fate and Fortune in Rural China: Social Organization and Population Behavior in Liaoning, 1774–1873*. Cambridge: Cambridge University Press, 1997.

Lee, James Z., and Wang Feng. *One Quarter of Humanity: Malthusian Mythology and Chinese Realities, 1700–2000*. Cambridge, MA: Harvard University Press, 1999.

Lentin, Ronit, editor. *Gender and Catastrophe*. London: Zed Books, 1997.

Leonard, Jane Kate, and John R. Watt, editors. *To Achieve Security and Wealth: The Qing Imperial State and the Economy, 1644–1911*. Ithaca, NY: Cornell East Asia Series, 1992.

Levenson, Joseph. *Confucian China and Its Modern Fate: A Trilogy*. Berkeley: University of California Press, 1968.

Li Fubin. "Qingdai zhonghouqi Zhili Shanxi chuantong nongyequ kenzhi shulun" (An account of land reclamation in the traditional agricultural areas of Zhili and Shanxi during the mid and late Qing). *Zhongguo lishi dili luncong* 2 (1994): 147–66.

Li, Lillian M. *Fighting Famine in North China: State, Market, and Environmental Decline, 1690s–1990s*. Stanford, CA: Stanford University Press, 2007.

———. "Introduction: Food, Famine, and the Chinese State." *Journal of Asian Studies* 41.4 (August 1982): 687–707.

———. "Life and Death in a Chinese Famine: Infanticide as a Demographic Consequence of the 1935 Yellow River Flood." *Comparative Studies in Society and History* 33.3 (1991): 466–510.

Li Sui. *Jinyou riji* (Diary of travels in Shanxi). Edited by Huang Jianhui. Taiyuan: Shanxi renmin chubanshe, 1989.

Li Wenhai. *Jindai Zhongguo zaihuang jinian* (A chronological record of disasters in Modern China). Hunan: Hunan jiaoyu chubanshe, 1990.

———, Cheng Xiao, Liu Yangdong, and Xia Mingfang. *Zhongguo jindai shi da zaihuang* (The ten great disasters of China's modern period). Shanghai: Shanghai renmin chubanshe, 1994.

———, and Xia Mingfang, editors. *Tian you xiongnian: Qingdai zaihuang yu Zhongguo shehui* (Heaven sends bad years: Disasters and Chinese society during the Qing dynasty). Beijing: SDX Joint Publishing, 2007.

———, and Zhou Yuan. *Zaihuang yu jijin, 1840–1919* (Disaster and famine, 1840–1919). Beijing: Xinhua shudian, 1991.

Liang Peicai (Qing). "Shanxi miliang wen" (A Shanxi essay on grain). In *Guangxu sannian nianjing lu*, 77–99. Taiyuan: Shanxi sheng remin weiyuan hui bangong ting, 1961.

Lin, Man-houng. "Late Qing Perceptions of Native Opium." *Harvard Journal of Asiatic Studies* 64.1 (June 2004): 117–44.

———. "Two Social Theories Revealed: Statecraft Controversies over China's Monetary Crisis, 1808–1854." *Late Imperial China* 12.2 (December 1991): 1–35.

Lin Yutang. *A History of the Press and Public Opinion in China*. Chicago: University of Chicago Press, 1936.

———. "Feminist Thought in Ancient China." *T'ien Hsia Monthly* 1.2 (1935): 127–50.

Lindqvist, Cecilia. *China: Empire of Living Symbols*. Translated by Joan Tate. Reading, MA: Addison-Wesley, 1991.

Linfen xianzhi (Gazetteer of Linfen County). 1933. Reprint, Zhongguo fangzhi congshu 415. Taipei: Chengwen chubanshe, 1968.

Linjin xianzhi (Gazetteer of Linjin County). 1923. Reprint, Zhongguo fangzhi congshu 420. Taipei: Chengwen chubanshe, 1976.

Little, Daniel. *Understanding Peasant China: Case Studies in the Philosophy of Social Science*. New Haven, CT: Yale University Press, 1989.

Liu Fengxiang. "Qianxi 'Dingwu qihuang' de yuanyin" (A brief analysis of the causes of the 'Incredible Famine of 1877–78"). *Jining shizhuan xuebao* 4 (2000): 1–3.

Liu Rentuan. "'Dingwu qihuang' dui Shanxi renkou de yingxiang (The influence of the "Incredible Famine of 1877–78" on Shanxi's population). In *Ziran zaihai yu Zhongguo shehui lishi jiegou* (Natural disasters and social structure in Chinese history). Edited by Institute of Chinese Historical Geography, Fudan University, 91–131. Shanghai: Fudan daxue chubanshe, 2001.

Liu Xing (Qing). *Huangnian ge* (Song of the famine years). 1897. Edited version published in *Yuncheng zaiyi lu* (Record of disasters in Yuncheng). Compiled and edited by Zhang Bowen and Wang Mancang, 105–14. Yuncheng: Yuncheng shizhi ban, 1986. Unedited manuscript copy owned by Nan Xianghai.

Lu Xun, *Selected Stories of Lu Hsun*. Translated by Yang Hsien-yi and Gladys Yang. Peking: Foreign Language Press, 1978.

Ma Guangren. *Shanghai xinwen shi, 1850–1949* (History of the press in Shanghai, 1850–1949). Shanghai: Fudan daxue chubanshe, 1996.

Macintyre, Kate. "Famine and the Female Mortality Advantage." In Dyson and Ó Gráda, *Famine Demography*, 240–59.

Mallory, Walter H. *China: Land of Famine*. New York: American Geographical Society, 1926.

Mann, Susan. *Precious Records: Women in China's Long Eighteenth Century*. Stanford, CA: Stanford University Press, 1997.

———. "Widows in the Kinship, Class, and Community Structures of Qing Dynasty China." *Journal of Asian Studies* 46.1 (1987): 37–56.

McAlpin, Michelle Burge. *Subject to Famine: Food Crises and Economic Change in Western India, 1860–1920*. Princeton, NJ: Princeton University Press, 1983.

Mencius. Translated and with an introduction by D. C. Lau. London: Penguin Books, 1970.

Missionary Herald, The. Baptist Missionary Society, 1876–1881. London.

Mittler, Barbara. *A Newspaper for China? Power, Identity, and Change in Shanghai's News Media, 1872–1912*. Cambridge, MA: Harvard University Press, 2004.

———. "'My Brother Is a Man-Eater': Cannibalism before and after May Fourth." In *Festschrift für Wolfgang Kubin*. Edited by C. Schwermann. Bonn: Bonn University Press, 2007.

Mokyr, Joel, and Cormac Ó Gráda. "Famine Disease and Famine Mortality." In Dyson and Ó Gráda, *Famine Demography*, 19–43.

Morash, Chris. "Famine/Holocaust: Fragmented Bodies." *Eire-Ireland* 32.1 (Spring 1997): 136–50.

———. *The Hungry Voice: The Poetry of the Irish Famine*. Dublin: Irish Academic Press, 1989.

———. *Writing the Irish Famine*. Oxford: Clarendon Press, 1995.

———, and Richard Hayes, editors. *"Fearful Realities": New Perspectives on the Famine*. Dublin: Irish Academic Press, 1996.

Morse, H. M. *The International Relations of the Chinese Empire*, vol. 2. London: Longmans, Green, and Co., 1918.

Muhlhahn, Klaus. "'Remembering a Bitter Past': The Trauma of China's Labor Camps, 1949–1978," *History & Memory* 16.2 (Fall–Winter 2004): 108–39.

Nathan, Andrew J. *A History of the China International Famine Relief Commission*. Cambridge, MA: Harvard University Press, 1965.

North China Herald and Supreme Court and Consular Gazette. Shanghai, 1876–1880.

O'Flaherty, Liam. *Famine*. 1937. Reprint, Dublin: Wolfhound Press, 2000.

Ó Gráda, Cormac. *Black '47 and Beyond: The Great Irish Famine in History, Economy, and Memory*. Princeton, NJ: Princeton University Press, 1999.

————. "Famine, Trauma, and Memory." *Béaloideas* 69 (2001): 121–43.
O'Sullivan, Patrick, and Richard Lucking. "The Famine World Wide: the Irish Famine and the Development of Famine Policy and Famine Theory." In *The Meaning of the Famine.* Edited by Patrick O'Sullivan, 195–231. London: Leicester University Press, 1997.
Pao Chao Hsieh. *The Government of China, 1644–1911.* Baltimore: Johns Hopkins Press, 1925.
Peking Gazette (Jingbao). Excerpts translated by the *North China Herald* and excerpts reprinted in the *Shenbao.* Shanghai, 1876–1880.
Peking United International Famine Relief Committee. *The North China Famine of 1920–1921, with Special Reference to the West Chili Area.* 1922. Reprint, Taipei: Ch'eng-wen, 1971.
Perdue, Peter C. *China Marches West: The Qing Conquest of Central Eurasia.* Cambridge, MA: Belknap Press of Harvard University Press, 2005.
Pillemer, David B. *Momentous Events, Vivid Memories.* Cambridge, MA: Harvard University Press, 1998.
Pinglu xian xuzhi (A continuation of the gazetteer of Pinglu County). 1932. Reprint, Zhongguo fangzhi congshu 426. Taipei: Chengwen chubanshe, 1968.
Pingyao xianzhi (Gazetteer of Pingyao County). 1883.
Poirteir, Cathal. *Famine Echoes.* Dublin: Gill & Macmillan, 1995.
————, editor. *The Great Irish Famine.* Dublin: Mercier Press, 1995.
Polachek, James. *The Inner Opium War.* Cambridge, MA: Harvard University Press, 1992.
Pomeranz, Kenneth. *The Making of a Hinterland: State, Society, and Economy in Inland North China, 1853–1937.* Berkeley: University of California Press, 1993.
Pong, David. *Shen Pao-chen and China's Modernization in the Nineteenth Century.* New York: Cambridge University Press, 1994.
Qi Yu Jin Zhi zhenjuan zhengxin lu (Statement of accounts for relief contributions for Shandong, Henan, Shanxi, and Zhili). N.p., 1881.
Qingdai qibai mingren zhuan (Biographies of seven hundred famous personalities of the Qing dynasty). Edited by Cai Guanluo. 1937. Reprint, Beijing: Zhongguo shudian, 1984.
Qingshiduo (Anthology of poems from the Qing period). 2 vols. Compiled by Zhang Yingchang. 1869. Reprint, Beijing: Zhonghua shuju, 1983.
Qingshigao liezhuan (Biographies in the draft history of the Qing dynasty). Compiled by Zhao Ersun. N.d. Reprint, Qingdai zhuanji congkan, 89–95. Taipei: Mingwen shuju, 1985.
Qinyuan xianzhi (Gazetteer of Qinyuan County). 1933. Reprint, Zhongguo fangzhi congshu 404. Taipei: Chengwen chubanshe, 1976.
Quinn, Peter. "Introduction: An Interpretation of Silences." *Eire-Ireland* 32.1 (Spring 1997): 7–19.
Rankin, Mary. *Elite Activism and Political Transformation in China: Zhejiang Province, 1865–1911.* Stanford, CA: Stanford University Press, 1986.
————. "'Public Opinion' and Political Power: *Qingyi* in Late Nineteenth Century China." *Journal of Asian Studies* 41.3 (May 1982): 453–84.

Rawski, Evelyn Sakakida. *Education and Popular Literacy in Ch'ing China.* Ann Arbor: University of Michigan Press, 1979.

Read, Bernard E. *Famine Foods Listed in the Chiu Huang Pen Ts'ao.* Reprint, Taipei: Southern Materials Center, 1982.

"Report on the Famine in the Northern Provinces of China." Irish University Press Area Studies Series. *British Parliamentary Papers.* China, 42.2 (1878): 1–19.

Richard, Timothy. *Forty-five Years in China: Reminiscences.* New York: Frederick A. Stokes Company, 1916.

Riskin, Carl. "Seven Questions about the Chinese Famine of 1959–1961." *China Economic Review* 9.2 (1998): 111–24.

Rowe, William. *Saving the World: Chen Hongmou and Elite Consciousness in Eighteenth-Century China.* Stanford, CA: Stanford University Press, 2001.

Said, Edward. *Orientalism.* New York: Pantheon Books, 1978.

Sands, Barbara. "Agricultural Decision-Making under Uncertainty: The Case of the Shanxi Farmers, 1931–1936. *Explorations in Economic History* 26 (1989): 339–59.

———. "An Investigation into the Nature and Extent of the Market in Shanxi Province, China: 1928–1945." PhD diss., University of Washington, 1985.

Scheper-Hughes, Nancy. *Death without Weeping: The Violence of Everyday Life in Brazil.* Berkeley: University of California Press, 1992.

Schwarcz, Vera. *Bridge across Broken Time: Chinese and Jewish Cultural Memory.* New Haven, CT: Yale University Press, 1998.

———. "Circling the Void: Memory in the Life and Poetry of the Manchu Prince Yihuan (1840–1891)." *History & Memory* 16.2 (Fall–Winter 2004): 32–66.

———. "The Pane of Sorrow: Public Uses of Personal Grief in Modern China." *Daedalus* 125.1 (Winter 1996): 119–48.

Sen, Amartya. "Food, Economics, and Entitlements." In *The Political Economy of Hunger: Selected Essays.* Edited by Jean Dreze, Amartya Sen, and Athar Hussain. Oxford: Clarendon Press, 1995.

———. "Nobody Need Starve." *Granta* 52 (Winter 1995): 219–20.

———. *Poverty and Famines: An Essay on Entitlements and Deprivation.* Oxford: Clarendon Press, 1981.

Shanxi tongzhi (Gazetteer of Shanxi Province). Compiled by Zeng Guoquan and Wang Xuan. 1892.

Shenbao (The Shenbao Daily News). Shanghai, 1876–1881.

"Si sheng gao zai tu qi," shou juan (Pictures reporting the disaster in the four provinces, opening volume). In *Qi Yu Jin Zhi zhenjuan zhengxin lu.*

Snyder-Reinke, Jeffrey. "Dry Spells: Rainmaking, Power, and the State in Late Imperial China." PhD Diss., University of Michigan, 2006.

Sommer, Matthew. *Sex, Law, and Society in Late Imperial China.* Stanford, CA: Stanford University Press, 2000.

Spence, Jonathan D. *The Chan's Great Continent: China in Western Minds.* New York: W. W. Norton, 1998.

———. *The Death of Woman Wang.* New York: Viking Press, 1978.

———. *The Search for Modern China.* New York: W. W. Norton, 1990.

Stanley, John. *Late Ch'ing Finance: Hu Kuang-Yung as an Innovator.* Cambridge, MA: Harvard University Press, 1961.

Struve, Lynn. "Confucian PTSD: Reading Trauma in a Chinese Youngster's Memoir of 1653." *History & Memory* 16.2 (Fall–Winter 2004): 14–31.

———, editor. *The Qing Formation in World-Historical Time.* Harvard East Asian Monographs 234. Cambridge, MA: Harvard University Asia Center, 2004.

———, editor and translator. *Voices from the Ming-Qing Cataclysm: China in Tigers' Jaws.* New Haven, CT: Yale University Press, 1993.

Sun Anbang, compiler. *Qing shilu: Shanxi ziliao huibian* (Veritable records of the Qing dynasty: A compilation of materials regarding Shanxi). 3 vols. Taiyuan: Shanxi guji chubanshe, 1996.

Sung, Marina H. "The Chinese Lieh-nü Tradition." In *Women in China: Current Directions in Historical Scholarship.* Edited by Richard W. Guisso and Stanley Johannesen, 63–74. Youngstown, NY: Philo Press, 1981.

Tan, Qixiang, editor. *The Historical Atlas of China.* Vol. 8, *Qing Dynasty Period.* Beijing: Cartographic Publishing House, 1982.

Tao Fuhai. "Qing Guangxu Dingchou Jin, Shaan, Yu da han kuixi" (Analyzing the great drought in Shanxi, Shaanxi, and Henan in the third year of the Guangxu reign). In *Pingyang minsu congtan* (A collection of Pingyang folk customs). Taiyuan: Shanxi guji chubanshe, 1995.

The Threatened Famine in Western and Southern India. Cmnd. 1707; 1754. 1877.

Tóibín, Colm, and Diarmaid Ferriter. *The Irish Famine: A Documentary.* London: Profile Books, 2001.

Tsu Yu-yue. *The Spirit of Chinese Philanthropy: A Study on Mutual Aid.* 1912. Reprint, New York: AMS Press, 1968.

Tu Wei-ming, editor. *The Living Tree: The Changing Meaning of Being Chinese Today.* Stanford, CA: Stanford University Press, 1994.

Turner, Victor. *The Forest of Symbols: Aspects of Ndembu Ritual.* Ithaca, NY: Cornell University Press, 1967.

Twitchett, Denis, and John K. Fairbank, general editors. *The Cambridge History of China.* Vol. 10, *Late Ch'ing, 1800–1911, Part 1.* Edited by John K. Fairbank. Cambridge: Cambridge University Press, 1978.

———, general editors. *The Cambridge History of China.* Vol. 11, *Late Ch'ing, 1800–1911, Part 2.* Edited by John K. Fairbank and Kwang-Ching Liu. Cambridge: Cambridge University Press, 1980.

Vittinghoff, Natascha. "Readers, Publishers and Officials in the Contest for a Public Voice and the Rise of a Modern Press in Late Qing China (1860–1880)." *T'oung Pao* 87. 4/5 (2001): 393–455.

Wagner, Rudolf. "The Early Chinese Newspapers and the Chinese Public Sphere." *European Journal of East Asian Studies* 1.1 (March 2001): 1–33.

———. "Ernest Major's Shenbaoguan and the Formation of Late Qing Print Culture." Unpublished manuscript.

———. "The Role of the Foreign Community in the Chinese Public Sphere." *China Quarterly* 142 (June 1995): 421–43.

———. "The *Shenbao* in Crisis: The International Environment and the Conflict between Guo Songtao and the *Shenbao*." *Late Imperial China* 20.1 (June 1999): 107–38.

Wakeman, Frederic, Jr. "Civil Society and the Public Sphere Debate." *Modern China* 19.2 (1993): 121–31.

———, and Wen-hsin Yeh, editors. *Shanghai Sojourners*. China Research Monograph 40. Berkeley: Institute of East Asian Studies, University of California Center for Chinese Studies, 1992.

Wang, Jianyin, editor. *Zhongguo chengyu da cidian* (Large dictionary of Chinese proverbs). Shanghai: Shanghai cishu chubanshe, 1987.

Wang Jingxiang. "Shanxi 'Dingwu qihuang' luetan" (A brief exploration of the "Incredible Famine of 1877–78" in Shanxi). *Zhongguo nongye shi* 3 (1983): 21–29.

Wang Xilun, *Yiqingtang wenji* (1912).

Wang Yongnian and Jie Fuping. "Dingchou zhenhuang ji" (Record of famine relief in 1877). *Yuncheng wenshi ziliao* (Yuncheng literary and historical materials) 2 (1988): 97–125.

Wanrong xianzhi (Gazetteer of Wanrong County). Beijing: Haichao chubanshe, 1995.

Warner, Marina. *Alone of All Her Sex: The Myth and Cult of the Virgin Mary*. New York: Vintage Books, 1983.

Wasserstrom, Jeffrey N., and Elizabeth J. Perry, editors. *Popular Protest and Political Culture in Modern China*, 2nd ed. Boulder, CO: Westview Press, 1994.

Watkins, Susan Cotts, and Jane Menken. "Famines in Historical Perspective." *Population and Development Review* 11.4 (1985): 647–75.

Weigelin-Schwiedrzik, Susanne. "Trauma and Memory: The Case of the Great Famine in the People's Republic of China." *Historiography East & West* 1.1 (2003): 38–67.

Will, Pierre-Étienne. *Bureaucracy and Famine in Eighteenth-Century China*. Translated by Elborg Forster. Stanford, CA: Stanford University Press, 1990.

———, and R. Bin Wong, with James Lee, Jean Oi, and Peter Perdue. *Nourish the People: The State Civilian Granary System in China, 1650–1850*. Ann Arbor: Center for Chinese Studies, 1991.

Williamson, Alexander. *Journeys in North China, Manchuria, and Eastern Mongolia; with some Account of Corea*. London: Smith, Elder & Co., 1870.

Wolf, Arthur P. "Is There Evidence of Birth Control in Late Imperial China?" *Population and Development Review* 27.1 (March 2001), 133–54.

Wolf, Margery. *Women and the Family in Rural Taiwan*. Stanford, CA: Stanford University Press, 1972.

Wolf, Margery, and Roxane Witke, editors. *Women in Chinese Society*. Stanford, CA: Stanford University Press, 1975.

Wong, R. Bin. *China Transformed: Historical Change and the Limits of European Experience*. Ithaca, NY: Cornell University Press, 1997.

———. "Food Riots in the Qing Dynasty." *Journal of Asian Studies* 41.4 (1982): 767–88.

———, and Peter C. Perdue. "Famine's Foes in Ch'ing China." Review of Pierre-Étienne Will's *Bureaucratie et famine en Chine au 18 siecle*. *Harvard Journal of Asiatic Studies* 43.1 (1983): 291–332.

Wu Jun. Collection of rubbings of stele inscriptions from the Yuncheng area, held in the Yuncheng shi Hedong bowuguan (Yuncheng City Hedong Museum). Yuncheng, Shanxi.

———. "Shanxi shike yanjiuhui Yuncheng diqu fenhui choubei gongzuo qing-kuang huibao" (Report on the preparatory work situation of the Yuncheng area branch society of the Shanxi Stone Inscription Research Association). *Hedong shike yanjiu* (Hedong stone inscription research), no. 1 (1994): 5–7, 28–32.

Wue, Roberta. "The Profits of Philanthropy: Relief Aid, *Shenbao,* and the Art World in Later Nineteenth-Century Shanghai." *Late Imperial China* 25.1 (June 2004): 187–211.

Xia Dongyuan. *Zheng Guanying zhuan* (Biography of Zheng Guanying). Shang-hai: Huadong shifan daxue chubanshe, 1985.

Xia Mingfang. "Cong Qingmo zaihai qun faqi kan Zhongguo zaoqi xiandaihua de lishi tiaojian: Zaihuang yu Yangwu Yundong yanjiu zhiyi" (The historical conditions of early Chinese modernization as seen from a cluster of natural disasters in the late Qing: Part I of research on disasters and the Westerniz-ation Movement). *Qingshi yanjiu* 1 (1998): 70–82.

———. "Qingji 'Dingwu qihuang' de zhenji ji shanhou wenti chutan" (An ini-tial exploration of the relief and reconstruction problems during the Qing-era "Incredible Famine of 1877–78"). *Jindaishi yanjiu* 2 (1993): 1–36.

———. "Zhongguo zaoqi gongyehua jieduan yuanshi jilei guocheng de zaihai shi fenxi" (An analysis of the impact of natural disasters on primitive accu-mulation during the early stages of industrialization in China). *Qingshi yan-jiu* 1 (1999): 62–81.

"Xian taiye bai chenghuang: xiju xiaopin" (The county magistrate pays respects to the city god: A short drama). Compiled by the Pingyao County Historical Relics Bureau. Unpublished manuscript, 2001.

Xia xianzhi (Gazetteer of Xia County). 1880.

Xie xianzhi (Gazetteer of Xie County). 1920. Reprint, Zhongguo fangzhi cong-shu 84. Taipei: Chengwen chubanshe, 1968.

Xiezhou Ruicheng xianzhi (Gazetteer of Xie Department and Ruicheng County). 1880.

Xuxiu Jiangzhou zhi (A continued and revised gazetteer of Jiang Department). 1879.

Xuxiu Jishan xianzhi (A continued and revised gazetteer of Jishan County). 1885.

Xuxiu Linjin xianzhi (A continued and revised gazetteer of Linjin County). 1880.

Xuxiu Quwo xianzhi (A continued and revised gazetteer of Quwo County). 1880.

Xuxiu Xizhou zhi (A continued and revised gazetteer of Xi Department). 1898. Reprint, Zhongguo fangzhi congshu 428. Taipei: Chengwen chubanshe, 1976.

Xu Yishi xianzhi (A continuation of the gazetteer of Yishi County). 1880.

Xu Zaiping and Xu Ruifang. *Qingmo sishinian Shenbao shiliao* (Materials on the *Shenbao* in the last forty years of the Qing). Beijing: Xinhua chubanshe, 1988.

Yang, Dali L. *Calamity and Reform in China: State, Rural Society, and Institu-tional Change since the Great Leap Famine.* Stanford, CA: Stanford Univer-sity Press, 1996.

Yang Jianli. "Wan Qing shehui zaihuang jiuzhi gongneng de yanbian: Yi 'Dingwu qihuang' de liang zhong zhenji fangshi wei li" (Changes in social disaster relief in the Late Qing: Taking two kinds of relief methods during the "Incredible Famine of 1877–78" as examples). *Qingshi yanjiu* 4 (2000): 59–76.

Ye, Xiaoqing. "Shanghai before Nationalism." *East Asian History* 3 (June 1992): 33–52.

Yicheng xianzhi (Gazetteer of Yicheng County). 1929. Reprint, Zhongguo fangzhi congshu 417. Taipei: Chengwen chubanshe, 1968.

Yonghe xianzhi (Gazetteer of Yonghe County). 1931. Reprint, Zhongguo fangzhi congshu 88. Taipei: Chengwen chubanshe, 1968.

Yongji xianzhi (Gazetteer of Yongji County). 1886.

Yuanqu wenshi ziliao (Yuanqu literary and historical materials) 4 (1988). Compiled by Zhongguo renmin zhengzhi xieshang huiyi Yuanqu xian weiyuanhui (Yuanqu County committee of the Chinese people's political consultative conference).

Yuncheng zaiyulu (Record of disasters in Yuncheng). Compiled and edited by Zhang Bowen and Wang Mancang. Yuncheng: Yuncheng shizi ban, 1986.

Yuncheng shi bowuguan bian (Yuncheng City Museum publication). Compiled by Wang Zhangbao. Yuncheng, 1989.

Zarrow, Peter. "Historical Trauma: Anti-Manchuism and Memories of Atrocity in Late Qing China." *History & Memory* 16.2 (Fall–Winter 2004): 67–107.

Zeng Guoquan. *Zeng Zhongxiang gong (Guoquan) shuzha* (Zeng Guoquan's correspondence). Compiled by Xiao Rongjue, 1903.

———. *Zeng Zhongxiang gong (Guoquan) zouyi* (Zeng Guoquan's memorials). Compiled by Xiao Rongjue, 1903. Reprinted in *Jindai Zhongguo shiliao congkan* (Modern Chinese historical materials) 44. Edited by Shen Yunlong. Taipei: Wenhai chubanshe, 1969.

Zhang Jie. *Shanxi ziran zaihaishi nianbiao* (A yearly record of Shanxi's natural disasters), 730 B.C.–1985 A.D. Taiyuan: Shanxi sheng chubanshe, 1988.

Zhang Kemin, editor. "Zhongguo jindai zaihuang yu shehui wending" (Disasters in modern China and social stability). In *Zhongwai lishi wenti ba ren tan* (An eight-person discussion of questions in Chinese and foreign history), 158–206. Beijing: Guojia jiaowei gaojiao shehui kexue fazhan yanjiu zhongxin, 1998.

Zhang Zhengming. *Jinshang xingshuai shi* (A history of the rise and fall of the Shanxi merchants). Taiyuan: Shanxi guji chubanshe, 1995.

Zhao Lianyue. "Renhuo jiazhong le tianzai: 1876–1879 nian 'Dingwu qihuang' bianxi" (Man-made disaster adds to natural disaster: Critical analysis of the 1876–1879 "Incredible Famine"). *Guangxi Youjiang minzu shifan gaodeng zhuanke xuexiao xuebao* 12.1 (1999): 41–43.

Zhao Shiyuan. "'Dingwu qihuang' shulue" (An account of the "Incredible Famine of 1877–78"). *Xueshu yuekan* 141.2 (1981): 65–68.

Zheng Guanying. *Jiuhuang fubao* (Good fortune received as recompense for famine relief). 1878. Reprint, 1935.

———. *Zheng Guanying ji* (Collected works of Zheng Guanying), 2 vols. Edited by Xia Dongyuan. Shanghai: Shanghai renmin chubanshe, 1982.

Zheng Guosheng. "Yipian beiwen" (One stele inscription). *Zhongguo qingnian* (China's youth) 5 (1961): 33–34.

Zheng Hesheng, editor. *Jinshi Zhong Xi shi ri duizhao biao* (A comparison chart for the Chinese and Western calendars in the modern world). Beijing: Zhonghua shuju, 1985.

Zheng Yi. *Scarlet Memorial: Tales of Cannibalism in Modern China*. Translated and edited by T. P. Sym. Boulder, CO: Westview Press, 1996.

Zhu, Guangqian. *Psychology of Tragedy* (Beiju xinli xue). Hefei: Anhui jiaoyu chubanshe, 1989.

Zhu Hu. *Difangxing liudong ji qi chaoyue: Wan Qing yizhen yu jindai Zhongguo de xinchen daixie* (The fluidity and transcendence of localism: Late-Qing charitable relief and the supersession of the old by the new in modern China). Beijing: Zhongguo renmin daxue chubanshe, 2006.

Zito, Angela. "City Gods and Their Magistrates." In *Religions of China in Practice*. Edited by Donald S. López, Jr. Princeton, NJ: Princeton University Press, 1996.

Index

Text: 10/13 Sabon
Display: Sabon
Compositor: Integrated Composition Systems
Indexer: Alexander Trotter
Cartographer: Bill Nelson
Printer and binder: Thomson-Shore, Inc.